Clitics

In most languages we find 'little words' which resemble a full word, but which cannot stand on their own. Instead they have to 'lean on' a neighbouring word, like the *'d, 've* and unstressed *'em* of *Kim'd've helped'em* ('Kim would have helped them'). These are clitics, and they are found in most of the world's languages. In English the clitic forms appear in the same place in the sentence that the full form of the word would appear in, but in many languages clitics obey quite separate rules of placement. This book is the first introduction to clitics, providing a complete summary of their properties, their uses, the reasons why they are of interest to linguists and the various theoretical approaches that have been proposed for them. The book describes a whole host of clitic systems, and presents data from over 100 languages.

ANDREW SPENCER is Professor of Linguistics in the Department of Language and Linguistics at the University of Essex.

ANA R. LUÍS is Assistant Professor of Linguistics in the Department of Language, Literature and Culture of the University of Coimbra.

CAMBRIDGE TEXTBOOKS IN LINGUISTICS

General editors: P. AUSTIN, J. BRESNAN, B. COMRIE, S. CRAIN,
W. DRESSLER, C. EWEN, R. LASS, D. LIGHTFOOT, K. RICE,
I. ROBERTS, S. ROMAINE, N. V. SMITH

Clitics
An Introduction

Clitics
An Introduction

ANDREW SPENCER

University of Essex

ANA R. LUÍS

University of Coimbra

CAMBRIDGE UNIVERSITY PRESS
Cambridge, New York, Melbourne, Madrid, Cape Town,
Singapore, São Paulo, Delhi, Mexico City

Cambridge University Press
The Edinburgh Building, Cambridge CB2 8RU, UK

Published in the United States of America by Cambridge University Press,
New York

www.cambridge.org
Information on this title: www.cambridge.org/9780521682923

First published 2012

Printed in the United Kingdom at the University Press, Cambridge

A catalogue record for this publication is available from the British Library

ISBN 978-0-521-86428-2 Hardback
ISBN 978-0-521-68292-3 Paperback

For Marina

Contents

Tables

Preface

This book is an exploration of a very intriguing collection of linguistic beasts. Clitics is a fascinating subject. To study them adequately you really need to be concerned with all aspects of linguistics, from detailed phonetics to the analysis of discourse and conversation. Much of the interest they provoke is precisely because they sit at the interface between sound structure, word structure and sentence structure (not to mention the lexicon and language use). Partly for this reason, pinning down the notion of clitic is a little like trying to catch minnows with your bare hands. This has made it more difficult than usual to organize and arrange our material. In many cases it's hard to understand the point of, say, a phonological analysis of a set of clitics until you've seen the syntactic analysis of them, but without the phonological analysis it's difficult to understand the syntax. For this reason we've written some of the book cyclically, introducing some concepts at a basic level and returning to them later in the book to explore them in more detail. We've tried to reduce unnecessary overlap as far as possible but the reader will sometimes see similar examples cropping up in different places. In addition we've tried to perform a balancing act over choice of language examples. On the one hand it's important to see as much of the richness of clitics in the world's languages (and for us it's interesting to encounter or revisit many of those languages), but on the other hand it's much easier to understand some of the complexities of an unfamiliar language if you see it in several different contexts. For this reason we've tended to concentrate on languages that have been discussed a good deal in the literature, or with which we're more or less familiar, or both.

In some respects we've written this in bad faith. There's an important sense in which we don't actually believe in the existence of clitics. However, we do believe that it's worthwhile to study in great detail the kinds of properties that have been ascribed to clitics. In this way we gain a much better understanding of the complex interactions between phonology, morphology and syntax. For this reason, clitics are an excellent testing ground for linguistic theory.

We have tried in this book to set out the principal issues and to point the reader to some of the main research literature. Our survey has had to be very selective. There are many interesting and important clitic systems that we've ignored or skirted over and many important contributions that we've only mentioned in passing or not all. We hope that those whose contributions are not discussed here will not be offended.

We have greatly benefitted over the years from talking to friends and colleagues about clitics, and several of these have advised us about aspects of this book. These include Ricardo Bermúdez-Otero, Olivier Bonami, Bob Borsley, Grev Corbett, Wolfgang Dressler, Alice Harris, Martin Haspelmath, István Kenesei, Marian Klamer, Ryo Otoguro, Bojana Petrić, Ingo Plag, Gergana Popova, Louisa Sadler.

None of these is to be held responsible for anything you don't like in the book.

Finally, a very special thanks to Marina.

Conventions and abbreviations

For languages written with some version of the Latin alphabet we have generally reproduced the orthography of that language. This means that some diacritics will have different values in different languages; for instance, an acute accent on a vowel may mean stress (Spanish), a long vowel (Czech, Hungarian), high tone (Yoruba), rising tone (Mandarin Chinese) or nothing at all (French). For languages written in a non-Latin system we have used whatever transcription we are familiar with or whatever transcription seems easiest on the reader. For Slavic examples readers might want to be aware of the following equivalences: č = ʧ, š = ʃ, ž = ʒ, ḱć = c.

We have largely followed the Leipzig Glossing Conventions: affixes are separated by a dash affix-stem in examples and glosses, and where we don't separate the property in the example its abbreviation is combined with a dot: *cats* ⇒ cat.PL. Sometimes for clarity we will separate clitics (or putative clitics) from their hosts by an equals sign =: *the cat='s whiskers* ⇒ cat=POSS. In the morpheme-by-morpheme glosses we will sometimes label a gloss 'CL' for clarity. Abbreviations for morphosyntactic properties are given in SMALL CAPITALS. Occasionally the 'gloss' for a word is just that word in small capitals, e.g. untranslatable discourse particles. We have generally followed the transcriptional and glossing practice of our sources, but we have freely adapted some of the originals to bring their abbreviatory conventions into line with ours. Thus, we might see, say, a hypothetical gloss 'Clt.M.Sg.Dat' which might appear in our text as MASC.SG.DAT.CL. On the other hand, when morphosyntactic properties are referred to in running text we generally use lower case rather than small capitals, for purposes of readability. Thus, an element that is glossed, say, '3SG.ACC' might be referred to in the text as 'the 3sg.acc form' or (more likely) 'the 3sg accusative form'.

We have tried to identify clitics in the examples (though not in the running text) putting them in **boldface**. On a number of occasions this is a risky ploy because the whole point of our discussion at that point is to raise the question of whether the element is really a clitic or not. The reader should therefore bear in mind that a boldface element is an element to which we wish to draw attention, it doesn't mean an element which can be definitively characterized as a clitic.

Abbreviations

2P	second position
ABL	ablative (case)
ABS	absolutive (case)
ACC	accusative (case)
ADJ	adjective
ADLAT	adlative (case)
ADV	adverb(ial)
AGR	agreement
AgrS	subject agreement head (Minimalism)
AOR	aorist
AP	adjective phrase
APPL	applicative
ART	article
AUG	augmented (number)
AUX	auxiliary (verb)
BCR	Backward Coordinate Reduction
CL	clitic
COMP	complementizer
ComplexPred	complex predicate
COND	conditional
CONJ	conjunctive particle (Hittite)
COP	copular
DAT	dative (case)
DECL	declarative
DEF	definite
DEM	demonstrative
DEP	dependent (HPSG feature)
DP	determiner phrase
ERG	ergative (case)
EXCL	exclusive (1st person plural)
EZ	ezafe (HPSG feature)
FCR	Forward Coordinate Reduction
FOC	focus(sed)
FUT	future
FV	final vowel (Bantu)
GEN	genitive (case)
H	high (tone)
HPSG	Head-Driven Phrase Structure Grammar
HUM	human
IMPER	imperative
IMPF	imperfect
INAN	inanimate

INDEF	indefinite
INDIC	indicative
INF	infinitive
INST	instrumental (case)
INTR	sentence introductory particle (Hittite)
L	low (tone)
LFG	Lexical Functional Grammar
LOC	locative
LPART	l-participle (Slavic)
LV	Light verb
MID	middle (voice)
N	noun
NEG	negation, negative
NEUT	neuter
NOM	nominative (case)
NONHUM	non-human
NON-NOM	non-nominative
NONPAST	non-past
NONREFL	non-reflexive
NONSPEC	non-specific
NP	noun phrase
NPAST	nonpast
NUM	number
OBJ	object
OM	object marker (Bantu)
PAF	possessor agreement
PAUC	paucal
PASS	passive
PERF	perfect
PFM	Paradigm Function Morphology
PHON	phonology (HPSG feature)
ph-af-nom-wd	phrasal affix nominal word (HPSG type feature)
PL	plural
pl-nom-wd	plain nominal word (HPSG type feature)
PM	person marker (Udi)
POSS	possessive, possessor
POSS-S	English 'possessive 's'
PPT	Principles and Parameters Theory
PRED	predicate (LFG)
PRES	present
PROG	progressive
PRT	particle
PX	possessor

Q	interrogative marker
QUOT	quotative particle (Hittite)
RECIP	reciprocal
REFL	reflexive
RRC	reduced relative clause (Persian)
SEM	SEMANTICS (HPSG attribute)
SG	singular
SM	subject marker (Bantu)
Spec	specifier
SUBJ	subject
SUBJUNCT	subjunctive
SVO	subject-verb-object (word order)
SYN	SYNTAX (HPSG attribute)
TAM	tense-aspect-mood
VSO	verb-subject-object (word order)
VP	verb phrase

1 Preliminaries

1.1   Introducing clitics

Consider the sentence *Pat's a linguist*. If we transcribe the sequence *Pat's* phonetically we can see that it forms a single syllable, /pæts/, which expresses both the subject of the sentence 'Pat' and the verb. A more transparent way of representing the structure would be to pronounce the sentence as *Pat is a linguist*. But in the sequence *Pat's* the verb *is* has been shortened to just a single consonant and has been attached to the noun *Pat* in the manner of a suffix. In one sense, then, /pæts/ is composed of two words, even though it's pronounced as a single word. Put differently, the *'s* is phonologically just the final part of /pæts/ but in terms of the sentence structure it functions as the main verb of the sentence.

This type of behaviour makes *'s* a typical instance of a clitic. In the present case the clitic is a form of a word which is phonologically attached to another word, its host. The *'s* corresponds to another form of the same word which doesn't show the same reliance on a phonological host. In *Pat is a linguist* we can pause between *Pat* and *is* or even insert another word: *Pat, apparently, is a linguist*. Similarly, if we want to confirm that Pat really is a linguist we can put the main emphasis or accent on the word *is* and say *Pat (really) IS a linguist*. None of these things is possible with the clitic form *'s*. The full form *is* therefore behaves like a genuine word, while the clitic *'s* behaves more like a suffix. A clitic which attaches to the right edge of its host, like a suffix, is called an enclitic. A clitic which attaches to the left edge of its host is called a proclitic.[1] (There are also endoclitics which attach inside their host, in the manner of an infix, though these are much rarer.)

In terms of their function and meaning, the clitic *'s* and the full form *is* are essentially the same thing. Since it is not a fully-fledged word we might want to say that *'s* is an affix like the plural *-s* or like the 3sg ending *-s* in *eats*. Like clitics, affixes cannot exist independently but need something to attach to. However, clitics are not ordinary affixes. A genuine affix only attaches to words of a particular category, such as a noun (for plural) or a verb (for person-number agreement). But the clitic *'s* attaches to whatever word it happens to be next to, even the pronoun *you* in *The woman standing next to you's a linguist*. In the next chapter we'll discuss other auxiliary verbs in English that have clitic forms (such as the *'ll* of *we'll see*).

English, then, has elements which behave phonologically like affixes because they have to be attached to some host, but which don't behave morphologically like affixes given that they attach to words of any category. Furthermore, they have the function and meaning of words and may even correspond to a full word form, but they don't have the autonomy of words. A further aspect of our example is worth noting. When syntacticians analyse sentences such as *Pat is a linguist* or *Pat is reading a book*, they generally take the verb form *is* to form a constituent with *a linguist* or *reading a book*. There are no syntactic theories which would regard the subject noun phrase *Pat* and the verb *is* as forming a syntactic constituent (well, almost none). Yet in the forms with a cliticized verb we have no choice but to say that *Pat's* is a single morphosyntactic unit: it's a single word form, after all. Thus, the clitic illustrates an important analytical problem: how to analyse the construction in such a way that the verb forms a constituent with its complement at one level while forming a word with the phrase to its left at the morphophonological level.

English also has another element which shares some of these properties, illustrated in *the Queen's hat*. Here the *'s* has a totally different function, broadly speaking to indicate possession. Again, it looks a little like a suffix, for instance the plural *-s* in *the Queens of England*. But there is a subtle difference. The plural *-s* must attach to the noun it pluralizes. If we wish to speak about the set of women comprising Mary Tudor, Elizabeth I, Victoria and so on we have to say *the Queens of England*, not **the Queen of Englands*. However, when we wish to name the hat that the Queen of England possesses, the possessive *'s* attaches to the last word of the phrase *the Queen of England*, not to the word denoting the person that actually owns the hat. In other words we say *the Queen of England's hat*, not **the Queen's of England hat*. A more precise way of putting this is to say that the possessive *'s* attaches to the rightmost edge of the possessor phrase; it doesn't attach to the head of the possessor phrase, *Queen*, unlike the plural suffix, which shows exactly the opposite behaviour. Because the possessive *'s* attaches to whatever word comes last in the phrase, it can attach to a word of any class, as in *the girl you met yesterday's hat*. Very much like the *'s* in *The woman standing next to you's a linguist*, the English possessive is phonologically dependent on a preceding word regardless of its category.

The examples we've seen so far involve just a single clitic, but there are many languages which allow clitics to occur in strings or clusters. In such languages, the ordering of the clitics is very strict, even if word order for ordinary words is very free. A simple example of such a cluster is found in a collection of dialects known nowadays officially as Serbian-Bosnian-Croatian-Montenegrin, after the principal countries in which it is spoken, but which we will refer to by a variant of its older composite name, Serbian/Croatian. In (1) (Browne 1974) we see two clitics, one pronominal, the other a clitic form of the auxiliary verb:

(1)   Taj pesnik **mi**   **je**   napisao knjigu
         that poet   to.me AUX.3SG wrote   book
         'That poet wrote me a book'

As we will see, these clitics have to come in this order. Their placement as a cluster permits one variant, however. The cluster can break up the noun phrase *taj pesnik* 'that poet', as in (2):

(2)   Taj **mi**   **je**   pesnik napisao knjigu
        that to.me AUX.3SG poet   wrote   book
        'That poet wrote me a book'

Even from our very brief characterization we can see that clitics are special in terms of their phonology (i.e., sound structure), their syntax (i.e., sentence structure) and their morphology (i.e., word structure). In other words, clitics lie on the interfaces between the major modules according to which grammar is organized. Moreover, clitics represent various stages in the processes of grammaticalization. In these processes, ordinary words such as demonstrative adjectives, spatial prepositions, verbs and so on begin to acquire the properties of function words, becoming, say, pronouns, case markers or auxiliary verbs. These function words may then lose the ability to bear accent and acquire the typical properties of clitics. But the process often continues, so that an accentless clitic starts being associated with a particular kind of host. A clitic pronominal argument may become an obligatory satellite to a verb, in which case it may develop into an agreement affix, or it may become an affix on a noun signalling possession. A clitic case marker derived from a preposition may become a genuine affixal case marker. An auxiliary verb may become fused with the lexical verb to become a tense/aspect/mood affix and so on. The problem is that such processes are typically gradual, and may not even affect all lexemes of the relevant word class. In that case the descriptive linguist is often faced with very difficult analytical choices.

Broadly speaking there are two aspects to the problem of identifying clitics. First, we need to decide whether we are dealing with an ordinary word represented in the syntax like other words, or whether we are dealing with an element whose syntax is special or idiosyncratic, or indeed an element which is simply not represented syntactically as a word in the first place. Second, we need to decide whether we are dealing with a clitic or with an affix.

As we will see, many of the elements labelled clitics in theoretical and descriptive discussions correspond to function words in other languages (or earlier varieties of that language). If an element fails to behave like a normal function word and shows idiosyncratic or restricted behaviour, we might then use this as evidence that we have a clitic. However, we often find that the evidence is contradictory. Take the case of definite articles in English and French. Phonologically, the articles are weak in both languages and are therefore candidates for clitic status, specifically proclitics. However, their placement seems to be determined by ordinary syntactic principles. When we contrast the two languages we find that there's an interesting difference. In English it's possible to elide an article in a coordinated phrase (we will say that the definite article takes wide scope over the coordinate phrase):

(3)   The [[boys from Paris] and [girls from Milan]] were present

However, in French this is not possible: the article has to be repeated on the second conjunct (*les filles de Milan* as in (4b); omitting it leads to ungrammaticality (4a) (Miller 1992, 12):

(4) a.   * Les garçons de   Paris et   filles de   Milan étaient présents
                 the boys   from Paris and girls from Milan were   present
      b.   Les garçons de   Paris et   les filles de   Milan étaient présents
                 the boys   from Paris and the girls from Milan were   present
                 'The boys from Paris and the girls from Milan were present'

This sort of behaviour is not characteristic of function words, and isn't even characteristic of clitics. Rather, it's the sort of property we expect to see of an affix. On the other hand, different forms of the French definite article can themselves be conjoined, which is a property of function words, but not normally a property of affixes or of clitics (Miller 1992, 151):

(5)   On peut dire le   ou la   pamplemousse
          One can say 'le' or 'la' pamplemousse
          (*pamplemousse* means 'grapefruit')

The rider 'not normally' is important because we frequently find affixes, especially derivational affixes, which can be conjoined. Examples are frequent in English: *pre- and post-war, in- and out-going mail, ...*

However, there are additional reasons why it can be difficult to establish the identity of clitics from reading the research literature. Because clitics and affixes share important properties, and because they often overlap in their functions, theoreticians will sometimes feel the need to draw attention to such overlaps and similarities by means of their choice of terminology. An intriguing case in point occurs when Baker et al. (1989, 223) are discussing the nature of the passive participle in English, that is, the *-en* suffix of the verb *broken* in a sentence such as *The vase was broken by Tom*. The authors draw parallels with the use of certain types of clitic reflexive pronoun in Romance languages such as Spanish, which often give rise to constructions which are syntactically very like the periphrastic passive construction of English. They then say of the English passive *-en* suffix: "We regard its essential properties to be like those of clitics." At the same time, but independently, Suñer (1988) is describing the pronominal clitics of Spanish, arguing that on morphophonological and morphosyntactic grounds these elements are essentially affixes. Neither group of authors is necessarily 'wrong', of course. Each is trying to focus attention on specific properties of the construction in hand (and there are very good reasons to think of the Romance pronominals as a deviant type of affixal system rather than as a kind of clitic system). But it is easy to see how imaginative use of terminology can become less than helpful and may even degenerate into a downright abuse of terminology.

    The upshot is that clitics can be confused with affixes and vice versa. If we analyse something as a clitic when in fact it really has the properties of an affix, then we should really leave the job of analysis to the morphologist. This is the conclusion of a much-cited and very important paper by Zwicky and Pullum (1983), which shows that the English -*n't* negation formative has all the properties of an inflectional affix and none of the properties of a clitic. The diagnostic tests proposed by Zwicky and Pullum have become a cornerstone of analysis for those studying clitics, and we will discuss their work in more detail in Chapter 5.

At the same time, clitics are often treated as a deviant kind of word, and hence as the domain of syntax. We will see in the course of our book that the behaviour of clitics tends to be nothing if not idiosyncratic. The result is that any model of syntax that tries to encompass clitic phenomena as though they were ordinary syntax will end up having to accommodate very idiosyncratic behaviour, which generally leads to a considerable complication of the grammar. Arguably, it's a better strategy to ensure that the overall architecture of grammar has a relatively simple and straightforward syntax, leaving idiosyncrasy and complexity to the morphological description.[2] We would argue that, while clitics often demonstrate syntactic properties, it's also often important to distinguish them from other types of unaccented function word. We will therefore survey the various ways in which clitics are atypical types of word and the ways they differ from affixes. Some types of clitics are distinguished in essentially phonological terms while other types are distinguished in terms of their morphological and syntactic properties. The problem of clitics is thus in some ways unique in linguistics because it encompasses almost all components of grammar.

Among the questions we will be addressing, directly or indirectly, are the following. Are clitics essentially affixes, or essentially words, or a special category of their own? Is there a universally valid way of distinguishing between affixes, full words and clitics? Is there a universally valid way to identify clitics for any arbitrary language? To a large extent the goal of this book is to unravel the criteria that have been proposed to answer these questions and to determine to what extent those criteria are successful. As we proceed we will see that failure to establish clear criteria has sometimes led to genuine confusion.

We have tried as far as possible not to take for granted too much linguistic theory. We will presuppose familiarity with the basic notions of contemporary linguistics, but we will provide very introductory discussion of some of the more important notions as we proceed. This particularly relates to recent morphological theory, which is probably less well known and less understood than phonology and syntax amongst general linguists.

We must also bear in mind that terminological usage can differ considerably from one theoretical framework to another, quite apart from the idiosyncratic usage of individual authors. The important thing is to understand the concepts which underly the terminology so that we can 'translate' easily from one framework of description to another. At the same time, in the descriptive grammatical tradition, in which linguists try to write definitive and exhaustive grammars of a language, we often find that different experts working on different language groups will use the same terms but with different meanings, or alternatively will use different terms to describe essentially the same phenomenon. This problem is not unique to linguistics, of course, but it's very important to be aware of it. Even very experienced linguists can been misled into thinking that two languages exhibit the same phenomenon just because the grammars use the same term, and progress has often been made by realizing that two phenomena in different languages which are traditionally given different names are actually just instantiations of the same phenomenon. We will repeatedly see that the notion 'clitic' is particularly susceptible to such terminological confusion, but it's by no means the only notion.

1.2   About the book

Throughout this book we will discuss phenomena that don't involve clitics directly but which we believe are essential to an understanding of how clitics work. This is particularly true of the morphosyntax of agreement, where we present an overview in Chapter 6 and elsewhere of morphological agreement systems so as to facilitate comparison with pronominal clitic systems. A recurrent theme running through the book is the difficulty of finding principled ways of distinguishing clitics from other elements, especially affixes. Another theme is the tendency of linguists, especially syntacticians, to discuss non-clitic systems using the vocabulary of the clitic. For these and other reasons, it's therefore necessary to have explicit comparisons between more-or-less typical affixal morphology and more-or-less typical clitic systems. For these reasons, we have tried to provide a basic descriptive overview of the types of morphological (mainly inflectional) system that is, most relevant to an understanding of how clitic systems work. In our experience, even knowledgeable linguists are sometimes not fully conversant with the full variety of morphological systems in the world's languages, or with the full richness of the types of interaction between morphological forms and syntactic structures and processes. For this reason, a fair deal of our book is not actually about clitics, but rather about inflectional paradigms, agreement systems, and so on. We make no apology for this: it is completely impossible to understand the crucial conceptual and theoretical issues that clitics raise without a proper understanding of how morphology works.

Where syntax is concerned we have had to provide only the very curtest of surveys. The main reason for this is that we are not syntacticians and therefore we lack the expertise required to do justice to the complexity of the most influential syntactic theories. Another reason is space: the book would have to be double its size if we were to present a proper comparison of just the three main syntactic models that we discuss. A third reason has to do with the development of (what we have chosen to call) Principles and Parameters Theory (PPT) of syntax. These models, starting with the Trace Theory of movement (Chomsky 1973), have had an enormous impact on the way that clitic systems are conceived of and analysed. However, the development of the model, from Trace Theory to Government Binding theory (Chomsky 1981) to various forms of the Principles and Parameters model and then to the various forms of the Minimalist Program (Chomsky 1995b) has been extremely complex. The analyses conducted in one version of PPT will often be partly or even largely incompatible with analyses conducted in an earlier version (sometimes by the same author), and keeping track of all the theoretical implications requires the skill of a syntactician who is deeply immersed in that tradition. This is much less of a problem with the constraints-based models, Head-Driven Phrase Structure Grammar (HPSG) and Lexical Functional Grammar (LFG).[3]

As may already be clear, one of the principal problems with talking about clitics is delineating the domain of discourse and deciding when to call an element a clitic as opposed to anything else. The main difficulties, as we've said, are distinguishing clitics from affixes, especially inflectional affixes, and distinguishing clitics from function words. Now, we can only understand the notions of affix and function word against the background of an appropriate model of morphology and syntax. Different models, however, provide different characterizations, so it's necessary to bear in mind when reading the research literature on clitics precisely what background assumptions an author is making. We'll see that the theoretical literature, very broadly speaking, focusses either on the phonological properties of clitics, or their morphological properties, or their syntactic properties. More ambitious studies try to combine two or even all three of these aspects, but that is, still a very daunting task, necessary though it is. Most authors concentrate on one aspect of the problem, and from the point of view of theoretical debate and controversy the most important divide is between the morphological approaches and the syntactic approaches. Some linguists try to accommodate all clitic phenomena in a morphological model. A prime example of this is Stephen Anderson's contention that all clitics are phrasal affixes, that is, clitics are essentially morphological elements. The relation to syntax is then essentially the way that the positioning of the clitics is defined with respect to phrases rather than words or stems. Other linguists try to accommodate all clitic phenomena in a model of syntax. A number of practitioners of the PPT approach to syntax take this stance, for example. For many of these linguists the peculiar formal (for us, morphological) properties of clitics are rather uninteresting idiosyncrasies that can be largely ignored. Still other linguists regard the most interesting aspect of clitics as their interface properties between morphology and syntax (and phonology).

This book is organized as follows: Chapters 2 and 3 offer a descriptive survey of the main functions of clitic systems (Chapter 2) and their basic types, as defined by their placement properties (Chapter 3). In Chapter 2 we will encounter the basic data relating to clitic systems as well as one of the fundamental problems. We will see that clitic systems regularly express the same kinds of morphosyntactic properties as inflectional systems. With verbs we see tense-aspect-mood properties (often through cliticized auxiliary verbs) and agreement properties via cliticized pronominals. With nouns we see clitics expressing definiteness, case and possession (the latter through cliticized pronominals). However, we also see properties that are more properly associated with the whole clause, such as types of evidential marker (expressing the degree to which the speaker vouches directly for the veracity of a statement) and markers of interrogative mood. Related to these are the discourse markers, expressing subtle, often untranslatable nuances of attitude or emphasis. These are less easy to view as types of inflection, even though they often occur in the same cluster as the more inflectional types of clitic. For those models that try to assimilate clitic phenomena to the domain of morphology clitics of this sort are problematical.

Chapter 3 presents a descriptive overview of clitic types, based on patterns of placement and distributional properties of clitics. Most clitics are banned from occurring clause-initially and tend to select very specific non-initial positions (such as the second position in the clause). This chapter also examines placement domains, distinguishing broadly between nominal clitics (i.e., which have scope over nominal phrases) and verbal clitics (i.e., which have scope over verb phrases). The chapter opens, however, with a presentation of two early 'typologies' of clitics. In a sense it's premature to discuss the different types of clitic at such an early stage in our discussion, because it's difficult to see what a typology is describing without seeing a wide variety of clitic systems and their behaviours. Clitic typology is therefore a question we'll be returning to at various points, and especially in Chapter 8, when we discuss the various theoretical approaches to clitics.

The next three chapters are devoted to phonological, morphological and syntactic aspects of clitic systems. In Chapter 5 on clitics and morphology and Chapter 6 on clitics and syntax we have tried as far as possible to present a descriptive overview, without exploring the various theoretical approaches to the phenomena we discuss. This is a somewhat artificial enterprise, of course, and at various points we will introduce a minimum of theoretical machinery to aid the description.

Chapter 4 is devoted to the phonological properties of clitics and their interaction with phrase phonology, examining the inherently unstressed, unaccented nature of clitics and their dependency on a stressed lexical item. We will look at data that suggest that clitics sometimes seek a prosodically defined host, rather than one defined in terms of syntactic position or word class. We will also look at the effects clitics have on the phonology of their hosts. In some cases, for instance, the clitic is incorporated into the prosodic structure and affects such processes as stress placement or vowel harmony, while in other cases the clitics remain outside the prosodic structure, and in yet other cases clitics have their own unique prosodic properties, not shared by affixes or function words. Some types of clitic are defined primarily in terms of their phonological or prosodic behaviour (the so-called simple clitics), and we give an overview of some typical examples next in the chapter. We conclude the chapter by asking how to represent the prosodic structure of clitic-host combinations. This will require us to summarize very briefly the main theoretical point of debate on the phonological representation of clitics, whether there is a special prosodic unit or constituent, the Clitic Group, that defines the phonology of the clitic+host, independently of other types of prosodic unit.

In Chapter 5 we turn to the morphological aspects of clitics. There are two sides to this question. First, there is the issue of how to distinguish clitics from affixes (to the extent that this is possible). We start with the celebrated Zwicky–Pullum criteria for drawing this distinction, which has been extremely influential in all subsequent discussion. We will see here, and later in the book, examples that are often described in terms of cliticization but which are best described as affixes. This applies most obviously to the English negation affix *n't* that motivates the Zwicky–Pullum study, but it applies also to pronominal clitics in Romance languages, Modern Greek and elsewhere.

Second, independently of whether we treat clitics as a species of affix, we can ask in what ways clitics resemble morphological objects as opposed to lexical items. For instance, clusters of clitics often have properties that we associate more with strings of affixes: the clusters usually assume a fixed, partly idiosyncratic order which often goes against what the rest of the syntax of the language dictates, and adjacent clitics often show idiosyncratic types of allomorphy that are not otherwise found between adjacent words. We then look at phenomena that motivate the claim that clitics are essentially morphological in kind, especially the phenomenon of edge inflection, in which it appears that an inflectional property is expressed by modifying whatever word happens to appear at the edge of the relevant phrase. The notion of edge inflection has been controversial and we'll return to it in somewhat more detail in Chapter 8 when we look at theoretical approaches to clitics.

Chapter 6 discusses various ways in which clitics interact with syntactic structure. We begin by looking at weak (non-prominent, unaccented) function words that are generally not treated as clitics (or if they are, as merely phonological clitics). As we saw above in our brief discussion of French definite articles, unaccented function words can behave like clitics or even like affixes, while retaining the basic syntactic properties of words. One particularly important aspect of this problem relates to the behaviour of pronominal clitics. There are a number of questions here, most of which revolve around two basic questions: when does a weak pronoun become a clitic, and hence not an ordinary function word? When does a clitic pronoun become an affix? To understand the issues we'll need to survey briefly the notion of agreement: much of the debate revolves around the question of whether a clitic pronoun system resembles an agreement system, and so its necessary to understand just how complex and multifarious agreement systems based on uncontroversial affixal morphology can be.

We then investigate three aspects of pronominal clitics which have exercised theorists looking for a unified account of pronominal clitics. First, we look at subject clitics. It is common in the world's languages to find pronominal clitics serving as, or cross-referencing, subjects, but it is less common in the standard varieties of Romance languages, and those varieties that have subject clitics have, apparently, developed them independently of the object clitics. For syntacticians this has sometimes led to important questions about the nature of the clitic systems of those language varieties generally. We next consider two phenomena which are very common and which appear to offer completely contradictory evidence about the nature of clitics. In a number of languages, especially the more familiar Romance languages, a clitic pronoun object is in complementary distribution with an overt noun phrase object. This has motivated a syntactic approach to clitics under which they are simply weak pronouns occupying the position of the verb's object. However, in many languages overt noun phrase objects (and subjects) can, or sometimes must, be doubled by a clitic. This clitic doubling gives rise to constructions which can look very much like agreement systems in languages with affixal agreement morphology. On the other hand, in many languages we find subordinate clause constructions in which a pronominal realizes the object of the subordinate clause verb, but that pronominal is cliticized to the matrix verb. In other words, alongside *Martina wants [to.read=it]* we find *Martina it=wants [to.read]* (or even *Martina=it wants [to.read]*). This clitic climbing is generally taken to imply that the clitic pronouns are syntactic objects which can be raised, that is, moved from a subordinate clause to the higher matrix clause. We will see, however, that comparisons either way with syntax or morphology are highly misleading. It's perfectly possible to provide a syntactic account of clitic doubling or a morphological account of clitic doubling.

We conclude the chapter with a discussion of aspects of the syntax of non-argument clitics. First, we look at the 'Ethical Dative' type of construction, in which the pronominal expresses discourse meanings of a subtle and hard-to-define kind, even though it retains (some of) its properties as a pronominal. We conclude by rehearsing the very complex syntactic patterning of the clitic cluster in Tagalog, a language which combines a rich array of pronominal clitics with an even richer array of discourse marker clitics.

In Chapter 7 we bring together a number of points raised in earlier chapters and ask to what extent we can draw a clear dividing line between clitics, words and affixes. It will emerge that no universal concept of 'clitic' is available. Rather, some languages seem to make use of reasonably well-defined 'word-clitic-affix' categories, while others permit intermediate formatives which can behave like one category in some contexts and like another category in others. In those cases, each type of formative has to be described in its own terms, and it is not even always possible to make general typological statements about what kind of properties imply what other properties.

In this chapter we look at affixes that can be (or perhaps still are) mistaken for clitics and at affixes which have prosodic or morphosyntactic properties similar to those of (some types of) clitics or syntactically represented function words, such as free word order or the ability to inflect. We also look at 'mixed' instances of clitics, which behave like clear affixes in some contexts and like clear clitics in others. Systems such as these are extremely important for theoretical analyses of clitics: any theory that treats clitics as pure morphology will have to account for the syntactic behaviour of the clitics, while any theory that treats clitics as pure syntax will have to account for the morphological behaviour. We conclude the chapter with a brief examination of the relation between clitics and a particular class of word, the ubiquitous 'particle'.

Chapter 8 provides a brief overview of the main theoretical approaches to the phenomenology of clitics. We will not give a detailed explanation of these approaches, since it would require a book of this length to do that for just a single one of the major theoretical models. Instead, we will attempt to present the conceptual underpinnings of each model in as non-technical a way as possible. The main types of approach are those which present clitics as essentially morphological elements and those which present clitics as essentially syntactic objects. We look at several approaches deploying Paradigm Function Morphology, Optimality Theory and Distributed Morphology. The latter is an approach in which the morphological analysis is tightly bound up with syntactic analysis. We look in more detail at models of syntax and clitics in the next part of the chapter, where we consider the way that clitic systems have been treated in HPSG and LFG (in the case of the section dealing with HPSG we focus on the way that theory has been used to model edge inflection). We return to the question of how to establish a typology of clitics, including our own views on what constitutes a 'canonical clitic', before looking in more detail at the way that various approaches, principally Minimalist approaches, have handled various features of clitics, including Wackernagel (2P) placement, clitic cluster formation, clitic climbing and clitic doubling.

The final chapter presents very brief conclusions in which we concur with Arnold Zwicky (perhaps perversely, given the title of the book) that the term 'clitic' is best thought of as an umbrella term for a variety of properties which may or may not coincide. Although it may be useful in individual languages to set up a special sub-category of clitic to capture various distributional or formal generalizations, there is no obvious sense in which clitics represent a uniform, universal category. Rather, a complete grammatical description of a language has to establish for each element, and sometimes for each class of contexts in which an element is used, just what clitic-like or non-clitic-like properties that element has. That being said, the group of phenomena that we commonly call 'clitics' represents one of the more fascinating and challenging aspects of linguistic theory, combining as they do aspects of phonology, morphology, syntax, semantics and lexical representation in a bewildering variety of ways.

1.3   Works on clitics

Our book is not an exhaustive survey of the literature on clitics, much less a surrogate bibliography of the subject. However, we will here note those books and surveys which we have found particularly valuable or which we believe have been particularly influential. A complete bibliography of works on clitics up to 1991 can be found in Nevis et al. (1994).

A General works on clitics

Anderson (2005)
Crysmann (2002) (HPSG treatment)
Denniston (2002) (Ancient Greek particles)
Everett (1996)
Halpern (1995)
Klavans (1982)
Wackernagel (1892) (Ancient Greek)
Zwicky (1977)

Halpern (1998) (handbook article)
Nevis (2000) (handbook article)

B Collections of papers on clitics

Beukema and den Dikken (2000)
Borer (1986)
Chicago Linguistics Society, 1995, Parasession on clitics
Gerlach and Grijzenhout (2000)
Halpern and Zwicky (1996)
Heggie and Ordóñez (2005)
Kallulli and Tasmowski (2008)
van Riemsdijk (1999b)

C Studies of individual languages or language groups

Avgustinova (1997) (Bulgarian)
Benacchio and Renzi (1987) (Romance contrasted with Slavic)
Bošković (2001) (South Slavic)
Bonet (1991) (Catalan)
Franks and King (2000) (Slavic)
Gerlach (2002) (Romance)
Harris (2002) (Udi)
Journal of Slavic Linguistics, **12**(1–2), 2004
Kari (2003) (Degema)

Kupść (2000) (Polish)
Luís (2004) (European Portuguese)
Miller (1992) (French)
Monachesi (1999, 2005) (Italian, Romanian)
Perlmutter (1971)
Rivas (1977) (Romance, especially Spanish)
Tegey (1977) (Pashto)

D Works on (prosodic) words and the phonology of clitics

Berendsen (1986)
Dixon and Aikhenvald (2002)
Hall et al. (2008)
Hall and Kleinheinz (1999)
Kaisse (1985)
Peperkamp (1997)
Selkirk (1984) (especially chapter 7)
Toivonen (2003)
Vigário (2003) (European Portuguese)

We have found some of these references exceptionally useful. Anderson (2005) is an extremely valuable survey of many of the issues dealt with in this book. Anderson's book sets out a particular theoretical position on clitics (one with which we have a great deal of sympathy) but it also serves as a very good introduction to the general issues. Franks and King (2000) is a masterly survey of very complex and often confusing facts from the Slavic languages, together with a detailed but very accessible summary of research questions within the Principles and Parameters framework. We have availed ourselves of the data and analyses in these two works throughout our book. The earlier works of Zwicky (1977) and Klavans (1982) are still valuable and relevant and make an excellent introduction to the key issues. Zwicky and Pullum (1983) should be required reading for all linguists. Harris' (2002) monograph deals with an unusual clitic system in just one language, but the book is an object lesson in how to do theoretically informed descriptive linguistics (or descriptively informed theoretical linguistics) and is worth reading for its sheer elegance.

2   The functions of clitics

2.1   Introduction

In this chapter we give an overview of the main functions of clitics. Most clitics are straightforward function words, and so their functions are virtually the same as the functions of inflectional morphology and of full-form function words generally across languages. We will summarize the major functions, concentrating on broadly verbal properties, clausal properties (which are similar to the verbal properties), nominal properties and 'other' properties. We briefly illustrate the parity of function between clitics and inflections by pointing up instances of inflection which parallel the clitics we have discussed. One of the reasons why this comparison is important is because inflections are generally thought to arise in historical language change through a stage of cliticization.

Although the parallels between clitics and inflections are close, there are one or two differences in patterning, too. One important class of words which often become clitics is adverbials, with meanings such as *here*, *there*, *then*, *now*, as well as *still*, *yet*, *already*, *never*, and many others. These tend not to be grammaticalized as inflections. Similarly, many languages have discourse particles which take the form of clitics. Discourse particles can be thought of as a special class of adverb which have the function of helping the speaker manage the structure of the conversation (examples are given below in Section 2.6.3). These, too, are rarely expressed by inflection.

2.2   Verbal functions

The functional categories associated with verbs include tense, aspect and mood marking as well as polarity (i.e., negation), in addition to agreement properties derived from pronouns, such as person, number, gender, animacy, definiteness and so on. Many languages have inflections that indicate the speaker's attitude to the truth of a statement; for instance, whether the speaker knows a fact from personal experience, from inference or from hearsay. Some languages have different inflections on the verb depending on whether we are making a statement (declarative mood) or asking a question (interrogative mood). These categories are also often realized by clitics.

The English clitic auxiliary system is one of the most well-known instances of a clitic system, and we used the example of the auxiliary *'s* to introduce the notion of clitic in Chapter 1. In (1–5) we see examples of full form auxiliaries and their clitic equivalents:

(1) a. Harriet is reading
    b. Harriet**'s** reading

(2) a. Dick has left
    b. Dick**'s** left

(3) a. The kids have been warned
    b. The kids**'ve** been warned

(4) a. Sue would have complained
    b. Sue**'d** have complained

(5) a. Tom will have been looking for Harriet
    b. Tom**'ll** have been looking for Harriet

In each case we have an auxiliary verb which can be expressed by a phono-logically reduced form consisting of a single consonant (possibly syllabic, and possibly preceded by schwa). The position of the clitic in the phrase corresponds to the position of the full form auxiliary (it comes immediately after the subject of the clause in these examples). The auxiliary verb helps to express such categories as progressive aspect (1), perfect aspect (2, 3) and modal meanings (4), including future time reference (5).

As we saw in Chapter 1, these reduced auxiliary forms don't resemble affixes very much. First, it would be unusual (but not impossible) for a tense/aspect/mood affix to attach to a noun. More importantly, however, we have seen that the reduced form attaches to words of any category. Further examples are given in (6):

(6) a. The girl over there**'s** reading
    b. The guy you were talking to**'s** already left
    c. The girl nearest him**'d** have complained
    d. The man who phoned**'ll** have been looking for Harriet
    e. The kids responsible**'ve** been singing

In (6) the auxiliary attaches respectively to an adverb *there*, a preposition *to*, a pronoun *him*, a verb (but part of a relative clause modifying the subject noun) and an adjective *responsible*. True affixes are generally very selective about the word class they attach to and never show this degree of freedom. We will see in Chapter 4 that this oversimplifies the picture somewhat, but the general point is clear. We will refer to this lack of selectivity as promiscuous attachment.

It's also important to see that the reduced auxiliary forms are not ordinary (if unstressed) words. This is clear in the case of the *'ll* and *'d* clitics when they correspond to *will/shall* and *would/should* respectively. There is no productive phonological process even in the most colloquial speech which would derive the forms /d/ or /l/ from /wʊd/ or /wɪl/. This is an idiosyncratic property of these words in their capacity as auxiliary verbs. Other auxiliaries such as *was/were* do not have such reduced forms, and the nouns *wood* and *will* do not have reduced forms either.

English is not the only language to have clitic auxiliaries. Several of the Slavic languages have such clitics, too. A well-known example, which we will return to, is that of Serbian/Croatian. In this language the verb *be* is used as a copular and it has a full form and a clitic form (just as in English). In (7) we see the clitic form *su* '(they) are':

(7)   Devojke **su**   u sadu
          girls   3PL.BE in garden
          'The girls are in the garden'

This clitic form is unstressed. If we wish to focus on the verb we use a full form, *jesu*:

(8)   Devojke JESU   u sadu
          girls   3PL.BE.FOC in garden
          'The girls ARE in the garden'

There are other respects in which the clitic form *su* differs in its properties from the full form *jesu*. In Serbian/Croatian a subject phrase can be omitted if it is obvious from the context. This is seen in (9):

(9)   JESU u sadu
          3PL.BE in garden
          '(They) ARE in the garden'

The clitic requires a host to its left (that is, it is an enclitic). This means that it cannot appear at the beginning of a sentence, because it would have nothing to encliticize to (see (10a)). Since the clitic form cannot be given stress, we can't focus it either (see (10b)):

(10) a.   * **Su**   u sadu
                  3PL.BE in garden
        b.   * **SU**   u sadu
                  3PL.BE in garden

The clitics of Serbian/Croatian exhibit a very important property, which distinguishes them sharply from the auxiliary clitics of English. They have to appear in the second position in the sentence. Word order in Serbian/Croatian is very free, and this means that almost any phrase can begin the sentence. The clitic comes immediately after this first phrase (11a, b) but nowhere else. For instance, it cannot appear after the second phrase (11c):

(11) a.   U sadu   **su**
              in garden 3PL.BE
              '(They) are in the garden'

b.   U sadu **su**   devojke
        in garden 3PL.BE girls
        'The girls are in the garden'

c.   *Devojke u sadu   **su**
        girls   in garden 3PL.BE

This principle of second position is extremely widespread in clitic systems, and we'll be discussing it in some detail throughout the book. Clitics which obey this principle we will call 2P clitics. They are often referred to as Wackernagel clitics after the Swiss philologist Jacob Wackernagel, who first described such constructions in the classical Indo-European languages (Wackernagel 1892 (see Chapter 3)).

In English the auxiliary clitics appear in the same position in the sentence that the full form auxiliaries appear. In Serbian/Croatian the positioning of the clitics is defined according to strict rules which are totally different from the rules governing the rest of the sentence. At a purely descriptive level it is sometimes useful to distinguish clitics which show more or less the positioning you would expect from the rest of the grammar from clitics which seem to obey entirely separate principles of ordering. Zwicky (1977) called the first type 'simple clitics' and the second type 'special clitics' and you will often see this terminology in the literature. We will occasionally draw the same distinction, though in Chapter 5 we will see that it's a distinction which can lead to misunderstanding.

It's important to appreciate that there is nothing specific about these tense/aspect/mood categories which forces a language to express them with clitics rather than with affixes or with periphrastic constructions involving full words. For instance, the perfect aspect is found in a good many languages, including Spanish and Swahili. In Spanish it is expressed by the auxiliary verb *haber* 'have' and the perfect participle:

(12) a.   El muchacho ha partido
            the boy   has left
            'The boy has left'

     b.   Las muchachas han partido
            the girls   have left
            'The girls have left'

     c.   Hemos partido
            we.have left
            'We have left'

There is no reduced form of the auxiliary verb so here we are dealing with a construction formed from two words, much like the English construction with full form auxiliaries. Spanish also has a progressive aspect formed with the auxiliary verb *estar* 'be' and a participle form of the verb ending in *-ndo*: *Las muchachas están partiendo* 'The girls are (in the process of) leaving'. Again, the auxiliary is not a clitic.

On the other hand, Swahili has a perfect aspect form which is expressed by means of the prefix *me-*. Compare (13a), a simple past form, with (13b), the perfect form:

(13) a. Hamisi a-li-soma   kitabu
         Hamisi 3SG-PAST-read book
         'Hamisi read the book'
    b.   Hamisi a-me-soma   kitabu
         Hamisi 3SG-PERF-read book
         'Hamisi has read the book'

Similarly, many languages express a progressive or continuous aspect using affixal morphology. Inflectional future tense and conditional mood (corresponding roughly to English *will/would*) is found in many languages, including all the modern Romance languages.

From this brief survey of auxiliaries we can see four typical properties of clitics:

1   Clitics are generally unstressed (and unstressable). Even in languages which lack a category of word stress, we find that clitics are elements that cannot be focussed or emphasized by being given special emphatic accent.

2   Clitics require a host to attach to. Either the clitic attaches to the right of a host (enclitic) or to the left (proclitic).

3   Clitics attach promiscuously, that is, they do not select words of a particular class.

4   Clitics often have different syntax from fully-fledged words. In some cases this means that the position of the clitic is determined by entirely separate principles from the syntax of the rest of the language (special clitics, for instance 2P clitics), in other cases the basic position of the clitic is the same as that of a full-form word with similar function (simple clitics), but in practice there may be restrictions that apply specifically to clitics because of their need to attach to a host in a particular direction.

2.3   Clausal properties

We now give examples of properties expressed by clitics that relate to the clause as a whole, though to some extent it is artificial to distinguish these from verbal clitics, because properties of the clause tend to be expressed on verbs in inflection. In each case we will provide just one or two properties that distinguish the clitic from a full word or an affix.

We have seen that Serbian/Croatian has 2P auxiliary clitics. Czech has a very similar set of 2P clitics. However, Czech has a large number of adverbial particles included amongst the clitics. One of these, *prý*, has the function of an evidentiality marker, comparable to that of the word *apparently* in *Apparently, Harriet has already left*, or the phrase *(so) they say*. These expressions indicate that the speaker believes the truth of the assertion that they are making but doesn't actually have first-hand evidence for its truth; for instance, the speaker didn't actually witness Harriet leaving. Instead, the speaker surmises this from indirect evidence (her coat isn't hanging on the coat hanger) or has been told by someone else (hearsay). The English particle/adverb *apparently* is like any other adverb and can appear in various positions in the sentence: *Apparently, Harriet has already left*, *Harriet, apparently, has already left*, *Harriet has apparently already left*, *Harriet has already left, apparently* or even *Harriet has already, apparently, left*. Adverbs in Czech normally exhibit a similar freedom of placement, but not the particle *prý*. In (14) we see that it can occur only in the second position in the sentence:[1]

(14) a.   Eva **prý** již   napsala   ten dopis
           Eva PRY already has.written that letter
           'Apparently, Eva has already written the letter'
    b.   (***prý**) Eva již (***prý**) napsala (***prý**) ten dopis (***prý**)

Word order in Czech is very free, so in principle more or less any word or phrase can appear in first position, but the clitic always follows the first phrase:

(15) a.   Již **prý** napsala ten dopis
           '(She's) already written the letter, apparently'
    b.   Napsala **prý** ten dopis
           '(She's) written the letter, apparently'
    c.   Ten dopis **prý** již napsala
           'The letter, (she's) already written, apparently'

Many languages express yes-no questions (or polar questions) by means of an uninflected particle. In Polish and Latvian the particle comes at the beginning of the sentence, in Japanese and Chinese it comes at the end of the sentence (we discuss the Chinese case in Chapter 4). Finnish has an interrogative clitic, *ko/kö*. Word order in Finnish is very free, but the word or phrase which is the focus of a question is placed at the beginning of the clause. The interrogative clitic attaches to that word, irrespective of the word's class. Thus, the *ko/kö* marker is a 2P clitic. (We will discuss this case in a little more detail in Chapter 4.)

Yes-no questions have a special status with respect to meaning because we can focus the question on different constituents of the clause. In English we can do this by means of special syntactic constructions (*Was it Dick that wrote the letter?*) or by means of intonation and accent (*Did DICK write the letter (or Tom)? Did Dick WRITE the letter (or type it)?*). In other languages an interrogative particle can serve the purpose of intonation. In Imbabura Quechua the interrogative particle *chu* attaches to whatever constituent is the focus of the question (see (16a)). If the question has neutral focus (with no particular constituent receiving special focus) the particle attaches to the verb (see (16b)):

(16)   Imbabura Quechua (Cole 1982, 15)
    a.   wasi-man=**chu** ri-ju-ngui
             house-to=Q   go-PROG-2
             'Are you going TO THE HOUSE?'
    b.   wasi-man ri-ju-ngui=**chu**
             house-to go-PROG-2=Q
             'Are you going to the house?'

The *chu* particle has no inherent stress of its own and requires a host to attach
to. It is therefore a clitic, though one whose placement is determined by the
information structure of the clause.

   Evidential meanings are often expressed by full-form adverbs or particles,
such as English apparently. However, these markers are like the Czech clitic
prý in that they are not obligatory. In many languages evidentiality is an obligatory inflectional category. Thus, in Turkish, if the speaker has not witnessed an
event for themselves, they must use the evidential form of the verb using a suffix
–miş (Lewis 1967). The Amazonian language Tariana has five different evidential markers (Aikhenvald 2003). In a number of languages verbs take different
inflections depending on whether they are in the declarative or the interrogative
mood (e.g. Yup'ik, Reed et al. 1977).

   There is one verb- or clause-level function which we have yet to mention
and that is negation (or more generally, polarity). However, we will leave this
case, since it turns out that most of the better-known instances of apparent clitic
negation are best analysed as affixation. This is even true of English, as we will
see when we look at the work of Zwicky and Pullum (1983) in the next chapter.
We will therefore not illustrate negation here.

2.4   Nominal functions

   Clitics can express typical nominal functions such as case, definiteness, possessor agreement and (more rarely) number. In Chapter 1 we saw that
English has a possessive clitic *'s*. Of course, in English possession can also be
indicated by a full word, the preposition *of*. In many languages possession is indicated by means of an affix on the possessor noun, usually known as a genitive
case marker. In some respects one can think of the English *'s* as a clitic genitive case marker. Equally, in many languages possession is indicated by means
of an agreement construction, in which it is the possessed noun that is marked
morphologically.[2] This is illustrated in (17) for Hungarian:

(17)   Possessor agreement in Hungarian
             autó   car
             autó-m   my car
             autó-d   thy car
             autó-ja   his/her car
             etc.

The Hungarian possessor endings show all the properties of affixes and none of the properties of clitics. However, in the Austronesian language Tukang Besi, spoken in Sulawesi, Indonesia, the formative that appears to be a possessive suffix is actually a clitic:

(18)   Tukang Besi (Donohue 1999, 73; see also Dryer 2005b, 234)
   a.   te   kene=**su**
       NON-NOM friend=1SG.POSS
       'my friends'
   b.   te   wunua molengo=**su**
       NON-NOM house old=1SG.POSS
       'my old house'

The marker -*su* indicates a 1sg possessor, just like the suffix -*m* in Hungarian *autóm* 'my car'. However, unlike the Hungarian suffix, the Tukang Besi possessive marker can sometimes attach to the rightmost word in the noun phrase, just like the English '*s*, depending on whether the noun phrase as a whole has nominative or non-nominative function in its clause (Donohue 1999, 304). If the non-nominative case marker *te* is replaced by the nominative marker *na* in (18b), for instance, we find the order N-POSS ADJ: *na wunua=su molengo*. The possessive marker in (Modern) Greek also shows variability of placement characteristic more of clitics than of affixes.

In Chapter 1 we gave the French definite article as a (possible) illustration of a proclitic. There we saw that the English definite article is rather similar to the French in this respect, though it has enough properties of a fully fledged word to make it difficult to treat it as a standard instance of a clitic. In other languages, definiteness is marked by means of clitics which appear at the right edge of the phrase (enclitic) or after the first word of the noun phrase, as in the Bulgarian examples shown in (19):

(19) a.   (edna) interesna   kniga
       one   interesting book
       'an interesting book'
   b.   kniga=**ta** (e interesna)
       book=the (is interesting)
       'the book (is interesting)'
   c.   interesna=**ta**   kniga
       interesting=the book
       'the interesting book'
   d.   anglijska=**ta** kniga
       English=the book
       'the English book'
   e.   interesna=**ta**   anglijska kniga
       interesting=the English   book
       'the interesting English book'

The examples in (19) show that the definite clitic is a 2P clitic, but 'second position' is defined within the noun phrase rather than the whole clause. We will return to this distinction in Chapter 3.

Again, we can contrast such constructions as the French and the Bulgarian with languages like German in which the definite article is a full-form word which occurs only at the beginning of the noun phrase. At the same time there are languages in which definiteness is marked by means of inflectional affixes. In Arabic, for instance, a noun is made definite by means of the prefix *al-* (*l-* after vowels): *kitaab(u)* 'definite clitic '(a) book', *al-kitaab(u)* 'the book'. Arabic nouns even trigger a process of definiteness agreement by which an adjective modifying a definite-marked noun has to repeat the definiteness marker: *al-kitaab-u l-kabiir-u* 'the large book' (literally: 'the-book the-large' (Ryding 2005, 239-44)).

In many languages nouns take affixal inflections which indicate the grammatical function of the noun phrase in the clause. A typical example is Latin, in which nouns distinguish the following cases: nominative (subject), accusative (direct object), dative (indirect object), genitive (possessor), ablative (from a place, instrument and other meanings) and finally vocative (used for direct address to a person or thing). Some of these functions are often expressed by full words in other languages. Thus the functions of dative, genitive and ablative are expressed by prepositions in English (*to, of, by/with/from*) and by postpositions in Japanese (*Tookyoo e* 'towards Tokyo', *Kyooto de* 'in Kyoto', *Oosaka kara* 'from Osaka').[3] In other languages, the elements which mark case functions or grammatical functions are clitics. In some descriptions of such languages these are referred to as clitic prepositions/postpositions, while in other descriptions they are referred to as clitic case markers. For our purposes it doesn't greatly matter how we describe them, provided we recognize that their morphological and syntactic behaviour is neither that of fully-fledged words, nor that of bona fide affixes.

Indo-Aryan languages such as Hindi are rich in clitic postpositions. A list of these is given in (20):

(20)   Clitic postpositions in Hindi

Clitic	case name	function
ne	ergative	subject of transitive verb
ko	accusative/dative	direct or indirect object
se	instrumental	by means of, with
kaa	genitive	of
mẽ	locative1	place
par	locative2	place

These postpositions are not affixes. Hindi nouns do take inflectional endings and these express singular/plural number and direct/oblique/vocative case. However, those endings are genuine suffixes and thus they cannot take wide scope over coordinated nouns.

The subject and object function of these postpositions is illustrated in (21) and the possessor function in (22):

(21)   raam=**ne** ravii=**ko** piiṭaa
              Raam-NE Ravi-KO beat
              'Raam beat Ravii'

(22) a.   raam aur raani=**kaa** bhaaii
              Ram and Rani=KAA brother
              'the brother of Ram and Rani'
     b.   raam=**ke**   aur raani=**ke**   bhaaiyõ
              Ram=KAA and Rani=KAA brothers
              'Ram's brothers and Rani's brothers'

(The form =*ke* in (22b) is the form assumed by KAA when the possessed noun is plural.)

As indicated in the glosses, the genitive postposition in (22a) applies to the complete conjunct, *Ram and Rani*. We often say in such cases that the postposition 'takes (wide) scope' over the whole conjunct. The result is that Ram and Rani themselves are brothers. However, in (22b) the postposition relates solely to the noun it immediately follows ('takes narrow scope'), implying that there are two distinct sets of brothers. Exactly the same effect is found with the English possessive clitic: *Ram and Rani's brother* refers to one person who is brother to both Ram and Rani (so that Ram and Rani themselves are brothers), while the expression *Ram's and Rani's brothers* can refer to two different groups of brothers (and Ram and Rani don't have to be related to each other).

In some languages such case markers appear as 2P clitics. In (23) we see an example from the Yawuru language of Western Australia (Hosokawa 1991, 36, cited by Dryer 2005a, 211):

(23)   kayukayu=**ni** buru inanyarndyarrayirr mudiga
              soft=ERG   sand caught   motorcar
              'The soft sands caught our car'

The clitic *ni* marks the subject of a transitive clause (ergative case), but it attaches to the first word of the noun phrase, much like the definiteness marker in Bulgarian.

A case which is very rarely discussed in the theoretical literature is the vocative (see Daniel and Spencer 2009). This is the case form of a noun which denotes the person or thing the speaker is addressing in speech, for instance in an imperative. An archaic equivalent in English would be the use of the particle *O*, as in *O ye of little faith*, or *O Lord, remember not our transgressions*. In Latin many nouns have a specially inflected case form for this function. Thus, the word *dominus* 'lord' has the vocative case form *domine*, as in *adiuva me, Domine* 'help me, (O) Lord'. A number of languages regularly use a particle such as archaic English 'O', including Ancient Greek (where the particle is also 'o'). However, in English and Greek the particles are stressed and so look more like function words than clitics (though how they are to be represented in the syntactic structure is anybody's guess). In other languages, however, such particles have more the character of (unstressed) clitics. A case in point is Arabic, where the particle is *yaa*: *yaa Rashiidu* 'O Rashid!' (Ryding 2005, 170). This is a relatively unusual instance of a case marker which is a proclitic. However, because noun phrases in Arabic begin with the noun, especially where we have a proper noun, the particle can't be said to exhibit promiscuous attachment.

2.5   Argument functions

2.5.1   Argument and agreement marking

Even though agreement markers tend to be affixes and arguments tend to be full words, there is no necessary correlation between affixal status and agreement marking, on the one hand, and word status and argument marking, on the other. That is why argument marking and agreement can also be encoded by clitics. Clitics with this function are called pronominal clitics and generally express person, number, gender and case features.

2.5.2   Argument clitics

When pronominal clitics function as arguments they occur in complementary distribution with overt subjects or objects, satisfying the subcategorization properties of the verb they are semantically related to. Subjects and objects often behave differently in one and the same language, and we will therefore look separately at object clitics and subject clitics. We first consider instances in which the clitics function more or less like a pronoun in English, in that they express the argument of the verb on their own, and cannot co-occur with a full-form word bearing the same function.

Object arguments

We begin with object arguments of verbs, without necessarily distinguishing between direct and indirect objects (in the languages we discuss here both functions are expressed by clitics).

In Serbian/Croatian, the direct object of a verb can be encoded either by a full pronoun or by a clitic form. In (24) we see the clitic form *je* 'her.ACC' (not to be confused with the 3sg auxiliary verb form *je* discussed earlier in the chapter):

(24)   Jovan **je**   vole
            Jovan ACC.3.SG.FEM loves
            'Jovan loves her'

If we compare the clitic form *je* with its full form *njû* 'her.ACC', we see that they differ in various ways. For example, the clitic has a short vowel which can never bear tone, unlike *njû* which has a long vowel with a falling tone (signalled by the circumflex accent). Similarly, the clitic can never bear contrastive stress, unlike the full form:

(25)   * Jovan **JE**   vole
                 Jovan her.CL.FOC loves
                 (Intended: 'Jovan loves her (and not, say, Maria))'
(26)   Jovan vole NJÛ
                 Jovan loves her
                 'Jovan loves her'

The clitic *je* is also different from its full form *njû* in that it requires a host to its left, exactly like the clitic auxiliary addressed in Section 2.2. This effectively means that both clitic auxiliaries and clitic pronouns in Serbian/Croatian are enclitic. Therefore, while full pronouns can occur in sentence-initial position, clitic pronouns cannot:

(27)   Njû vole Jovan
                 her loves Jovan
                 'Jovan loves her'
(28)   * **Je**   vole Jovan
                 her.CL loves Jovan

It is then clear that clitic forms lack the phonological autonomy of a full word. Further evidence of this is given in (29, 30). Example (29a) shows that *je* can never occur in isolation, unlike its stressed counterpart, *njû* (29b), and that it can never be coordinated with another pronominal form, whether a word or a clitic, (30a). Full pronouns, such as *njû* 'her.ACC' and *mène* 'me.ACC', on the contrary, can be coordinated, as shown in (30b). In (30a, b) *ga* 'he.ACC' is the masculine third singular clitic and *njèga* 'he.ACC' the corresponding full form (circumflex accent signals falling tone on a long vowel, while grave accent signals rising tone on a long vowel):

(29) a.   Koga znaješ?   ***JE**
           who you.know her.CL.FOC
     b.   Koga znaješ?   NJÛ
           who you.know her.ACC(full form)
           'Who do you know?' 'Her.'

(30) a.   *Maria **ga**   i **je**   znaje
           Maria him.CL and her.CL knows
           (Intended: 'Maria knows him and her')
     b.   Marija znaje njèga i   njû
           Maria knows him and her (full forms)
           'Maria knows him and her'

Clitic pronouns differ from full words in other ways as well. In Serbian/Croatian, not only clitic auxiliaries but also clitic pronouns must appear in the second position after the first constituent in the clause, very much like clitic auxiliaries in this language (see Section 2.2). This is shown in (31). Full pronouns, on the contrary, are just like lexical nouns in that they can appear in almost any position in the clause, as in (32):

(31) a.   Jovan **je**   vide svaki dan
            Jovan her.CL sees every day
            'Jovan sees her every day'
     b.   Vide **je**   svaki dan
            sees her.CL every day
     c.   Svaki dan **je**   vide
            every day her.CL sees
            '(He) sees her every day'

(32) a.   Jovan vide njû svaki dan
            Jovan sees her every day
            'Jovan sees her every day'
     b.   Njû vide Jovan svaki dan
            her sees Jovan every day
            '*Her*, Jovan sees every day'

An interesting question arises with 2P clitic systems such as that of Ser-
bian/Croatian. Languages generally take 'second position' to mean 'after the
first constituent'. However, in many languages (including the classical languages
originally studied by Wackernagel) the host can be just a single word, even if that
means that the clitic cluster breaks up a syntactic constituent. This is illustrated
in (33):

(33) a.   [Svaki **je**   dan] vide ovoj čovek
            each her.CL day sees that man
     b.   [Ovoj **je**   čovek] vide svaki dan
            that her.CL man   sees every day
            'That man sees her every day'

In (33a) the clitic has broken up the noun phrase 'every day', functioning as a
time adverbial, and in (33b) it has broken up the subject noun phrase, intervening
between the determiner 'that' and the head noun. This type of behaviour is quite
untypical of words, because we don't expect a lexical item to break up a phrase,
all the more so if it is not even semantically related to it. In particular, full-
form pronouns such as *njû* cannot break up phrases. For instance, we couldn't
have (33c):

(33) c.   * [Svaki njû dan] vide ovoj čovek
            each her day sees that man
            (Intended: 'That man sees her every day')

The fact that clitics occupy such a restricted position is quite at odds with
the fact that word order in this language is extremely free. The contrast between
the placement of clitics and full-form words is therefore quite striking. However, Serbian/Croatian is far from unusual in this respect, indeed, if anything the
typical pattern is for rigid clitic order in a language to co-occur with very free
word order elsewhere in that language.

Clitics whose syntax is different from other words are often referred to
generally as special clitics. Not all clitics have unique placement or ordering

properties. Clitic pronouns in German show more or less the positioning of their corresponding full forms. They belong to the group of clitics which are generally known as simple clitics. In (34) and (35), the clitic forms *'s* and *'n* occur in the same position as the full forms *es* 'it' and *ihn* 'he.ACC', respectively.

(34) a. Er hat es gewusst
          he has it known

      b. Er hat**'s**   gewusst
          he has.it.CL known

          'He knew it'

(35) a. Ich habe ihn gesehen
          I   have him seen

      b. Ich hab**'n**   gesehen
          I   have.him.CL seen

          'I have seen him'

In (34b, 35b) the verb=clitic combinations are pronounced as a single word /hats/ and /habn̩/.

However, it would be misleading to think that such clitic forms show the same distribution of the full words. Note that, like all clitic forms so far presented, German clitic pronouns are unstressed and therefore need a stressed host to 'lean' on. This means that, like clitics in Serbian/Croatian, they show many of the properties of clitics, such as not bearing contrastive stress (36), not occurring clause-initially (37) and not appearing in isolation (38) (where capitalization indicates that the clitic is intended as bearing accent):

(36) * Ich hab **'N**   gefragt, nicht sie
        I   have him.CL.FOC asked   not   her
        (Intended: 'I asked him, not her')

(37) * **'N**   hab ich gefragt
        him.CL.FOC have I   asked
        (Intended: 'Him, I asked')

(38) Was haben Sie gesehn? ***'S**
        what have   you seen   it.CL
        (Intended: 'What did you see? It')

Like typical clitics, they are not constrained to attach to words of a particular class. In (39a) the clitic pronoun *'s* attaches to a full subject pronoun and in (39b) it attaches to a noun.

(39) a. Kannst du**'s**   mir   geben?
          can   you.it.CL to.me give

          'Can you give it to me?'

      b. Wenn Mutti**'s**   mir   gegeben hätte
          if   Mummy.it.CL to.me given   had

          'If Mummy had given it to me'

Clitic pronouns in Romance languages such as Spanish or Italian share several of the properties of clitics, such as phonological deficiency. However, in most

Romance languages they obey a constraint which says that they must appear adjacent to a verb form (either a lexical verb or an auxiliary verb). Ordinary nouns, including full forms of pronouns, are not subject to such a constraint. In this respect the Romance pronominal clitics have a distinct syntax from full-form words, and so would be regarded as special clitics.

(40)   **Me-lo**=dió solo hoy
            me-it=gave only today
            '(He) gave it to me only today'

In (40), the clitic string *me-lo* 'me-it' appears as the first element. This is possible because the clitic string is proclitic (i.e., it needs a host to its right). So, while Serbian/Croatian object clitics are always enclitic, most Romance clitics can be either proclitic (typically before indicative and subjunctive verb forms) as in (40), or enclitic (after imperative, infinitive and gerund) as in (41).

(41)   Da=**me-lo**, por favor!
            give=me-it please
            'Give it to me, please!'

Subject arguments

In addition to clitic pronouns which encode an object function, there are also clitics pronouns that function as subject arguments, in other words, subject pronouns are also prone to weakening and ultimately cliticization. Spoken French provides a well-known example . The clitic forms in (42) are contrasted with the full forms.

(42)   French pronominal clitics

			clitic	full form
1	Singular		je [ʒə]	moi [mwa]
2	Singular		tu [ty]/ t' [t]	toi [twa]
3	Singular			
		Masculine	il [il]	lui [lɥi]
		Feminine	elle [el]	elle [el]
1	Plural		nous [nu]	nous [nu]
2	Plural		vous [vu]	vous [vu]
3	Plural			
		Masculine	ils [il]	eux [ø:]
		Feminine	elles [el]	elles [el]

As is often the case with clitic systems, for some person/numbers the clitic form is identical to the full form except for being inherently unaccented. However, where the clitic and full forms differ, the clitic forms show the kinds of properties we've seen with object clitics. For instance, they cannot be modified, conjoined, contrastively stressed or used in isolation (Cardinaletti and Starke 1999, 44):

(43) a.   Seul lui/*il viendra   demain
            only he/CL will.come tomorrow
            'Only he will come tomorrow'

      b.   Pierre et   lui/*il   viendront demain
            Pierre and him/CL will.come tomorrow
            'He and Pierre will come tomorrow'

      c.   C'est lui/*il qui viendra   demain,   pas Marie
            It.is   he/CL who will.come tomorrow, not Marie
            'It's him who will come tomorrow, not Marie'

      d.   Qui viendra demain? Lui/*il
            Who will   come   tomorrow? Him/CL

Clitic subjects are often doubled by full form pronouns in a syntactically dislocated position:

(44)   Lui, **il** viendra   demain
            he   CL will.come tomorrow
            'He will come tomorrow'

Moreover, the clitic forms have to be placed adjacent to the verb and cannot be separated by a parenthetical, unlike the full-form pronouns.

(45) a.   Lui/Jean, souvent, mange du fromage
            he/Jean often   eats   of cheese
            'Often, he/Jean eats cheese'

      b.   * **Il**, souvent, mange du fromage
            CL often   eats   of cheese
            'Often, he eats cheese'

A number of languages have subject clitics. According to Kari (2003) subject proclitics are the only pronominal clitics in Degema, a Benue-congo language (the language, has a variety of non-subject enclitics expressing tense-aspect-mood properties). Luiseño, an Uto-Aztecan language, has subject clitics in addition to a variety of tense-aspect-mood clitics. A number of Salishan languages have subject clitics but object affixes, for example Lummi (Steele et al. 1981). The only pronominal clitics of the Nakh-Daghestanian language Udi are the subject markers, but they have rather unusual properties, which we describe below in Section 7.4.2

Clitic arguments – summary

Our survey has argument clitics which share the properties that they are unstressed (and hence can't be modified), cannot be coordinated and cannot occur in isolation. Their syntax is different from that of full words, and even so-called simple clitics, such as those of German, do not appear in exactly the same position as the corresponding full personal pronoun: German clitic pronouns cannot occur clause-initially, especially if they are enclitic.

There are important respects in which the clitic pronouns surveyed above differ from affixes. A feature of the Serbian/Croatian and German clitics is that they don't select the class of the base they attach to, and can thus take words of any category as their host (that is, they show promiscuous attachment). Romance clitic pronouns are different in this respect, in that they have to attach to a verb form, whether an auxiliary verb or a lexical verb. This is a characteristic of a number of clitic pronoun systems. Such systems are in some ways intermediate between true clitic systems and true affix systems, and for this reason we will return to them later in the book.

We now turn to systems of argument marking which can be said to constitute agreement systems.

2.5.3   Agreement marking

Affixal agreement

In an agreement relation, the element agreeing with the argument co-occurs with the argument to which it is coreferential. That is, we need to have simultaneously in the clause the controller of agreement (e.g. the subject/object phrase) and the target of agreement, that is, the agreeing word (generally a verb). It is also one of the properties of the agreeing element (or agreement marker) that it shares a similar (though not complete) set of person, number and case features with the argument. Although we tend to think of agreement as being morphologically marked, either through word form alternation or simply through affixation, agreement can also be encoded through clitics.

There are a great many examples of languages in which subject and/or object agreement is signalled through affixation on the verb. Chukchee is a language in which a transitive verb has to mark agreement with both subject and object (46):

(46) a.   ənan ine-lʔu-gʔi   gəm
            he   3SG.SUBJ-saw-1SG.OBJ me
            'He saw me'
     b.   kejŋe ne-lʔu-gʔen   ətləgən
            bears 3PL.SUBJ-saw-3SG.OBJ father
            'The bears saw the father'

As is usual with such agreement systems, the agreement markers themselves can function as arguments without necessarily co-occurring with an overt noun phrase or pronoun:

(47) a.   ine-lʔu-gʔi
            3SG.SUBJ-saw-1SG.OBJ
            'He saw me'
     b.   ne-lʔu-gʔen
            3PL.SUBJ-saw-3SG.OBJ
            'They saw him'

In this case the agreement markers can be thought of as a kind of incorporated pronominal (see Chapter 6).

Clitics as object agreement markers

We will say that a clitic is functioning as an agreement marker when the argument clitic is obligatorily present even when the argument itself is expressed by an overt noun phrase. In the clitics literature such a situation is often referred to as clitic doubling. The idea is that the clitic doubles the argument phrase (or, according to some theoretical accounts, the clitic is the real argument and the overt noun phrase doubles the clitic).

In Macedonian, definite/specific direct objects and all indirect objects are obligatorily cross-referenced by a pronominal clitic (Spencer 1991, 359–62). Franks and King (2000, 251) cite examples (48–49):[4]

(48)   Marija *(**go**)   poznava učenik-ot/Vlado/nego
           Marija 3SG.OBJ knows   pupil-DEF/Vlado/him
           'Marija knows the pupil/Vlado/him'
           (Vlado is a male personal name.)

(49)   Marija (***go**)   poznava eden učenik
           Marija 3SG.M.OBJ knows one pupil
           'Marija knows a pupil (some pupil or other)'

The -ot suffix of *učenik-ot* 'the pupil' is the definite article (itself a kind of clitic). Example (48) therefore illustrates that a definite direct object such as a proper name, a full-form (emphatic or contrastive) pronoun or a noun with a definite article must be doubled by the clitic. The clitic therefore functions as a kind of agreement marker. As was the case with Chukchee agreement, the overt noun phrase can be omitted, as in (50):

(50)   Marija **go**   poznava
           Marija 3SG.M.OBJ knows
           'Marija knows him'

The doubling is contingent on certain semantic constraints being met: in particular, the object has to be specific or identifiable (any definite noun phrase is ipso facto specific). Franks and King (2000, chapter 7) discuss these factors in some detail and also discuss whether it is appropriate to call such a relationship 'agreement'. We will deal with this question in much greater detail in Chapter 5. For the present we will simply mention that there are abundant cases of affixal agreement systems which are subject to similar or even more stringent semantic restrictions, so there can be no objection in principle to thinking of such doubling as a kind of agreement.

The clitics in Macedonian are very much like the clitics of Romance languages in the sense that they are constrained to appear adjacent to a verb (either an auxiliary or a main verb). In this respect they are becoming more like prototypical affixes. However, the clitic system of Bulgarian, while very similar to that of Macedonian, retains vestiges of the Wackernagel or 2P organization described for Serbian/Croatian in Section 2.2. Here, too, direct and especially indirect objects are generally doubled by a clitic if they are specific (see Franks and King 2000, 51–8 for examples and discussion). We will return to various aspects of these systems later in the book.

Clitics as subject agreement markers

In Udi, subject agreement markers obligatorily cross-reference the subject for person and number features (Harris 2000, 2002). As Harris shows in meticulous detail, the subject markers conform to all the criteria true of clitics. Unlike verbal affixes, these markers may attach to a rather broad range of lexical items: not just a verb (51), but also a negative particle (52) or a noun (53), among others. In all cases they clearly need a host to their left and would therefore be unable to occur clause-initially.

(51)   boš-t'-al-le
        in-LV-FUT-3SG
        'S/he will plant'
(52)   nana-n   te-**ne**   buɣa-b-e   p'a   ačik'ašey
        mother-ERG NEG-3SG find-DO-AOR II   two   toy.ABS
        'Mother did not find two toys'
(53)   yaq'-a-**ne**   ba-st'a
        road-DAT-3SG in-LV.PRES
        'On the road he opens it'

The same subject markers have the remarkable property of occurring as enclitics on inflected verb forms, or even as endoclitics, placed inside verb stem morphemes. We'll discuss this aspect of their behaviour in Section 7.4.2

2.6   Other functions

We conclude with a few examples of clitics subserving functions which are not normally thought of as inflectional (though they can be realized with inflections in other languages).

2.6.1   Conjunctions and prepositions

It's very common for highly frequent conjunctions such as 'and', 'or' and 'but' to become phonologically reduced, as when *William and Mary* is pronounced /wɪljəmṇmɛːɹɪ/ ('William 'n' Mary'). Some languages, however, have conjunctions which are always clitics. A particularly interesting example, which we shall return to, is provided by Latin. One way of saying 'and' in Latin is to add the clitic =*que* to the second member of the coordinated phrase:

(54)   senatus populus=**que** Romanus
            senate people=and Roman
            'the Roman senate and people (SPQR)'

The reason this is a clitic and not a suffix is that it attaches to words of any category (promiscuous attachment):

(55) a.   arma virum=**que** cano
            arms man=and I.sing
            'I sing of arms and the man' (*Aeneid* I, 1.1)   noun=*que*
      b.   inferret=**que**   deos Latio,
            brought.in=and gods to.Latium
            'and imported the gods to Latium' (*Aeneid* I, 1.6)   verb=*que*
      c.   multos=**que** per annos errabant
            many=and   for years they.wandered
            'and they wandered for many years' (*Aeneid* I, 1.31)   adjective=*que*

An example of a conjunction which occurs in the normal syntactic position of conjunctions would be the reduced form of English *and* pronounced as a syllabic /n̩/: *Chomsky 'n' Halle, Laurel 'n' Hardy*. In English it's also common for monosyllabic prepositions to be pronounced without any stress (and hence with a reduced vowel): *for four dollars* /fə fɔː dɒləz/ (British English pronunciation). Such prepositions alternate with stressed full forms, of course. In Russian, two prepositions (almost always) lack a full form because they are single consonants: *v* 'in' and *s* 'with'. These have exactly the same distribution as other, stressed, prepositions, such as *na* 'on' or *bez* 'without' but they have to procliticize to the following word. Compare *(na) (očen') (bol'šix) (ploščadjax)* 'on very large squares' and *(bez) (ètix) (pjati) (mašin)* 'without these five cars' and *(v očen') (bol'šix)(domax)* 'in very large houses' and *(s ètimi) (pjatju) (mašinami)* 'with these five cars', where the brackets enclose phonologically independent words.

2.6.2   Adverbs

Certain of the Romance languages have a form of the adverb 'there' which is generally regarded as a clitic, as in the French *y* of (56):

(56)   Jean **y** va
            Jean Y goes
            'Jean goes there'

This is the position where pronominal clitics are found (comparable to the 2P pronominal clitics of Serbian/Croatian, but occurring immediately before the verb). Like the pronominal forms, the *y* clitic cannot occur in any other position:

(57) a.   * Jean va   **y**
             Jean goes Y
      b.   * **Y**, Jean va
             Y Jean goes

It is not normally possible for a genuine adverb of place to appear in such a position, because adverbs appear after the verb (58b, 59b):

(58) a.   Jean va   à Paris
           Jean goes to Paris
           'Jean goes to Paris'
     b.   * Jean à Paris va
           Jean to Paris goes

(59) a.   Jean va   là
           Jean goes there
           'Jean goes there'
     b.   * Jean là   va
           Jean there goes

The *y* clitic is somewhat unusual, in that it is the only clitic in French with such an adverbial function. There is no clitic form of *ici* 'here', for instance. Moreover, although the clitic systems of Romance languages tend to be fairly uniform, with similar forms and functions, some of the Romance languages lack such adverbial clitics. They are lacking in Spanish and Portuguese, but Italian, Catalan and Provençal/Occitan have a similar 'there' clitic, and Sardinian has no less than three locative clitics (Jones 1993).

2.6.3   Discourse functions

Discourse particles are words which convey rhetorical effects, emphasis, the attitude of the speaker and so on, often in ways that are extremely difficult to pin down. In English they are represented by about a hundred expressions of the kind *actually, well, you know, sort-of, then, in fact, after all*, as in *Well, they were actually going to leave sort of earlier, you know*. Such particles have been studied within the rubric of pragmatics (for instance, in Relevance Theory, see Blakemore 2002) and especially in Conversation Analysis (Schegloff 2007), which has devoted considerable research effort to unravelling the functions of particles in turn-taking and in attitudinal factors in discourse. In some languages, discourse particles play such an important role that their study has entered the pedagogic tradition, and second-language learners are expected to study them as part of the grammar of the language. This is true of Classical (though not Modern) Greek (cf. Denniston 2002[5]), Russian (Vasil'eva, 1974) and especially German (where they are generally referred to as *Modalpartikeln*, Abraham 1991, or *Abtönungspartikeln*, Weydt 1969).

In many languages, the conversational or discourse particles are essentially adverbs. However, in many languages, words of this sort can turn into clitics. This type of clitic is similar to the adverbial type in many respects, and, like the adverbials, the discourse clitics tend not to correspond to inflectional categories. We start with a very simple example. In Russian, words can be given a contrastive interpretation by means of the enclitic particle =*to* (which is spelled '-to' but always pronounced with a reduced vowel [tə]):

(60) a.   Ja=**to** ne   rabotaju doma
             I=TO NEG work   at.home
             'I don't work at home (someone else might) ...'
      b.   Doma=**to**   ja ne   rabotaju
             at.home=TO I NEG work
             'I don't work at home ... (though I do work in the office)'
      c.   Daj mne nožik=**to**
             give me   knife=TO
             'Give me the/a knife' [probably with impatient expression]
      d.   Govorit′=**to** po-russki govorju no čitat′ ne   umeju
             to.speak=TO Russian I.speak but read NEG can
             'I can speak Russian but I can't read it'

This is an example of a clitic whose position is determined entirely by the meaning – it attaches directly to the word or phrase it modifies. In this respect it's
similar to the question particle of Imbabura Quechua. In Ancient Greek, however, many of the discourse particles are 2P, that is, Wackernagel clitics. Greek
had a great wealth of such particles, so we'll just illustrate with one paired set.
A contrast between two ideas was often expressed by means of the particles *men*
... *de*... (sometimes translated rather clumsily as 'on the one hand ... on the
other hand'). In example (61) (from Plato, via Weir Smyth (1920, 656)), we see
the two particles intervening between the definite articles which modify the two
subject nouns 'soul' and 'body', a typical position for such 2P clitics:[6]

(61)   he: **men** psy:k^{h}é: polyk^{h}rónión esti to **de** sô:ma ast^{h}enésteron
         the MEN soul   long-lasting is   the DE body weaker
         'The soul lasts for a long time, the body is weaker'

All of the Greek clitic particles which we have illustrated here are of the discourse marker type. Greek also had pronominal clitics, which generally appear
after the discourse markers. The pronominal clitics actually belong to a different
cluster from the discourse particles, however. Garrett (1996, 88) points out that
there are sentence constructions in which a subordinating conjunction such as ɛí
'if' or a wh-word subordinator such as тís 'which, what' appears in non-initial
position in the clause and some other word occupies first position. In such cases
we find that the discourse participles (connective clitics, so called because they
are thought of as connecting successive utterances) are hosted by the clause-
initial word while the pronominal clitics (sentential clitics, so called because
their function is internal to the sentence in which they are found) are hosted
by the later-position subordinator. This is illustrated in (62), from the earliest
literary stage, the Homeric variety of the Ionian dialect, and in (63), from the
Attic dialect of the classical period, where the connective, discourse clitics are in
boldface and the pronominal, sentential clitics are in italics:[7]

(62)   épos =**d'** eí =*per* =*ti* bébaktai   deinón
         word **TOP** if *FOC some* has.been.spoken dangerous
         'But even if some dangerous word has been spoken ...' (*Odyssey* 8.408-409)

(63)   ha **dè** tálain' álok^hos tíni   =*moi*   óleto moírai
the **TOP** wretched wife.NOM *WHAT.DAT.SG* DAT.1SG.CL perished fate.DAT
'But by what fate did my wretched wife perish?' (Euripides, *Phoenissae* 1566)

In a number of languages, however, clitics with discourse functions are found inside clusters that include grammatical clitics, such as auxiliary verb clitics, pronominal clitics or mood clitics. Garrett (1996) demonstrates that Hittite was one of those languages. Hittite distinguished the two types of function semantically in its clitic system, in that it had two connective clitics, *(y)a* conjunctive (CONJ), and *(m)a* topic (TOP), as well as a host of sentential clitics expressing adverbial, discourse and other meanings, together with a set of clitic pronouns:

(64)   Hittite pronominal clitics

	Nominative	Accusative	Dative
1sg	——	mu	mu
2sg	——	ta, ddu	ta, ddu
3sg common	aš	an	ši
3sg neuter	at	at	ši
1pl	——	naš	naš
2pl	——	šmaš	šmaš
3pl common	e, at	uš, aš	šmaš
3pl neuter	e, at	e, at	šmaš

The Hittite example (65) contrasts with the Greek examples: the pronominal enclitic isn't attracted to the subordinating conjunction, the relative pronoun *kuit*, but is cliticized to *nu*, one of the sentence-introductory particles that frequently begin sentences in Hittite.[8]

(65)   nu=**nnaš** É-ir kuit   ēššuen
NU=DAT.1PL house REL.PRON made.1PL
'the house that (we) built us ...' (Garrett 1996, 88)

A wide variety of clitics can appear in this second position, each occupying its own slot in a clitic template (much as in Serbian/Croatian) of the form conjunction – *wa(r)* quotative (indicating direct speech) – pronominal/reflexive – adverbial (Lauffenburger 2008, 100–9).[9]

Pashto is another example of a language in which discourse clitics combine with sentential clitics (discussed in Chapter 4). A particularly good example of such a language is Tagalog (Schachter and Otanes 1972, 411–36), discussed in some detail in Chapter 6.

2.7   Conclusions

We've seen a variety of functions which can be expressed by full-form function words, by affixes or other morphological devices, or by something in between, namely clitics. Of the principal nominal properties, clitics frequently express case, possession and definiteness. Of the verbal categories, clitics regularly express Tense-Aspect-Mood (TAM) categories, including such categories as interrogative mood and negation. A particularly important category is that of pronominal argument, which often turns into a kind of agreement system. We'll discuss pronominal clitics in a good deal of detail at various points in the book. Finally, we've also seen that clitics often realize meanings that are realized by locative or temporal adverbs or by various kinds of discourse marker expressing evidentiality or other discourse- and context-related meanings. All of these meanings and functions can be seen in inflectional systems, reflecting the well-known fact that inflections generally arise when clitics become morphologized as affixes.

To conclude, we will summarize the main properties of clitics that we have appealed to in this chapter in order to distinguish them from words and affixes. In subsequent chapters we'll be discussing these diagnostics in much more detail and developing further diagnostics.

1	Clitics express functional (inflectional) categories or discourse functions.
2	Clitics are generally unstressed (and unstressable).
3	Clitics require a host to attach to.
4	Clitics show low selectivity towards their host (promiscuous attachment).
5	Clitics typically appear in rigidly ordered clusters (templates).
6	Clitics and clitic clusters often have different syntax from fully-fledged words. A particularly common phenomenon is the 2P clitic (cluster), in which the clitics have to be placed after the first constituent (word/phrase) of the phrase or clause they relate to.
7	Pronominal clitics often serve as the argument of the verb, but in some languages the clitics can be doubled by full noun phrases, giving the appearance of subject-verb or object-verb agreement.

3   Types of clitic system

3.1   Introduction

Scholars from diverse linguistic traditions have observed that the behaviour of clitics is neither that of an independent word nor that of an affix, but enjoys what Klavans (1982) calls 'dual citizenship'. Among the classical studies on clitic phenomena, two oft-cited and influential papers stand out, namely Wackernagel (1892) and Zwicky (1977). In Section 3.2 we offer a summary of these studies, which represent two early attempts at identifying and classifying the idiosyncrasies of clitic placement. Section 3.3 offers a descriptive overview of a number of well-documented (though not necessarily uncontroversial) placement patterns. Having surveyed the meaning and function of clitics in the previous chapter, we look in somewhat more detail at the distributional properties of clitics and the various positions within which clitics occur cross-linguistically. We first briefly introduce the notion of clitic cluster and then explore the way that clitics or clusters of clitics are positioned within their domain (the clause, the noun phrase, occasionally the verb phrase). Placement patterns vary significantly: while some clitics may show a strong preference for the second position in the clause, others are banned from the edge of the sentence, and yet others must be adjacent to a specific word category. We will also show that even a concept such as 'second position' can mean different things in different languages. Clitics very often express functional properties akin to (or even identical to) inflectional categories in a language, which in practice means inflectional properties of nouns and of verbs. A clitic's linear positioning usually associates it in some way with the noun or verb whose properties it expresses, and so the noun and verb serve to define domains for clitic placement. In Section 3.4 we examine these domains. On the other hand, a good many clitics express properties of entire clauses or, in the case of discourse clitics, of utterances. Section 3.5 is devoted to such clause-domain clitics.

3.2   Typologies of clitics

In this section we review three highly influential attempts at characterizing the notion clitic. These three studies serve in many respects as the foundations of all studies on clitics. We start with a synthesis of a remarkable nineteenth-century philological study of word order in early Indo-European languages. We next consider the first major attempt to place clitics on the contemporary linguistics map – Zwicky's celebrated overview of clitics. We then briefly summarize the principal ideas behind the very insightful categorization of clitic systems proposed by Judith Klavans, which remains a point of departure for many studies of clitics. In Chapter 8 we'll return to the question of clitic typology from the vantage point of more recent theoretical studies, though the issues raised in these three studies will remain as relevant as they were.

3.2.1   On Indo-European word order (Wackernagel 1892)

One of the most cited and perhaps also one of the most unread studies[1] in linguistics is Wackernagel's monograph-length paper, *Über ein Gesetz der indogermanischen Wortstellung* ('On a law of Indo-European word order'), on second-position clitics in Indo-European. In this study, the Swiss philologist Jacob Wackernagel (1853–1938), examines the behaviour of unstressed items in Ancient Greek which show a strong preference for the second position in the clause, after the first accented word. As the example in (1) shows, while the appositional noun phrase *theios Oneiros* can surface as a discontinuous constituent, the clitic pronoun *moi* 'to me' follows the first word. Positioning the clitic after the third or fourth word would result in an unattested pattern.[2]

(1) t^heîós=**moi**   enýpnion é:lt^{h}en óneiros
           divine.NOM=to.me dream   came Oneiros.NOM
           'divine Oneiros came to me as a dream' (IL.2.56) (Taylor 1996, 478)

Wackernagel and his contemporaries were acutely aware of the contrast that existed in Ancient Greek between the relative free order of words and the rigid positioning of clitics (p. 367). The idiosyncratic placement of unstressed particles was already at the centre of a heated debate between those who tried to provide a grammatical explanation for the clitic position by claiming that it was triggered by the category of the preceding word and those who had already observed that the explanation was simply dependent on the number of words preceding the clitics. In effect, the idea that unstressed items in Ancient Greek prefer to occur after the first word, regardless of the category of the host, had already been proposed at the time, in particular by Abel Bergaigne (pp. 342–3), as Wackernagel himself observes. Wackernagel's paper (effectively a monograph) provides an impressive amount of empirical data, largely in support of Bergaigne's position, a position which defines today's view on second position clitics in both Ancient Greek and Vedic Sanskrit.

In addition to the overall observation that unstressed pronouns and other unstressed particles in Ancient Greek occur preferably in second position, Wackernagel makes other specific claims about the phonological and the syntactic properties of such second-position clitics. As to their phonology, clitics are defined as phonologically weak items with an 'enclitic nature' (p. 359). This then shows that Wackernagel is aware of the fact that the reason why these clitics cannot appear sentence-initially is due both to their phonological weakness and to their direction of attachment (pp. 367, 377).

Another property of these clitics, as noted by Wackernagel (pp. 337–8, 345, 358) and illustrated above in (1), is their ability to break up phrases. Here are some additional examples of this. In (2), for example, the clitic occurs between the preposition *amphi* and the noun *auton* and in (3) it occurs between the determiner *tô:n* and the noun *állo:n* in sentence-initial position.

(2)   [auton=**d'**   amp^h i] gérontes ak^h aiô:n   e:geréth onto
          him.ACC DE around elders   Achaeans.GEN gathered
          'the elders of the Achaeans gathered around him' (IL.19.303)

(3)   [tô:n=**d'**   állo:n]   tís   **ken** hê:isi   p^h resin   ounómat' eípoi
          the.GEN=DE others.GEN who PRT those.DAT hearts.DAT names
             could.speak
          'who could speak with his heart the names of the others' (IL.17.260)

He even cites instances of what appear to be tmesis (the term is from the Greek 'cutting') in which the word *oukéti* 'no longer', formed from the particle *éti* and the negative particle *ou(k)*, is split by the pronominal clitics *me*, *moi* (p. 358).

Since second-position clitics target specific positions in the sentence, it comes as no surprise to find that clitics are not sensitive to the category of the preceding word. As the examples in (2) and (3) illustrate, clitic particles can occur after a pronoun and after a determiner.

In modern linguistics, the promiscuous property of clitics is regarded as one of the main criteria for the distinction between clitics and affixes (Zwicky and Pullum 1983). In Wackernagel's time, the unrestricted nature of enclitics was far from obvious, which is also why Wackernagel writes his paper as a critical response to other philologists, in particular Albert Thumb, who had suggested that the position of enclitics was dependent on the category of the previous word (pp. 334–5). Instead, Wackernagel notes, precisely because the position of enclitics is defined in linear terms (i.e., as the second word), there is usually not even a semantic or syntactic relationship between the enclitic and its preceding prosodic host (pp. 337–8, 346).

As has been stressed by Stephen Anderson (Anderson 1993, 2005) Wackernagel (in his section XII, p. 425) extends his analysis of second-position placement of unaccented elements in Greek and Latin to the verb-second phenomenon of modern German (albeit tentatively). We will not consider this extension, however, and leave the reader to consult Anderson's discussion and the copious syntactic literature on this topic.[3]

Summing up, Wackernagel's monograph, which emerged as part of an ongoing debate on the nature of 2P clitics in ancient Indo-European, highlights a number of important properties of 2P clitics which are still at the centre of debate.

These include the property of promiscuous attachment or low selectivity, the ability of a clitic to break up phrases, and the clitic's phonological dependency on a host. Strictly speaking, however, for Wackernagel, 'second position' defines a position which follows the first full word. The conception of syntax current in Wackernagel's time did not lay the same stress on the notion of 'phrase' as most current theories of syntax, which are heavily based on the American Structuralist notion of '(immediate) constituent'. Subsequent work on clitics has shown that, if anything, it is more common for second-position clitics to be limited to the position after the first phrase in the clitic's domain (so-called 2D clitics – see below). This is the case in Czech, for instance. It is relatively rare to find a language in which clitics are constrained to occur only after the first word in the domain (so-called 2W clitics), though it is not uncommon for a language to permit both options, so that the clitic occurs either after the first word or after the first full phrase, as in Serbian/Croatian or Luiseño. Consequently, in current language descriptions, a Wackernagel clitic is a clitic that can be positioned either after the first word or after the first phrase. Similarly, the term Wackernagel's Law has been generalized from defining the tendency for clitics to appear after the first word to defining the tendency to appear after the first word or phrase.

3.2.2   On clitics (Zwicky 1977)

Wackernagel examined one clitic type within a small set of related languages. Future researchers who examined clitic systems likewise concentrated on specific groups of languages. An influential study of Slavic clitics was published in 1935 by Roman Jakobson (subsequently republished as Jakobson 1971) in which he argued that the fate of Wackernagel clitics in the three main groups of Slavic languages depended on the accentual system of each language (fixed stressed, moveable stress, and so on). Thus, the 'inflecting clitics', that is, the pronominal and auxiliary clitics, were lost in Russian, which has moveable stress, but were kept in West Slavic languages such as Czech and Slovak. Jakobson's short article was expanded considerably and his model applied to Romance by Benacchio and Renzi (1987). Perlmutter (1971) was a significant contribution to the study of Romance (especially Spanish) clitic systems, as it introduced the notion of a template for the clitic cluster. Other important studies of the clitic systems of individual languages or groups include Rivas (1977) on Romance clitics in the Chomskyan framework, Tegey (1977), whose data on Pashto will be discussed in Chapter 4, and Browne (1974), whose meticulous survey of the principal facts of the Serbo-Croat clitic cluster formed the foundation for nearly all subsequent work in theoretical linguistics.

However, the first major attempt to classify clitic phenomena within a genuinely cross-linguistic perspective is that of Zwicky (1977). Based on the defining properties of clitic phenomena in a wide range of unrelated languages, Zwicky formulates a clitic typology which is mostly known for its two-way distinction between simple clitic and special clitics. This bipartite classification can be broadly defined as a distinction between clitics with a fairly regular (or simple) syntax and clitics with a more idiosyncratic (or special) syntax. So, underlying Zwicky's study is the claim that clitics, despite their unifying phonological weakness, differ with respect to their distributional properties and their relation with the full form (if one exists).

For Zwicky, then, a simple clitic corresponds to a phonologically weak function word, such as a preposition, an auxiliary verb, a definite marker, among others, which is phonologically weak and so must adjoin phonologically to an adjacent full (accented) word. In Zwicky's own words, the presence of simple clitics captures the fact that "a free morpheme, when unaccented, may be phonologically reduced, the resultant form being phonologically subordinate to a neighbouring word" (Zwicky 1977, 5). In addition to their weak phonology, one further crucial property of simple clitics is their syntax, which is regular, i.e., identical to that of their free (i.e., stressed) counterparts. English personal pronouns and prepositions are often cited as examples of simple clitics. In (4a) and (4b), they surface in their weak form and occur in the same position as their non-clitic correspondent.

(4) a.   She met him
           Full form: [mɛt hɪm]
           Clitic form: [mɛtɪm]
    b.   Mary looked at me
           Full form: [at]
           Clitic form: [ət]

As phonologically unaccented items, simple clitics are assumed to be syntactically unexceptional and any restrictions on their placement follow from their lack of accent. This explains why they can neither be stressed nor constitute an utterance on their own:

(5) a.   She met him [ˈhɪm/*ɪm] not her [ˈhɜː/*ə]
    b.   Who did she see? Him [ˈhɪm/*ɪm].

A special clitic is "an unaccented bound form" which "acts as a variant of a stressed free form with the same cognitive meaning and with a similar phonological makeup" (Zwicky 1977, 3). As to the phonological relation between special clitics and their full forms, clitics can bear some phonological resemblance to the full form, although they are best viewed as lexically listed items rather than as phonologically derived forms. Like simple clitics, they are assumed to be unaccented and to attach prosodically to a full word.

Syntactically, special clitics constitute a theoretical challenge because, by definition, there are no free forms with the same distribution as special clitics (that is what makes them special). For example, clitic pronouns[4] in Spanish are generally placed before the verb, but unmarked declarative word order in this language is Subject-Verb-Object:

(6) a.   Maria **lo**   compró
           Maria 3SG.MASC.ACC bought
           'Maria bought it'

b.   Maria compró un libro con poemas
            Maria bought a   book with poems
            'Maria bought a poetry book'

Similar examples can be given from other Romance languages. Thus, Romance clitics are special because their placement patterns require special syntactic treatment. Other examples of special clitics include the 2P clitics, say, of Serbian/Croatian, whether 2W or 2D, since in both cases it is evident that they do not follow the general rules of word order (and in particular they have none of the freedom of ordering found with true words and phrases).

Although it is the simple/special typology of clitics that has entered mainstream linguistic description, the original typology proposed in Zwicky (1977) contained in effect a third class of clitics, namely, the class of bound words. These are other types of unaccented forms which have no accented counterpart. Distributionally, they are "semantically associated with an entire constituent" (p. 6) and phonologically attached to the margins of this constituent. As an example of a bound word, Zwicky gives English possessive 's (POSS-S). In (7), the POSS-S is associated to a noun phrase and attached phonologically to the last word of the noun phrase:

(7)   [The Queen of England]'s hat

Our brief survey of Zwicky's typology reveals that the distinction between simple clitics, special clitics and bound words is largely based on two distinguishing features, namely, (a) the syntactic distribution of clitics and (b) the relationship between the clitic form and its full form counterpart. By cross-referencing these two criteria, we obtain effectively three different classes: clitics with a stressed form and simple syntax (i.e., simple clitics); clitics with a stressed form and special syntax (i.e., special clitics); and clitics with special syntax but no full form counterpart (i.e., bound words). Recall that all clitics are assumed to be unaccented and hence prosodically dependent.

(8)   Zwicky's original typology of clitics

	full form	simple syntax
Simple clitic	yes	yes
Special clitic	yes	no
bound word	no	no

Although the basic typology has been extremely influential, some of Zwicky's claims have been subject to a certain degree of criticism. Thus, the distinction between special clitics and bound words seems to rely solely on Zwicky's claim that bound words, unlike special clitics, never have a full-form counterpart. But a clitic can sometimes be very different from its full-form counterpart, both in phonological form and in morphosyntactic behaviour, and it then becomes very difficult to know whether we can really say that a clitic has a full form. But that would mean that the clitic had become (or was becoming?) a bound word. Thus, the utility of the notion bound word turns on how clearly we can relate full and reduced forms of function words. As Anderson (2005) points out, this is not really a very important question. He observes that we must focus on the properties that special clitics and bound words have in common, namely, their unique and idiosyncratic placement requirements. Note that both in the case of special clitics and bound words, the position occupied by clitics is not available to full words. For Anderson, therefore, whether these clitics have any relation with a (putative) full form does not shed any light on the placement restrictions imposed on clitics (see also Klavans 1982). Interestingly, the class of bound words was tacitly subsumed under the class of special clitics by Zwicky and Pullum (1983), and explicitly by Zwicky (1985a).

One further problem with Zwicky's typology is the original distinction between simple clitics and special clitics. The dichotomy is meant to highlight the fact that weak phonology (i.e., lack of accent) is not synonymous with special syntax, but Zwicky (1977, 6) himself is the first to recognize that "the line between these types of clitics is not always clear". One reason for such difficulty has to do with the observation that simple clitics do not all exhibit the same degree of syntactic simplicity. For instance, a phrase-initial preposition occurs before the noun both as a stressed full form or as an unstressed clitic, as in (4b) above. However, in sentence-final position, only the full form is allowed:

(9)   What are you waiting for [fɔ:(r)]/*[fr̩/fə]?

Similarly, clitic auxiliaries in English do not exhibit exactly the same distribution as their corresponding non-clitic auxiliaries. As shown in (10), they cannot occur before elision sites, even though they are phonologically enclitics and therefore attached to the preceding stressed word (Kaisse 1985):

(10)   John's tired and Mary is [mɛ:rɪɪz/*mɛ:rɪz] too.

In order to accommodate the fact that some simple clitics show a more restricted distribution than their full forms, we may therefore need to define simple clitics along the lines of Halpern (1998), namely, as clitics that may be positioned in a subset of the positions within which the full forms are found, rather than as clitics that have the same distribution as their full-form counterparts as in Zwicky (1977). Under this broader definition, we capture the fact that simple clitics differ from special clitics in that they can appear in some of the positions that are occupied by their corresponding full forms, while special clitics never can. In effect, as suggested above, the positions of special clitics are never available to their full forms (in case such forms exist).

The assumption that clitics are incapable of bearing stress or other forms of prominence has also been subject to a fair deal of criticism, and is explicitly rejected as a principal diagnostic in Zwicky (1985a). Anderson (2005) has proposed to redefine Zwicky's typology, arguing that simple clitics owe their clitic status to their phonological weakness, while special clitics owe it to their special syntax. As we have already pointed out, the placement restrictions which characterize special clitics are not applicable to free words and can be found in both accented and unaccented clitics. On the contrary, the syntax of simple clitics is largely unproblematic.

We will largely follow the more recent literature in (a) rejecting the notion of bound word as a special category, and (b) treating simple clitics as instances of lowered prominence. This means that the principal interest of clitics lies in the so-called special clitics, and from now on when we use the term 'clitic' it will usually mean special clitic.

3.2.3 Klavans' typology

Perhaps the most systematic attempt to provide a typology of clitics following Zwicky's pioneering 1977 study was that of Judith Klavans (1982, 1985). She argued that we can account for the placement patterns of clitics by factoring those patterns into a collection of parameters. A given clitic system is then obtained by setting the values of those parameters. We will illustrate the basic idea by means of a hypothetical example and then briefly discuss Klavans' own proposals.

Suppose a language expresses definiteness by means of a clitic within the appropriate noun phrase, such as that shown bracketed in (11):

(11)   Cats chase [small white mice] relentlessly

The clitic could be placed at the beginning (left edge alignment) or the end (right edge alignment) of the NP, as in (12a, b):

(12) a.   Cats chase [the=small white mice] relentlessly
     b.   Cats chase [small white mice=the] relentlessly

However, this is slightly misleading, because in (12) we're assuming that a clitic placed on a left edge will take as its host the following word (i.e. will be a proclitic) and a right edge clitic will be an enclitic. This is a reasonable assumption because it guarantees that the clitic will be pronounced within the NP to which it relates, but as we've seen clitics in some languages attach to the 'wrong' word in the 'wrong' phrase. Thus, a further logical possibility for attachment would be that seen in (13):

(13) a.   Cats chase=the [small white mice] relentlessly
     b.   Cats chase [small white mice] the=relentlessly

In both (12a) and (13a) the clitic is oriented with respect to the first element (left edge) of the NP. The difference between the two examples is that in (12a) the clitic seeks out its phonological host to the right, while in (13a) it seeks out its host to the left, and hence appears outside its NP. The examples in (12b) and (13b) are the mirror-image of the left-edge examples.

The distinction between the placements in (12) and (13) motivate two distinct parameters. The first Klavans calls Dominance (though perhaps a more felicitous term is 'Anchoring', alluded to in Anderson 1992 and adopted in Anderson 2005). This has the values First/Last (corresponding to the more contemporary terms 'left edge', 'right edge'). The second parameter is phonological attachment, which Klavans calls Liaison. This has the values Enclitic/Proclitic. The two parameters of Anchoring and Liaison account for four patterns, three of which are relatively common (it's difficult to find good examples of the type illustrated in (13b)).

However, these two parameters aren't sufficient to describe the full range of clitic types that we're familiar with. We've seen a number of cases in which a clitic attaches to the right of the first element in a domain, the 2P or Wackernagel position. This is illustrated in (14a), and in (14b) we give the mirror-image of 2P:

(14) a.   Cats chase [small=the white mice] relentlessly
      b.   Cats chase [small white the=mice] relentlessly

Klavans accounts for these two additional placement possibilities by proposing a further parameter, which we can call the Before/After parameter: Is the clitic located Before or After the First/Last word in the domain? In (14a) the clitic is After the First word, while in (12a) it's located Before the First word. Similarly, in (14b) the parameter settings are Before, Last, while in (12b) they are After, Last.

This extra parameter essentially allows us to define the 2P position, though it also defines a further 'anti-Wackernagel' position that is hardly attested, if at all. Klavans takes her parametrization to its logical conclusion and argues that there are (or must be) clitic systems of the kind illustrated in (15):

(15) a.   Cats chase [small the=white mice] relentlessly
      b.   Cats chase [small white=the mice] relentlessly

The general consensus (Anderson 1992, 2005, Marantz 1988, Sadock 1991, Spencer 1991) is that this typology is too rich, and several of the logical possibilities simply aren't attested (though Cysouw 2005 provides a detailed defence of patterns in which the clitic finds itself in the 'wrong' phrase, that is, when the clitic is attached to a host which is in a different phrase from that of the word whose features the clitic is realizing). The problem seems to be with the Before/After parameter. Note that this parameter isn't actually independent of the Anchoring parameter, since 'Before/After' can only be defined with respect to the word chosen as the anchor point.

The Before/After parameter is added specifically to allow the typology to describe the 2P placement pattern. However, it seems that this pattern is better thought of as simply a preferred place for clitics (and other elements such as finite verbs). Anderson (1993, 2005) advances this claim in detail (arguing for an explanation in terms of the interaction of constraints within an Optimality Theoretic model). The special status of second position, regardless of how it's encoded in grammatical theory, is entirely lost on Klavans' typology. (The special status of the Wackernagel 2P position is also inherent in the account proposed for 2P clitics by Halpern 1995.)

Another difficulty with Klavans' approach is that it fails to account for instances in which the placement is defined in terms that are not purely positional. In particular, there are well-attested cases in which the clitic is positioned with respect to a pragmatically defined unit such as a focussed phrase (for instance, the subject marker clitics of Udi, Chapter 7) or a prosodically defined unit, such as the first phonological phrase of a domain (Bošković 2001, Chung 2003).

Klavans intended her account to include the famous pronominal clitics of the Romance languages. However, she noted that the positioning of those clitics seems to be defined relative to a named category, that is, the verb. This suggests that an additional value is required for the Anchor parameter, namely, 'head of the phrase'. However, as Klavans (1985) herself notes, a clitic that is placed with respect to a lexical head is pretty close to being an affix, so that perhaps Romance clitics are really an odd sort of affix, rather than being an odd sort of clitic.

Despite its shortcomings, Klavans' typology has been very influential amongst those seeking to analyse clitics as an essentially morphological phenomenon.[5] This is particularly true of Anderson (1992), who takes up one particular theme in Klavans' approach, namely, the fact that clitic placement is not defined in terms of the normal rules of syntax. Klavans argues, in fact, that a clitic is really a kind of affix, but one whose placement is defined by reference to syntactic structure, a 'phrasal affix'. Anderson (1992, 1993, 2005) strongly emphasizes this aspect, claiming in effect that all clitics are phrasal affixes, including those that attach to the head of a phrase.[6]

3.3   Patterns of placement

3.3.1   Introduction

In this section we will look at some well-documented cases of 'special' clitics form a variety of typologically and genetically diverse languages. Some of the placement patterns we will address have been discussed before, either in this chapter or in the previous one. We cannot do justice to the complexity of the clitic systems we will be describing, nor can we hope to cover all the theoretical and descriptive issues raised. What we aim to do, therefore, is to present what we see as the key questions that have emerged over the past forty years or so of research.

We will restrict our attention to clitics whose positioning is determined for the main part by morphosyntax. In Chapter 4 we will see instances of clitics whose placement seems to be determined by phonological factors, specifically, the placement of phrasal accent. This is true of the clitic system of Pashto, the Bulgarian interrogative clitic *li* and the pronominal clitics of Chamorro. Before we look at the way that clitics are positioned we must briefly mention what happens when several clitics come together in a single clause or phrase.

3.3.2   Clitic clusters

So far we have mainly been concerned with individual clitics. However, a very important property of clitics is their ability to combine into clitic strings, usually known as clitic clusters. Even though languages differ with respect to the number of clitics a given clitic string can take, rigid ordering is typical of almost all languages with clitic systems, especially those clitics that realize inflection-like functions such as tense-aspect-mood-polarity properties or pronominal arguments.[7] For example, the ordering between clitic pronouns and clitic auxiliaries in Serbian/Croatian is given in (16).

(16)   Aux - Dat - Acc - Refl - *je* (3sg auxiliary)

Note that the ordering restrictions within a clitic cluster can be very idiosyncratic. In (16), for example, we can see that all clitic auxiliaries must precede clitic pronouns, except for the clitic auxiliary *je* 'BE.3SG.PRESENT', which must come last in the cluster. On the other hand, the pronominal clitic *je* '3SG.FEM.ACC' appears in the same position as all the other accusative clitics. Idiosyncratic linear orderings such as this are often referred to as templates, and the kind of system that exhibits such ordering is often referred to as templatic morphology (Simpson and Withgott 1986) (though this term is also used for a somewhat different phenomenon, namely, the root-and-pattern morphology of Semitic languages and other language groups).

   When several clitics co-occur, it is the clitic cluster as a whole, i.e., the string of clitics in the order given in (16), that gets positioned after the first word/phrase. In (17), the clitics *mi* 'me.DAT' and *ga* 'it.ACC' form a rigidly ordered clitic string.

(17) a.   Jovan **mi   ga** kupuje svaki dan
          Jovan for.me it buys   every day
     b.   Svaki dan **mi ga** Jovan kupuje
          each day me it Jovan buys
     c.   Kupuje **mi ga** Jovan svaki dan
          buys   me it Jovan every day
          'Jovan buys it for me every day'

We will discuss the significance of the clustering property of clitics in much more detail in Section 5.4 and we'll discuss the ways that different linguistic models capture the clustering in Chapter 8.

3.3.3   Second-position clitics

        Recall that 'second position' can be defined in linear terms, in which case it means 'after the first accented word', or it can be defined in structural terms, in which case it means 'after the first accented phrase'. In order to distinguish between the two types of placement possibility, in our survey of the data we will use the terminology introduced by Halpern (1995, 15): placement after the right edge of the first phrase of the clause is called 2D placement ('2D' for 'second (constituent) daughter'), while placement after the first (full, phonological) word is called 2W placement ('2W' for 'second word'). We will see next that while some languages allow their clitics to alternate freely between 2W and 2D, some languages restrict their 2P clitics to either one or the other.

Serbian/Croatian, Luiseño and Ngiyambaa (2W/2D)

In Chapter 2 we saw examples of Wackernagel or 2P clitics in Serbian/Croatian, a language which has been the subject of a good deal of discussion in the recent theoretical literature. Here we expand on our earlier description to illustrate the typical 2P properties of this clitic system. Recall that Serbian/Croatian has auxiliary verb clitics and pronominal clitics (as well as a question particle whose behaviour will be discussed in detail in the next chapter). The auxiliaries are present tense forms of the verb BE used in forming the 'periphrastic' past tense,[8] together with a special inflected form of the verb (the 'l-participle').

The auxiliary has three persons and two numbers. It occurs in a full (stressed, accented) form as well as in a clitic form. The clitic forms and their corresponding full forms are given in (18) (see Spencer 1991, 352, Browne 1993, 339).

(18)   Clitic and full-forms of Serbian/Croatian auxiliary BITI 'to be'

Person/ Number	Full form	Clitic
1sg	jèsam	sam
2sg	jèsi	si
3sg	jëst(e)	je
1pl	jèsmo	smo
2pl	jèste	ste
3pl	jèsu	su

In the full form the auxiliary behaves just like any other lexical verb. As we saw in Chapter 2, this full form is only used when the auxiliary itself is in focus. Although we have referred to this verb as 'auxiliary', it is also the copular verb and the verb of existence/location as we mentioned in Chapter 2 (see examples (7) and (11) from that chapter). When used as a copular in the present tense it is still a clitic (unless it is focussed, of course). In the periphrastic past tense form of the copula we use the *l*-participle *bil* and the appropriate present tense form of the copula. In (19, 20) we see the copula combined with dative case clitic pronouns *mi, nam* 'to me', 'to us'. The clitic forms are in bold face and the copula is underlined.

(19) a.   Onaj les   **mi**   <u>je</u>   vrlo drag
         that forest 1SG.DAT 3SG.AUX very dear
         'That forest is very dear to me'

   b.   Onaj les   **mi**   <u>je</u>   bil   vrlo drag
         that forest 1SG.DAT 3SG.AUX BE.LPART.SG very dear
         'That forest was very dear to me'

(20) a.   Ova polja <u>su</u>   **nam**   vrlo draga
         these fields 3PL.AUX 1PL.DAT very dear
         'There fields are very dear to us'

   b.   Ova polja <u>su</u>   **nam**   bila   vrlo draga
         these fields 3PL.AUX 1PL.DAT BE.LPART.PL very dear
         'The fields were very dear to us'

The clitic clusters in (19a, 20a), in which the verb is the present tense form of the copula, show exactly the same ordering properties as the clusters in (19b, 20b) where the verb is the past tense auxiliary. In particular, the 3sg form *je* in (19) has the unusual property of coming last in the cluster, while other auxiliary forms, such as the 3pl form *su* in (20), come first.

In (19) and (20) the auxiliary clitic and the clitic pronouns are positioned after the first phrase, *onaj les, ova polja*. However, these clitics also display the property noted in Chapter 2, examples (33a, b), of attaching to the first full accented word of the clause, even if this is inside a phrase. This is illustrated in (21) and (22):

(21)   Onaj **mi**   **je**   les   bil   vrlo drag
          that   1SG.DAT 3SG.AUX forest BE.LPART.SG very dear
          'That forest was very dear to me'

(22)   Ova **su**   **nam**   polja bila   vrlo draga
          these 3PL.AUX 1PL.DAT fields BE.LPART.PL very dear
          'The fields were very dear to us'

Notice that the l-participle forms *bil, bila* don't form part of the clitic cluster and therefore appear where we would expect to see a main verb.

There are other languages in which 2P clitics can alternate freely between 2W and 2D, such as Luiseño, an Uto-Aztecan language of Southern California. As in Serbian/Croatian, auxiliary and pronominal clitics are bound to the second position, even though constituents can appear in any order. Free constituent order in Luiseño is illustrated in (23), where semantically identical sentences differ with respect to the order of constituents, but not with respect to the position of the tense/aspect and subject agreement clitics which occur after the first phrase.

(23) a.   noo **nu po** heyin
          I   1SG FUT will.dig
          'I will dig' (Akmajian et al. 1979, 4)
     b.   heyin   **nu po**   noo
          will.dig 1SG FUT I
          'I will dig' (Steele et al. 1981, 29)

2D placement is also observed in (24) with a more complex clitic sequence containing a modal auxiliary, a tense/aspect clitic and a subject agreement clitic.

(24) a.   mariya **xu**   **p**   **po** xwaani 'ari
          Mary   MODAL 3SG.SUBJ FUT John   kick
          'Mary should kick John' (Steele 1978, 13-14)
     b.   * **xu**   **p**   **po** mariya xwaani 'ari
          MODAL 3SG.SUBJ FUT Mary   John   kick
     c.   * mariya xwaani **xu**   **p**   **po** 'ari
          Mary   John   MODAL 3SG.SUBJ FUT kick
     d.   * mariya xwaani 'ari **xu**   **p**   **po**
          Mary   John   kick MODAL 3SG.SUBJ FUT

The Luiseño clitic cluster can alternate freely between 2W and 2D. This means that clitics can optionally appear after the first constituent as in (25a) or after the first word as in (25b). In analogy to Serbian/Croatian, in 2W position, clitics can optionally interrupt multi-word constituents when such constituents occur in sentence-initial position. In (25b), the clitic appears as the second word, giving rise to a syntactic structure in which the head noun *wiiwiš* is separated from the modifier *'axaat* (Steele 1976, 597). It would be impossible for lexical items such as nouns or pronouns to occur between the noun and the adjective.

(25) a. wiiwiš 'axaat **up** na'q
         wiwish delicious 3SG is:burning
         'The delicious wiwish is burning'
     b. wiiwiš **up** 'axaat na'q

Ngiyambaa is a Pama-Nyungan language of Australia known for its very flexible word order. As a non-configurational language, it allows not only free order of constituents but also discontinuous constituency. Such freedom of word order contrasts markedly with the strict placement of certain clitics which must necessarily occur either after the first word or after the first full phrase. In (26a), for example, the pronominal enclitic *=ndu* attaches to the first word *ʔadhay* 'tasty' while it attaches to the whole phrase *ʔadhay guya* 'tasty fish' in (26b).

(26) a. ʔadhay =**ndu** guya dha-yi gambira
         tasty   2NOM fish eat-PAST yesterday
         'You ate a tasty fish yesterday' (Klavans 1982, 71)
     b. ʔadhay guya =**ndu** dha-yi gambira
         tasty   fish 2NOM eat-PAST yesterday

Similarly, in (27), clitics such as *ba*, *bara* and *baga*, which express different degrees of assertion (Kiefer 1998, 279), are fixed to the same rigid position in the clause. In (27a), *bara* occurs after the first word and in (27b) after the first phrase.

(27) a. bangaba: bara dhibi   ʔa:nhi winaru
         white.ABS emph bird.ABS saw   woman.ERG
         'A woman saw (a) really white bird' (Klavans 1982)
     b. bangaba: dhibi bara ʔa:nhi winaru

Like many languages of Australia, Ngiyambaa is 'non-configurational', that is, it permits its phrases to be discontinuous, so that the members of a given phrase need not be adjacent to each other. (This is a phenomenon which is often referred to as 'Scrambling' in the syntactic literature.) Previous studies have noted that when 2W is possible it also seems to be possible to put non-clitics in between the two parts of a putative constituent (Kroeger 1993). In this case, then, what has often been cited in the literature as 2W position might instead be best viewed as a 2D position (Halpern 1995, 49). The idea is that when a phrase is broken up by Scrambling, each component word itself becomes a kind of phrase. Thus, the effects of 2W placement might really be the result of placing the clitic after the first phrase, which just happens to be a single word that has been displaced from the rest of its phrase. In other words, rather than a structure of the kind (28a) we might have a structure of the form (28b):

(28) a.   2W placement:

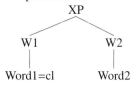

   b.   2W placement as 2D placement + Scrambling

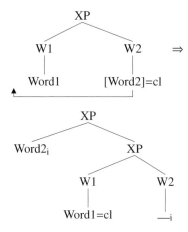

It would be wrong, however, to imagine that languages fall into two neat types with respect to this kind of variation. Occasionally we find instances in which a language appears to belong firmly to the 2D (phrase) only pattern, but allows limited cases of 2W placement. Finnish is a case in point. Below we discuss Finnish discourse particles, pointing out that they (mainly) pattern as strict 2D clitics. However, when a clitic particle attaches to a noun phrase containing an interrogative word such as *missä* 'which?', that word can sometimes attract the clitic to itself, as seen in (29) for the particle *-han/hän* (Nevis 1986, 31, 82).

(29) a.   missä   maassa=**han**
             which.INESS land.INESS=HAN
   b.   missä=**hän**   maassa
             which.INESS=HAN land.INESS
             'in which land?'

Summary: In some languages, 2P clitics can alternate between 2W and 2D. As we will see next, this option is not available in other clitic systems. Some languages with 2P clitics only allow one of these positions; that is, in some languages clitics which occur in second position can appear only after the first word

Table 3.1 *Pronominal forms in Czech*

Person/Number	Accusative Full	Accusative Clitic	Genitive Full	Genitive Clitic	Dative Full	Dative Clitic
1sg	mě	mě	mě	mě	mně	mi
2sg	tebe	tě	tebe	tě	tobě	ti
3sg m	jeho	ho	jeho	ho	jemu	mu
3sg n	je	ho	jeho	ho	jemu	mu
3sg f	ji	ji	jí	jí	jí	jí
1pl	nás	nás	nás	nás	nám	nám
2pl	vás	vás	vás	vás	vám	vám
3pl	je	je	jich	jich	jim	jim
Refl	sebe	se	sebe	se	sobě	si

(e.g. Ancient Greek) while in other languages the clitic can appear only after the first full phrase (e.g. Czech). However, there is not necessarily a strict line of demarcation between the two types (Finnish).

Czech, Slovene and Warlpiri (primarily 2D)

As we saw in Chapter 2, Czech, a language which is closely related to Serbian/Croatian, has an auxiliary clitic system in which the present tense of the verb BE functions as the auxiliary for the periphrastic past tense. Czech, like Serbian/Croatian, has clitic forms for accusative, dative and genitive pronouns, as shown in Table 3.1 (after Franks and King 2000, 98, slightly simplified).[9] Although Slavic languages generally exhibit very free word order, the position of clitics in Czech, as in other Slavic languages with clitics, is defined very rigidly.

Neither pronominal nor auxiliary clitics in Czech can break up a clause-initial constituent, unlike in Serbian/Croatian. Examples such as (30), in which the pronominal cluster splits up the first phrase of the clause, would be grammatical in Serbian/Croatian but are completely ungrammatical in Czech:

(30) a. Tohle staré kolo **se ti** jednou rozpadne
This old bicycle REFL you.DAT once fall-apart.3SG
'This old bicycle will fall apart on you one day' (Toman 1986, 124)

b. * Tohle **se ti** staré kolo jednou rozpadne

Similarly, the Czech pronominal clitic *mi* 'me-DAT' cannot occur inside the sentence-initial noun phrase *ten básník* 'that poet', as we can see from (31b). It must instead occur after the whole phrase, as in (31a):

(31) a. Ten básník **mi** čte ze své knihy
That poet me.DAT read.3SG from his book
'That poet is reading to me from his book' (Fried 1994, 158)

b. * Ten **mi** básník čte ze své knihy

Languages with 2P clitics can sometimes allow their clitics to surface in other positions in the clause. Czech is one such language, in which reflexives show some deviation from 2D. For example, in (32b) *se* occurs in third position because the pre-clitic position can be occupied by a topicalized constituent. Crucially, however, in third position Czech clitics do not break up full phrases:

(32) a.   Vždyt' **se**   Petr odstěhoval
          but   REFL.ACC Peter moved-away
          'But Peter has moved out'
     b.   Vždyt' Petr **se**   odstěhoval
          but   Peter REFL.ACC moved-away
          'Peter, however, has moved away' (Fried 1994, 160)

Slovene is another Slavic language which allows free constituent order like Serbian/Croatian and Czech. Although geographically closer to Serbian/Croatian, Slovene has a clitic system which is more similar to that of Czech. To begin with, as in Czech, Slovene clitics can only be positioned after a full phrase. Thus, in Slovene the noun phrase *moje srce* 'my heart' in (33b) cannot be broken up by the clitic *je* 'AUX.3SG':

(33) a.   in moje srce **je**   bilo   veselo
          and my   heart AUX.3SG be.LPART happy
          'and my heart was happy'
     b.   * in moje **je**   srce bilo   veselo
          and my   AUX.3SG heart be.LPART happy

Unlike Czech or Serbian/Croatian, Slovene also allows clitics to alternate between 2D and initial position, as shown in (34), where the 1sg auxiliary clitic *sem* appears in clause-initial position. What seems uncontroversial about (34) is the fact that the clause-initial clitic attaches to the following full word, forming a single phonological unit with it. Since Slovene clitics can either procliticize (34) or encliticize (33), we must conclude that they are prosodically neutral (Bennett 1986).

(34)   Ko **sem**   **se**   vzdranila,   sem   ležala   na postelji
          when AUX.1SG REFL awake.LPART AUX.1SG lie.LPART on bed
          'When I awoke, I was lying in bed'

Another language in which clitics occur primarily in 2D position is Warlpiri, a Pama-Nyungan language of Central Australia. As in Ngiyambaa, another Pama-Nyungan language, grammatical function in Warlpiri is conveyed through case marking rather than through word order. Case marking allows constituents to appear basically in any order (i.e. Warlpiri is 'non-configurational'), as shown in (35), where the (transitive) subject always takes ergative case and the object always takes nominative case:

(35) a.   Yankirri-rli maju-manu yakajirri
          Emu-ERG bad-made   berries.NOM
          'Emu spoilt the berries' (Laughren 2002, 84)

b.   Yakajirri   maju-manu yankirri-rli
      berries.NOM bad-made   emu-ERG
c.   Yankirri-rli yakajirri maju-manu
d.   Maju-manu yankirri-rli yakajirri
e.   Maju-manu yakajirri yankirri-rli
f.   Yakajirri yankirri-rli maju-manu

Warlpiri also allows free word order at the sub-clausal level. An example of discontinuous constituency is given in (36), where the relationship between nouns and modifiers is signalled by their identical case: ergative case on *berry* and *bad*, and the nominative case on *emu* and *small* (Laughren 2002, 84):

(36) a.   Yakajirri-rli maju-ngku yankirri   wita   maju-manu.
           berry-ERG   bad-ERG   emu.NOM small.NOM bad-made
           'The bad berries hurt the little emu'
     b.   Yakajirri-rli yankirri   maju-ngku wita   maju-manu.
           berry-ERG   emu.NOM bad-ERG   small.NOM bad-made

In contrast to the flexible order shown by full words, the clitic sequence is restricted to one fixed position, namely, as 2D clitics. As shown in (37), the clitic complex follows a range of constituent types that can occur clause initially: an interrogative phrase in (37a), a coordinated phrase in (37b) or a locative phrase in (37c). The clause-initial position which precedes the clitic sequence must be characterized in syntactic terms, as a position that can be filled by a single-word phrase (37a) or multi-word phrase (37b–c):

(37) a.   Ngana-patu **ka**   **lu**   wangka-mi?
           who-PL.NOM TENSE 3PL.SUBJ speak-NPAST
           'Which ones are speaking?' (Laughren 2002, 94)
     b.   Wati-ngki manu karnta-ngku **ka**   **lu**   ngarri-rni
           man-ERG and   woman-ERG TENSE 3PL.SUBJ tell-NPAST
           'Men and/or women tell (him off)' (Laughren 2002, 95)
     c.   Ngulya-ngka jinta-ngka **ka**   **lu**   paka-rni
           burrow-LOC one-LOC   TENSE 3PL.SUBJ hit-NPAST
           'They kill (them) in the one burrow' (Laughren 2002, 95)

As we can see from (37), Warlpiri clitics are rigidly ordered inside the clitic cluster: auxiliary clitics (expressing tense, aspect or mode) precede pronominal clitics (encoding subject or non-subject features) (Laughren 2002). However, as extensively noted in the literature, both auxiliary and pronominal clitics can be preceded by a 'complementizer' type category (C), such as *kuji, kaja, kala* or *yi*, which realize tense and modal properties. When they are hosted by such C-type elements, Warlpiri clitics can optionally surface in clause-initial position. An example of the alternation between 2D and initial position in Warlpiri is illustrated in (38), where the pronominal clitic *lu* is enclitic to *kala* 'PAST'.

(38) a.   kala **lu**   warru-pu-ngu   yapa-patu-rlu kuyu
           PAST 3PL.SUBJ around-kill-PAST person-PL-ERG animal.NOM
           'The people used to kill animals all over' (Laughren 2002, 92)

b.   yapa-patu-rlu kala **lu** warru-pu-ngu kuyu

c.   kuyu kala **lu** warru-pu-ngu yapa-patu-rlu

According to Legate (2008), the discussion of Warlpiri clitics in the literature has been flawed by a number of misconceptions. She scotches a number of earlier proposals (including analyses in which the placement of the clitics was based on the phonological property of the number of syllables on the host) and points out that earlier analysts have often confused a complementizer element for a member of the clitic sequence. She provides the following list of complementizers and auxiliary clitics (Legate 2008, 7):

(39)   Warlpiri complementizers and clitic auxiliaries

Complementizers		Auxiliaries	
kuja	'that'	*ka*	Present Imperfective
kaji	'if/when'	*lpa*	Past Imperfective
yinga	'for, since'	∅	Perfective
yungu	'for, since'		
kala	remote past		
kala	potential		
kapi	future		

The labels, especially for the complementizers, are arbitrary, of course. In particular, the complementizers with time referential labels name elements that co-occur with particular expressions of time reference; they are not tense (or aspect) markers in their own right.

The problem is that complementizer elements have largely the same distribution as clitics, except that the true clitic cluster can never appear in absolute initial position in the clause whereas the complementizers can. Legate therefore proposes that a complementizer, whether overt or null, always serves as the syntactic host for the clitics. However, the clitics as morphological objects are enclitics and require an overt host to their left. When the complementizer is overt it can appear in initial position and can host the clitic cluster. When the complementizer is null the clitic cluster requires some other element to begin the clause and serve as host.

In general, Warlpiri clitics cannot break up phrases, according to Legate. Now, there are plenty of attested examples in which it seems that just this has happened, but Legate argues that this is an illusion caused by the intervention of clitics between two independent phrasal units that are semantically linked. In particular, a modifier may take the same case ending as the noun head it modifies. Under those circumstances it appears that the modifier is a separate phrase (indeed, one sometimes sees English glosses of such examples along the lines 'the dog, the big one' in place of 'the big dog'). However, when the modifier doesn't have its own case marker then it forms a constituent with its head, and Legate shows that precisely that kind of phrase can't be broken up by the clitics. Thus, in (40a) the phrase *kurdu yalumpurlu* 'child that-ERG' is unsplittable because case isn't marked on the head noun *kurdu*. However, in

(40b) it is possible to split up the phrase because both members are case-marked
(Legate 2008, 20):

(40) a.   * Kurdu=**ka-jana**   yalumpu-rlu maliki-patu jiti-rni
              child=PRES.IMPF.AUX-3PL.OBJ that-ERG   dog-PAUC   tease-NONPAST

      b.   Kurdu-ngku=**ka-jana**   yalumpu-rlu maliki-patu
              child-ERG=PRES.IMPF.AUX-3PL.OBJ that-ERG   dog-PAUC
              jiti-rni
              tease-NONPAST
              'That child is teasing the dogs'

There is one exception to the ban on splitting constituents. Warlpiri verbs
often have preverbs. In many cases these are loosely concatenated adverb-like
elements that can readily be separated from their verb stem. Such preverb + verb
combinations can also be readily split by clitics. However, there is a class of more
tightly cohering preverbs known as semi-productive preverbs that can't be split
away from their verb by any other type of phrase. These preverbs are not completely morphologized as fully-fledged prefixes, however, because they can be
separated by the clitic cluster. Legate (2008, 51–2) illustrates with two examples
using the preverbs *yitaki* 'tracked' and *pirri* 'scattered':

(41) a.   Yitaki-rra=**jana**   ma-nu   parnman-kurlangu-rlangu
              tracked-THITHER=3PL.OBJ get-PAST mother.in.law-having-kinship.pair
              kuja=**lpa-lu**   ya-nu
              DECL.COMP=PAST.IMPF.AUX-3PL.SUBJ go-PAST
              'He went off tracking his mother-in-law and his wives, following where they
              had gone'

      b.   Pirri=**ka-lu**   nguna-mi   miyi manu kuyu
              scattered=PRES.IMPF.AUX-3PL.SUBJ lie-NONPAST food and   meat
              kiji-rninja-warnu
              throw-INF-after
              'The food and meat lie scattered after being thrown'

In effect, these examples are Warlpiri's answer to the phenomenon of tmesis in
classical languages.

Summary: Within our second group of 2P clitics, we have included clitics
whose position is defined primarily in syntactic terms. These are clitics which
appear preferably after the first full phrase and which encliticize to the preceding
word. We have also shown that, despite their preference for 2D, these clitics can
also occur clause-initially, either as enclitics or proclitics.

Ancient Greek, Sanskrit and Tagalog (primarily 2W)

Another type of 2P clitic occurs primarily after the first phonological word, what
Halpern (1995) refers to as 2W placement. This seems to have been a feature
of Indo-European. Clearcut cases of 2W clitics are also found in Avestic (Indo-
Iranian) and in Vedic Sanskrit, as pointed out by Wackernagel (1892, 402–3),
citing his contemporaries.[10] The cluster is illustrated in (42) (Hock 1996, 215):

(42) ádant   **ha sma á   etásya**   puránnam
      eat-3PL.PRES PRT PRT PRT DEM.GEN.SG.MASC earlier.food.ACC.NEUT
      'They eat his earlier food'

We also find 2W outside the Indo-European language family. For example, Tagalog, an Austronesian language spoken in the Philippines, has a large variety of clitics, including pronominal clitics, aspectual clitics and the question marker *ba*.

The pronouns distinguish three persons and singular/plural number with an inclusive/exclusive distinction for non-singular first person forms, corresponding respectively to 'I and you(singular)' and 'I and some third party or parties'. Schachter and Otanes treat the inclusive first person as a kind of non-plural dual and the exclusive as a kind of plural dual. They have three 'case' forms corresponding to the three main clausal functions they have. Schachter and Otanes (1972, 88) label these the '*ang*-form', '*ng*-form' and '*sa*-form' after the particles found with corresponding full noun phrases. The *sa*-form pronouns are not clitics so we will disregard them here. Schachter (1973) and, following him, Anderson (2005) call the *ang*-form pronouns 'Topic' forms and the *ng*-form pronouns 'Complement' forms, after their default usages.[11] The relevant forms are tabulated below (ignoring irrelevant variations):

(43)   Tagalog clitic pronouns

	Non-Plural		Plural	
	Topic	Comp	Topic	Comp
1sg	ako	ko	kami	namin
dual	kata	nita	tayo	natin
2nd	ka	mo	kayo	ninyo
3rd	siya	niya	sila	nila

2sgTopic+   kita (*ka + ko)
1sgComplement

Note that the sequence of 2sgTopic acting on 1sgComplement is expressed by a portmanteau (disyllabic) form.

Schachter and Otanes (1972, 184–93) discuss the rather complex patterning of clitics. The main principle is that the three monosyllabic clitics *ko, ka, mo* precede all other clitics, including non-pronominal clitics. When a sequence of two disyllabic clitics occurs they can be found in either order, but the order Complement(*ng*)-form < Topic(*ang*)-form is more common. Examples are:

(44) a.   Nakita **ka   niya/namin/nila**
           saw   you.SG he/we/they
           'He/We/They saw you'
     b.   Nakita **ko siya/kayo/sila**
           saw   I him/you.PL/them
           'I saw him/you/them'

  c. Nakita **kita**
    saw I.TOPIC>you.SG.COMPLEMENT
    'I saw you'
(45) a. Nakita **namin siya**
    saw we him
  b. Nakita **siya namin**
    saw him we
    'We saw him'

Tagalog clitics occur primarily after the first accented word. Since Tagalog clauses are typically verb-initial, this means that the clitics tend to occur after the verb, as shown in (46a). However, other word classes are permitted to appear clause-initially, such as the fronted wh-word *bakit* 'why', and the sentential negation marker *hindi*. Such words are then able to host the Wackernagel cluster as shown in (46b, c):[12]

(46) a. Tinawag **niya** ang bata
    called s/he ANG child
    'S/he called the child'
  b. Bakit **ka niya** tinawag
    why you s/he called
    'Why did s/he call you?'
  c. Hindi **ka niya** tinawag
    NEG you s/he called
    'S/he didn't call you'

A feature of Tagalog clitics is that in sentences with fronted topics there is a difference in the distribution of discourse particle clitics and pronominal clitics (Anderson 1992, 2005). In (96) we see sentences with the interrogative clitic *ba* and the pronominal clitic *sila* 'they':

(47) a. Sasayaw **ba sila** ng panganggo bukas ng gabi
    dance Q 3PL.NOM NG fandango tomorrow NG night
    'Will they dance a fandango tomorrow night?'
  b. Bukas **ba** ng gabi 'y sasayaw **sila** ng panganggo
    tomorrow Q NG night AY dance 3PL.NOM NG fandango
    'Will they dance a fandango tomorrow night?'

In the verb-initial sentence (47a) both the question particle and the pronominal clitic occur in second position immediately after the verb. However, in the sentence (47b), where the adjunct phrase *bukas ng gabi* 'tomorrow night' occurs as a sentence-initial topic, the clitic cluster *ba sila* is broken up: while the question particle *ba* appears in 2W position within the fronted topic phrase, the clitic pronoun appears in 2W position within the clause. We discuss further aspects of the Tagalog system in Section 6.5.

Bulgarian (between 2P and verb-adjacent/non-initial)

Bulgarian is a South Slavic language closely related to Serbian/Croatian. It, too, has a system of pronominal and auxiliary verb clitics that form a cluster with a set ordering. However, although there are certain respects in which the Bulgarian system resembles a standard Wackernagel system, such as that of Czech or Serbian/Croatian, there are important differences. We will follow the description in Franks and King (2000, 48) occasionally supplemented by data from grammars and from informants (a particularly good description is that of Hauge 1976, summarized in Hauge 1999, 191f.).

The auxiliary clitics are reduced forms of the present tense of the verb 'to be', which is used to form a variety of tense/aspect forms with the passive participle and with the l-participle. In addition, the verb 'to be' has clitic forms in the present tense in its original use as a copular verb (just as in other Slav languages). The forms are given in (48):[13]

(48)   Bulgarian present tense clitic forms of BE

	Singular	Plural
1st	săm	sme
2nd	si	ste
3rd	e	sa

The pronominal clitics occur in two forms, just as in other Slav languages: an accusative case form and an oblique ('dative') case form. This is interesting in the context of Bulgarian (and Macedonian, whose clitic forms are very similar) because, unlike other Slavic languages, Bulgarian/Macedonian has lost its nominal case marking morphology. The forms are given in (49):

(49)   Bulgarian pronominal clitics

	Singular		Plural	
	Acc	Dat	Acc	Dat
1st	me	mi	ni	ni
2nd	te	ti	vi	vi
3rdM/N	go	mu	gi	im
3rdF	ja	i		

	Acc	Dat
reflexive	se	si

The reflexive is neutral between singular/plural and the 3pl forms are neutral for gender.

This does not exhaust all the elements that can be considered as part of the clitic cluster, but it does form the core of that cluster. The basic ordering of these clitics is given in (50):

(50)   Basic ordering of Bulgarian clitics (simplified list)
          Aux < Dat < Acc < e (3sg)

The cluster is clearly very similar to that of the other Slav languages we have seen, but with an added twist (also found in Serbian/Croatian): the 3sg form of the auxiliary/copular occurs at the right edge of the cluster while all the other auxiliaries occur at the left edge. This fact alone shows that we are not dealing with any normal syntactically placed elements. Such highly idiosyncratic ordering is characteristic of affixal systems (and clitic systems), not of syntax.

Some examples are:

(51)   Bulgarian clitic cluster (Franks and King, 2000, 61)

  a.   Dal   **si**   **mu**   **gi**

       gave.MASC AUX.2SG 3SG.MASC.DAT 3PL.ACC

       'You gave them to him'

  b.   Dala   **mu**   **gi**   e

       gave.FEM 3SG.MASC.DAT 3PL.ACC AUX.3SG

       'She gave them to him'

From the examples seen so far we might imagine that the Bulgarian clitic cluster was a typical Wackernagel type, and to some extent this is true: the simple cluster illustrated in (51) can never appear in absolute clause initial position, as seen from (52):

(52) * **Mu**   **gi**   e   dala

       3SG.MASC.DAT 3PL.ACC AUX.3SG gave.FEM

However, unlike strict Wackernagel clitics, the cluster can often be preceded by more than one constituent (Avgustinova 1994, 55):[14]

(53)   Na snimkata sigurno **săm**   **ti**   **ja**   pokazvala

       on picture.DEF certainly 1SG.AUX 2SG.DAT 3SG.FEM.ACC showed

       'I've probably shown her to you on the picture'

The two initial constituents have to be intonationally separated, as in the case of the two adverbials in (53).

Now, word order for non-clitic constituents is very free in Bulgarian. The orders shown in (54) represent only some of the possibilities:

(54) a.   (Tja) sigurno dava tazi kniga na majka mi

       (she) probably gives that book to mother my

       'She is probably giving that book to my mother'

  b.   Na majka mi (tja) sigurno dava tazi kniga

  c.   Tazi kniga (tja) sigurno dava na majka mi

  d.   Tazi kniga dava (tja) sigurno na majka mi

Nonetheless, it turns out the 'that' cluster obeys an additional constraint, which is rather stronger than the tendency to occupy Wackernagel position: it must immediately precede the lexical verb (Franks and King 2000, 234–8). Thus, while the examples of (55) are fine, other orders in which the cluster is separated from the verb are impossible, (56):

(55) a.   Tja sigurno **ì**   **ja**   e   dala tazi kniga

       she probably 3SG.FEM.DAT 3SG.FEM.ACC 3SG.AUX gave that book

       'She has probably given her that book'

  b.   Tja **ì ja** e dala sigurno tazi kniga

  c.   Tazi kniga sigurno **ì ja** e dala

(56)   *Tja **ì ja** e tazi kniga dala

Bulgarian has a variety of constructions in which forms of the auxiliary verb 'to be' are used in forms other than the present tense. Such forms are not clitics and have a strong tendency to serve as the host of the clitic cluster (Avgustinova 1997, 48). The basic facts are summarized succinctly in Hauge (1999, 194–5). There are four groups of auxiliary forms to consider (all are forms of the verb BE).

(i) Past tense forms (finite), inflected for person/number, used for forming the pluperfect:

	Singular	Plural
1.	bjax	bjaxme
2.	beše/be	bjaxte
3.	beše/be	bjaxa

(ii) The l-participle form (inflected for singular/plural number and for masc/fem/neut gender in the singular), used for forming the Renarrated (Evidential) Mood: *bil, bila, bilo, bili*.

(iii) Alternative forms to the (clitic) present tense form *săm*, used principally to form the Future:

	Singular	Plural
1.	băda	bădeme
2.	bădeš	bădete
3.	băde	bădat

(iv) Conditional forms, inflecting for person/number:

	Singular	Plural
1.	bix	bixme
2.	bi	bixte
3.	bi	bixa

The past tense auxiliary forms in (i) and the l-participle forms (ii) can appear either immediately after the second-position clitic cluster or before the cluster (as though it were part of the cluster itself) (the examples in (57) are from Avgustinova 1997, 48, the others are from Hauge 1999):

(57) a.   Az **mu**   bjax   dal knigata
             I   3SG.MASC.DAT 1SG.AUX.PAST gave the.book
             'I had given the book to him'

      b.   Az bjax   **mu**   dal knigata
             I   1SG.AUX.PAST 3SG.MASC.DAT gave the.book

(58) a.   Te =**mu**   bili   kazali
             they =to.him AUX.LPART told

      b.   Te bili   =**mu**   kazali
             they AUX.LPART =to.him told
             'They told him, apparently'

With Future tenses formed from *bǎda*, … the clitics are always followed immediately by the auxiliary:

(59) a. **Šte ja** bǎde   pročel
        FUT it AUX.FUT read
        'He will read it'
    b. * Bǎde   **šte ja** pročel
        AUX.FUT FUT it read

With the conditional auxiliary the clitics are always hosted by the main (lexical) verb:

(60) a. Az bix   **mu   go** dal
        I   AUX.COND to.him it give
        'I would give it to him'
    b. * Az **mu   go** bix   dal
        I   to.him it AUX.COND give

Avgustinova (1997) discusses such constructions in some detail. We illustrate with examples of the pluperfect. In (57) we saw that the pronominal clitic *mu* cannot be separated from the past tense auxiliary *bjax* which goes to form the pluperfect. In (61) we see further evidence of that generalization:

(61) a. (Az) dal **mu**   bjax   knigata
        I   gave 3SG.MASC.DAT 1SG.AUX.PAST the.book
        'I had given him the book'
    b. * Az **mu** dal bjax knigata
    c. * Az bjax dal **mu** knigata

When the verb is itself the first element of the clause, we obtain something like a Wackernagel effect, in that the clitic cluster must follow immediately after the verb, whether the lexical verb (62b) or the auxiliary (62a) (Avgustinova 1997, 48–9):

(62) a. Bjax   **ja**   vidjal
        1SG.AUX 3SG.FEM.ACC saw
        'I had seen her'
    b. Vidjal **ja** bjax
    c. ?? Vidjal bjax **ja**
    d. * Bjax vidjal **ja**
    e. * Az **ja** vidjal bjax

In (62d, e) the string is ungrammatical because the clitic *ja* is separated from the finite auxiliary. In (62c) the clitic follows the auxiliary but it doesn't occupy the canonical Wackernagel position so its acceptability is highly degraded compared with (62a, b).

The tendency for the clitics to occupy second position but to immediately precede the (finite) verb is also seen in early varieties of Romance such as Medieval Spanish, Italian and French. In early Romance varieties the verb could appear in clause-initial position, in which case the clitics would follow immediately after it.

The second position effect was retained in subordinate clauses, except that the clitics followed the subordinating conjunction. The phenomenon was studied by the nineteenth-century linguists A. Tobler and A. Mussafia, and it bears their names in Romance linguistics. Fontana (1996) provides an interesting discussion along with a comparison with similar phenomena in Germanic languages. Fischer (2003) discusses the interesting development of the clitic system in Old Catalan. Most traditional and generative accounts have claimed that the Tobler–Mussafia placement of clitics is ultimately governed by phonological pressures to put the clitic cluster after a suitable host, but Fischer claims that in Old Catalan, at least, the clitics are syntactic heads and are placed by syntactic principles in accordance with the Minimalist Program.[15]

In effect, then, Bulgarian exhibits the Tobler–Mussafia property (see also Halpern 1995 for explicit comparison of Bulgarian with early Romance, and Macedonian with modern Romance languages).

Finally, recall that we mentioned the complementizers in Warlpiri that can host the clitic cluster. Bulgarian, too, has a pair of rather idiosyncratic cluster hosts: the invariable future particle *šte* and the negation element *ne*. These are unusual in the sense that they behave like clitics themselves, yet they can also host the rest of the clitic cluster. We will discuss these elements in more detail in Chapter 5.

3.3.4   Verb-oriented clitics

Macedonian is a language which is very closely related to Bulgarian (the two languages are mutually intelligible), yet it has a rather different clitic system. The basic system is summarized in Spencer (1991, 358–62) and in Franks and King (2000, 67–89). Like Bulgarian, Macedonian has a set of pronominal clitics for direct and indirect objects and clitic forms of the verb BE. The clitic pronouns are shown in (63), where it can be seen that they are virtually identical to those of Bulgarian (there are slightly larger differences between the two languages in the shapes of the full-form pronouns).

(63)   Macedonian pronominal clitics

	Singular		Plural	
	Acc	Dat	Acc	Dat
1st	me	mi	ne	ni
2nd	te	ti	ve	vi
3rdM/N	go	mu	gi	im
3rdF	ja	i		

	Acc	Dat
reflexive	se	si

The Macedonian clitic cluster is also very similar to that of Bulgarian.[16] However, its placement is crucially dependent on the main verb and shows few signs, if any, of Wackernagel positioning. In finite clauses (that is, clauses which are not imperative or gerunds) the cluster is prefixed to the main verb or to its finite auxiliary form:

(64) a.   **Mi   go** dade Vera včera
            to.me it   gave Vera yesterday
            'Vera gave me it yesterday'

      b.   Takov ton   ne **mi   se**   dopaǵa
            such   tone NEG to.me REFL pleases
            'I don't like that kind of tone'

      c.   **Sme   gi**   imale kupeno knigite
            AUX.1SG them have bought the.books
            'We have (reportedly) bought the books' (Franks and King 2000, 70, 71)

With imperatives and gerunds the cluster is suffixed to the verb:[17]

(65) a.   Zemi   **ja**!
            take.IMPER it
            'Take it!'

      b.   Zemajḱi   **mu   ga**, počna da   bega
            taking.GERUND he.DAT it   began COMP run
            'Taking it from him, he began to run' (Spencer 1991, 359)

(66) a.   Nosi   **mi   go**
            bring.IMPERATIVE to.me it
            'Bring it to me!' (Franks and King 2000, 83)

      b.   Ne donesuvajḱi   **mi   go** toa na vreme ...
            NEG bringing.GERUND to.me it   that on time
            'Not bringing me it on time ...' (Franks and King 2000, 84)

This verb-oriented pattern of clitics is more familiar, of course, from the Romance languages, and the Macedonian clitic system shows striking similarities to that of languages such as Spanish and Italian.

3.3.5   Other placement types

In this subsection we look at cases in which the clitic or clitic cluster doesn't form part of the phrase that it applies to but in which it is placed in positions other than the Wackernagel position. Specifically, we survey cases in which the clitic is apparently put in the 'right' place by rules of syntax but appears to attach to the 'wrong' element as its host. A number of cases of this kind are discussed by Cysouw (2005) (he refers to such clitics as 'ditropic', i.e., 'being in two places', a term due to Embick and Noyer 2001). The existence of some types of ditropic clitic system has been doubted in the past, and Cysouw goes to some lengths to demonstrate that there are well-established and incontrovertible cases of such ditropism. Then we look at clitics which are promiscuous in the sense that they can attach to more or less any word category and can appear in more or less any part of the clause (Polish floating inflections).

Ditropic clitics

An important type of clitic distribution is found when an element is syntactically associated with a phrase in one direction but phonologically bound to a word in the opposite direction. This is seen in English auxiliary clitic forms. In an expression such as *Tom's a linguist* or *Tom's reading a book* we see that the clitic auxiliary *-s* forms a morphophonological unit with the subject noun *Tom*, yet syntactically the auxiliary is in construction with the following noun phrase or verb phrase.

Kwak'wala (in the older literature known as Kwakiutl) is a member of the Northern Wakashan languages spoken on the seaboard of British Columbia. The clitic system is described in Anderson (1984) and especially Anderson (2005). The language as a whole has two distinct types of clitic system, one of which we will discuss later in the book when we talk about prosodic or phonological domains for clitics. Here we illustrate the other set of clitics, with a single (oft-cited!) example from Anderson (1984):

(67)   kw'ix̣ʔid=**ida** bəgwanəma=**x̣**=**a** q'asa=**s**=**is**   t'əlwagwayu
       clubbed=the   man=OBJ=the   otter=INSTR=his club
       'The man clubbed the otter with his club'

Two types of clitic are illustrated here. The forms *x*, *s*, labelled OBJ, INSTR, cross-reference the direct object and the instrument (though these are just the basic functions of these elements). The formatives glossed 'the' are a type of determiner providing deictic information about the noun they relate to. The formative glossed 'his' is a possessive pronominal marker.

From the point of view of syntax, the determiners and the possessor element =*is* 'his' are clearly in construction with the following phrase, but morphophonologically they can be shown to be hosted by the preceding word. Another language with clitics of this sort that has been discussed in the literature is Yagua, a virtual isolate spoken by about 3,000 people in Peru. In that language a direct object is often doubled by a clitic. The canonical clausal word order is verb-subject-object (VSO). The clitic is always to the left of the direct object it doubles, but it is an enclitic. This means that willy-nilly it attaches to a host which is not related to the object it doubles. We will discuss the case of Yagua in a little more detail when we come to illustrate clitic doubling in Chapter 6, where we will see that the clitic can attach to the subject, to the verb or to an adverbial. This case isn't exactly like the Kwak'wala case because the clitic isn't a functional element of the object phrase as such (like a determiner), but the overall placement patterning is somewhat similar, in that the syntactic position of the clitic is determined syntactically (it is to the immediate left of the direct object phrase, wherever that is) but the morphophonological position of the clitic is at variance with that placement.

A particularly interesting type of ditropic clitic has been reported for the Pama-Nyungan Australian language Kugu Nganhcara (Klavans 1985, Cysouw

2005). A dative pronoun is cross-referenced by an enclitic *ngu*. This appears immediately before the final word of the clause, which has to be the main verb. However, elsewhere in the clause word order is free so the host for the clitic can be any word:

(68) a.   nhila   pama-ng nhingu pukpe-wu kuʔa=**ngu**   wa:
            he.NOM man-ERG him.DAT child-DAT dog.DAT=CL gave
            'The man gave the dog to the child'
    b.   nhila pama-ng nhingu kuʔa pukpe-wu=**ngu** wa:
    c.   kuʔa pama-ng nhingu pukpe-wu nhila=**ngu** wa:
        etc.

Polish has a very interesting and theoretically important set of clitics that cross-reference subjects in past tense constructions. The clitics, derived historically from auxiliary verbs, are able to attach to the l-participle form of the verb and to more or less any word to the left of the verb in the clause. When such a clitic attaches to a non-verbal element it is effectively behaving ditropically. The placement is different from that of Kwak'wala or Nganhcara, however, in that there is no obvious sense in which the clitic is placed anywhere by the syntax. The system will be described in more detail in Chapter 4.

Other patterns

The patterns surveyed briefly here don't exhaust by any means the types of clitic positioning found cross-linguistically. One important type of clitic, which will be discussed in greater detail in Chapter 4, is that which attaches to a prosodically defined constituent (an accented word or a phonological phrase of some kind). In other cases, such as that of Udi discussed in Chapter 7, the clitic attaches to that element in the sentence under focus (the focus position in Udi is defined as the constituent immediately before the verb). In yet other cases we may find that there are very few restrictions on where in the clause or phrase a clitic can attach. This is the case with the Polish floating or mobile inflections, for instance, discussed in Section 4.4.3.

3.4   Domains of placement

Clitics are primarily functional elements, that is, they resemble inflections. As we saw in Chapter 2, the principal lexical categories they apply to are those of the noun and the verb. The verb is the lexical head of the whole clause so that clitics associated with verb features can equally be thought of as being associated with clausal features. On the other hand, clitics associated with nouns often relate solely to relations within the noun phrase. We can think of the noun phrase and the clause as constituting the domain over which the clitic has scope. The clitic (cluster) itself gets placed within that domain by selecting a host of a particular grammatical or prosodic type, or by selecting a host in a particular syntactic position, such as left/right edge of the phrase, or after the first element of the phrase. In many descriptions of clitic systems we are told that a clitic cluster attaches to the lexical head of the noun phrase or the verb phrase. However, when a clitic selects a noun or verb head as its host, it becomes very difficult to distinguish the construction from ordinary affixation. For the present we will simply present a few examples of systems in which the standard descriptions tend to present the markers attached to nouns/verbs as clitics and leave till various later points in the book discussion of whether these are really clitics, or really affixes, or something else.

3.4.1   Noun phrase domain clitics

We will first look at clitics which are placed with respect to the noun phrase domain. In the examples cited in Chapter 2 we saw clitics realizing the property of definiteness, 'case' marking (in the form of clitic postpositions) and possession, and we also saw clitic coordinating conjunctions in Latin. In Section 2.4 we cited examples of possessor clitics in Tukang Besi. The 1sg possessor clitic *su* attaches to a host which is at the right edge of the noun phrase. This is essentially the patterning found with a more familiar possessor clitic, the English *'s*, often called the 'Saxon genitive'. This clitic attaches to whatever word appears at the right edge of the noun phrase, whatever the category of that word happens to be:

(69)   The English 'saxon genitive'
    a.   [the Queen of England]'s hat   noun
    b.   [the girl you met]'s name   finite verb
    c.   [the man responsible]'s name   postnominal adjective
    d.   [the boy that seemed tired]'s name   predicative adjective
    e.   [the girl we were talking to]'s name   preposition
    f.   [the woman you met yesterday]'s name   adverb

Some examples of this kind sound awkward, though this is partly because of the rather complex and poorly understood principles which determine when we use the *'s* as opposed to the preposition *of* (see Rosenbach 2005 and the references cited there for recent discussion). The *'s* can only be placed at the very edge of the phrase, never inside that phrase, even though this means that it is often separated from the word it most directly relates to, the lexical head noun.

We saw in Chapter 2 that Bulgarian has a definite article which appears in the 2P position with the noun phrase. The order of words within the noun phrase enjoys a certain amount of freedom, but in general, attributive adjectives come before the head noun, while prepositional phrase modifiers, participial phrases and relative clauses come after the head noun. When the noun phrase begins with one or more prenominal modifiers, the definite article attaches to the first of the modifiers (usually an adjective, of course). One interesting feature of this placement is seen when the prenominal adjective is itself modified by a degree modifier such as *mnogo* 'very'. Then, we find that 2P is defined as the first full constituent, not the first full word. In other words, we have 2P patterning but not 2W patterning:

(70) a.   mnogo interesna=**ta**   kniga
              very   interesting=the book
              'the interesting book'

    b.   * mnogo=**ta/to** interesna   kniga
            very=the   interesting book

The form of the definite article is determined by the form of the host. In (70a) the article matches the FEM.SG ending *-a* of the adjective (which itself agrees in number/gender with the head noun). In (70b) we see that the article is not allowed on the degree modifier *mnogo*, whether it matches the final vowel of *mnogo* (**mnogo=to*) or whether it reflects the feminine sg agreement with *kniga* 'book' (*mnogo=ta*). Facts such as these make it difficult to treat the Bulgarian definite article as a genuine clitic. We will see later (Section 5.5) that a better way of analysing the Bulgarian (and Macedonian) articles is to treat them as a type of affix, though one which attaches to phrases in much the same way as a Wackernagel clitic, resulting in a kind of 'Wackernagel inflection'.[18]

A less controversial example of a 2P clitic in the Bulgarian noun phrase is found with possessive marking (Franks and King 2000, 55–8). Possessive pronouns take the form of clitics, homophonous to the verbal pronominal clitics:

(71)   Bulgarian possessive clitics

    a.   mnogo-to=**ti**   novi knigi
          many-DEF=your new books
          'your many new books'

    b.   večno   mlada-ta=**ni** stolica
          eternally young-DEF=our   capital
          'our eternally young capital'

Notice that the possessive clitic attaches to a word form already marked with the definite article.

A rather different pattern is found with possessive markers in Modern Greek. In that language we see more variability in the positioning of the possessive clitic, as shown by Joseph and Philippaki-Warburton (1987, 163) (see also Cysouw 2005).

(72)   Greek possessives as variable 2P clitics
    a.   to ómorfo   éksipno skilí **mu**
          the beautiful smart   dog   my
          'my beautiful smart dog'
    b.   to ómorfo éksipno **mu** skilí
    c.   to ómorfo **mu** éksipno skilí

3.5   Clause-domain clitics

We next turn to the clause-domain clitics. We've seen several typical examples of 2P clause-domain clitics such as those found in Serbian/Croatian, discussed in Chapter 2. In the case of Serbian/Croatian, the clitics are pronominal arguments or auxiliary verbs (though in Czech we've seen that discourse markers such as the evidential particle *prý* can also form part of the clitic cluster). Many languages, however, have discourse particles that behave as clitics, often appearing in 2P position. In most cases the domain of such particles is the whole clause (or indeed the whole utterance).

A case in point is the various discourse markers of Finnish. Like Quechua, Polish, Japanese and many other languages, Finnish has an interrogative clitic. Its form is *=ko/kö* and it follows classical Wackernagel placement. Karlsson (1987, 68–70) provides an overview of how this clitic is used. Taking the affirmative sentence (73) we can form the four yes-no questions in (74):

(73)   Pekka saapui Turkuun aamulla
        Pekka arrived at.Turku in.the.morning
        'Pekka arrived at Turku in the morning'

(74) a.   Saapui=**ko** Pekka Turkuun aamulla
           arrived=KO Pekka at.Turku in.the.morning
           'Did Pekka arrive at Turku in the morning?'
     b.   Pekka=**ko** saapui Turkuun aamulla
           Pekka=KO arrived at.Turku in.the.morning
           'Was it Pekka who arrived at Turku in the morning?'
     c.   Turkuun=**ko** Pekka saapui aamulla
           at.Turku=KO Pekka arrived in.the.morning
           'Was it at Turku that Pekka arrived in the morning?'
     d.   Aamulla=**ko**   Pekka saapui Turkuun
           in.the.morning Pekka arrived at.Turku
           'Was it in the morning that Pekka arrived at Turku?'

In all these cases we see the back vowel variant of the interrogative clitic. In (75) we see front and back variants:

(75) a.   Menet=**kö** ulos?
           go.2SG=KO out
           'Are you going out?'   [Front vowel host]
     b.   Olet=**ko**   sairas?
           be.2SG=KO ill
           'Are you ill?'   [Back vowel host]
     c.   Presidentiksi=**kö** Koivisto valittiin?
           As.president=KO Koivisto was.elected
           'Was Koivisto elected PRESIDENT?'[19] [Front vowel host]
     d.   Tuli=**ko**   Pekka Turkuun
           come=KO Pekka to.Turku
           'Did Pekka come to Turku?' [Back vowel host]

Notice that *menet and presidentiksi* are front vowel words because they contain
no back vowels, while *olet* and *tuli* are back vowel words, even though they end
in a front vowel. The vowels /i, e/ are transparent to harmony in Finnish in such
cases and so it is the back vowel of the stem that determines the harmony. This
illustrates the fact that the clitic participates in a phonological alternation that is
not purely phonological, but which in part is influenced by lexical factors.

Finnish has a variety of other particles, many of which are 2P clitics.
(Being discourse particles they are often very difficult to translate, hence our
rather approximate glosses.) Two common ones are *-han/hän* 'indeed' and the
emphatic particle *-pa/pä* (Karlsson 1987, 193, with the translations given by A.
Chesterman; see also Nevis 1986, 29):

(76)   Finnish 2P discourse particles *-han/hän*:
   a.   Minä=**hän** rakastan sinua
         I-HAN   I.love   you
         'I LOVE you!'
   b.   Rakastan=**han** minä sinua
         I.love=HAN   I   you
         'Of course I love you'
   c.   Sinua=**han** minä rakastan
         you=HAN   I   I.love
         'You are the one I love'

(77)   Finnish 2P discourse particles *-pa/pä*:
   a.   On=**pa** täällä kuuma!
         Is-PA   here   warm
         'It really is hot here!'
   b.   Tuossa=**pa** on iso joukko
         there-PA   is big group
         'There's a really big group!'

Notice that although *-pa/pä* serves to add emphasis to an utterance, in (77) it
attaches to a word which itself is unemphasized, because it happens to occur in
sentence-initial position.

The discourse clitics can stack up on each other. Thus, we often see combinations of *-ko/kö* and *-han/hän*:

(78)   Finnish 2P discourse particles *-ko+han*:

         On=**ko=han** Pentti kotona?
         is-KO-HAN   Pentti at.home
         'I wonder if Pentti is at home'

One of the Finnish discourse particles, *-kin*, has the interesting property of
appearing enclitic to the finite head (verb) of the clause (Karlsson 1987, 192; see
also Nevis 1986, 11, Anderson 2005, 80):

(79)   Finnish V-oriented discourse particle *-kin*:
    a.   Eikö   hän ole=**kin** ihana!
          NEG-Q he   is=KIN wonderful
          'Isn't he wonderful!'
    b.   Kalle on=**kin** täällä
          Kalle is=KIN here
          'Kalle is in fact here'
    c.   Menin=**kin** kotiin
          I.went=KIN home
          'I did go home'

Since the verb is the principal constituent of any typical clause, it isn't surprising to find that clitics which relate to the clause as a whole are placed close to or even adjacent to the verb. The clitic system of the Austronesian language Kambera is interesting in this regard, because here we are dealing with clitics which are placed with respect to the phrase, and not hosted by just the verb, but the phrase that hosts the clitics is clearly built around the verb rather than around the clause as a whole. This can be seen from example (80), which illustrates a subject phrasal proclitic, *ku*, a complement phrasal enclitic, *nya*, and a possessive clitic, *nggu*.

(80)   Napa [**ku**=   [hili beli   pàku] =**nya**$_j$]$_S$ [na umbuk   =**nggu**]$_j$
        later 1SG.NOM= again return first   =3SG.DAT ART grandson =1SG.GEN
        'I'll first have to go back to my grandson again'

Notice that the proclitic *ku* is separated from the verb head *beli* 'return' by the adverb *hili* 'again', and the enclitic *nya* is separated from the same verb form by the adverb *pàku* 'first'. We will look at the very interesting Kambera system in rather more detail in Chapter 8.

At various points in the book we will look at other instances of formatives traditionally described as clitics that cluster around the verb, namely, the pronominal clitics of Romance languages and of Greek. We will see that such cases often more closely resemble affixation than genuine cliticization, and many authors treat such systems as affixational. In general, we expect the positioning of true clitics to be defined in terms of syntactic positions, such as 'the first word/phrase of a domain', rather than in terms of specific categories of word, such as 'verb' or 'noun'.

3.6   Summary

In this chapter we have looked at a variety of ways in which Wackernagel's original insights into the nature of clitic elements have been extended and enriched in more recent research. We first noted that clitics often 'hunt together' by forming clusters, whose linear ordering may appear to be very idiosyncratic compared to the rest of the syntax. This is an aspect of clitics which brings them closer to affixes than to syntactically represented function words, and we will explore this facet in much more detail at various points in the book. Then we noted that Wackernagel's original observations about Ancient Greek and other early Indo-European languages holds for a good many languages throughout the world: numerous unrelated languages and language groups have developed second position or Wackernagel clitic systems, either at clause level or the level of the noun phrase or both. Languages may choose to define 'second position' in various ways, as 'after the first full word' (2W) or 'after the first phrase' (2D) or 'after the first full word or the first phrase'.[20]

An interesting variant on the second-position placement is shown in Bulgarian and a variety of medieval forms of Romance, in which the first position in the clause can be occupied by a whole variety of constituents and the clitic cluster then follows that first constituent, but the element following the clitics has to be the main verb (with or without auxiliary verbs). The exception is when the first element in the clause is itself the main verb. The result is that the clitics are always adjacent to the verb. This is the Tobler–Mussafia patterning, and it would appear that it represents an intermediate stage for many languages on the way to the next pattern of placement, adjacent to the verb, represented by Bulgaria's closest neighbour, Macedonian.

In many languages a clitic appears at first to be positioned where we would expect from the syntactic principles of the language, but we find that it forms a morphophonological unit with a host that is entirely unrelated, so-called 'ditropic clitics'. An obvious example of this behaviour is that of the English auxiliary clitic, but more spectacular instances have been reported for languages such as Kwak'wala.

We concluded by briefly illustrating clitics whose domain is the noun phrase or the clause as a whole. Within the noun phrase we can in principle find the same range of complexity as within the verb phrase, but since noun phrases tend to be simpler in structure than verb phrases or clauses this complexity is not so obvious. Finally, we saw that discourse clitics realized at the clausal level may have very similar placement properties to the more inflection-like clitics.

4   Clitics and phonology

4.1   Introduction

In this chapter we look in more detail at the phonological properties of clitics. For many linguists the most important feature of clitics is the fact that they can't exist as autonomous words because they lack inherent stress, and therefore need a host (with stress) to 'lean on' phonologically. While this is an important aspect of clitichood, it can't be a defining property, otherwise we would never be able to define clitics in languages that lack a stress system. In Section 4.2 we therefore generalize the idea of 'lacking inherent stress' to 'lacking inherent prosodic prominence'. This means that we can define clitics in languages that have a tone system or an accent system but no stress system, for instance, Japanese.

In Section 4.3 we see how the placement of a clitic cluster is often a complex interaction of syntax, prosody and morphology, but in at least one familiar system, that of Pashto, it seems that it is just prosody that determines the placement. Another question arises with regard to the internal structure of the clitic cluster. In Bulgarian the stress of the host interacts in rather complex ways with the organization of the cluster.

Here we should anticipate arguments we will be advancing later in the book about a number of well-known clitic systems. It is frequently claimed that the Romance languages, Greek, Albanian and Macedonian have clitic systems (especially pronominal clitics). In these languages the pronominal elements attach to a verb form (either the lexical verb or an auxiliary verb). In Section 4.4 we will show that in some cases the pronominals appear to violate the normal stress pattern of the language, while in other cases they appear to be incorporated into the stress domain of the verb. Where the pronominal appears to be incorporated into the lexical stress domain, it thereby takes on some of the characteristics of an affix, whereas if it remains outside the normal domain of lexical stress, it is easier to treat it as different from an affix, i.e., as a clitic.

However, it is open to us to conclude that the clitics of these languages can just as easily be thought of as deviant types of affix. More precisely, we will argue that these systems represent formatives that are neither purely affixes nor purely clitics. However, we will also conclude that there is no obvious answer to the question 'What is the behaviour of a typical affix with respect to stress?', since this depends on exactly what type of stress system the language has. The reader should therefore bear in mind that some of the clitics we talk about in this section lack a number of clitic properties (particularly the property of promiscuous attachment) and may even show features normally associated only with affixes (such as triggering idiosyncratic allomorphy on the host). Having issued this caveat about the clitic nature of these formatives, we will continue to refer to them as clitics.

We conclude the chapter by looking at elements whose clitichood is defined purely in terms of their phonological properties, the phonological or simple clitics (Section 4.5) and then turn to the various ways proposed by phonologists for representing the phonological structures of clitic–host combinations. As we will see, some phonologists argue that clitics require us to set up a special phonological constituent, the Clitic Group, while others reject that view and argue that clitics are incorporated into other prosodic units such as the Phonological Word or Phonological Phrase (Section 4.6).

4.2   Clitics and prominence

Clitics are prototypically stressless, and yet clitics can occasionally bear stress. We will see how this comes about later in the chapter. For the present, however, we will adopt the standard view that clitics are inherently without stress of their own. However, it is insufficient to use lack of stress as a definition of clitichood for the simple reason that there are languages that seem to have clitics but that don't have a stress system.

Even languages without a stress system will often have a system of prominence in which one syllable is set apart from other syllables in a word or phrase. In Japanese, all syllables[1] of a word have either a high tone (H) or a low tone (L). There are several patterns. In the first pattern, (1a), the initial syllable is high and the rest low. In the second pattern, (1b), the first syllable has low tone, the next set of syllables are high, and the final syllable is low. In the final pattern, which accounts for about 80% of all Japanese words, the first syllable is low and all the others high.

(1) a.   H L L L ...
    b.   L H H ... H L
    c.   L H H H ... H

A standard way of accounting for this kind of patterning is to say that words with patterns (1a) and (1b) have a syllable that bears an abstract phonological property called accent. In pattern (1a) the accent is on the first syllable, while in pattern (1b) it falls on the last high toned syllable. This is represented in (2), where the underlined syllable is the accented one:

(2) a.   H̲ L L L ...
    b.   L H H ... H̲ L

The rules for tone placement now state that the accented syllable has high tone which falls to a low tone on the next and any subsequent syllables. All syllables preceding the accented syllable are also high except for the first which is low. In the default patterning in (1c) none of the syllables is accented and all the syllables are high except for the first.

The point of this is that Japanese has a number of function words that are accentless, including a group of elements somewhat similar to those of Hindi (Section 2.4) which are placed immediately after the final noun of a noun phrase. These include *ga* '(focussed) subject', *o* 'direct object', *ni* 'indirect object, locative', *no* 'possessor', *wa* 'topic'. Such postnominal particles are incorporated into the accentual scheme of the noun they come next to, forming a single prosodic word. We can see the effect of this by considering three nouns whose only phonological difference is accent: *hási* 'chopsticks', *hasí* 'bridge' and *hasi* 'edge'. In isolation they are pronounced as shown in (3a), where we can see that 'bridge' and 'edge' have the same tonal contour. When followed by a postpositive particle such as *wa* they have the tonal contours shown in (3b):

(3) a.   hási   H L   'chopsticks'
           hasí   L H   'bridge'
           hasi   L H   'edge'
     b.   hási wa   H L L   'chopsticks'
           hasí wa   L H L   'bridge'
           hasi wa   L H H   'edge'

The particles are not noun suffixes. For one thing they can attach to adverbs and to postpositional phrases headed by lexical postpositions; in other words, they exhibit promiscuous attachment. But in that case we can see that the particles have the prosodic properties of clitics, in that they attach to an element that bears an accent (but not a stress). Needless to say, no phrase or clause can begin with one of these particles.

A similar situation arises in Mandarin Chinese (Putonghua). One of the ways Chinese expresses yes–no (polar) questions is by a sentence-final particle, *ma*. This follows words of any category:

(4) a.   Nĭ hăo ma
           you good Q
           'Are you OK?'
     b.   Tā chīfàn ma
           he eat.rice Q
           'Is he eating (rice)?'
     c.   Nĭ zhīdao tā   ma
           you know him Q
           'Do you know him?'
     d.   Nĭ kàn le   ma
           you read PERF Q
           'Have you read (it)?'

e.   Zhège rén   shì shén ma
           this   person is who Q
           'Who is this person?'

Chinese lacks word stress. However, all lexical (content) words, as well as most function words, bear one of four tones. The interrogative particle lacks tone, so it's the equivalent of a stressless word in a language with stress. The four tones of Chinese are high-level (tone1, H), falling (tone2, H-L), low fall-low rise (tone 3, M-L-M) and high rise (tone 4, L-H).[2] Toneless syllables such as *ma* are incorporated into the tonal structure of the word to their left by continuing the tonal movement of that word. Thus, the pitch on *ma* in the sequence *hǎo ma* from (4a) is slightly higher than the (mid) pitch on *hǎo*, because that word has tone 3, a low rising tone, while the pitch on *ma* in the sequence *tā ma* in (4c) is a level high tone, because *tā* has tone 1, a level high tone. Although toneless function words in Chinese are not often discussed in the context of clitics (partly, no doubt, because there's no clear notion of 'word stress' in Chinese), the interrogative particle has the relevant properties of a clitic: it isn't a straightforward affix because it shows promiscuous attachment, but it isn't a prototypical word either, because its position in the sentence is fixed (it can only ever appear as the last element of a clause) and its tonal phonology is defined by the adjacent word.

Having noted that we can have clitics in a language without lexical stress, we will now consider the way that clitic systems and stress systems interact in languages with recognized stress systems. There are three situations of interest. The first is where the clitics have no effect on the stress pattern of the word to which they are cliticized. This is probably the majority pattern cross-linguistically. The second is where the clitics are incorporated into the stress contour of the word, so that a word with clitics looks very much like an affixed word or a monomorphemic word. The third situation is much more rare and more interesting, and this is where a formative which has the phonological or morphosyntactic properties of a clitic has idiosyncratic effects on the stress of its host. This is interesting because it's the kind of behaviour we would normally expect of an affix.

Before we look at specific cases, bear in mind that stress systems come in a variety of forms. In the simplest cases the stress algorithm is defined over word forms on the basis of the phonological shape of the word (for instance, 'stress the first/last syllable', 'stress the penultimate syllable if heavy and otherwise stress the antepenultimate' and so on). In other cases stress is conditioned morphologically, so that stress becomes part of the exponence of certain morphological properties. In other cases stress is assigned in a more or less arbitrary fashion to lexical items, so that the position of stress has the same status as, say, whether the first consonant is voiced or voiceless. In many languages stress obeys a complex combination of all these factors.

4.3   Phonologically defined domains of cliticization

4.3.1   Pashto

The clitic cluster of Pashto, an Indo-Iranian language spoken in Afghanistan, has an extremely simple placement rule: the cluster is attached to the first stressed word in the clause. However, this system has given rise to a good deal of debate because of the complexity of the morphology and syntax of the language, which has made it rather unclear what is meant by 'first stressed word'. We will therefore have to discuss some fairly complex details of morphosyntax before the overall system is revealed. The most exhaustive source of data for the language is Tegey (1977), and our analysis follows very closely that of Kaisse (1981), whose analysis is largely endorsed by Anderson (2005, 152–7).

The clitics appear in a cluster consisting of pronominal markers, modal markers and discourse markers. These are shown in (5):[3]

(5)   Pashto clitics

pronominal clitics		modal clitics		adverbial clitics	
me	1sg	*ba*	'will, might, …'	*xo*	'really, of course'
de	2sg	*de*	'should, ought'	*no*	'then'
ye	3				
am	1/2pl				
mo	1/2pl				

The order of clitics in the cluster is rigid:

(6)   xo   ba   am/mo   me   de   ye   no
        indeed   FUT   1/2PL   1SG   2SG   3   then
                                           should

The clitics follow the first phrase in the clause, even if this means that they come after the verb (which otherwise is placed in sentence-final position):

(7) a.   xušal   =**me** zyaati   ne   wah-i
           Khosal =1SG any more NEG hit-3SG.PRES
           'Khosal doesn't hit me any more'
    b.   zyaati   =**me** ne   wah-i
           any more =1SG NEG hit-3SG.PRES
           'He doesn't hit me any more'
    c.   wah-i   =**me**
           hit-3SG.PRES =1SG
           'He hits me'
    d.   zə ɣwarəm če   tor =**me** wuguri
           I want   that Tor =1SG see
           'I want Tor to see me'

Although the clitics attach to the first phrase in the clause, some element in that phrase has to be stressed. Otherwise, the clitic will attach to the leftmost stressed word. This can be seen from examples (8) (Anderson 2005, 154):

(8) a.   ra ta te   rɑ   škɑwə́ =**de**
                me for from.it here pick   =2SG
                'You were picking it for me from it'

     b.   rɑ sara wí =**de**
                me with be =let
                'Let it be with me'

     c.   rɑ sará =**de** wi
                me with =let be
                'Let it be WITH ME'

Example (8a) seems to begin with a postpositional phrase, which might there-fore be expected to host the clitic. However, the postposition, which itself is unstressed, takes an unstressed pronoun as its complement. It isn't until we reach the verb that the clitic finds a prosodically appropriate host.

So far we have seen adequate evidence to back up our claim that Pashto clitics attach to the first stressed constituent in the clause. However, there is a further twist when we consider more complex examples, and these have prompted some to argue that Pashto exhibits endoclisis. This term refers to a situation in which a clitic breaks up a morpheme or word form in violation of the principle of lexical integrity. The analogy is with infixation. We will return to the implications of this question in Chapter 8. For the present we will note that it is not necessary to argue that Pashto clitics can be endoclitics. The result will be that we can say that in essence clitic placement in Pashto is determined prosodically.

The patterns of interest arise from a stress shift that is morphologically motivated. In imperfective verb forms the stress is word final, whereas in the perfective aspect forms the stress is word initial. A further point which needs to be considered is the fact that verbs in Pashto, as is common in the Indo-Iranian group, are frequently complex, consisting of a Preverb and a verbal element. The Preverb sometimes has an identifiable meaning as an adverb or an incorporated noun, and the verbal element is generally a meaningful verb that can sometimes occur on its own. However, quite often either the Preverb or the verbal element or both are semantically opaque. A meaningless verbal element in such structures is often referred to as a 'light verb' (LV).

The perfective stress in complex verbs falls on the Preverb (Kaisse 1981, 206):

(9) a.   ṭel-wɑhé   (I) was pushing it
                ṭél-wɑhe   I pushed it

     b.   takwɑhə́   (I) was shaking it
                tákwɑhə   I shook it

     c.   pore-westə́   (I) was carrying it across
                poré-westə   I carried it across

If a verb is monomorphemic it acquires a meaningless prefix (similar to the Sanskrit or Greek 'augment') which serves to bear the shifted stress:

(10) a.   skundə́la   'was pinching'
      b.   wə́-skundəla   'pinched'

The question now arises as to where the clitics will be placed when a word undergoes stress shift in the perfective. The answer is that the clitic placement principles treat the stressed Preverb as an independent word, which can therefore serve as the host for the clitics. This can be seen in examples (11–15) where the (a) examples are in the imperfective aspect with verb-final stress and the (b) examples are in the perfective, with stressed Preverbs:

(11) a.   ṭel   wɑhé =**me**
           PREVERB push =1SG
           '(I) was pushing it'
     b.   ṭél   =**me** wɑhe
           PREVERB =1SG push
           'I pushed it'

(12) a.   tak   wɑhə́ =**me**
           PREVERB shake =1SG
           '(I) was shaking it'
     b.   ták   =**me** wɑhə
           PREVERB =1SG shake
           'I shook it'

(13) a.   pore   -westə́ =**me**
           PREVERB carry =1SG
           '(I) was carrying it across'
     b.   poré   =**me** westə
           PREVERB =1SG carry
           'I carried it across'

(14) a.   pox   kə́ṛay =**me** da
           COOK DO(LV) =1SG is
           'I was cooking it'
     b.   pox   =**me** kə
           COOK =1SG DO(LV)
           'I cooked it' (Kaisse 1981, 200)

(15) a.   pezandə́ =**de**
           recognize =2SG
           'You were recognizing (him)'
     b.   wə́   =**de**   pezandə
           PREVERB =2SG recognize
           'You recognized him'

So far we can simply conclude that most verbs in Pashto are complex and that the Preverb is visible in the syntactic representations over which clitic placement is presumably stated. However, there are further complications. First, there is a small class of verbs where stress can be final or initial in the imperfect. This stress alternation doesn't, however, affect clitic placement:

(16) a.   pə́rebdə =**me**
           beat   =1SG

b.   pərebdə́ =**me**
        beat   =1SG
        'I was beating (him)'

c.   *pə́ =**me** rebdə

This shows that the clitic placement principle is unable to 'see inside' such verbs in order to attach the clitic word-internally to the first stressed syllable. This is a useful datum, because Pashto words tend to be stress final, so that it isn't generally possible to tell whether the clitic is attached to the right edge of a word containing a stressed syllable, or to the right of the stressed syllable of that word. A subset ('about nine verbs' according to Kaisse) of this group of verbs with moveable stress in the imperfective is a group of verbs beginning with the vowel /a/. This is unusual in Pashto because verbs, whether simple or complex, almost always begin with a consonant. The *a*-component of these verbs acts as a Preverb in the perfective even though it has no meaning. In (17) and (18) we see the stressed *a*-Preverb serving as the host for cliticization (Kaisse 1981, 203):

(17) a.   axistə́lə =**me**
             buy   1SG

     b.   á   =**me** xistələ
             PREVERB 1SG buy
             'I was buying'

(18) a.   aɣustə =**me**
             wear   1SG

     b.   á   =**me** ɣustə
             PREVERB 1SG buy
             'I was wearing (it)'

The *a*-initial verbs exhibit further unusual behaviour in the perfective aspect tense forms, however (Kaisse 1981, 202). Perfective verb formation treats the *a*- initial verbs as though they were monomorphemic, and provides them with the supporting wə. However, this wə, along with the negative particle nə, triggers an idiosyncratic process of vowel coalescence, under which wə/nə + a becomes wá/ná. (Kaisse cites examples to show that this is not a regular phonological alternation, but is only found in verb forms such as this.) In (19a, b) we see the negation particle and the perfective particle, while in (19c) we see an example with a longer cluster for good measure:

(19) a.   ná   ye xli
             NEG 3SG buy
             'He isn't buying it'

     b.   wá   ye xla
             PERF 3SG buy
             'Buy it!'

     c.   wá   **xo   ba ye** nə   xle
             PERF then will 3SG NEG buy
             'You won't buy it then'

What this means in terms of Kaisse's analysis (which we follow here) is that
the underlying form of (19b) is really (20):

(20)   wə́   a   **ye** xla
            PERF PREVERB 3SG buy

There are two features of this handful of *a*- initial verbs worth remarking on.
First, the *a*- behaves like a Preverb with respect to clitic placement in the imperfective forms that have initial stress. If we don't regard the *a*- as a Preverb, then
we have to say that the clitic cluster is able to split up a word form, violating
the principle of lexical integrity. Indeed, some authors argue that this is exactly
how we should analyse such cases. Tegey (1977) himself claims that it would
be incorrect to treat the *a*- element as a prefix. Although this element was historically a prefix in some verb, it was not in all of them (including *a-x* 'buy').
However, it's quite common for reanalysis of simple forms to take place in historical change, especially where there are only a few exemplars. We therefore
follow Kaisse in treating the *a*- as a meaningless (perhaps reanalysed) Preverb.
The vowel coalescence alternation can now be defined as a property of just this
Preverb. The only remaining peculiarity of the *a*-initial verbs is the fact that they
still require the supporting *wə* element in the perfective. The normal pattern of
complex verbs is for the Preverb to receive the stress in the perfective (and for
this Preverb to then serve as the host for cliticization). However, this peculiarity
is more understandable when we consider that there are very few vowel-initial
Preverbs. Thus, the supporting *wə* provides a supporting consonant.

The upshot of this rather complex set of data is that the cliticization process
is actually rather simple. First, we have to assume that complex verbs (including
oddities like the *a*-initial verbs) consist of two words. The clitic cluster attaches
to the first stressed word. It doesn't split up a word.

4.3.2   Bulgarian *li*

One of the clitics of Bulgarian is the question particle *li*. This turns
an assertion into a yes-no question. It is also found in Serbian/Croatian, where it
comes at the very beginning of the clitic cluster. In Bulgarian, too, it generally
comes at the beginning of the cluster, but with a twist: it has to attach to a word
which bears stress. This is an important fact, because it shows that some clitics
at least are placed with respect to prosodic units and not by rules of syntax (cf.
Franks 2000, 9–14).

The description which follows is based on the excellent survey of the facts
provided by Hauge (1976) (see also Hauge 1999). Bulgarian has very free word
order, much like Serbian/Croatian, so that a phrase of any category can appear
at the beginning of a sentence. In a yes-no question marked with *li*, the first constituent will be focussed intonationally, and will hence function as the focus of
the question. This is seen in (21), where the focussed/stressed word is indicated
by capitalization:

(21)   MAŠA **li šte** otide dnes   na teatăr?
              Masha Q FUT go   today to theatre
              'Is it Masha who is going to the theatre today?'

However, if the information structure is neutral, so that the whole verb phrase is treated as the focus, then the intonational focus falls on the main verb, as shown in (22):

(22)   **Šte** OTÍDE **li** Maša   dnes   na teatăr?
              FUT go   Q Masha today to theatre
              'Is Masha going to the theatre today?'

In (22) the clitic *li* attaches to the stressed verb *otíde*. The future particle *šte* lacks inherent stress so it can't itself serve as the host for *li*.

  Bulgarian has pronominal clitics, such as *mu* 'him/it.DAT' and *go* 'him/it.ACC'. The future particle *šte* can function as the host for these clitics. However, the clitics, like *šte*, lack lexical stress of their own and so they can't host *li*. Thus, when we have a string of clitics following *šte* the clitic *li* has to cliticize to the first lexical word that can bear stress, which in the case of (23) is the verb *vărnéte*:

(23)   **Šte mu**   **go** VĂRNÉTE **li**?
              FUT to.him it   return   Q
              'Are you going to return it to him?'

The negation particle *ne* has somewhat unusual properties. It is itself unstressed, but it causes stress to be placed on the next word. In (24) this is the main verb:

(24)   Ne   ISKATE **li**?
              NEG you.want Q
              'Don't you want (it)?'

However, in the examples in (25) we can see that *ne*, like *šte*, can serve as the host of a cluster of clitics. In this case it is the clitic immediately following *ne* which receives stress. The clitic *li* then cliticizes to the stressed clitic:

(25) a.   Ne   **GO li** ISKATE?
              NEG it   Q you.want
              'Don't you want it?'

  b.   Ne   **MU**   **li go** DADOXTE?
              NEG to.him Q it   you.gave
              'Didn't you give it to him?'

  c.   Ne   **STE**   **li mu**   **go** DALI?
              NEG AUX.2PL Q to.him it   given
              'Haven't you given it to him?'

  d.   Ne   **ŠTE li** ste   mu   go DALI?
              NEG FUT Q AUX.2PL to.him it   given
              'Won't you have given it to him?'

The stressing of the clitic following *ne* is a purely phonological phenomenon, in the sense that it has nothing to do with focussing or sentence phrasal accent. The focus of the examples in (25) is in each case the lexical verb *iskate, dadoxte, dali*. However, because the clitic after *ne* is phonologically stressed, it can serve as the host for *li*.

Another language in which clitic placement is determined by prosodic categories is Chamorro, which we discuss in more detail in Section 8.4.

4.4   Clitics and stress

4.4.1   Stress-neutral clitics

Perhaps the most common prosodic property of clitics is that they are stress neutral, that is, they have no effect on the stress pattern of their hosts. This is true, for instance, of the Russian conversational particle *=to*, and Wackernagel or 2P systems are generally stress neutral, too. Thus, the 2P discourse particles of Classical Greek and the clitic cluster of Serbian/Croatian have absolutely no effect on the stress, tone or accentual systems of these languages. At the same time these clitic system don't induce any violations of otherwise well-motivated principles of stress or accentuation. There is no rule of Serbian/Croatian which says that a lexical word can't end in a string of unstressed syllables (indeed, many words do so without having any clitics attached). We can think of such clitic systems as being 'outside' the prosodic system generally. There still remains the important analytical question of how a clitic or clitic cluster is attached prosodically to its host. At the end of this chapter we survey recent approaches to Prosodic Phonology which address that question.

4.4.2   Clitics which fall outside the stress system ('outlaws')

There is another sense in which a clitic system can be outside the stress system: the clitics can behave as 'outlaws', violating normal rules. This arises in languages that constrain stress to be placed on a particular position within the word, such as the first syllable or the rightmost heavy syllable. When an affix is attached to a word in such languages the affix generally (but not always!) counts towards the calculation of stress placement. For instance, if a language places stress regularly on the penultimate syllable, then adding a monosyllabic suffix will cause the stress to be shifted one syllable to the right. When a monosyllabic clitic is attached to its host in such a language it will typically be invisible to the stress placement and will therefore result in a word that apparently has antepenultimate stress, in violation of the stress rule.

In Spanish, stress obeys the principle of the 'three-syllable window', which restricts the main stress to one of the last three syllables in the word. Although the position of stress can to some extent be predicted on phonological grounds, in the general case its position is determined lexically and morphologically. For instance, position of stress is fixed on the stem in *canto* 'I sing' but on the ending in the past tense form *cantó* 's/he sang'. Here stress is a partial exponent of the property of the past tense. There are no words in Spanish, whether monomorphemic or suffixed, that have stress further to the left than the third syllable. Cliticized verbs, however, can behave differently with respect to stress. We saw in Section 2.5 that Spanish has a pronominal clitic cluster which invariably attaches either to the left or to the right of a verb form host, wherever that verb form might be. In the case of a non-finite verb form with lexical stress on the theme vowel (e.g. *cantando* 'singing'), the three-syllable window is violated when two pronominal clitics (e.g. *me-lo*) encliticize to the verb, as in *cantando-me-lo* 'singing it to me'. The standard explanation for this behaviour is that the clitics are themselves unstressed and are not actually part of the stress domain of the host. They are therefore outlaws. A variety of languages exhibit similar behaviour including Catalan and Italian (both closely related to Spanish, of course). Occasionally we find that the clitic behaves in a more law-abiding fashion and is incorporated in the calculation of stress. We will give some illustrative examples of such types below.

4.4.3   Clitics which fall within the stress domain

We also find languages that have elements that have to be considered clitics by general criteria such as promiscuous attachment, but which behave like affixes with respect to stress assignment. A particularly striking case is that of Polish. The following data are based on Booij and Rubach's (1987) account (see also Spencer 1991, 370f.).

Polish has a set of auxiliary verb-like elements used in the 1/2 person forms of the past tense (along with a participial form of the verb ending in -*ł/l*). These are =*m* '1sg', =*ś* '2sg', =*śmy* '1pl', =*ście* '2pl'. The singular clitics lack a vowel of their own, so they are always preceded by an epenthetic vowel -*e*- when they attach to a consonant-final word. These clitics demonstrate (very) promiscuous attachment. Moreover, their position isn't determined by morphology, syntax or prosody. Essentially, they can attach to any stressed host to the left of the main verb (Sussex 1980 discusses constraints on their attachment). They take as host any word other than the negation element *nie* and prepositions. Some examples are provided in (26):[4]

(26)   Promiscuous attachment of Polish auxiliary clitics
    a.   i. Ja   to robił-e=**m**
           I   it did-E=1SG
       ii. Ja   to=**m** robił
          I   it=1SG did
     iii. Ja=**m** to robił
        I=1SG it did
        'I did it'

   b.   i. Co ty robił-e=**ś**
              what you did-E=2SG
         ii. Co=**ś**   ty robił
              what=2SG you did
              'What did you do?'

   c.   i. ... ale robił-e=**m**
              ... but did-E=1SG
         ii. ... ale=**m**   robił
              ... but=1SG did
              'but I did'

   d.   i. W domu to zrobili=**ście**
              in   house it did=2PL
         ii. W domu=**ście** to zrobili
              in   house=2PL it did
              'you did it at home'

   e.   i. Jeden mieli=**śmy**
              one   had=1PL
         ii. Jeden-e=**śmy** mieli
              one-E=1PL   had
              'we had one'

Given such placement it is clear that we are dealing with clitics. However, these elements display a number of clear affix-like properties. There are two lexical phonological alternations that are triggered by the clitics that are normally only triggered by (true) affixes. First, there is an alternation under which the vowel /o/ is raised to /u/ before a word-final voiced consonant.

(27)   o ⇒ u raising before word final voiced C
   a.   jak-ie=**m** mogł-a   [mogwa]
         how-E=1SG could-FEM.SG
         'How I(female) could'
   b.   jak-ie=**m** mógł   [mugw]
         how-E=1SG could-MASC.SG
          'How I(male) could'

The basic form of the vowel in the stem *mogł-* is /o/, which is the form which appears when the word is inflected with the vowel suffix *-a*. When there is no ending, however, as in the masculine singular form in (27b), the /o/ is raised to /u/. This is a very general alternation, though recent loan words fail to undergo it, so it can't be considered an automatic alternation. In other words it is part of the lexical phonology (see Gussmann 2007, 261–8, for a detailed defence of this claim).

The Raising alternation is blocked by clitics:

(28)   Blocking of Raising by clitics

         jak mogł-e=**m**
         how could-E=1SG
         'How I(male) could' (cf. 27b)

Another alternation in the lexical phonology of Polish is the well-known phenomenon of 'Yer Lowering'. The name of the alternation comes from the historical processes that gives rise to the alternation, under which a short high vowel ('yer' in Slavic philology) is either deleted or lowered to /e/. In the modern language the resulting alternation has the appearance of epenthesis triggered by a sequence of consonants. We can see it in a number of the examples already cited, where the lowered 'yer' is glossed as 'E'. The point is that this alternation is triggered by the two non-syllabic clitics, as illustrated by the adverb *jak* 'how, as': *jak-ie=m, jak-ie=ś*.

Finally, stress in Polish regularly falls on the penultimate syllable of the word. There are numerous exceptions to this rule (mainly loan words originating from Greek and Latin), in which the stress falls on the antepenultimate syllable: *uniwerzyty* 'university' (we represent stressed vowels by means of underlining). When a clitic is added to a word, whether it's the non-syllabic singular form or the syllabic plural form, the stress is often shifted in order to respect the penultimate placement rule. For instance, we have *robił* 'did' but *robiłe=m* 'did=1sg'.

We have thus seen three respects in which the auxiliary clitics behave like genuine affixes rather than like clitics, and this includes their effect on stress. Polish auxiliary clitics therefore represent a very mixed picture with respect to the clitic/affix distinction. Indeed, this is reflected in the term used to describe these clitics in traditional Polish grammar: 'mobile inflections'. Morphosyntactically they are clearly clitics (hence 'mobile'), while morphophonologically they are equally clearly affixes (hence 'inflections'). The force of this observation is strengthened by two further points. First, the two plural auxiliary clitics, =*śmy*, =*ście*, always block *o*-Raising. However, in 'cultivated speech' they fail to affect stress. Thus, in this style we hear *zrobili=ście* 'you did', with stress retained on the penultimate syllable of the verb form, rather than the more colloquial *zrobili=ście*, in which the stress is moved forward to the final syllable of the verb form . This shows that in principle the plural clitics can behave like clitics (though only with respect to stress).

A further interesting example is that of the conditional particle *by*.[5] This particle is unstressed normally and therefore is usually cliticized to a lexical host to its left. However, it fails to trigger the *o*-Raising alternation (29), and it doesn't affect stress (30):

(29)   mógłby   [mugwbi]
            (he) could COND
            'he could'

(30) a.   protestował
            protested
     b.   protestował by
            protested   COND
            'would protest'

The conditional particle itself can host the auxiliary clitics, as in (31):

(31)   Ja to zrobiłby=**m**
         I it did=COND=1SG
         'I would do it'

However, an intriguing twist to the story is that the particle can serve as the host to the auxiliary when the particle itself is not cliticized to the verb (32a) and it can even (for some speakers, at least) appear in absolute sentence-initial position and serve as a host for the auxiliary clitic (32b):

(32) a.   Ja to by=**m**   zrobił
          I it COND=1SG did

     b.   By=**m**   ja to zrobił
          COND=1SG I it did
          'I would do it'

The conditional particle, then, too, exhibits dual behaviour, except in this case it appears to behave sometimes like a clitic and sometimes like a prosodically autonomous word. This situation is not uncommon in clitic systems (for instance, we will see similar behaviour with the Bulgarian future particle *šte*).

Other languages in which clitics are incorporated into the stress pattern of the whole word include the Lucanian dialect of Italian (Peperkamp 1997, 176, 191f.). Thus, we have (33):

(33) a.   vínnə
          sell.IMPERATIVE
          'sell!'
     b.   vənní=**llə**
          sell.IMPERATIVE=it
          'sell it!'
     c.   vinnə=**mmí=llə**
          sell.IMPERATIVE=me=it
          'sell it to me!'

When one clitic is added the stress is brought forward to the final syllable of the verb stem (33b). When two clitics are added the verb stem is no longer in the stress domain and the stress falls on the penultimate syllable of the whole verb form (33c).

A slightly more complex pattern is found with Macedonian clitics (Spencer 1991, 360f.). In this language a string of clitics, including pronominals and other elements, attaches directly to a verb form either as a proclitic (before finite verb forms) or an enclitic cluster (after non-finite forms and the imperative). This is exactly like Romance languages such as Spanish. The proclitic cluster can appear in absolute sentence initial position:

(34)   **Mu**   **go** dádov
         to.him it I.gave
         'I gave it to him'

In this situation the clitics are not incorporated into the stress domain of the verb. Stress in Macedonian is almost always on the antepenultimate syllable. In (34) the stress remains on the first syllable of the verb form. If the proclitic string had been incorporated into the stress domain of its host the stress would have been *mu=gó=dadov*.

Verbs are negated by means of a proclitic *ne*. When this attaches directly to the verb it attracts stress to itself from mono- or disyllabic verbs:

(35) Né dade
      NEG he-gave
      'He didn't give'

Effectively, the negation element has been incorporated into the stress domain of the verb and has received the regular antepenultimate accent.

An interesting situation arises when we have a verb with proclitic pronominals and also negation. The negation element appears to the left of the proclitics, effectively becoming a proclitic itself. However, this time the proclitics are now within the verb's stress domain. This means that whichever pronominal is in antepenultimate position will get primary stress. This is seen in (36). In (36a) we see two pronominal clitics *mu, go*, while in (36b) we see the future tense clitic particle *će* and the reflexive clitic *se*:

(36) a.   **Ne** =**mu** =**gó** =dade
          NEG to.him it   he.gave
          'He didn't give it to him'
     b.   **Ne** =**će** =**sé** =venča
          NEG FUT REFL marry
          'They won't get married'

A similar thing is seen with interrogative pronouns such as *što* 'what?', *koj* 'who?':

(37) a.   Štó reče?
          what he.said
          'What did he say?'
     b.   Što **mú**   reče?
          what to.him he.said
          'What did he say to him?'

The Macedonian data illustrate an important point about clitic systems. Such systems are frequently in a state of gradual transition from a grammar with unstressed function words to a grammar with genuine affixes. But the shift from word to clitic to affix rarely takes place in a single step and in an across-the-board fashion. Rather, we see gradual grammaticalization, with some constructions becoming morphologized relatively early and other constructions, often closely related to the first, remaining in a relatively conservative form.

4.4.4   Clitics which have their own accentual properties

In Section 2.6 we mentioned the Latin clitic *que* 'and' /kʷe/. This is one of a number of clitics in Latin, some of which are like *que*, existing solely as clitics, and some of which are homophonous with lexical words. Other examples include *ne* 'question particle', *ve* 'or', *libet* 'whatever', *propter* 'for'. The clitic *libet* was originally the 3sg form of a verb *libeo* 'I please', while *propter* also functions as a lexical preposition with the same meaning (*propter eas res* 'because of these things', *propter magnam gloriam tuam* 'because of Thy great glory'). As we mentioned, the clitics show promiscuous attachment. For instance, the question particle *ne* attaches to the focus of the question.

Stress in Latin was determined in purely phonological terms by reference to heavy/light syllables and the right edge of the word. The Latin stress rule places stress on the penultimate syllable if that syllable is heavy (i.e. has a long vowel or a vowel + consonant) and if the penultimate is light the stress falls on the antepenultimate. In a disyllabic word the stress always falls on the first syllable. (The nature of the final syllable is always irrelevant to determining stress.) Examples are shown in (38), where a dot . indicates a syllable boundary, and stress is indicated by an acute accent ´:

(38) a.   ú.bi 'where'
      b.   é.a:s 'these (things)'
      c.   Cí.ce.ro: 'Cicero'
      d.   Ca.túl.lus 'Catullus'
      e.   Ha.dri.á:.nus 'Hadrian'
      f.   La.ví.ni.a 'Lavinia'
      g.   Cas.sán.dra 'Cassandra'
      h.   For.tú:.na 'Fortune'
      i.   á.li.quot 'a number of'
      j.   co:n.stí.tu.o: 'I place'

The one systematic exception to this patterning is found with the clitics. These attract stress to the last syllable of their host, no matter what the nature of that syllable.[6] With the monosyllabic clitics such as *que* and *ne* this means that we regularly get words in which the stress falls on the final syllable of the host word, and hence the penultimate syllable of the cliticized word, even if that penultimate syllable is light:

(39) a.   Laviniá=**que** 'and Lavinia'
      b.   Cassandrá=**que** 'and Cassandra'
      c.   Fortu:ná=**que** 'and Fortune'
      d.   ubí=**que** 'and where'
      e.   urbé=**que** 'and (in) the town'

Notice that we can't say that the /kʷ/ of /kʷe/ is a consonant cluster which therefore makes the previous syllable heavy. If that were the case we would find penultimate stress in words such as *aliquot* 'a number of' (see 38i). In addition, a clitic such as *ne* begins with just a single consonant, yet still exhibits the property of stress attraction.

The unique accentual properties of the clitics gives rise to intriguing minimal pairs where a commonly cliticized sequence gets lexicalized. A number of Latin words ending in *que* originated as cliticized forms and then became lexicalized, losing the 'and' meaning. Amongst these is *itaque* which means 'so, therefore'. This is formed historically from *ita* 'thus, in such a manner', a word which existed alongside the lexicalized form *itaque*. The adverb *ita* can, of course, be cliticized with *que*, in which case it will mean something slightly different from 'therefore' (in fact, the *que* may simply be conjoining the clause beginning with *ita* to the previous clause). The lexicalized form is stressed according to the Latin stress rule, hence, *ítaque*. However, the cliticized form is stressed according to the clitic accentuation principles, hence: *itáque* (Greenough et al. 1983, 7).

To sum up, the Latin clitics bring along their own stress, as it were, but place it on the final syllable of their host. This type of behaviour is not uncommon with affixes. The English suffixes *-ity* and *-ic* have this property, for instance: *ícon*, *icónic*, *iconícity*. Such behaviour makes the clitics look more like affixes.

A somewhat different situation is represented by (Modern) Greek. This language has two important sets of clitics. One is similar to the pronominal clitic set of Romance or Macedonian. As in those languages the clitics tend to be placed as proclitics except after imperative form verbs. Greek words respect the 'three syllable window' we saw with Spanish. A disyllabic imperative verb form such as *δóse* 'give' is stressed on the first syllable. When two pronominals are encliticized to such a word form the three-syllable window is violated. In this case an additional stress is found on the first of the two clitics: *δóse=mú=to give=to.me=it* 'give it to me!' This contrasts minimally with the Spanish example we saw earlier: *dándo=me=lo* 'giving it to me'. In the Spanish case the clitics are 'outlaws' with respect to stress. In Greek the clitics are more accommodating, but under their own terms.

The Greek examples illustrate systems in which clitics impose their own stress patterns on the hosts to which they attach, though not in quite the drastic way that Latin clitics do this. Nonetheless, a full account of data such as the Greek examples will have to stipulate certain aspects of the stress pattern of cliticized words.[7] The problem is that there is no general principle of Greek accentuation which will tell us how to stress a disyllabic word that hosts two clitics, and which thus violates the three-syllable window. The violation could have been removed, for instance, by shifting the stress on the verb forward one syllable. Alternatively, it could have been the final clitic that received stress. And there's no particular reason why both the verb and the clitic receive stress: the violation of the stress window would have been removed if just one of the clitics had received stress (as happens in the Lucanian dialect of Southern Italian which we introduced in Section 4.4 and which will be discussed in rather more detail in Section 4.6). Other languages that relieve a stress violation by putting an additional stress onto the clitic cluster include Neapolitan Italian.

Greek also has nominal enclitics expressing possession: *to spíti* 'the house', *to spíti=mu* 'my house' (literally 'the house=of.me'). Here, only one clitic is found with each host. However, the same problem can arise with the stress window when the clitic is added to a word with antepenultimate stress such as *avtokínito* 'car'. Again, an additional stress appears, but not on the clitic. Instead we obtain the stress pattern *avtokínitó=mu* 'car=of.me', 'my car'. The rightmost stress appears to be the main stress here, with the original primary stress becoming a secondary stress. Again, it's not obvious why that stress has to remain (or why the noun gets two stresses, rather than the additional stress being placed on the clitic).

4.5   Phonologically weak function words ('simple' clitics)

4.5.1   Introduction

Function words in some languages have both a strong form and a weak form. One reasonably robust set of examples of this type of clitic would be the definite and indefinite articles in English. While the strong forms are used for contrastive emphasis, the weak forms only appear with reduced vowels and no stress, even at a slow and careful speaking rate, and are therefore unemphatic. Such phonologically weak function words are traditionally referred to as 'simple' clitics. As shown in Chapter 3, the literature quite often draws the distinction between simple clitics, which are found in the same syntactic positions as full-form words and whose clitichood is defined in purely phonological terms, and special clitics, whose placement is idiosyncratic compared to other words. However, while the English articles may be reasonably good exemplars of simple clitics, many of the clitics that are often so regarded turn out not to be so simple when we examine their syntactic behaviour more carefully. To illustrate the problem we will look at other function words in both English and German.

4.5.2   Phonological properties

Function words in English and German generally have a strong and a weak form. In (40) we see full-form and clitic forms for a variety of personal pronouns and definite determiner forms in German (Prinz 1991).

(40)   German personal pronouns and determiners (selection)

	strong	weak	
pronouns			
du	duː	də	2sg
sie	ziː	zə	3sg.fem
ihm	iːm	m̩	3sg.masc.dat
ihn	iːn	n̩	3sg.masc.acc
es	es	s	3sg.neut.

determiners			
dem	deːm	m̩	def.masc./neut.sg.dat
den	deːn	n̩	def.masc.acc.sg
die	diː	d(ə)	def.nom.pl/def.fem.acc.sg

In (41) we see a small selection of English auxiliaries, pronouns, prepositions and conjunctions (where the alternatives for *are*, *her*, *for* are to accommodate rhotic and non-rhotic accents respectively).[8]

(41)   Some English clitics

	strong forms	weak forms
auxiliary verbs		
are	ɑː(ɹ)	ɹ̩, ə
will	wɪl	l, l̩
had	had	d, d̩
have	hav	v, v̩
is, has	ɪz, haz	z
pronouns		
them	ðɛm	m̩
her	hɜː(ɹ)	ɹ̩, ə
him	hɪm	ɪm
you	juː	jə
others		
and	and	n̩
for	fɔː(ɹ)	fɹ̩, fə
to	tuː	tə

The weak forms in English and German illustrate the phonotactic deficiency mentioned above. They have a reduced vowel (e.g. [fə]), a syllabic consonant (e.g. [l̩] 'will') or no vowel at all (e.g. [z] 'is, has'). Lacking a fully-fledged vowel, such forms cannot in principle be stressed. Because of this phonological property, they only appear in unstressed positions and never occur on their own. In (42), the full, stressed form of the German '3sg.fem' pronoun forms a one-word utterance, [ziː], while the weak form, [zə], cannot:

(42)   Wen hast du gesehen?   Sie   = [ziː], ≠ [zə]
             who have you seen   3.SG.FEM.ACC
             'Who did you see? Her.'

For the same reason, no emphasis can be given to weak forms, whether in the form of contrastive or emphatic stress.

One other property of weak forms is that they need a host which is not itself prosodically deficient, that is, a stressed lexical item. In example (43) we see the reduced form of the German definite article *dem*. This clitic form attaches to a stressed host to its left, as shown in (43a), where the definite article occurs after the preposition *mit*. However, in (43b) the article is sentence-final, so there is no possible host in the correct position:

(43) a.   Wir haben mit dem [mitm] Franz darüber geredet.
           we have with DEF.MASC.SG.DAT about-it spoke
           'We spoke with Franz about it'

   b.   Dem *[m] Kind hat sie eine Geschichte erzählt.
           DEF.NEU.SG.DAT child has she one story told
           'She told the child a story'

The determiner in (43a) constitutes an independent syntactic element, and its unstressed form is assumed to be phonologically dependent on the preceding host. However, while phonological dependency is a defining characteristic of any clitic, German determiners also seem to be selective with respect to the host. This seems to suggest that their attachment may not be simply phonological (see Chapter 5).

4.5.3   The relation between weak form and strong form

The examples in (40) and (41) suggest that for each strong form the language provides one or more weak forms. Metaphors such as 'weak' or 'reduced' form also suggest that clitics are somehow derived through phonological 'reduction' or 'weakening'. However, not all of the elements which are commonly called clitics have a corresponding strong form. This is true of the English possessive clitic 's, for instance. This raises the question as to whether the existence of strong/weak counterparts is of relevance to the characterization of clitics (cf. Chapter 3).

Because clitics such as those shown in (40) and (41) bear a certain resemblance to their full forms, earlier attempts at accounting for clitics treated such weak forms as genuine phonological reductions of strong forms. Clitic pronouns which bore little or no resemblance to stressed forms (as is partially the case with Serbian/Croatian pronouns) were simply treated as lexically listed items. For weak forms, the idea was that phonological rules could explain the weakening of the syllable nucleus or the deletion of consonantal segments. However, from the 1970s phonologists have resisted the temptation to relate partially suppletive forms by means of phonological rules, and given this perspective it soon becomes apparent that many of the English clitic forms could not possibly have been derived through productive rules because there were simply no rules of English phonology that could derive those forms. They are therefore best regarded as lexically listed clitic forms. For instance, the 'reduction' of *will* to [l̩] or [əl] is better thought of as a historical phenomenon, not part of the synchronic grammar of English. In particular, there is no sense in which the strong form could be regarded as the phonological 'underlying form' of the weak form.

So, this means that a given lexeme is associated with two or more forms with different phonological shapes to convey the same basic set of morphosyntactic properties. For this reason it is an unfortunate use of terminology to refer to weak forms as 'reduced'. As soon as one accepts that the weak forms given in (41) are lexically listed, the logical conclusion is that the relation between clitics and strong forms is the same, whether we are talking about English function words or

Serbian/Croatian auxiliary verbs. But this should not be surprising: as Anderson (2005, 12) points out, it would be rather odd to try to define a linguistic entity such as a clitic by reference to whether or not there exists a form with exactly the same meaning which can be stressed.

4.5.4   Syntactic 'simplicity'

Although phonologically weak function words (or simple clitics) ought to be syntactically trivial, their phonological properties will often interact in important ways with their syntactic behaviour. We will effectively apply traditional structuralist methods and ask what kind of distribution clitics have in linguistic expressions. Although we expect the distribution of a simple clitic to be identical to that of a full-form correspondent, we have seen already that in practice there may be positions that are excluded for phonological reasons (see the clitic form of the determiner *dem* in (43b)). In this section we provide further evidence that shows that the distribution of so-called simple clitics is sometimes regulated by more than just phonological conditions.

The clitics in (40) and (41) tend to have properties of their own that are completely independent of the full form. In particular, their direction of phonological attachment is often lexically specified, as either proclitic or enclitic. In the same way that the German proclitic indefinite article cannot appear sentence finally, so an enclitic, such as the clitic *'s* form of *has* in English, cannot appear in sentence-initial position, as illustrated by the contrast between (44a) and (44b):

(44) a.   Ana's [z] written this
      b.   *S' [z] Ana written this?

Compare (44) with (45), where we have the full-form auxiliary:

(45) a.   Ana HAS written this
      b.   HAS Ana written this?

The full form of the auxiliary is only appropriate in spoken English if it is focussed (i.e. fully stressed). This means that sentence (46) pronounced with unstressed but full form auxiliary is in effect ungrammatical in the spoken variety in discourse neutral contexts (though it can be found as the expression of a particular type of discourse-level emphasis, and it is also possible to interpret it as the spoken token of a sentence of written English):

(46)   Ana has [həz] written this

However, when the auxiliary is fronted it can appear without stress (and hence with a schwa vowel), and indeed this is the only possible form in spoken English when the auxiliary is not itself accented:

(47)   Has [həz] ANA written this?

But note that the unaccented form [həz] is not the same as the true clitic form [z], at least not in Standard English.

If the distribution of strong/weak forms of auxiliaries were determined solely by phonology such observations would be a mystery. In particular, there is nothing phonologically wrong with a string such as [zana], so it's entirely unclear why (44b) isn't the natural spoken form of the inverted clause, rather than (47).

Such examples suffice to show that there are additional factors at work over and above phonology. At the very least we have to say that the clitic 's form is an enclitic and can't appear as a proclitic. However, lack of a host in the right place doesn't of itself seem to account for all the distribution restrictions of English auxiliaries. If the 's form simply required a host to its left, then we could not explain why (48) is unacceptable:

(48)   *But's [bəts] Ana written this?

A similar problem arises with German examples such as (49):

(49)   Ich weiß nicht, ob   die ([diː]/?[də]) Frau   uns gesehen hat
        I   know not   whether the   woman us   seen   has
        'I don't know whether the woman saw us'

The clitic variant of the definite article *die* should in principle be able to find a host either in the subordinating conjunction *ob* or in the following noun, yet neither pronunciation seems possible.

Such examples suggest that it is misleading at best to think of simple clitics as just ordinary words with reduced pronunciation. German pronoun strings provide further illustration of this. If clitics are merely phonological variants of full-form words then their positioning should be determined entirely by rules of syntax. Where the resulting order fails to provide an appropriate phonological host, the string will be ruled as unacceptable. What we don't expect is a situation in which the order of elements in an expression including clitics is distinct from that predicted from the syntax of the language. In (50) we see the dative pronoun is followed by the accusative pronoun:

(50) a.   Ich habe ihr   es   gegeben
           I   have her.DAT it.ACC given
     b.   Ich hab ihr='s   gegeben
           I   have her.DAT=it.ACC given
           'I gave it to her'

In both the full-form variant and the clitic variant we see the order dative < accusative. However, the alternative order shown in (50c) is also possible:

(50) c.   Ich habe='s   ihr   gegeben
           I   have=it.ACC.CL her.DAT given
           'I gave it to her'

Moreover, before a subject pronoun, the dative < accusative order of pronouns is only acceptable with a weak form, as in (51b). In the absence of weak forms, the opposite order is found, as in (51c) (though that order is also possible when the accusative pronoun is a clitic, as seen in (51d)):

(51) a.   * Wenn er ihm   es   gibt
                  If   he him.DAT it.ACC gives
       b.   Wenn er ihm's   gibt
                  If   he him.DAT it.ACC.CL gives
       c.   Wenn er es   ihm   gibt
                  If   he it.ACC him.DAT gives
       d.   Wenn er='s   ihm   gibt
                  If   he=it.ACC him.DAT gives
                  'If he gives it to him'

The 'simplicity' of many simple clitics is further undermined by the observation that some phonological clitics have more than one weak form, and these are not in free variation. A particularly intriguing instance of this, to which we will return, is provided by the syllabic and non-syllablic variants of auxiliaries in English. After a subject form pronoun certain auxiliaries appear as a single, non-syllabic consonant. In examples (52a, b) the pronoun is accented:

(52) a.   SHE'd [ʃiːd] be interested
       b.   YOU'll [juːl] make a good Head of Department

However, non-pronominals cannot be followed by a non-syllabic clitic form. Rather the clitic has to be a syllabic consonant (possibly pronounced with a schwa):

(53) a.   LEE'd [liːd̩]/*[liːd] be interested
       b.   YU'll [juːl̩]/*[juːl] make a good Head of Department

Clearly, whatever is responsible for the different distribution of syllabic and non-syllabic variants is more than just pure phonology.

Whilst there no doubt are instances of stressed and stressless function words whose distribution is purely syntactic, it seems that all the interesting cases arise precisely when that simple pattern is disrupted.

4.5.5   The morphophonological interaction between clitic and host

Even when clitics occur in exactly the same position as their full form, they can affect the phonology of the host in ways which full forms would not. Of interest here are those cases where a supposedly simple clitic triggers non-automatic, idiosyncratic allomorphy on its host. We have already seen the case of the Polish floating inflections, whose syntactic distribution is that of a special clitic, but which trigger lexical, non-automatic morphophonological alternations on their hosts (Section 4.4). The English auxiliary clitics provide particularly striking examples of this when combined with subject pronoun forms: *we~we're* [wiː]~[wɜː], *you~you're* [juː]~[jɔː], *they~they're* [ðeɪ]~[ðɛː]. These examples are especially important because these auxiliaries, unlike the Polish floating inflections, are supposed to have the distribution of full-form auxiliaries, as determined by syntax. It is therefore somewhat puzzling to see them triggering idiosyncratic allomorphy, a property which is typically associated with affixes.

4.5.6   Summary: the simple clitic

If we were to take Zwicky's original distinction between simple and special clitics at face value, we would expect the simple clitic and its corresponding full form to have the same distribution, that is, they would be in free variation. However, the cases we have surveyed fail to meet the expectations in their entirety. The idea behind the notion of the simple clitic rested on two assumptions: some clitics derive phonologically from a full form and they are syntactically unexceptional. However, in a number of those cases that are often presented as simple clitics in the literature, neither assumption can be upheld: phonological derivation is synchronically not a relevant aspect and the syntactic behaviour of the clitic is clearly not so simple. Our discussion here complements that of Anderson (2005, 23), who argues that the clitichood of a simple clitic should rest solely on its phonological dependence (without prejudicing the question of whether there is any full form or not).

4.6   Clitics and prosodic structure

In this section we ask how linguists have sought to represent the phonological side of cliticization in terms of an articulated theory of phonology. We will lay out what we take to be a consensus view about the representation of prosodic categories such as the phonological phrase and phonological word, without entering into the technicalities of debate in this area.

There are several theoretical issues that relate to the phonological representation of clitics. The first is the nature of the relation between phonology and syntax. This is a complex issue and we will not go into it in detail. It is generally agreed that there is a broad correspondence between the types of structures implied by phonology and those implied by syntax. Thus, in the default case an object defined as a word or phrase in the syntax will correspond to a phonologically defined word or phrase. However, it is also generally agreed that there are mismatches and that there are principles dictating the way that phonologically defined units can differ from corresponding syntactic units. Much of the research conducted under the rubric of Prosodic Phonology concerns these types of phonology-syntax mismatches.[9]

Where clitics are concerned we can ask whether clitic elements themselves are identified as linguistic objects. One way of doing this is simply to propose a feature such as [+clitic] or a type *clitic* which rules can appeal to. A more subtle way of achieving this is to treat clitics as lexically stored and accessible objects and to code cliticness into lexical representations. In the model of Prosodic Phonology developed by Inkelas (1989), for instance, affixes are furnished with subcategorization frames stating what kinds of word or stem they attach to, and in what linear order. She extends this approach to clitics. Thus, an enclitic/proclitic can be defined as an element that selects a prosodic word to its left/right and creates another prosodic word:

(54)   Subcategorization frames for clitics
                enclitic: $(_{\omega} (_{\omega} \ldots)$ ___)
                proclitic: $(_{\omega}$ ___ $(_{\omega} \ldots))$

The alternative is to treat clitics as a kind of epiphenomenon and to define their phonological properties in terms of independent properties that clitics actually have. It is the essence of the approach developed by Selkirk (1995), whose ideas have been applied to clitic systems in a wide range of languages, including more recently the clitic system of Serbian/Croatian (Werle 2009).

An important question, then, arises from studying the phonology of clitics, indeed, what we may think of as the central existential question surrounding clitics: do they exist as a distinct linguistic category? This is a question that relates to all aspects of clitics, not just their phonology and we will return to it at various points throughout the book.

4.6.1   The Prosodic Hierarchy

Phonologists have noted that a variety of phonological processes such as vowel reduction, assimilation, consonant aspiration, epenthesis and so on may apply in different ways to one and the same string of segments depending on the way those segments are organized. For instance, in English it's very common for the /t/ of a word ending in the /st/ cluster to be dropped: *fast* /fas/. However, the /t/ is not dropped in the word *faster* /fastə/, */fasə/. This is not because the /t/ is in the middle of the word or because it comes before a suffix. In the word *fastness* we generally drop the /t/: /fasnəs/. The reason is that the *t*-dropping process occurs when the /t/ is in the coda of a syllable rather than the onset of a syllable.

The syllable is just one of the phonological domains over which phonological generalizations can be stated. Careful examination of the phonological behaviour of different types of expression has shown that there are several such domains. A very influential model of prosodic domains was first proposed by Nespor and Vogel (1986). In their model, the domains are organized into a Prosodic Hierarchy, in which each domain is contained inside the next higher domain. A simplified version of the Prosodic Hierarchy is shown in (55):

(55)   Prosodic Hierarchy
            U   Utterance
            I   Intonational Group/Phrase
            Φ   Phonological Phrase, Φ-phrase
            ω   Prosodic/Phonological Word, p-word
            Σ   Foot
            σ   Syllable

In the most straightforward cases all syllables are grouped into feet with a single accented/prominent syllable, all feet are grouped into phonological words, which are grouped into a Phonological Phrase, all Phonological Phrases are grouped into an Intonational Phrase (Intonational Group) and all Intonational Phrases are grouped into an Utterance. This holds for languages which make use of prominence relations such as lexical stress. The foot is a common way of representing stress relationships. Where a word has several stressed syllables we assume that it is articulated into several feet, each of which is headed by a stressed syllable. The domains of phonological word, phonological phrase and intonational group correspond very roughly to the morphosyntactic domains of morphosyntactic word, syntactic phrase and clause.

   The phonological word is by default the pronunciation of a morphosyntactic word, but it is also the domain of phonological processes that 'apply within words'. The phonological phrase is the correlate of a syntactic phrase, though how exactly this correlation is defined depends on the language. In English, for instance, the syntactic phrase (verb phrase) *bake me a cake* will be pronounced as a single phonological phrase at normal speaking rate and speaking style. On the other hand *bake me a cake as fast as you can* would normally be pronounced as two phonological phrases, even though syntactically you could argue that it was really just an extended verb phrase and hence still one syntactic phrase and not two. The intonational phrase is the domain of intonation contours. The sentence *Are you going to bake me that cake today?* has a single intonation contour stretching over the whole utterance, characteristic of a question, while the sentence *I'm baking you that cake just as fast as I can* has a single intonation contour characteristic of an assertion. Each utterance consists of several phonological phrases. Finally, a single sentence such as *Are you going to bake that cake or do I have to go into the kitchen and bake the thing myself?* consists of (at least) two Intonational Groups.

   The categories of phonological word and phonological phrase have played a particularly prominent role in discussions of clitics. Essentially, the idea is that a clitic is a non-prominent word that has to combine phonologically with a more prominent host. Typically, the analyst proposes that the clitic forms a single phonological (prosodic) word with its host. Bošković (2001) has argued (along with others) that the intonation group plays a role in the rather complex distribution of the Wackernagel cluster in Serbian/Croatian. We will return to that question in Chapter 8. Before we discuss the way that these prosodic notions have been deployed we need to see how they operate in practice.

First, we should distinguish morphosyntactic words from phonological words, since the two notions need not be coextensive. There are instances in which a single morphosyntactic word consists of more than one phonological word, as well as the converse, where a single phonological word realizes two morphosyntactic words. To see an instance in which a morphosyntactic word may consist of more than one phonological word, consider a language such as Finnish, which exhibits the phenomenon of vowel harmony. Within a simple, native Finnish word all the vowels are front (written as {i, y, e, ö, ä}) or back (written as {u, o, a}). All affixes in Finnish are suffixes and most of them have two variants, one with front vowels for front vowel stems and one with back vowels for back vowel stems. The systematic exception occurs with /i/, which is neutral with respect to harmony and can occur with either front or back stems. The suffix -ssa/ssä 'in' exhibits the vowel harmony alternation: *Helsingi-ssä* 'in Helsinki' but *Tapiola-ssa* 'in Tapiola', *Oulu-ssa* 'in Oulu'. There is a systematic set of exceptions to the rule of vowel harmony within stems, and that is when the stem is a compound. Finnish has many compounds made by combining two words: *pääkaupunki* 'capital city' from *pää* 'head' *kaupunki* 'town'. When such a word takes a harmonizing suffix such as -ssa/ssä it is the final component which determines the vowel harmony. This is true no matter how many stems with the contradictory harmony precede the final stem: *pää-kaupungi-ssa* 'in the capital' (the -nk-~-ng- alternation here is regular). One way to analyse such a situation is to say that the domain of vowel harmony is the phonological word, but that compounds consist of more than one phonological word. The prosodic structure for a suffixed compound such as *pääkaupunki* is therefore ($_\omega$pää)($_\omega$kaupungi-ssa) in which the suffix forms part of the same phonological word as the final component.

A more subtle instance of the mismatch between phonological words and morphological words is seen in a well-known conundrum found in English. The comparative suffix -er attaches to monosyllabic adjectives or disyllabic adjectives: *bigger, commoner, simpler, easier* but not **immenser, *frequenter, *difficulter*. Now consider the word *unhappier*. This is phonologically well formed and yet it appears to violate the restriction against suffixing -er to words of more than two syllables, since it seems to have the structure [[unhappy] er]. We might imagine that we could solve this problem by saying that we prefix *un-* to *happier* to give the structure [un[happier]]. However, this would contradict the semantics. The meaning of *unhappier* is 'more unhappy', rather than 'not happier'. Thus, we can't say **Tom is unhappier than Harriet* to mean 'Tom is not more happy than Harriet (though both are happy)'. Rather, we must use it in a context such as *Tom is unhappy about this but Harriet is unhappier* (or *Harriet is the unhappier of the two*). In these examples both Tom and Harriet are actually unhappy. This shows that the semantic structure is [[un happy] er] and this structure violates the phonological restriction on -er (Pesetsky 1985).

Puzzles of this sort are sometimes called 'bracketing paradoxes', because we seem to require two incompatible constituent structures or 'bracketings' for one and the same expression. Linguists have suggested a variety of solutions to this problem. The simplest of these is to accept that the word has two structures, one phonological, the other morphosemantic (see, for instance, Booij and Lieber 1993). But in that case we can say that the existence of such a mismatch between the morphosemantics and the phonological requirements constitutes a further argument in favour of an independent representation of prosodic structure.

Phonological phrases are often co-extensive with syntactic phrases, but there are well-known instances of mismatches. One context in which we find such mismatches in English is with nested relative clauses, found in nursery rhyme examples such as (56):

(56)   ($_\phi$ this is the cat) ($_\phi$ that killed the rat) ($_\phi$ that ate the malt) ($_\phi$ that lay in the house that Jack built)

The syntactic constituent structure of such an example would be something like (57):

(57)   [this] [is [the cat [that killed [the rat [that ate [the malt [that lay in [the house [that Jack built]]]]]]]]]

In the syntactic structure we have a series of phrases within phrases. In the phonological representation this nested structure is flattened out to a string of phonological phrases whose boundaries cut across the syntactic boundaries. Clearly, this is essentially the same kind of mismatch as that found with *unhappier*.

In the next subsection we will see that a number of authors have argued that clitics should be treated as extraneous elements that are adjoined to different prosodic units to give different phonological effects. Specifically, we will see that some clitics can be analysed as being adjoined to phonological words while others can be thought of as adjoined to phonological phrases. However, for some phonologists this leads to an uncomfortable theoretical disparity. In the classical version of Prosodic Phonology (Nespor and Vogel 1986) prosodic structure is organized according to the Strict Layer Hypothesis: each unit on the Prosodic Hierarchy must be a direct (immediate) constituent of the next higher unit. But if a clitic is adjoined to a prosodic phrase it will violate the Strict Layer Hypothesis.

The solution proposed by Nespor and Vogel (1986) to this problem is to set up an intermediate level between the phonological word and the phonological phrase, the clitic group (see also Nespor 1999, and Vogel 2009[10]). They argue that there are phonological reasons for recognizing such a unit. Here we summarize one of the arguments from Nespor (1999).[11]

In Italian, verb-clitic combinations observe a process of *troncamento*, truncation of the final vowel of certain verb forms before the clitic:

(58)   dare   **gli**   ⇒ dar**gli** (*dare**gli**)
         give.INF to.him
         'to give to him'

(59)   andare **ci**   ⇒ andar**ci** (*andare**ci**)
         go.INF there
         'to go there'

This process can be observed before other types of word, including homophonous function words such as *gli* 'the', but then it is optional and not obligatory:[12]

(60)   vuole scrivere   gli indirizzi ⇒ scriver gli/scrivere gli

          wants write.INF the address

          'wants to write the address'

(61)   andare via   ⇒ andar via/andare via

          go.INF away

          'to go away'

Nespor argues that this process is obligatory when it takes place within the Clitic Group but optional when it takes place between Clitic Groups:

(62)   Clitic Groups in Italian

          ($_\phi$ (CliticGroup ($_\omega$ dare) ($_\omega$ gli)))

          ($_\phi$ (CliticGroup ($_\omega$ scrivere))) (CliticGroup ($_\omega$ gli) ($_\omega$ indirizzi)))

   The notion of Clitic Group has not earned widespread recognition amongst phonologists and is explicitly rejected, for instance, by Anderson (2005), Booij (1988), Booij (1996a), Selkirk (1995), Truckenbrodt (1999), Werle (2009), Zec and Inkelas (1991), among others.

4.6.2   Representing clitics

          In this section we look at some of the proposals that have been made for integrating clitics into prosodic structure without the mediation of the Clitic Group (Selkirk 1995, Booij 1996a). There are two basic senses in which we can say that a clitic is 'part of' another structure in the hierarchical prosodic arrangement of words. In the first sense the clitic is attached to the right or left of a prosodic unit (word or phrase) and is treated exactly like any other syllable or unit in that phrase. We can call this 'incorporation' and illustrate it in (63):

(63)   Clitic incorporation

          original prosodic word/phrase   cliticized prosodic word/phrase

          ω/ϕ ω/ϕ

          σ_1 σ_2 ... σ_n σ_1 σ_2 ... σ_n clitic

The second notion of 'part of' is adjunction, in which a slightly more complex structure is created, as shown in (64):

(64)   Adjunction

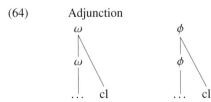

We can now ask which of these types of representation best reflects the phonology of clitics.

A convenient discussion of the issues is provided by Peperkamp (1997, 176f.). She contrasts the pronominal enclitics in three varieties of Italian. In Standard Italian the clitics fall outside the stress domain of the host, much as in Spanish. In Neapolitan the clitics receive stress so as to respect the three-syllable window but the host retains its stress (as in Greek). Lucanian, as we have seen, is like Neapolitan except that the host loses its accent. Peperkamp represents these three situations as shown in (65):

(65)   Three types of clitic incorporation in Italian varieties

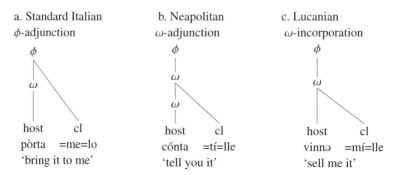

| a. Standard Italian | b. Neapolitan | c. Lucanian |
| φ-adjunction | ω-adjunction | ω-incorporation |

How exactly such representations can be deployed to account for the stress patterns depends on the theory of stress and the theory of phonology generally that one adopts, and we won't enter into those issues here.

Peperkamp doesn't herself discuss cases such as the Latin clitics. A simple way to treat such clitics is to say that they have a lexical (or perhaps better morphological) representation which includes a stress position for the preceding syllable (this is essentially the analysis proposed by Inkelas (1989) for suffixes such as *-ity*). We would assume that the clitic is incorporated into the phonological word, but that it places a stress on the previous syllable. The representation would therefore be something along the lines of (66):

(66)   Latin *que*, ω-incorporation with pre-stressing

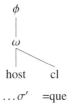

Finally, to accommodate cases such as Bulgarian *li* we need to invoke some grammatical principle that guarantees that the clitic is adjacent to a stressed word (though not necessarily a stressed syllable). This is a complex matter, since the rule has to be able to treat a clitic in a clitic cluster as a kind of word (at least as far as stress is concerned). This means that the *li* clitic is constrained to attach to the right edge of a stress foot. A suggestion is given in (67):

(67)   Bulgarian clitic *li*, ω-incorporation to foot

However, precisely how this will work depends on exactly what theory of prosody and phonology is adopted.

4.7   Conclusions

In this chapter we have surveyed the principal phonological and especially the prosodic properties of clitics. We have taken a fairly broad characterization of 'clitic', including any element that differs significantly in its behaviour from the standard inflectional affixes of the language. In some cases aberrant behaviour with respect to stress is one of the most salient properties of the clitic. Our conclusions are summarized as follows:

Clitics can be defined with respect to any type of prosodic prominence: stress, pitch accent, lexical tone. The general characterization of the prosody of a clitic is that it is inherently non-prominent (e.g. unstressed) and requires a host that can be prominent. The prosody of the host can be very important for defining the placement of clitics. Thus, in Pashto the clitic cluster attaches to the first stressed element of the clitics' domain, while in Bulgarian it is the question clitic *li* which attaches to the first stressed element, even where that element is itself a clitic in a clitic cluster.

Elements that are clitics by one set of criteria (e.g. promiscuous attachment) can behave like affixes with respect to phonological criteria. For instance, they can be incorporated into the normal stress system of the word, and they may even trigger lexical morphophonological alternations. Thus, the pronominal clitics of the Lucanian dialect of Italian behave like affixes with respect to word stress, while the Polish 'mobile inflections' not only affect word stress as though they were affixes, they even trigger allomorphy which only affixes can trigger. On the other hand, clitics may be 'outlaws' with respect to stress systems, remaining, so to speak, invisible to lexical stress rules (Standard Italian and Spanish enclitics are like this). Other clitics occupy an intermediate position: they introduce additional stresses, sometimes on the clitics themselves, so as to respect a restriction on stress placement, but they co-occur with the original lexical stress (Neapolitan Italian, Greek). Finally, there are the clitics of Latin, which impose a unique stress pattern on their hosts, unlike that found with normal affixes, but which don't actually bear stress themselves.

We next addressed the question of whether there are elements that are clitics purely by virtue of the phonological dependence and lack of prosodic prominence, that is, 'phonological clitics'. We investigated a number of cases and came to the conclusion that it can be difficult to find clear examples of pure phonological clitics. Even if we factor out the independent effects of phonological constraints, we find that putative examples of phonological clitics tend to develop other clitic-like attributes in addition to their lack of prominence. Indeed, it's this property which tends to bring them to the attention of grammarians. A number of the cases often cited as standard examples of 'simple' clitics turn out to be far from simple. In particular, they often have a different syntactic distributional pattern from the full-form words that they are supposed to be phonological reductions of.

Finally, we saw how linguists have sought to represent the main types of interaction between clitics and phonological structure (especially prosodic structure). Phonologically speaking the canonical clitic lacks its own prosodic structure and is loosely associated with its host. When that association is at its loosest we get the 'outlaws', clitics that fail to participate in the overall prosodic organization and give the appearance of being invisible to principles of stress placement. However, that association can get tighter as the clitic comes to increasingly resemble a bona fide affix. This is clear with the pronominal clitics that attach to verbs almost in the manner of an affix. But even if the clitic exhibits promiscuous attachment, it may still have prosodic properties of its own, as in the case of the Latin clitics. In such instances we see a strong mismatch between the morphosyntactic properties of the clitic, such as promiscuous attachment and the expected phonological properties. The case of the Polish floating/mobile inflections is particularly striking in this regard, since we effectively have elements that are prototypically affix-like in their morphophonological behaviour but prototypically clitic-like in their morphosyntactic behaviour.

5   Clitics and morphology

5.1   Introduction

       In this chapter we look at morphological aspects of clitics. There are two aspects to this. First, all investigators are agreed that in many of those constructions that are conventionally labelled as clitic systems the clitics themselves behave like affixes, morphological elements, rather than words. We therefore need to survey these morphological modes of behaviour. We'll start by summarizing a celebrated and still important set of criteria for distinguishing clitics from affixes (what in future we will simply refer to as the 'Zwicky–Pullum criteria'). Applied to the English negation 'clitic' *n't*, these criteria yield a perhaps surprising conclusion. We then return to a phenomenon briefly introduced in Chapter 3, the clitic cluster. We will find that within the cluster the clitics behave much more like affixes than anything else, no matter how they might behave as a cluster. To set the scene for that demonstration we briefly survey the behaviour of uncontroversial affixes in the verb forms of Classical Nahuatl. We then turn to a more controversial issue. When we speak of clitics as phrasal affixes, we are thinking of a clitic as a morphological object (an affix) that happens to be attached to whatever happens to come at the edge of a phrase, rather than a true affix which seeks out a particular type of word within the phrase. Now, given current approaches to morphology, there are two ways of thinking of affixation. We can treat it in the manner of classical structuralist linguistics and regard it as essentially the addition of a morpheme to another string of morphemes. However, as we will see in Chapter 8, a very influential alternative model of inflectional morphology is current, under which inflectional affixation is treated more as a set of morphophonological processes that applies to the root or stem form of a lexeme. Under such realizational approaches to inflection, we can ask whether phrasal affixation, too, can be thought of as a set of morphophonological processes applying to the edge of a phrase. This is what is generally known as edge inflection. We'll enumerate a number of cases of edge inflection that have been discussed of late in the literature. Finally, we look at a rather remarkable type of edge-of-phrase phenomenon, the famous 'definitive accent' of the Polynesian language Tongan.

5.2   Clitics and affixes – the Zwicky–Pullum criteria

There have been many points throughout this book at which it has been difficult to decide whether a given formative is 'really' a clitic or 'really' an affix. It is now time to confront this problem head-on and see whether we can develop a set of hard-and-fast criteria for distinguishing the two notions. We will begin with discussion of arguably the most influential paper on this topic, that of Zwicky and Pullum (1983). These authors developed a set of criteria for clitichood and affixhood because they wanted to ask a very specific question: is the *-n't* formative in English a clitic or an affix? We'll turn to their answer to that question in the next section. To begin with we'll summarize the criteria they developed.

The Zwicky–Pullum criteria (see Stump 1998, 20f. for discussion):

i   Host selectivity: Clitics can exhibit a low degree of selection with respect to their hosts while affixes exhibit a high degree of selection with respect to their stems.

ii   Arbitrary gaps in the set of combinations are more characteristic of affixed words than of clitic groups.

iii   Morphophonological idiosyncrasies are more characteristic of affixed words than of clitic groups.

iv   Semantic idiosyncrasies are more characteristic of affixed words than of clitic groups.

v   Lexical integrity: Syntactic rules can affect words, but cannot affect clitic groups.

vi   Clitic-affix ordering: Clitics can attach to material already containing clitics, but affixes cannot.

The common thread that runs through these criteria is that affixes are associated with words and hence with the kinds of idiosyncrasies to which words are subject. Clitics, however, are associated with phrases and hence show the kind of regularity and well-behavedness that we more usually associate with syntax. Of course, this is just an approximate way of thinking of this difference: there are properties of words that are very regular, while there are also irregularities, exceptions and idioms in syntax. But the general trend is clear: idiosyncrasy and exceptionality is more typical of words than of phrases.

The first criterion states that affixes are choosy about the kinds of hosts they attach to, while clitics are not. We have referred to this lack of selectivity on the part of clitics as promiscuous attachment. Affixes usually attach just to a particular word class, and often only to specific subclasses of that word class. Thus, it's impossible to inflect a Spanish noun as though it were a verb and vice versa, and it's impossible to give a 3rd conjugation Spanish verb exactly the same inflections as a 1st conjugation verb. Moreover, derivational affixes are also very selective. In some cases the selectivity can be accounted for in terms of meaning, but very often specific affixes select specific types of base to attach to. For instance, the English suffix *-ness* attaches to a great many adjectives to give a nominal meaning 'name of the property denoted by Adjective'. But this suffix isn't used with certain adjectives, such as *sincere* (*sincer-ity*) or *warm* (*warm-th*). True clitics typically don't exhibit this selectivity. We've seen a variety of examples of this in a variety of languages (for example, the English possessive *'s*).

One of the more puzzling aspects of inflectional paradigms is the fact that we frequently find that paradigms have arbitrary gaps in them. Occasionally this can be explained in terms of meaning or phonology: some forms would either be meaningless or unpronounceable. For instance, the adjective WRONG can't really be said to have the comparative/superlative forms **wronger/wrongest* because either something is right or wrong, and therefore cannot be 'more/most wrong'. On the other hand, there is a phonological constraint on the formation of the comparative/superlative forms: the only adjectives that can take the *-er/est* suffixes are those consisting of one syllable or one syllable + y: *bigger, happier*. A form such as **curiousest* is therefore impossible because of the phonological constraint. However, in many languages there are completely arbitrary gaps in inflectional paradigms. A well-known instance from Russian is provided by the word MEČTA 'dream'. This is a regular noun and should have a genitive plural form **mečt*, just like the (fairly recently borrowed) word MAČTA 'mast (of yacht)', *mačt* 'of masts'. However, the genitive plural doesn't exist (though all the other forms of the paradigm do). Similar instances of accidental gaps in inflectional paradigms can be found throughout the inflecting languages.

Clitics, however, are not meant to show such gaps. For instance, the Latin clitic conjunction *=que* 'and' is supposed to attach to the second conjunct of any coordinated phrase, and the Finnish interrogative clitic *=ko/kö* is supposed to attach to any word that can appear at the beginning of the clause and as the focus of a question.

By 'morphophonological idiosyncrasy' we mean alternations in phonological form that are not the result of completely regular phonological processes that affect all words or word combinations of a given phonological type. In Turkish, for instance, the genitive case suffix has two forms *-in* and *-nin* depending on whether the noun stem it attaches to ends in a consonant or a vowel: *ev* 'house' *ev-in* 'of a house', *gece* 'night' *gece-nin* 'of the night'. This is an idiosyncratic fact about this one affix. The superficially similar 2sg possessive affix shows different allomorphy with consonant/vowel-final stems: *-in/n*: *ev-in* 'your house' but *gece-n* 'your night'. The 3sg possessive suffix is *-i*. However, when followed by any case suffix it takes the form *-in*: *ev-i* 'his house' (nominative), *ev-in-i* 'his house' (accusative), *ev-in-de* 'in his house' (locative). Again, this is the type of word-oriented idiosyncrasy that is not supposed to be manifested by clitics.

In these examples it is the affix itself that shows the idiosyncratic alternation. In other examples we see such alternations in the bases or stems to which the affixes are attached. For instance, when we add the suffix *-ity* to *electric* to get *electricity* we shift the word stress (*eléctric* ⇒ *èlectrícity*) and we change the final consonant (*electri[k]* ⇒ *electri[s]ity*). Both of these changes are specific

to a small number of affixes. A disyllabic affix such as *-able* doesn't condition
stress shift, for instance, and the sequence /iti/ doesn't automatically cause /k/ to
alternate with /s/ (otherwise the word *kitty* would be unpronounceable). This sort
of behaviour is definitely not what we would expect of a clitic.

Semantic idiosyncrasies are very common with derivational affixes, of course,
but they are also found with inflections. In Russian there is an instrumental case
which has a variety of uses, the principal one being that of 'instrument' as in 'hit
the nail with a hammer'. The words for the seasons, and for periods of the day
(day, night, evening, morning), however, take the instrumental case to express
point of time within which an event takes place: 'in spring, summer ...' and
'at night, during the day ...'. Other temporal words either don't use the instrumental at all in this way (year, month, minute, hour), though in the plural the
instrumental can be used with some of these latter words to mean 'for years,
days, hours ...', that is, to express duration, not point in time. Again, clitics are
supposed to be free of this idiosyncrasy: a given clitic is supposed to express a
single meaning in all contexts.

The lexical integrity criterion is somewhat different from the rest in that it
aligns clitics more with affixes than with words. The notion of lexical integrity
is a somewhat vexed one. It refers to the idea that a word is an indivisible unit
as far as rules of phrase structure are concerned. In syntax we expect to see the
internal structure of phrases being changed in various ways: words making up
phrases appear in various orders, get moved to the front of a clause, get elided,
parenthetical expressions can be inserted between words and so on. This is not
supposed to happen to the internal structure of a word. Clitics attach to word
forms as their host and form a string that is itself, phonologically speaking, a
word. This criterion states that a host=clitic combination behaves like a word
syntactically, too, in the sense that it is no more possible to split the clitic from
its host than it is to split an affix from its stem.

The positioning of affixes is a purely lexical matter in the sense that the grammar determines affix position with respect to word structure, without taking
account of any other criteria (for example, the kinds of phrases the resulting
word might enter into). On the other hand, we tend to think of clitics as being
added to their host after the phrasal structure has been determined (for instance,
we add a clitic to the last word of a phrase). Given this, if an affix and a clitic are
attached to the same word, the natural relative order is for the affix to be placed
first and the clitic afterwards, so that the affix is closer to the stem (more internal)
than the clitic.

The Zwicky–Pullum criteria have a good deal of heuristic value and they
nicely capture our intuitions about what sort of behaviour clitics and affixes
should exhibit. One of the important points about this list, however, is that there
are plenty of instances of things that are traditionally called clitics violating
one or other of these criteria (and equally, we find things traditionally called
affixes violating the criteria). These criteria therefore indicate tendencies and
are not defining characteristics that allow us to determine with absolute certainty

whether a given formative is an affix or a clitic. (It should be stressed that Zwicky and Pullum themselves were careful to draw attention to this caveat.) The reason Zwicky and Pullum drew up the criteria, however, was rather more parochial than the grand morpho-typological project we might imagine. They were interested in looking at the properties of one formative in English grammar, the negation particle -n't. It will be instructive to see how well -n't fares against these criteria, therefore.

5.3 English -n't

Clausal negation in English is almost always expressed by the formative -n't. This is usually referred to as a clitic, mainly because -n't is seen as a reduced form of *not*. It seems to have the same distribution as *not* and hence it is assumed to be a simple clitic. However, following Zwicky and Pullum, we can subject -n't to the six criteria to see whether it behaves more like a clitic or like an affix.

Criterion (i): How selective is -n't? In short 'very'. The formative only attaches to finitely inflected forms of auxiliary verbs: *aren't, didn't, can't, haven't* but not to lexical verbs (*likesn't, *wroten't*), or to non-finite forms of auxiliaries (*to do-n't, *to haven't, *beingn't, *beenn't*).

Criterion (ii): Arbitrary gaps result from the fact that not all inflected auxiliary forms take the negation marker: *amn't,[1] *mayn't*.

Criterion (iii): In general, the -n't formative only has one form (though the /n/ will often be reduced and trigger nasalization of any immediately preceding vowel, depending on exactly what the host is). However, it clearly triggers highly idiosyncratic allomorphy on its host, as seen in *do* /duː/ ~ *don't* /dount/, *can* /kan/ ~ /kaːnt/, *will* /wil/ ~ *won't* /wount/ and others.

Criterion (iv): Clausal negation with -n't exhibits semantic idiosyncrasies that are best seen by looking at negated forms of modal auxiliary verbs. Zwicky and Pullum (1983, 509) cite the examples in (1) to illustrate the way that the scope of negation is affected by choice of the stressed full form *not* over the reduced -n't.

(1) a.   A good Christian can nót attend church and still be saved
    b.   A good Christian cánnot/can't attend church and still be saved

Example (1a) says that church attendance is not obligatory for Christians (*It is possible for a good Christian not to attend …*), while (1b) implies that it's wrong for Christians to attend church (*It is not possible for a Christian to attend …*). This shows that the form *can't* found in (1b) cannot be derived from the straightforward combination of *can + not* seen in (1a).

Criterion (v): When an auxiliary hosts -n't there are no other elements that can intervene (including short interjections or parentheticals). No syntactic rule can separate -n't from its host.

Criterion (vi): The -n't formative comes after tense and agreement inflections, as in *do-es-n't, ha-d-n't*.

The result of the survey of properties is that *-n't* qualifies as a clitic only on Criterion (vi), arguably the least informative of all the criteria. On the other hand, it triggers completely idiosyncratic allomorphy on several of its hosts. This is a very characteristic feature of highly lexicalized affixation. Since *-n't* is compatible with affixhood according to most of the criteria, and scarcely compatible with clitichood according to most of them, the conclusion that Zwicky and Pullum draw is that *-n't* must be an affix. This has interesting implications for the grammar of English, because it means that negation is, in fact, an inflectional category, although one that is only ever expressed on an auxiliary verb. Although this is a more-or-less automatic consequence of Zwicky and Pullum's arguments, and although there has been no refutation of their paper, the idea that negation is an inflectional category in English has not be taken up with any enthusiasm in the descriptive literature (a major exception is Huddleston and Pullum 2002, 91).

5.4   The morphology of clitic clusters: templates

In this section we look at clitic combinations, that is, clitic clusters. We focus on the most actively studied type of clitic cluster, namely, that of the pronominal clitic. Before turning to the clitics proper we will first look at a reasonably representative case of an affixational system, in which the pronominal elements have most or all of the properties of affixes and few or none of the properties of clitics. Against the background of this typical morphological system we will then look at a number of weak pronouns traditionally treated as clitics. We will discover that some of these pronominal systems really resemble loose affixation more than clitic systems. This should not perhaps come as a great surprise after what we have just witnessed with English *-n't*. We will also see that even uncontroversial clitic systems such as 2P systems can show a number of the features characteristic of strings of affixes.

5.4.1   Inflectional clusters

In this subsection we look briefly at a verb system of Classical Nahuatl, the language of the Aztecs, rulers of pre-colonial Mexico. In this language, subject and object agreement (and agreement with other arguments) is expressed through verbal inflection.[2] For those who read French a great deal of interesting information is provided by the grammar of Launey (1999). The spelling in the following examples is a simplified version of the traditional post-colonial spelling system (the official orthography reflects spelling conventions for Latin American Spanish, which are a little confusing for those unfamiliar with the language). Nahuatl doesn't allow clusters of more than two consonants word-internally and doesn't allow any clusters at the margins of words, and any clusters which arise from affixation are broken up by epenthetic 'i'.[3]

Nahuatl verbs cross-reference the subject and object of the verb, marking 1st, 2nd, 3rd person and singular/plural number. There is no gender. In Table 5.1 we

Table 5.1 *Classical Nahuatl intransitive conjugation*

Present Indicative 'sleep', root: *kochi*		
	Singular	Plural
1	ni-kochi	ti-kochi-h
2	ti-kochi	an-kochi-h
3	kochi	kochi-h

Table 5.2 *Classical Nahuatl transitive conjugation*

Present Indicative 'call', root: *notza*		
Subj: 1sg Obj	Singular	Plural
1	ni-no-notza	——
2	ni-mitz-notza	n-ame:ch-notza
3	ni-k-notza	ni-kin-notza
Subj: 2sg		
1	ti-nech-notza	ti-tech-notza
2	ti-mo-notza	——
3	ti-k-notza	ti-kin-notza
Subj: 3sg		
1	nech-notza	tech-notza
2	mitz-notza	amech-notza
3	ki-notza	kin-notza
3 refl	mo-notza	
Subj: 1pl		
1	——	ti-to-notza-h
2	ti-mitz-notza-h	t-amech-notza-h
3	ti-k-notza-h	ti-kin-notza-h
Subj: 2pl		
1	an-nech-notza-h	an-tech-notza-h
2	——	am-mo-notza-h
3	an-ki-notza-h	an-kin-notza-h
Subj: 3pl		
1	nech-notza-h	tech-notza-h
2	mitz-notza-h	amech-notza-h
3	ki-notza-h	kin-notza-h
3 refl	mo-notza-h	

see an intransitive verb. In Table 5.2 we see a transitive verb cross-referencing both subject and object. Some combinations do not give legitimate word forms, for instance, there is no reflexive form for 1st, 2nd persons in which the subject and object have a different number (in other words, just as in English, you can't say things like 'I saw ourselves' or 'we saw myself').

There are also two indefinite object prefixes, *tla* 'something' and *te:* 'someone'. Examples: *kaki* 'hear': *ni-tla-kaki* 'I hear something', *ti-te:-kaki* 'we hear someone'. The prefixes here represented as *ni-*, *ti-*, *xi-*, *ki-* are really just *n-*, *t-*, *x-*, *k-*, with epenthetic *-i-*. The 3pl object prefix *kin-* has the form *kim-* before a vowel.

Some examples of transitive verbs are:

(2) a.   ni-k-kwa in tlaxkalli (*kwa* 'eat')
          'I eat the tortilla'
    b.   an-kin-notza-h in siwa-h (*notza* 'call')
          'You (pl) call the women'
    c.   ti-ki-kaki-h in tekwtli (*kaki* 'hear')
          'We hear the lord'
    d.   ni-k-kaki
          'I hear him/her/it'
    e.   ti-kin-kaki-h
          'We hear them'

With indirect objects, *maka* 'give':

(3) a.   ti-nech-tla-maka
          'You (sg) give something to me'
    b.   ti-kin-tla-maka-h in kokone
          'We give something to the children'
    c.   ni-te-tla-maka
          'I give something to someone'
    d.   ni-k-te-maka in tlaxkalli
          'I give the tortilla to someone'

These are all examples in the present indicative. Various tenses and moods are formed, mainly by adding suffixes to the verb stem, before the plural *-h* marker (which always appears word finally). The system is very regular and would normally be thought of as 'agglutinating', except that the word final *-h* plural marker marks plurality in a redundant fashion in 1st, 2nd person forms.

An interesting situation is seen with the optative mood (with the meaning of a wish or exhortation). In that mood the subject affixes are somewhat different from those of the indicative mood as shown in Table 5.3. As we can see, the plural suffix is *-kan* and not *-h*, and the 2nd person prefix is *xi-*, not *ti-/an-*.

The pronominal markers can be used alone, in which case they function in the same way as unemphatic pronouns in English. With overt subjects and objects the markers remain obligatory, in other words they function as agreement markers. The affixes cannot be separated from the verb and they always appear in a strict linear order (in striking contrast to the almost completely free word order found with lexical words, including a set of independent personal pronouns used for emphasis and contrast).

The Nahuatl system is fairly typical of a language with an agreement system expressed by pronominal affixes. Although there is a clear patterning, there are

Table 5.3 *Classical Nahuatl: Indicative vs Optative*

	Present Indicative	Present Optative
	'I weep'	'would that I wept'
1sg	ni-choka	ni-choka
2sg	ti-choka	xi-choka
3sg	choka	choka
1pl	ti-choka-h	ti-choka-kan
2pl	an-choka-h	xi-choka-kan
3pl	choka-h	choka-kan

interesting deviations from pure agglutination, characteristic of inflectional systems. One set of instances is found with double object verbs, taking a direct and an indirect object. The principles of affix order are as follows (as summarized by Sullivan (1988, 35–6) and Andrews (1975, 42)): the general order is specific < reflexive (*no, to, mo* etc.) < nonspecific human (*te*) < nonspecific nonhuman (*tla*). These basic orders are illustrated in (4) (Andrews 1975, 46f.):

(4) a.   specific < reflexive
ni-k-no-maka
1SG.SUBJ-3SG.OBJ-1SG.REFL-give
'I give it to myself'

b.   reflexive < nonspecific nonhuman
ni-no-tla-maka
1SG.SUBJ-1SG.REFL-NONSPEC.NONHUM-give
'I give something to myself'

c.   specific < nonspecific human
ni-k-te-maka
1SG.SUBJ-3SG.OBJ-NONSPEC.HUM-give
'I give it to someone'

d.   nonspecific human < nonspecific nonhuman
ni-te-tla-maka
1SG.SUBJ-NONSPEC.HUM-NONSPEC.NONHUM-give
'I give something to someone'

In addition to this, the plural direct object prefix takes the form *-in/im* rather than *-kin/kim* after an indirect object prefix (5):

(5)   ni-mitz-im-maka
1SG.SUBJ-2SG.OBJ-3PL.OBJ-give
'I give them to you'/'I give you to them'

Notice that (5) is ambiguous. Either of the two object markers can be interpreted as the direct or the indirect object.

Finally, where we have a combination of 3rd singular direct and 3rd singular indirect object we only find one prefix (6):

(6)   ni-mitz-maka
           1SG.SUBJ-2SG.OBJ-give
           'I give it/them to you'

In contradistinction to (5) the *mitz-* prefix can only denote an indirect object. The 3rd person direct object is not overtly marked. Moreover, the omitted 3rd person object can be interpreted as either singular or plural (so that on one reading (6) is synonymous with (5)).

Nahuatl has ways of creating causative and applicative verbs, with meanings such as 'have someone wash something' (causative) or 'wash something for someone' (applicative), or 'have someone wash something for someone' (applicative of causative). These permit pronominal objects expressed as prefixes (Andrews 1975, 108f.):

(7) a.   te-te-tla-pakaltilia
           NONSPEC.HUM-NONSPEC.HUM-NONSPEC.NONHUM-have.wash.for
           'He has someone wash something for someone'
    b.   nech-te-tla-pakaltilia
           1SG.OBJ-NONSPEC.HUM-NONSPEC.NONHUM-have.wash.for
           'He has someone wash something for me'
    c.   ni-k-no-te-pakaltilia
           1SG.SUBJ-3SG.OBJ-1SG.REFL-NONSPEC.HUM-have.wash.for
           'I have someone wash it/them for me'

Where two or more object prefixes are specific in reference all but one have to be omitted, as can be seen by comparing (8a, b):

(8) a.   mitz-pakaltia
           2SG.OBJ-have.wash
           'He has you wash it/them'
    b.   nech-pakaltilia
           1SG.OBJ-have.wash.for
           'He has you wash it/them for me'

The last added object 'for me' in (8b) is the one which remains overt. The original object prefix 'you', seen in (8a), is dropped.

Andrews (1975, 45) points out that some writers make further changes to the prefix order where a direct object is human and the indirect object is nonhuman (as in 'show the slave to the snake' or some such). In such (rather rare) situations the writer may retain the prefix denoting a human in preference to the non-human.

Classical Nahuatl morphology illustrates a fair number of the phenomena typically seen with affixal systems. We can now contrast that uncontroversially inflectional system with the pronominal system of a language which is traditionally said to have pronominal clitics.

5.4.2   Morpho-lexical clusters

      In this subsection we briefly describe a number of properties of two pronominal clitic systems, that of Italian and that of Luiseño. We will see that the elements within the clitic cluster interact with each other in many respects like affixes rather than like syntactically represented words (Simpson and Withgott 1986).

    We begin with the Italian clitic cluster. In Chapter 6 we will discuss some of the syntactic aspects of the Italian system. Here we look at the morphological properties, following Monachesi (1999, chapter 2). The basic clitic cluster has six positions, as seen in (9) (Monachesi 1999, 23):

(9)   Italian clitic cluster

I	II	III	IV	V	VI
personal	locative ci	reflexive si	accusative	impersonal si	partitive ne

We use the (non-standard) term 'personal clitics' to refer to 1st and 2nd person clitics representing direct or indirect objects, and 3sg clitics representing indirect objects. Their forms are shown in (10):[4]

(10)   Italian pronominal clitics

Person	Number	
	Singular	Plural
1	mi	ci
2	ti	vi
3 Masculine	gli	
3 Feminine	le	

    The 'accusative' clitics are shown in (11):

(11)

	Singular	Plural
Masculine	lo	li
Feminine	la	le

The locative *ci* means 'there'. It has a stylistically marked variant *vi*. The partitive *ne* cross-references quantified phrases, corresponding to *of them* in constructions of the form 'she bought three of them'. The reflexive *si* is an all-purpose pronoun used for 3rd person reflexives (1st, 2nd person reflexives are expressed by the personal clitics). The impersonal *si* is used in special syntactic constructions lacking a subject.

    We now show that clitics have a number of properties that make them similar to affixes. The first is the strict ordering represented in the template. A further important property is the internal allomorphy many of the clitics exhibit. The clitics *mi, ti, si, ci, vi* take the form *me, te, se, ce, ve* when followed by the clitics from positions IV or VI in the template, while *gli* and *le* become *glie* in the same position.

(12) a.   **Te la**   offro   (>ti la)
            2SG 3SG.FEM I.offer
            'I'm offering it to you'

      b.   **Ce lo**   mando (>ci lo)
            LOC 3SG.MASC I.send
            'I send it there'

      c.   Mandar**glielo** =
            mandar   **glie lo**   (>gli/le lo)
            send.INFINITIVE 3SG 3SG.MASC
            'to send it to him/her'

At the same time, a sequence of phonologically identical clitics is not normally permitted. This could occur when 1pl *ci* co-occurs with locative *ci* or when 2pl *vi* co-occurs with the literary variant of *ci*, *vi*. In either case the *ci ci* or *vi vi* sequence is spelt out as *vi ci*:

(13) a.   **Vi ci**   portano
            1PL LOC they.take
            'They take us there'

      b.   **Vi**   **ci**   rivolgete
            2PL.REFL LOC you.turn
            'You turn to it ('there')'

Similarly, the sequence *si si* is replaced by *ci si*:

(14)   **Ci   si**   lava
            REFL IMPERS washes
            'One washes oneself'

The cluster exhibits arbitrary gaps. Thus, a 1st or 2nd person direct object clitic cannot co-occur with an indirect object clitic (examples from Monachesi 1999, 26):

(15) a.   * Martina **gli**   mi presenta
            Martina 3SG.MASC 1SG introduces
            (Intended: 'Martina introduces me to him')

      b.   * Martina **gli**   ti   presenta
            Martina 3SG.MASC 2SG introduces
            (Intended: 'Martina introduces you to him')

Clearly, these properties are not typical of syntactically composed words but are typical of the affixal systems exemplified by Nahuatl.

The Italian clitic system is far from unique in showing these affix-like properties. On the contrary, this is typical behaviour whenever we have clitic clusters. Similar behaviour is seen in the independently developed clitic systems of a number of Slavic languages such as Czech/Slovak, Serbian/Croatian, Bulgarian and Macedonian, in Greek, in Tagalog, in a number of Australian languages such as Warlpiri, and so on. We illustrate below some of the inflection-like behaviour shown by the clitic cluster of the Uto-Aztecan language Luiseño. Steele et al.

(1981, 23–58) describe what they call an auxiliary constituent for Luiseño, in our terms a second-position (Wackernagel) cluster. Of interest to us here is the fact that the elements of this cluster exhibit typical properties of multiple and extended exponence that we are accustomed to finding in affixal systems. The cluster has three position classes. We will call the elements occupying Position 1 and 3 'auxiliary particles' and those occupying Position 2 'subject markers', as illustrated in (16) (Steele et al. 1981, 26):

(16)   Luiseño auxiliary particle inventory

Position 1	Position 2	Position 3
ṣu xu	Subject Markers	il po kwa

In addition, Luiseño verbs distinguish a number of tense/aspect/mood forms, shown in (17) (Steele et al. 1981, 28):

(17)   Luiseño TAM suffixes

	Nonfuture		Future
Distant	Near		
quṣ 'durative' uk 'habitual' ax, 'ya 'completed'	q/wun, an 'durative'		an 'future'

The Position 3 auxiliary particles respect co-occurrence restrictions with respect to the TAM forms (18). Thus, the Position 3 marker -il can only co-occur with the quṣ 'durative', uk 'habitual' and ax, 'ya 'completed' tense/aspect suffixes (Steele et al. 1981, 29):

(18)   TAM~aux co-occurrences

Nonfuture		Future
Distant	Near	
Ø-...-il	Ø-...-Ø	Ø-...-po

From these facts it would appear as if the Position 3 markers simply mark the general classification of distant nonfuture, near nonfuture and future. However, it is clear that this is an oversimplification once we look at sequences involving the Position 1 marker ṣu. On its own (that is, without any Position 3 markers) ṣu marks interrogative mood. However, in conjunction with Position 3 il, po it signals one of two types of evidential, what Steele et al. refer to as 'supposition with external verification' and 'supposition from general knowledge'. This is shown in (19) (Steele et al. 1981, 29):

(19)   Co-occurrence of modal auxiliary markers

	Nonfuture		Future
	Distant	Near	
	ʃu-...-il	∅-...-∅	*ʃu-...-po*
	supposition with	interrogative	supposition from
	external verification		general knowledge

These patterns are illustrated in (20) and (21) (Steele et al. 1981, 29–31):

(20) a.   wunaalum **ʃu-m-po** pomyo'   qalwun
           they   ʃU-SM-PO their.mothers are
           'They must have mothers somewhere'
     b.   ku'aalum **ʃu-m-il** nowiiwiyk   yuchiwun
           flies   ʃU-SM-IL in.my.wiwish sank
           'I see that flies sank in my wiwiish'
     c.   wunaalum **ʃu-m-il** heyiwun
           they   ʃU-SM-IL are.digging
           'They are digging (but I didn't know it until just now)'
(21) a.   wunaalum **ʃu-m-∅** heyiwun
           they   ʃU-SM-∅ are.digging
           'Are they digging?'
     b.   wunaalum **ʃu-m-∅** heyiquʃ
           they   ʃU-SM-∅ were.digging
           'Were they digging?'
     c.   wunaalum **ʃu-m-∅** heyin
           they   ʃU-SM-∅ will.dig
           'Will they dig?'

The other Position 1 marker, *xu*, is a modal expressing logical neces-sity/obligation and wishes. The marker *ʃu* is in paradigmatic opposition to the modal marker of obligation, *xu*, in all its uses. The co-occurrence restrictions between Position 3 markers and tense don't hold when Position 1 is occupied by an overt marker. For instance, *il/po* can co-occur with the 'near nonfuture plural' suffix *wun* if (but only if) Position 1 contains *ʃu/xu*.

From these observations we can conclude that the Position 1, 3 markers do not have a single meaning, or even a small collection of meanings; rather, they contribute in a non-compositional way to the interpretation of the whole cluster in much the same way that elements in an affix string contribute to interpreta-tion in classic cases of multiple exponence/cumulation of the kind we saw with Nahuatl.

Further instances of deviation from strict agglutination are in evidence when we consider the Subject Markers. These fall into three sets, shown in (22) (Steele et al. 1981, 35):

(22)   Luiseño Subject Marker sets

	SG	PL		SG	PL
	Set 1			Set 2	
1st	n	cha	1st	n	cha(m)
2nd	—	um			
			non-1st	—	m
3rd	—	pum			

Set 3 (Plural, all persons): m

Their use depends on exactly what TAM properties are expressed (note that Set 3 consists of just a single marker *m*, used just for plural subjects). The subject marker sets show co-occurrence restrictions with the auxiliary particles. Only the combinations shown in (23) are permitted (Steele et al. 1981, 37):

(23)   Co-occurrence restrictions between Subject Markers and modal auxiliary particles

a.	∅	Set 1	∅
b.	∅	Set 2	Particle 3
c.	Particle1	Set 2/3	Particle 3
d.	Particle1	Set 2/3	∅

This kind of behaviour is typical of inflectional systems, such as that of Nahuatl, where, for instance, we saw that the pronominal affixes found in the indicative mood are different from those found in the optative mood. It is not what is expected of syntactically represented pronominals. One further indication of inflection-like behaviour is the existence of an unmotivated paradigm gap (Steele et al. 1981, fn.21, 131–2): the 1pl subject marker is incompatible with the combination *ʂu-... -il*. Luiseño also exhibits a variety of inflection-like deviations from agglutinative organization in its 'quotative mood' forms, which use the Position 1 particle *kun*, for which we refer the reader to Steele et al.'s description. What these data from Luiseño illustrate is the way that the clitic cluster can show just the sort of behaviour expected of an affix string, and not the sort of behaviour we normally associate with well-behaved syntactic constructions.

There are other respects in which clitic clusters can behave more like affixes than words. One phenomenon that is encountered with some regularity in phonology and affixal morphology is haplology. This is found in affixal systems when two distinct but homophonous affixes come together. For instance, in Turkish, nouns take a plural number suffix, *-ler/lar*: *ev* 'house', *ev-ler* 'houses'. Nouns also take suffixes marking the possessor: *ev-i* 'his/her house', *ev-ler-i* 'their house'. In theory, the form expected when we have a plural possessor of a plural noun, as in 'their houses', should be *ev-ler-ler-i*. However, two tokens of *ler* never come together so that *ev-ler-ler-i* is simplified to *ev-ler-i*. This word form is therefore ambiguous between 'his/her houses', 'their house' and 'their houses' (see Lewis 1967, 40).

We have seen one strategy for avoiding identical sequences in Italian: one of the forms changes. A similar strategy is adopted in Serbian/Croatian when the 3sg auxiliary clitic *je* immediately follows the 3sg feminine accusative clitic *je*. The sequence *je je* is ungrammatical and so the pronominal clitic is then realized as *ju* rather than *je* (Spencer 1991, 356, Franks and King 2000, 30). In fact, this strategy is phonologically based: the pronominal clitic alternates with the *ju* form no matter how the *je je sequence arises (Barešić 1988, 87).

(24) a. On **je**   sreo svoju prijateljicu
         He 3SG.AUX met his   (girl)friend
         'He met his (girl)friend'

    b. On **ju**   **je**   sreo
         He 3SG.FEM.ACC 3SG.AUX met
         'He met her'

(25) a. On pije   vruću kavu
         He drinks hot   coffee.FEM
         'He drinks hot coffee'

    b. Pije   **ju**   vruću
         He.drinks 3SG.FEM.ACC hot
         'He drinks it (= coffee) hot'

(26) a. Ona jede salatu
         she eats salad.FEM
         'She eats salad'

    b. Ona **ju**   jede
         she 3SG.FEM.ACC eats
         'She eats it (= salad)'

One further respect in which clitic clusters tend to behave like affix systems can be seen when we consider languages in which one or other of the clitics really has become an affix. An interesting example of this type of development is seen in the future markers of Serbian/Croatian, as described in Spencer (1991, 352, 357), Franks and King (2000, 20–1) (for further discussion, see Milićević 2005). The emphatic form of the future uses the verb HT(J)ETI 'want' as an auxiliary, but unemphatic forms of the future use the clitic variant of the auxiliary. The full and clitic forms are illustrated in (27):[5]

(27)   Serbian/Croatian future tense auxiliary HT(J)ETI 'want'

	Singular			Plural	
	Full	Clitic		Full	Clitic
1sg	hòću	ću	1pl	hòćemo	ćemo
2sg	hòćeš	ćeš	2pl	hòćete	ćete
3sg	hòće	će	3pl	hòće	će

The full form of the auxiliary is illustrated in (28):

(28)   Hoće vid(j)eti Mariju
           FUT.3 see.INF Marija.ACC
           'He/she/they will see Marija'

The form in which the future auxiliary takes the form of a standard Wackernagel clitic is shown in (29a), while in (29b) shows the clitic fused with the infinitive form:

(29) a.   Vidjeti **će**   Mariju
           see.INF FUT.3 Marija.ACC
           'He/she/they will see Marija'
     b.   Vidjeće   Mariju
           see.FUT.3 Marija.ACC
           'He/she/they will see Marija'

The crucial point is that the kind of morphophonological fusion seen in (29b) isn't found elsewhere in the phonology of Serbian/Croatian. Moreover, this fusion only takes place when the future auxiliary immediately follows an infinitive verb form (and then only if that form ends in /t/). With infinitives that end in /-ći/ such as *ići* 'go' we get no fusion. Thus, we are dealing with a clitic that triggers idiosyncratic allomorphy on specific subclasses of hosts, in other words an affix.

An element that interacts in complex ways with the clitic system in Slavic is the negation formative *ne*, described in Franks and King (2000, 270–2). They describe this as a proclitic which attaches to finite verbs. In West Slavic and East Slavic languages, when it realizes sentence or clausal negation the negation element behaves more like an affix. It invariably attaches to the finite verb or finite auxiliary of the clause and in some languages clearly forms a morphological word with that verb form. For instance, in Czech and Slovak, morphological words are stressed on their first syllable. Any negated verb form in those languages has stress on the negative element, suggesting that the negation is in fact a prefix. With the copular verb BE we find idiosyncratic allomorphy (though it's not clear whether it's the prefix or the stem that undergoes the allomorphy):

(30)   Czech BE (in IPA transcription)

	Affirmative	Negative
1sg	sem 'I am'	ˈnejsem 'I am not'
2sg	si (seʃ⁶)	ˈnejsi
3sg	je	ˈneɲiː
1pl	sme	ˈnejsme
2pl	ste	ˈnejste
3pl	sou	ˈnejsou

Similarly, in Serbian/Croatian the negation formative fuses with the verbs BE and HAVE. However, in contrast with Czech/Slovak, the Serbian/Croatian fused negated auxiliary supplants the clitic auxiliary. Thus, in Czech the forms given in (30) can't be used when the verb is used as an auxiliary:

(31) a.   Nečetl **jsem**   zajímavou knihu
            NEG.read 1SG.AUX interesting book
            'I didn't read an interesting book' [Czech]

     b.   * Nejsem   četl zajímavou knihu
            NEG.1SG.AUX read interesting book

(32) a.   Nisam   čitao zanimljivu knjigu
            NEG.1SG.AUX read interesting book
            'I didn't read an interesting book' [Serbian/Croatian]

     b.   * Nečitao **sam**   zanimljivu knjigu
            NEG.read 1SG.AUX interesting book

The negation element in Polish and in the East Slavic languages, Russian, Belarasian and Ukrainian, is likewise a prefix on a finite verb form. In Macedonian and Bulgarian we see a rather more complex picture, however. Mišeska Tomić (2006, 243) claims that the Macedonian clitic cluster template contains two slots for the negation element:

(33)   ?Inter < Subj < Neg < Mod < Mood < Neg < Aux < Dat < Acc < (s)e

We will ignore the slots labelled '?Inter' and 'Subj' as well as those to the right of the second 'Neg' slot. The slot labelled 'Mod' is for what Mišeska Tomić calls 'modal clitics', the future ('expectative') clitic *ḱe* (pronounced [ce]) and the conditional clitic *bi*. The slot for 'Mood' houses the clitic *da*, which she analyses as a 'subjunctive mood marker'. Franks and King (2000, 81) paint a rather different picture of the cluster, namely, (34):

(34)   DA < NE < ḰE/BI < Aux < Dat < Acc < (s)e

However, they note that DA is initial as a complementizer but follows ḰE as a modal, and they cite examples (35) showing that, although NE basically occurs before the verbal complex, "there is some latitude in its placement depending on what exactly is being negated" (Franks and King 2000, 78):

(35) a.   **Ne bi** **sum**   **mu**   **go**   dala   (peroto) (nemu)
           NEG COND 1SG.AUX him.DAT it.ACC (the.pen) (to.him)
           'I wouldn't be willing to give it/the pen to him'

     b.   **Da bi**   **ne** stasal!
           DA COND NEG arrive
           'If only he wouldn't come!'

     c.   Jas dojdov **ne** **da te**   spasam, ama . . .
           I   came NEG DA you.ACC I.save   but
           'I came not to save you, but . . .'

     d.   **Da ne** **te**   spasam!
           DA NEG you.ACC I.save
           'Let me not save you!'

Mišeska Tomić (2006, 245) provides an interesting example in which NE occurs twice:

(36)   **Ne ḱe da ne gi**   vide
             NEG FUT DA NEG them.CL you.saw
             'It couldn't be (true), that you didn't see them'

Bulgarian is very similar to Macedonian, and Mišeska Tomić (2006, 261) provides an almost identical template as the one she provided for Macedonian (Franks and King largely omit negation from their discussion of Bulgarian clitics). She cites the examples in (37):

(37) a.   **Ne bix   ti   go**   dala
             NEG COND.1SG 2SG.DAT 3SG.ACC give
             'I wouldn't give it to you'
     b.   **Da ne si   mu   go**   dala poveče!
             DA NEG 2SG.AUX 3SG.DAT 3SG.ACC give more
             'Don't give it to him any more, or else!'

The simple way of thinking of these constructions is to recognize that the DA formative introduces a clause, at least, as far as phrase structure syntax is concerned. The clitic cluster is defined with respect to a single clause. In constructions with DA there are two clauses and thus two opportunities for negation to be expressed. The situation is made complex by the fact that some uses of negated *da*-clauses correspond to monoclausal affirmative constructions. For instance, in Bulgarian the normal way to negate a future tense clause (which is formed with the particle *šte*) is with an impersonal fused negative form of the verb IMA 'have', *njama* followed by a *da*-clause that realizes the various clausal properties other than future tense:

(38) a.   **Az šte săm   mu   go**   dal
             I   ŠTE 1SG.AUX to.him it.ACC give
             'I will have given it to him'
     b.   **Az njama da săm   mu   go**   dal
             I   NJAMA DA 1SG.AUX to.him it.ACC give
             'I won't have given it to him'

What we see in (38b) is a periphrastic construction built from an entire clause (see Spencer 2003a for detailed discussion of periphrasis in Bulgarian). Once we recognize the clausal nature of *da*-phrases, we can see that the position of the negation clitic is (relatively!) easy to explain.

Recall that in Nahuatl the order of affixes is sometimes governed by semantically based rules, as illustrated in (4). Something similar is often observed with clusters of pronominal clitics. The standard example is French, where the order of 3rd person clitics is direct object < indirect object: *le lui* 'it to-him/her', whereas the order with 1st/2nd person indirect objects is the indirect object < direct object *me le* 'to-me it'. Combinations of 1st person with 2nd person are disallowed altogether.

The conclusions that we must draw are that elements that are traditionally called clitics may exhibit a good many features normally associated with affixes on the Zwicky–Pullum criteria when they combine into clusters: a fixed order, idiosyncratic alternations in ordering, haplology, idiosyncratic allomorphy, and accidental gaps, not to mention multiple exponence and cumulation. One might wish to argue that this sort of behaviour is to be expected from the Romance clitics. They cluster around the verb, and so we could argue (as many have) that they are actually a type of affix anyway. But exactly the same type of behaviour is widespread with 2P clitic systems such as those of Slavic and Luiseño.

5.5   Phrasal affixation and edge inflection

A recurrent theme throughout this book, and throughout the literature on clitics generally, is the idea that a clitic is a reduced word form which attaches to the edge of a phrase, but has the sort of grammatical function one would expect of an inflectional affix were it to occur on the head of that phrase. This is the phenomenon of phrasal affixation, which according to a number of linguists is the principal or even the only guise assumed by clitics. We saw in Section 3.2 that Klavans (1982) explicitly treats clitics as phrasal affixes, and she has been consistently followed in this by Stephen Anderson .

However, we've also seen ample evidence that there isn't a clear distinction to be drawn in purely formal terms between clitics and affixes. It's therefore not too surprising to find that in some cases those elements that function as phrasal affixes have crucial properties normally only associated with true affixes, that is, elements that attach to word stems. We will illustrate a number of constructions in a variety of languages that indicate that 'phrasal affixation' can involve genuine affixes, or even non-affixal inflection. To distinguish the two kinds of construction it is customary to speak of edge inflection when some word at the edge of the phrase undergoes inflectional morphology rather than just receiving a clitic. The usual assumption is that each word that can appear at the edge of the relevant phrase inflects for those 'edge features'. For instance, if we think of the English possessive as edge inflection this would mean that pretty well every word in the language, including otherwise non-inflecting words, has a 'genitive case' form in *'s*. In other words, admitting edge inflection can entail a significant restructuring of the inflectional morphology chapter of a language's grammar. For this reason, linguists have often balked at the idea of edge inflection. However, if it happens that only a restricted class of words can be found at the edge of the relevant phrase, then we might be more inclined to accept the idea of those words inflecting.

Let's consider in more detail the English possessive *'s*, which has been claimed to be a case of edge inflection (Lapointe, 1990, 1992). In general, this phrasal affix behaves in an entirely 'agglutinating' fashion in that it simply attaches to whatever (fully inflected) word form happens to end the noun phrase: *[the girl we met]'s name*, *[the book that was stolen]'s value* and so on. However, there is an interesting twist when the host for the phrasal affix itself ends in the possessive *'s* or with a regular plural affix. We should warn readers at this point that the judgements in these cases are rather subtle and there's a good deal of variation between native speakers (which doesn't necessarily correlate with dialect). The original observations and argument were first made in detail in Zwicky (1987). We will follow the discussion in Halpern (1995, chapter 4).

First, recall that the possessive *'s* element has three regular allomorphs, /z/, /s/, /əz/, whose distribution is conditioned purely by the phonology of the host: after any word ending in a (voiced or voiceless) sibilant we find /əz/, after a voiceless plosive /s/ and elsewhere /z/. This allomorphy is exactly the same as that of the plural *-s* and the 3sg *-s* endings. Since the /z/ allomorph is apparently the default form, we will speak of the *-z* element (clitic/affix). The starting point is the observation that the possessive /z/ is simplified to a single token of /z/ whenever it follows another token of the /z/ element:

(39) a.   the girls' /gəːlz/ names = the names of the girls
      b.   *the girls's /gəːlzəz/ names

(40)   the larger of the two cats' paws
                  = the paws of the larger of the two cats

This simplification of two identical tokens to a single token is haplology, much like that discussed for the Turkish plural suffix *-ler/lar* (Section 5.4.2). This is not a purely phonological phenomenon because non-plural words that happen to end in /z/ fail to trigger the haplology, as seen in (41) and the minimal pair in (42):

(41) a.   the fox's paws /fɒksəz/, not /fɒks/
      b.   the mice's tails /maisəz/, not /mais/
      c.   the cheese's aroma /tʃiːzəz/, not /tʃiːz/

(42) a.   the cats' dinners /kats/, not /katsəz/
      b.   the Katz's dinners /katsəz/, not /kats/

Many speakers give the same judgements with the possessive and the 3sg /z/, though here we find variability, and speakers will often just avoid the construction and opt for a paraphrase:

(43) a.   anyone who snores' mouth /snɔːz/, not /snɔːzəz/
              better: *the mouth of anyone who snores*
      b.   the people we met at Mary's car /mɛːrɪz/, not /mɛːrɪzəz/
              (much) better: *the car belonging to the people who we met at Mary's (place)*

The analysis of the English possessive as edge inflection is somewhat controversial. Anderson (2005, 89–94) provides a number of arguments against that analysis in favour of treating the process as one of phrasal affixation. In other words, he argues that the /z/ formative is an affix that attaches to the right edge of the noun phrase rather than a specially inflected form of any word that happens to be able to appear at the edge of a noun phrase (in effect, any word of English). This certainly solves the conceptual problem posed by the idea that all words in English effectively have a possessive inflectional form. We will examine the English possessor construction in rather more detail when we come to look at specific theoretical analyses of such phenomena in Section 8.8.[7]

However, it appears that we can't write off the notion of edge inflection solely by re-analysing the English possessor construction. We look now at a number of cases that seem to require us to countenance the idea of words taking inflected forms by virtue of their position at the edge of a phrase.

We saw in Chapter 3 that Bulgarian and Macedonian have developed a kind of definite article which behaves like a Wackernagel clitic within the noun phrase. However, a good deal of evidence from allomorphy also indicates that the article is more of an affix than a bona fide clitic. Recall from Chapter 2 that the Bulgarian/Macedonian article inflects for gender and number and encliticizes to the first word of the noun phrase, as in the Bulgarian examples in (44):

(44) a.   kniga-**ta**
            book-the
            'the book'

      b.   xubava-**ta** kniga
            nice-the   book
            'the nice book'

      c.   moja-**ta** kniga
            my-the book
            'my book'

      d.   moja-ta xubava kniga
            my-DEF nice   book
            'my nice book'

This seems to be classic Wackernagel positioning. However, in Chapter 3 we noted that things are a little more complex. When a phrase-initial adjective is itself modified by a scalar adverb or degree modifier, it's still the adjective which receives the definite article enclitic:

(45) a.   mnogo interesna-**ta**   kniga
            very   interesting-DEF book
            'the interesting book'

      b.   *mnogo-**ta/to** interesna   kniga
            very-DEF   interesting book

Other examples are discussed in Halpern (1995, 155).

A further interesting fact about Bulgarian is brought to light in Halpern's discussion. Bulgarian adjectives generally agree with their head noun in number and gender. However, there are a number of adjectives, mainly loans from Turkish or more recently from English, which are indeclinable. An example is *serbez* 'quarrelsome'. Not only do such indeclinable adjectives not take number/gender inflections, they don't take the definite article either (Halpern 1995, 168):

(46)   * serbez-**ăt/ta**   žena
            quarrelsome-DEF woman
            (Intended: 'quarrelsome woman')

On the other hand, it isn't possible to violate the 2P requirement and put the article on the head noun:

(47)   * serbez   žena-**ta**
            quarrelsome woman-DEF

This is not because such adjectives are in some way incompatible semantically with definiteness, as the grammaticality of (48) confirms:

(48)   tazi serbez   žena
            that quarrelsome woman
            'that quarrelsome woman'

Needless to say, there is no problem with indefinite noun phrases:

(49) a.   serbez   čovek
            quarrelsome man
            'a quarrelsome man'
     b.   serbez   žena
            quarrelsome woman
            'a quarrelsome woman'

Such behaviour is rather difficult to reconcile with the idea that the article is a promiscuously attaching clitic.

   Finally, there is a good deal of evidence from stem allomorphy that the article is more of an affix than a bona fide clitic (Halpern 1995, 150–6). Obstruents in Bulgarian are devoiced word-finally. This is true even if the word with a final obstruent is followed by an enclitic:

(50) a.   grad [grat] 'city'
     b.   grad=**li**=**e**
            city=Q=COP
            'is it a city?'

However, the article blocks this devoicing:

(51)   grad-**ăt** [gradăt]
            city-DEF
            'the city'

The article triggers a process of liquid-schwa metathesis, which is otherwise only found with affixation, not cliticization:

(52)   grăk   gărk-ăt
        'Greek'   'Greek-DEF'

The article can change the word stress, unlike clear-cut instances of clitics. Quite often the article itself attracts stress, even though clitics are supposed to be stressless elements:

(53)   vlást   vlast-tá
        power   power-DEF

Finally, adjectives undergo unique allomorphy in the MASC.SG form just when suffixed with the article. In just this context the consonant-final adjective stem is augmented with an element -i:

(54)   xubav 'nice'
    a.   xubav čovek
            nice   man
            'a nice man'
    b.   xubavi-jăt čovek
            nice-DEF   man
            'the nice man'

The conclusion to draw is that the definite article is morphologically an affix. One of its properties is to trigger irregular allomorphy on certain types of stem. This means that we have to say that nouns and adjectives inflect for the property 'definite' in Bulgarian/Macedonian.

    Anderson et al. (2006) note three additional cases of edge inflection. We will first sketch their description of the two languages Nias Selatan and Kuuk Thaayorre, before discussing their third example, Somali, in a little more detail.

    In Nias Selatan (Austronesian, spoken on the island of Sumatra) the absolutive case is marked by changing the first consonant of the first word of the phrase. This type of alternation is a widespread phenomenon in the world's languages and is known more generally in morphology as consonant mutation. However, consonant mutation in Nias Selatan is not completely regular and the exact form of a mutated word depends on what word is being inflected. For instance, the mutated form of öri 'village' is nöri while the mutated form of öri 'amulet' is göri.

    In the Australian (Pama-Nyungan) language Kuuk Thaayorre the ergative case is marked by a variety of lexically specified suffixes (-al, -ku, -e, -i, -arr and several others). A noun phrase is marked once for ergative, on its rightmost word, which could be a noun, an adjective, a possessive pronoun or a demonstrative. Any such phrase-final word (including the possessive pronoun, Gaby 2005, 13) can be inflected for ergative case, except a demonstrative. When the phrase ends in a demonstrative, it is the previous word that gets marked for ergative (see Gaby 2005, 14f.). The generalization here, then, is that the ergative case is signalled by selecting the appropriately inflected form of whatever word comes at the end of the noun phrase (where 'noun phrase' excludes determiners).

A particularly interesting and intricate example of edge inflection is shown by Somali and other Cushitic languages. We follow the discussion in Anderson et al. (2006) and Saeed (1999). Somali has two lexical tones, High and Low. Words generally have one of three accentual patterns (AP) (Saeed 1999, 22):[8]

(55) a.   AP1 High tone on the last syllable, Low tone elsewhere
     b.   AP2 High tone on the penultimate syllable, Low tone elsewhere
     c.   AP3 Low tone on all syllables

These patterns are illustrated in the declension of the proper name *Cáli* 'Ali' (Saeed 1999, 23):[9]

(56) a.   absolutive case (citiation form)   Cáli   AP1
     b.   nominative case   Cali   AP3
     c.   genitive case   Calí   AP2

Paradigm (56) illustrates a typical declension pattern for Somali nouns. There is a base form (labelled 'absolutive case') from which can be derived nominative, genitive and vocative case forms. The nominative is formed in a variety of ways, the commonest being to replace any High tone with a Low tone, that is, replacing AP1 with AP3 as seen in (56). However, there are other ways of forming the nominative. Some nouns have stress on the final syllable in the absolutive (that is, their basic accent is AP3). Such nouns form their nominative by using AP1:

(57) a.   absolutive case   tuké 'crow'   AP2
     b.   nominative case   túke   AP1

Some nouns require a suffix -*i* in addition to shifting their accent pattern: *náag* 'woman', *naagi* 'woman.NOM', while other nouns form their nominative in still further ways, for instance, *nínka* 'the man.ABS', *nínku* 'the man.NOM'.

The crucial point is that case is marked on Somali noun phrases just once, at the right edge of the phrase (Saeed 1999, 66). Thus, in (58) we see that it is the adjective *dhèer* 'tall' that is marked for nominative case, while the head noun *nínka* remains in the absolutive:

(58) a.   nínka   dhèer
           man.ABS tall.ABS
           'the tall man.ABS'
     b.   nínka   dheeri
           man.ABS tall.NOM
           'the tall man.NOM'
     c.   * nínku   dhèer
           man.NOM tall.ABS
     d.   * nínku   dheeri
           man.NOM tall.NOM

In examples (59) and (60) we see that even the verb at the end of a relative clause may be inflected for the case of the phrase of which it's a constituent (see also Saeed 1999, 212 for further examples and discussion):

(59) a.   nínka   warqádda keená
            the.man.ABS letter   brings
            'the man who brings the letter (ABS)'
      b.   nínka   warqádda keenaa
            the.man.ABS letter   brings
            'the man who brings the letter (NOM)'

(60) a.   warqádda nínku   keenó
            letter   the.man.NOM brings.ABS
            'the letter the man brings (ABS)'
      b.   warqádda nínku   keenaa
            letter   the.man.NOM brings.NOM
            'the letter the man brings (NOM)'

Since the actual form of a case, whether nominative, genitive or vocative, can't be predicted in all instances, we have to accept that case marking is inflectional. But this means that we have to realize case on a noun phrase by inflecting the word on its right edge.

5.5.1   Clitics as phonology: Tongan 'definitive accent'

Before we leave the topic of edge inflection it's worth looking at one particular system that has been claimed to be a case of edge inflection but which in fact appears to be something more interesting, the 'definitive accent' in the Polynesian (Oceanic) language Tongan. Stress in Tongan falls almost always on the penultimate syllable of a word. One systematic exception is with enclitics. The subject pronominals and the demonstratives *ni*, *na* 'this, that' encliticize to the previous word and attract the stress to its final syllable. Churchward (1953, 6–10) characterizes the definitive accent as a kind of supplementary marker used with nominal phrases that are already in some sense definite. It consists of shifting the stress to the final vowel of the nominal phrase "just as it would be if an enclitic were added" (Churchward 1953, 7). We can see from examples (61) that the process affects the right edge of a definite phrase (in bold), not just the noun itself:

(61) a.   fále   áko
            house learn
            'school'
      b.   'i he fale **akó**
            in the school
            'in the school'
      c.   'i he fale ako **fo'oú**
            in the school   new
            'in the new school'
      d.   he fale   kuo nau fakataha **aí**
            the building PERF they assemble in.it
            'the building in which they have assembled'

Tongan has two articles, commonly labelled the definite article, *he/e*, and the indefinite article, *ha*. However, the definite article is really more of a specificity marker. Churchward (1953, 25) characterizes their use and their interaction with definitive accent by comparing the examples in (62):

(62) a.   Ha'u mo e   **afó**
        come you DEF.ART fishing.line.DEF
        'Bring the fishing line'

     b.   Ha'u mo e   afo
        come you DEF.ART fishing.line
        'Bring a fishing line'

     c.   Ha'u mo ha   afo
        come you INDEF.ART fishing.line
        'Bring a fishing line'

In (62b) 'fishing line' is distinguished from other objects, while in (62c) the speaker is referring to one fishing line out of all the fishing lines.

Examples (63a, b) make the point that definitive accent targets the noun phrase headed by the nominal that is definite.

(63) a.   'Oku mahino 'a e   me'a na'a nau fai **'aneafí**
        PRES clear   PRT DEF.ART thing PAST they do yesterday
        'The thing which they did yesterday is clear' (Churchward 1953, 7–8)

     b.   Na'a ke 'alu ki he   **fakatahá**   'aneafi?
        PAST you go to DEF.ART meeting.DEF yesterday
        'Did you go to the meeting yesterday?' (Churchward 1953, 9)

In (63a) the word *'aneafi* 'yesterday' is part of the postpositive relative clause modifying 'thing', but in (63b) *'aneafi* is modifying the main clause verb and is not part of the noun phrase headed by 'meeting'.

Recall that Tongan has two clitic demonstratives, *ni, na*. In fact, these form part of a larger paradigm of demonstratives, illustrated in (64):[10]

(64)   Tongan demonstratives

Clitic	Pronoun	Locative	Adverb
—	*ē*	*hē*	*pehē*
	this	here	like this
	that	there	like that
ni	*eni*	*heni*	*peheni*
this	this	here	like this
na	*ena*	*hena*	*pehena*
that	that	there	like that

The clear implication is that the missing 'clitic' cell is occupied by the definitive accent process. The accentual shift arose originally as the result of cliticization of a definiteness marker or demonstrative to the end of the noun phrase (perhaps of the form *a*), which, as a clitic, triggered accent shift. The clitic itself was subsequently lost, leaving the accent shift as its only trace.

Anderson (1992, 2005) has argued that what we have here is an instance of a special clitic which is not a phrasal affix but rather a phrasal phonological process. An alternative viewpoint is that of Poser (1985), who treats the definitive accent as an instance of edge inflection. The difference between the two accounts is this: if the accented forms arise from edge inflection, then what we have is a set of words inflected for definiteness which happen to be the kinds of words that can end a noun phrase. As can be seen from just the handful of examples we've cited, this probably includes most of the words in the language, given that the definitive accent can apply to the final word of a relative clause. The basis of the edge inflection analysis is the claim that the definitive accent is the kind of phonology that can't arise naturally from general phonological processes affecting phrases but has to be part of the lexical phonology, that is, those (sometimes idiosyncratic) patterns of allomorphy that affect individual word forms but which don't apply automatically. Anderson provides a number of arguments against this lexical analysis of the accent shift, arguing that it can be considered an ordinary postlexical phonological alternation. In that case it constitutes so to speak 'edge phonology'.

It might be thought that this is a rather strange type of process: the realization of a morphosyntactic property by means of a phonological alternation imposed at the right edge of a phrase. However, it should be borne in mind that non-affixal, processual morphology is actually quite common as a means of head inflection. There are hundreds of languages that express morphosyntactic properties by means of prosodic alternations such as tone/accent shift, stress shift, vowel lengthening/shortening, as well as non-prosodic means such as consonant mutation, vowel ablaut, nasalization and so on. A convenient summary of some of the more obviously phonological examples of this type of 'affixation of a phonological feature' are provided in Akinlabi (1996), for instance. Given the existence of non-affixal processual morphology effecting head marking, and given the possibility of phrasal affixation, we would actually expect there to be cases of non-affixal processes targeting phrase edges in this fashion.[11]

5.6   Summary: clitics as morphology

In this chapter we have addressed two related issues. First, we have summarized the ways in which clitic systems can resemble affixal systems, and hence can appear to be very different from syntactically represented function words. It is phenomena such as these that have led a number of authors to treat clitics as essentially morphological objects, and hence not necessarily subject to the normal principles of word-and-phrase syntax. Second, we have introduced some of the theoretical controversies surrounding the role of clitic systems in the architecture of grammar: are clitics really a kind of affix rather than a kind of word? The similarities between the behaviour of clitic clusters and affix strings is very striking. This is particularly true of clitic clusters that occupy positions where neither bona fide function words nor head-marking affixes are normally found, namely, in second position, as in Slavic and Luiseño. If clitics exist, distinct from affixes and function words, then presumably the 2P exemplars are the clearest, yet even in those systems, affix-like behaviour is rampant, distinguishing clitics starkly from function words.

In Chapter 7 we will return to the question of how affixes relate to clitics by considering cases of affixal systems that have retained (or perhaps even acquired) significant clitic-like properties. In the next chapter, however, we turn to properties of clitic systems that tie them in with syntactic phenomena. Although we will be looking at the syntactic behaviour of clitics in that chapter, we will of necessity be making comparisons with affixational morphology (for instance in comparing clitic doubling constructions with bona fide agreement systems), so the question of how clitic systems relate to morphology will remain with us.

6   Clitics and syntax

6.1   Introduction

This chapter will discuss various ways in which clitics interact with syntactic structure, in as theory-neutral a way as possible. This will involve examining the syntactic positions of clitics, the syntactic factors determining them and the syntactic role of clitics in phenomena such as agreement, doubling and climbing. We will see that behaviour generally associated with clitics, especially lack of 'doubling' of overt NP arguments and clitic climbing, can be found in otherwise canonical agreement systems. This sometimes has important consequences for theoretical models that attempt to deal with clitic systems.

6.2   Distributional idiosyncrasies

We will begin by surveying some of the peculiarities of function words that are not necessarily analysed in the literature as clitics, and which in any case are not special clitics. In Section 6.2.1 we look at properties that align ordinary function words with clitics, and in Section 6.2.2 we look at properties that align function words with affixes.

6.2.1   Clitic-like behaviour

In many cases we find that unaccented function words have properties that make them look more like clitics than full words. The most obvious such property is phonological: unaccented function words are phonological clitics, at least in languages with some sort of accentual system (for instance, word stress). However, there are other respects in which function words might resemble clitics more than lexical words. One very common instance of this concerns word order. In many languages the order of words within the clause or within, say, a noun phrase can be very free. Russian is a good example of this. Within a noun phrase, adjectives, demonstratives and possessive pronouns can be placed more or less anywhere, resulting in very subtle differences in emphasis as in (1):

(1) a.   tvoja novaja kniga
          your new   book
          'your new book'

b.	novaja tvoja kniga
c.	kniga tvoja novaja
d.	kniga novaja tvoja
e.	tvoja kniga novaja
f.	novaja kniga tvoja

Here the most neutral order is that of (1a), but all the others can be heard in Standard Spoken Russian.[1]

Now, exactly the same variation in word order is found when the noun phrase is the complement to a preposition such as *o* 'about' or *okolo* 'near'. However, there are severe restrictions on the placement of the preposition itself: it must occur first in the phrase.

(2) a.   o   tvojej novoj knige
          about your new book
          'about your new book'

b.	o novoj tvojej knige
c.	o knige novoj tvojej
d.	*tvojej o knige novoj
e.	*tvojej novoj o knige
f.	*tvojej novoj knige o

Examples such as (2d, e, f) are completely ungrammatical. Polysyllabic prepositions such as *okolo* 'near' are sometimes placed at the very end of the phrase in very colloquial styles, and a handful of prepositions can be used as postpositions in the standard language, such as *radi* 'for the sake of, out of': *interesa radi/radi interesa* 'out of interest', but the great majority of prepositions have a very fixed placement.

Similar phenomena are seen with auxiliary verbs in many languages. As we saw in Section 3.3, Bulgarian represents a particularly complex and interesting example of this theme. Recall that in Bulgarian we find auxiliary verb forms that behave entirely like 2P clitics. These are the present tense forms of the verb BE. We also find verbs with grammatical functions that have more or less the same word order properties as full-form lexical verbs. In between these we find inflected clitic forms of what was originally the past tense of the verb WANT used to convey conditional mood, as well as an invariable form *šte*, used for the future tense. These clitic forms are unusual in that they can appear at the beginning of the clause and can host the clitic cluster themselves, whereas true clitics require a lexical word as host. Finally, there are auxiliary verbs that are not clitics but that have restricted word order possibilities compared with lexical verbs.

German has a set of auxiliary verbs expressing perfect aspect, passive voice, future tense and various modal meanings. The perfect (HABEN 'have') and passive (WERDEN 'become') auxiliaries take the past participle form of the verb while the future and modal auxiliaries take the infinitive form of the verb. In subordinate clauses verbs always come at the end of the clause. Depending on the meaning we can therefore have different orders of lexical verbs, as in (3):

(3) a.   ... dass er sie die Torte zu probieren überredete
          ... that he she the cake to try   persuaded
          '... that he persuaded her to try the cake'
    b.   ... dass sie ihn zu überreden probierte
          ... that she him to persuade tried
          'that she tried to persuade him ...'

In (3a) the verb *persuade* applies to (takes in its scope) the verb *try*, while in (3b) the semantic scope relations are the other way around. This is reflected naturally in the word order, where the verb with the wider scope appears nearer the edge of the phrase than its complement. However, the order found with the combination aspectual auxiliary and infinitive modal auxiliary is fixed and doesn't always conform to what we would expect given usual patterns of word order and semantic scope:

(4) a.   ... dass er sie hat überreden können
          ... that he her has persuade been.able
          '... that he has been able to persuade her'
    b.   *... dass er sie überreden können   hat
          ... that he her persuade been.able has

6.2.2   Affix-like behaviour

While it may seem counter-intuitive, weak function words can sometimes behave more like affixes than like clitics. One common phenomenon is found with coordinated phrases. A full-form word can relate to a coordinate phrase without needing to be repeated. For instance, the adjective *old* in *old men and women* can modify both *men* and *women* together. Similarly, the verb *reads* applies to both coordinated noun phrases in *reads cheap novels and children's comics*. Borrowing a term from logic, we often say that the word *old* or *reads* takes wide scope over the two conjuncts (colloquially people say that the word scopes over the conjuncts).

What is the situation when unaccented function words have the opportunity to take wide scope over conjoined phrases? For instance, in a language with unaccented prepositions or with a definite article, can a single occurrence of a preposition or the article take scope over a coordinated phrase, as in *the (happy) [boys and girls]* or *on [the table or the chair]*? Here we find a good deal of cross-linguistic variation and quite frequently disagreement between speakers.

The reason this is of importance is that it is widely recognized that true affixes must always be repeated on conjuncts. For instance, it's impossible for the plural suffix on *girls* to scope over *boy* in **happy boy- and girl-s*. This is Criterion 3 proposed by Miller (1992, 157) for distinguishing affixes and clitics. On the other hand, many linguists would say that it is a feature of clitics that they DO take wide scope over conjuncts. This is Criterion 1 in Miller (1992, 155). Thus, given these assumptions, the reduced form *em* of the pronoun *them* in *wash and dry'em* cannot be an affix, though it could be a clitic. The behaviour of unaccented function words in Portuguese and similar languages is therefore somewhat puzzling. Not only do those words behave unlike full-word forms, they behave more like affixes than clitics. Indeed, Miller (1992) uses such evidence to argue that weak form function words such as definite articles and some prepositions in French actually are affixes, specifically phrasal affixes.

We'll return to this issue in Section 7.3 when we'll see that elements that are generally treated as affixes can often take wide scope themselves (this is the phenomenon often known as 'suspended affixation'). This means that scope or repeatability of an element gives us very little clue as to whether that element is a word, clitic or affix.

6.3   The morphosyntax of agreement

One important aspect of the syntax of pronominal clitics is their relation to agreement morphology (which often arises from the grammaticalization of clitic structures, of course). For this reason it will be necessary to review some of the key aspects of agreement against the background of clitic morphosyntax. We will not try to summarize the various theoretical approaches to agreement (an excellent source for such information is Corbett 2006) but rather we will point up those properties of agreement systems, especially the non-canonical agreement systems, that are most relevant for comparison with clitic systems, drawing preliminary comparisons with clitic systems. These comparisons will be expanded in the following section.

As we showed in Chapter 2, pronouns are function words that typically reflect grammatical, morphosyntactic properties such as person, number and gender (as well as case, definiteness and a host of other properties). Now, when a pronoun such as English *she* in (15) picks up the referent of another noun it can be thought of as being the target of a special kind of agreement relation.

(5)   The doctor walked in. She was wearing a white coat.

As Corbett has pointed out in various places (Corbett 1991, 248–59, Corbett 2006, 41–2, 227–8), there is no non-arbitrary way of characterizing agreement in all its manifestations in such a way as to rule out (15) and its counterpart in innumerable languages, as an instance of (non-canonical) agreement. Given this, clitic pronouns are a fortiori quite likely to exhibit (this type of) agreement, simply by virtue of being pronouns.

To help us to individuate clitics and distinguish them from affixal morphology, we could restrict our definition of agreement to something like the canonical inflectionally expressed verb–subject agreement found in countless languages. Let us assume such a distinction and turn now to typical clitic systems.

The most salient property that pronominal clitics seem to have is that they fulfil the role of the subject or object of the verb, just like non-clitic, full-form pronouns. One consequence of this is that we cannot have both a clitic and a full noun phrase expressing the same grammatical argument. For instance, in Serbian/Croatian we can say either (6a) with a full noun direct object or (6b) with a clitic object but not (6c), in which we try to combine both:

(6) a.   Ja   **sam**   video Jovana
       1SG.NOM AUX.1SG saw   Jovan.ACC
       'I saw Jovan'

    b.   Ja   **sam**   **go**   video
       1SG.NOM AUX.1SG 3SG.ACC saw
       'I saw him'

    c.   *Ja   **sam**   **go**   video Jovana
       1SG.NOM AUX.1SG 3SG.ACC saw   Jovan.ACC

We have to be careful here, however. An example such as (6c) is perfectly fine provided *Jovana* is separated from the rest of the clause intonationally, as a kind of afterthought. In this respect Serbian/Croatian is identical to, say, English. Thus, we cannot have an example like (7a) if the object noun *John* is pronounced in one intonational phrase with the rest of the sentence. This is true whether we pronounce the pronoun as a full form with secondary stress (i.e. as in [ˈsɔːˌhɪm]) or as a phonological (as in [ˈsɔːɪm]). Instead, we have to separate it, as indicated in writing by a comma (7b):

(7) a.   * I saw him John
    b.   I saw him, John

In Serbian/Croatian we have examples such as (6a) above with just a noun phrase direct object. In a language with pronominal agreement affixes such as Nahuatl such a construction would be ungrammatical (see Chapter 5). The pronominal affix is required by the agreement rules of the language. Another way of saying this is that clitic pronouns and full-form noun phrases are typically in complementary distribution, while pronominal agreement affixes signal a grammatical dependency between the verb form and the object noun phrase.

In many treatments of clitics these simple and well-known facts are taken to show that the clitic is actually a word and that it is represented in the syntactic structure just like any other word. From this it immediately follows that clitics and full-form noun phrases are in complementary distribution: a monotransitive verb cannot have more than one object, so that the Serbian/Croatian and English examples (6c) and (7a) are ungrammatical for the same reason that, say, *Mary saw John a photograph* is ungrammatical. In other words, there is no 'doubling' of the clitic pronominal by another NP, in contrast to the situation with agreement, where in the typical case the agreement morphology has to co-occur with the overt argument phrase (otherwise it would probably not be thought of as agreement). This was the reasoning behind the earliest treatments of pronominal clitics in generative grammar, and especially the treatment of French syntax in Kayne (1975). A brief survey of the relevant history is found in Spencer (1991, 384–90) and van Riemsdijk (1999). As a result, clitic pronominals have generally been analysed within Principles and Parameters syntax as just like full-form pronominals except for their unusual morphophonological properties.

Despite its initial appeal, a syntactic movement approach to the morphosyntax of clitics faces a number of serious problems. In point of fact, drawing a simple line between agreement (affixal) morphology and pronominal clitics is problematical in both directions: there are clitics that behave like standard agreement markers, and there are agreement systems that show some of the behaviour of clitic systems.

One important question is a long-standing debate concerning the supposed difference between agreement markers proper and so-called pronominal affixes. This debate is intimately connected to the existence or otherwise of generative grammar's 'PRO-drop parameter'. An extremely detailed and illuminating survey of the issues is provided in Corbett (2003), and important discussion is also found in Evans (2003) and Mithun (2003).

In some languages with subject agreement an overt subject is required even if the properties of that subject can be deduced from the agreement morphology. Thus, in German, 1st, 2nd and 3rd persons are distinguished in the singular by different agreement suffixes, yet a finite clause requires an overt subject, at the very least a pronoun, as seen in (8):

(8)   Conjugation of German verb HOLEN 'bring'

	Singular	Plural
1st	*(ich) hol-e	*(wir) hol-en
2nd	*(du) hol-st	*(ihr) hol-t
3rd	*(er/sie/es) hol-t	*(sie) hol-en

Scandinavian languages (Swedish, Norwegian, Danish) are similar to German.

In Russian, the situation is slightly more complex. It's very common for subjects and objects to be omitted in Russian, but only when it's possible to recover their referents from the context. Otherwise, pronouns have to be used, especially as subjects. If pronouns are used when the referent has already been mentioned this seems to have very little effect on the discourse structure. However, in the present tense it is usually possible to determine exactly the person and number properties of the subject, while in the past tense the number and gender properties of the subject are expressed, as shown in (9) (the symbol ′ after a consonant indicates palatalization):

(9)   Conjugation of Russian verb GOVORIT′ 'to speak'

Present tense		
	Singular	Plural
1st	(ja) govor′-u	(my) govor′-im
2nd	(ty) govor′-iš	(vy) govor′-ite
3rd	(on/ona/ono) govor′-it	(on′i) govor′-at

Past tense		
	Singular	Plural (all genders)
Masculine	govor′-i-l	
Feminine	govor′-i-l-a	govor′-i-l′-i
Neuter	govor′-i-l-o	

Russian is therefore not to be regarded properly as a PRO-drop language. Other languages that behave similarly include Latvian (a member of the Balto-Slavic family of Indo-European and therefore related to Russian) and Chukchee (completely unrelated to Russian).

In French a subject is also obligatory, though in that language there is less evidence of the grammatical properties of the subject in the verb morphology, especially in the spoken variety. In the present and imperfect tenses there are only three distinct forms: from *passer* /pase/ 'to pass' we have in the present tense /pas/ singular (all persons) and 3pl, /pasõ/ 1pl, /pase/ 2pl; in the imperfect we have /pasɛ/ singular (all persons) and 3pl, /pasjõ/ 1pl, /pasje/ 2pl, though in periphrastic tenses with the auxiliaries 'to be/have' we see greater differentiation, with five distinct person number forms. In English, there is no differentiation of person/number at all except for the 3sg of the present tense and then only for non-modal verbs (though the progressive aspect and passive voice distinguish three different forms in the present tense, of course, because they use the auxiliary BE). On the other hand, Spanish, Portuguese and Italian are regarded as PRO-drop languages (indeed, Italian was the first such language to be discussed in these terms).[2]

German and Russian (as well as English and French) are therefore to be regarded as obligatory subject languages (though the subject in German, as in French and English, is perhaps 'more' obligatory than that of Russian). This situation can be contrasted with the situation in other Slavic languages such as Polish, Czech, Serbian/Croatian or Bulgarian, in which we generally see null subjects rather than pronominal subjects and in which a pronoun generally bears emphasis if it appears in subject position. In the earlier generative literature, obligatory subject and null-subject languages were said to reflect different settings of a universal (innate) property, the PRO-drop parameter.[3]

The concentration on European languages is somewhat misleading, of course. Languages as diverse as Chinese, Japanese, Vietnamese and Thai (which belong to different families or even different phyla) have the same kind of discourse-sensitive null-subject/object constructions as Russian, yet these languages lack agreement morphology altogether. It's therefore a little puzzling why there was ever such a focus on languages such as Italian/Spanish/Polish with so-called 'rich agreement morphology' (whatever that means). Mindful of this point, Neeleman and Szendrői (2007) have argued that what characterizes subject and object PRO-drop languages is the morphological structure of the pronominals. In a language in which the subject/object or singular/plural pronominals are formed by agglutinative morphology, PRO-drop is possible, otherwise not. Thus, English is not a PRO-drop language because its pronominals are formed suppletively. They treat Russian as a PRO-drop language and argue that its pronominals are inflected by regular morphology. This is false, since Russian pronouns show a variety of unique idiosyncrasies in both their endings and their stem forms. But then Russian isn't really a PRO-drop language, so perhaps Russian isn't really a counterexample to their claims. On the other hand, Latin certainly was a (subject and object) PRO-drop language, and that language had very idiosyncratically formed personal pronouns. The Neeleman/Szendrői hypothesis is therefore false.

When we look at null-subject languages with 'rich agreement morphology' (i.e. ignoring the innumerable null-subject languages that lack agreement morphology), we observe a feature that acquired some importance for pre-generative structuralist linguists as well as for generative linguists: in null-subject languages the verb morphology that marks the subject effectively serves as the expression of the subject. For this reason descriptive linguists working on certain language groups referred to such morphology as a pronominal affix or an incorporated pronominal. Among languages that cross-reference direct or indirect objects morphologically we don't seem to find a corresponding obligatory object property, and so object marking almost always has the character of a pronominal affix. This way of looking at verb morphology brings with it certain entailments if the metaphor of the incorporated pronoun is taken to its logical conclusion: if a subject or object pronominal affix serves to express the subject or object of the verb, then that must mean that any overt pronoun or NP which apparently occupies the argument position must actually be some kind of adjunct. In other words, in a language in which *The girl kissed the boy* is expressed schematically as *The girl she-kissed-him the boy* then the phrases *the girl/the boy* cannot be the real subject/object of *kiss*, because those roles are expressed by the incorporated pronominals. In effect, we have a grammatical construction that in some respects is comparable to a dislocation structure of the kind *That girl, she kissed that boy*, or *She kissed him, that boy*.

This line of argument was pursued in an influential paper by Jelinek (1984). A typological extension of the idea was pursued by Baker (1996), who argued that such languages instantiate a Polysynthesis Parameter according to which they obey the property in (10) (Baker 1996, 14):

(10)   Polysynthesis Parameter
             Every argument of a head element must be related to a morpheme in the
             word containing that head.

Here, 'related to' means related by agreement or by incorporation. Baker's theory made a number of interesting predictions, which, however, seem not to be borne out universally.[4]

As Corbett (2003, 2006) points out in his discussion of pronominal affixes, it is somewhat counter-intuitive to say that Russian and French belong to one language type (by virtue of being obligatory subject languages and hence having true subject agreement suffixes) while Bulgarian belongs to an entirely different type, in which apparent subjects are really just adjuncts. Moreover, even when we consider languages that cross-reference core arguments with pronominal affixes, we find that there is a certain amount of variation in the morphosyntactic properties of the construction, depending on how closely the pronominal affix retains genuinely pronominal properties. Mithun (2003) provides a very interesting pair of case studies comparing and contrasting Yup'ik, an Eskimoan language, and the Athabaskan language Navajo. In Yup'ik the pronominal affixes retain the definiteness property normally associated with full-form pronouns. A pronominal affix may not cross-reference an indefinite object argument at all (though subject pronominal affixes can cross-reference indefinite subject NPs; Mithun 2003, 249). Either the clause is reconfigured in such a way as to obviate the need for reference to that object, or the object is 'demoted' to an oblique case adjunct and the verb acquires intransitive agreement morphology (what is sometimes called the 'antipassive construction', though Mithun herself does not describe the Yup'ik alternation in those terms):

(11)   Kitumek   tangellrua
         Kitu-mek   tangerr-llru-u-a
         someone-ABL see-PAST-INTR.INDIC-1SG
         'I saw somebody'

Navajo, on the other hand, does permit indefinite arguments, and they are cross-referenced in the same way (broadly speaking) as definite arguments. (Note that neither Yup'ik nor Navajo have a category of definiteness expressed on noun phrases.) The Yup'ik examples will be relevant when we consider clitic doubling in Bulgarian and Macedonian.

Nonetheless, the distinction between pronominal affixation and agreement still seems to be quite popular. We will follow Corbett in arguing that there is no good reason to draw such a categorial distinction (however useful it might occasionally be as a descriptive heuristic).

The status of null-subject/object languages and the nature of pronominal affixes is important for the study of clitics for this reason: a pronominal affix or incorporated pronominal is effectively a clitic masquerading as an affix. Therefore, if there are pronominal affixes then they should behave exactly like clitics with respect to crucial aspects of morphosyntax. In particular, the phrases that are 'doubled' by the pronominal affix should be adjuncts and not true arguments of the predicate. Similarly, any phrase doubled by a clitic should be an adjunct. In reality we observe a much more complex picture.

One problem is that agreement morphosyntax itself is much more complex than we have described. A useful survey of the possibilities is provided by Doron (1988). For instance, we find that there are languages in which agreement morphology is subject to restrictions making it similar to a clitic construction. For instance, in Breton, a Celtic language spoken in Northern France, the verb is marked for the number/person of the subject. But in non-negative clauses the verb fails to show number marking (that is, it defaults to the singular form) if there is an overt subject, either a full noun or a pronoun. Stump (1984, 292) refers to this as the Complementarity Principle. The pattern is shown for Breton in (12) (Borsley et al. 2007, 18; see also Anderson 1982):

(12) a.   Bremañ e   lennont   al levrioù
           now   PRT read.PRES.3PL the books
           'Now they are reading the books'
     b.   Bremañ e   lenn   ar vugale   al levrioù
           now   PRT read.PRES.3SG the children the books
           'Now the children are reading the books'
     c. * Bremañ e   lennont   ar vugale   al levrioù
           now   PRT read.PRES.3PL the children the books

In (12a) we see that a covert pronominal plural subject is expressed by the verb suffix *-ont*. In (12b) we see that an overt plural NP subject requires the (default) 3sg verb form, and a plural marked verb form is ungrammatical in such a construction (12c).

The Complementarity Principle is also seen in Irish, as in these examples from McCloskey and Hale (1984):

(13) a.   Chuirfinn   (*mé) isteach ar an phost sin
           put.COND.1SG (I)   in   on the job   that
           'I would apply for that job'
     b.   Chuirfeadh   sibh isteach ar an phost sin
           put.COND.3SG you in   on the job   that
           'You would apply for that job'
     c.   Chuirfeadh   Eoghan isteach ar an phost sin
           put.COND.3SG Owen   in   on the job   that
           'Owen would apply for that job'

Again, in (13a) we see that 1sg morphology on the verb is incompatible with the presence of an overt pronominal subject. Likewise, in (13b) the verb does not agree with the 2sg subject pronoun, rather it takes the default 3sg morphology found in (13c) when there is an overt 3rd person singular noun phrase.

In a model of morphosyntax such as that of transformational grammar it is natural to account for this complementarity by saying that the agreement suffix/pronominal affix is originally represented syntactically as a pronominal subject, and that it then gets incorporated into the verb by means of a movement transformation. Anderson (1982) and McCloskey and Hale (1984) explicitly provide analyses of Breton and Irish respectively in terms of incorporation of a pronominal element by the verb in the syntax. In other words, the only difference between the subject marking morphology in Breton/Irish and the object clitics of French are in the degree of morphological cohesion that these elements exhibit with respect to their 'host'.

However, the situation illustrated by the Celtic languages Breton and Irish is not universally found even within the rather small Celtic family. In Welsh, closely related to Breton, we see the same Complementarity Principle with respect to

overt noun phrases, except that the verb does agree for number when the subject
is a pronoun:

(14) a.   Cerddon   nhw adre
           walk.PAST.3PL they home
           'They walked home'
     b.   Cerddodd/*Cerddon   Aled a   Sara adre
           walk.PAST.3SG/walk.PAST.3PL Aled and Sara home
           'Aled and Sara walked home.' (Borsley et al. 2007, 17)

The same agreement pattern is found with inflecting prepositions. A number of
the commonest prepositions in Celtic languages take agreement suffixes cross-
referencing the complement of the preposition. A sample paradigm for the Welsh
preposition *am* 'about' is seen in (15) (Borsley et al. 2007, 17):

(15)   Paradigm for *am* 'about' in colloquial Welsh

	Singular	Plural
1st person	amdanaf i	amdanon ni
2nd person	amdanat ti	amdanoch chi
3rd person	amdano fe	amdanyn nhw

Borsley et al. point out that, again, an overt noun phrase doesn't trigger
agreement, while an overt pronoun does:

(16)   am/*amdanyn   myfyrwyr
        about/about.3PL the.students
        'about the students'

In other languages, agreement rules can be even more complex (see, for instance,
Doron's (1988) discussion of Hebrew and Chamorro).

   The Bantu languages provide particularly interesting examples of agreement
patterns. Typically, a Bantu verb marks the subject with an obligatory marker
(SM), but in some languages it is also possible to cross-reference the direct object
under a variety of discourse and semantic conditions that tend to differ from
one language to the next. An early discussion of this situation is Bresnan and
Mchombo's (1986, 1987) analysis of the object marker (OM) in Chicheŵa. The
basic word order in Chicheŵa is SVO, with the direct object obligatorily adjacent
to the verb, much as in English (there is no case marking in Bantu languages).
With this word order we generally do not find the OM on the verb. However,
when the OM does appear, any permutation of the original SVO order is now
possible. Bresnan and Mchombo apply a variety of tests to show that the object
in this case is actually a dislocated phrase, cross-referenced anaphorically by
the OM. This is comparable to English topicalized sentence constructions with
pleonastic pronoun, such as *That book, I read it yesterday*.

   Variation in object marking is discussed in some detail for some nineteen
Bantu languages by Marten et al. (2007). For instance, the OM is obligatory
in Swahili if the object is animate (Marten et al. 2007, 261):[5]

(17) a.   ni-li-mw-on-a   Juma
              SM.1SG-PAST-OM1-see-FV 1.Juma
              'I saw Juma'

      b.   * ni-li-on-a   Juma
              SM.1SG-PAST-see-FV 1.Juma

However, for Bemba, a sentence such as (17b) would be grammatical:

(18)   n-álì-món-à   Chìsàngá
              SM.1SG-PAST-see-FV 1.Chisanga
              'I saw Chisanga'

Marten et al. cite Bresnan and Moshi (1990), who point out that in Kivunjo Chaga the OM is obligatory with a pronoun:

(19)   n-á-í-kì-lyí-í-à   m-kà kyô
              FOC-SM1-PRES-OM7-eat-APPL-FV 1-wife 7.PRO
              'He/she is eating it for/on the wife'

The upshot of this wider perspective on agreement morphosyntax is that we cannot really take complementary distribution between clitic and overt NP argument to be diagnostic of syntactic movement. Even where we find this complementarity we could still be dealing with a species of agreement, and hence with inflectional morphology rather than a syntactically represented pronoun subject to syntactic movement.

Finally we turn to a phenomenon that we may call 'long-distance agreement', the morphological parallel to clitic climbing. A survey of various types is provided by Polinsky (2003), who points out that many of them probably reduce to more familiar types of syntactic construction such as Raising-to-Object (comparable to the English construction *We expected her [to leave early]*). However, in other cases we seem to be dealing with genuine long-distance effects in which a verb in a matrix clause agrees with a nominal in the subordinate clause. For instance, Polinsky and Potsdam (2001) provide a detailed analysis of long-distance agreement in the Daghestanian language Tsez, and Polinsky (2003) provides a detailed survey of the phenomenon in a variety of languages. Now, the agreement phenomena described for Tsez are rather different from the kind of phenomena we will see with clitics in the next section. However, there are at least two sets of phenomena that have been described in the literature that perhaps do parallel the behaviour of clitics, in that they involve exactly the same kinds of matrix predicates.

The first example is that of Hungarian subject agreement. Hungarian transitive verbs have two distinct sets of subject marker for 3rd person objects depending on whether the direct object is (broadly speaking) definite/specific or not. When the object is not definite, the subject agreements are exactly like those of intransitive verbs, but with definite objects we find the agreements of the so-called 'definite conjugation' (20), where 1st>2nd denotes a special form used for 1st person (singular or plural) acting on 2nd person (singular or plural):

(20)   Hungarian AD 'give', present tense

	indefinite conjugation	definite conjugation
1sg	látok	látom
2sg	látsz	látod
3sg	lát	látja
1pl	látunk	látjuk
2pl	láttok	látjátok
3pl	látnak	látják
1st>2nd		látlak

With a certain class of predicates, including a number of predicates generally treated as auxiliary verbs, the matrix verb takes the definite conjugation markers when its complement is a transitive verb with a definite object. These include *fog* 'future auxiliary', *szeret* 'like', *akar* 'want', *utál* 'hate' and others. Thus, we have examples such as (21) with the future auxiliary *fog*:

(21) a.   Ezt   a   könyvet   feltétlenül el   fog-om   olvas-ni
           this.ACC DET book.ACC definitely PREVERB FUT-1SG.DEF read-INF
           'I will definitely read this book'

   b.   Meg   fog-ok   tanul-ni   autót   vezetni
         PREVERB FUT-1SG.INDEF learn-INF car.ACC drive.INF
         'I will learn to drive a car'

   The second example is that of long-distance agreement in Chukchee, as discussed in Spencer (1991, 388), based on examples taken from Inenliqej and Nedjalkov (1967). In Chukchee finite verbs agree with both subjects and objects using a complex set of portmanteau prefixes and suffixes, whose exact form depends on the tense, mood and aspect of the verb as well as on the precise combination of person/number/grammatical relation properties. A number of verbs with phasal meanings ('begin/finish') and modal meanings ('be able/unable') take an infinitival clause complement. Chukchee is an ergative language, so an intransitive subject and a direct object appear in the absolutive case, while a transitive subject appears in the ergative case. In the case of some matrix predicates, when the infinitival complement is intransitive, the matrix verb takes intransitive agreements (agreeing solely with the subject), while when the infinitival complement is transitive, the matrix verb takes transitive agreements (infinitive forms in Chukchee are non-finite and hence show no agreement whatsoever). Inenliqej and Nedjalkov (1967, 256) cite the following examples:

(22) a.   ətlon   ləwawə-rkən   qut-ək
           s/he.ABS not.able-3SG.SUBJ stand-INF
           'S/he is unable to stand'

   b.   ənan   ləwawə-rkən-en   rəlqutet-ək orgoor
         s/he.ERG not.able-3SG.SUBJ>3SG.OBJ start   motor
         'S/he is unable to start the motor'

(23)   a.   cakəget   ləgaŋe-rkən   uwintet-ək
             sister.ABS not.manage-3SG.SUBJ light.fire-INF
             'Sister isn't managing to light a fire'

b.   caketta   ləgaŋe-rkənen   uwint-ək penjolgən
      sister.ERG not.manage-3SG.SUBJ>3SG.OBJ light   fire
      'Sister isn't managing to light the fire'

c.   ətlon   moo-gʔe   kelitku-k
      s/he.ABS began-3SG.SUBJ study-INF
      'S/he began to study'

d.   ənan   moo-nen   rəgjulew-ək ekək   iwini-k
      s/he.ERG began-3SG.SUBJ>3SG.OBJ teach-INF   son.ABS hunt-INF
      'S/he began to teach his son to hunt'

The verb rəlqutetək in (22b) is the causative of the verb qutək in (22a), while
the verb uwintetək 'light a fire' is an intransitive verb derived by suffixation
of -et to the transitive verb uwintək 'to light (a fire)'. Inenliqej and Nedjalkov
point out that the long-distance agreement effect is preserved across speakers
and under ellipsis:

(24) a.   əmto, kətepalgən təm-ən?
           So   ram.ABS   kill-2SG.SUBJ>3SG.OBJ
           'So, did you kill the ram?'

     b.   tə-lwaw-ən
           1SG.SUBJ-not.able-3SG.OBJ
           'I couldn't'

They list the following verbs as permitting long-distance agreement: gjuletək
'learn (to do)', qitpewək 'begin to do assiduously', ləwawək 'be unable',
ləgaŋek 'not succeed/manage to do', mgok, mook, ŋook 'begin', məcek 'forget
how to', ŋərkəlatək 'be embarrassed about doing',[6] plətkuk 'finish', tegjeŋək
'want', ʔelerek 'be bored doing'. They also mention a number of verbs which
alternate with the causative form in re- when their complement infinitival is
transitive:

(25) a.   ətlon   paa-gʔe   tipjejŋek
           S/he.ABS stop-3SG.SUBJ sing.INF
           'S/he stopped singing'

     b.   ənan   rə-paa-w-nen   jaak   irʔən
           s/he.ERG CAUSE-stop-CAUSE-3SG.SUBJ>3SG.OBJ wear.INF parka.ABS
           'S/he stopped wearing a parka'

(26) a.   ətlon   torəmgo-gʔe   kelitkuk
           s/he.ABS again.begin-3SG.SUBJ study.INF
           'S/he took up studying again'

     b.   ənan   rə-torəmgo-w-nen   rəgjulewək
           s/he.ERG CAUSE-again.begin-CAUSE-3SG.SUBJ>3SG.OBJ teach.INF
           ŋinqej
           child.ABS
           'S/he started to teach the child again'

Finally, for amusement, we mention a curious construction which translates as 'once (upon a time)'. This is formed from the expression *qol* 'once' + auxiliary verb, where the verb is either the intransitive ('be') auxiliary *itək* or the transitive ('have') auxiliary *rənək*.[7]

(27) a.   qol it-gʔi,   ətlon ekwet-gʔi   amnoŋetə
           once BE-3SG.SUBJ he.ABS went-3SG.SUBJ tundra.DAT
           'One day he set off for the tundra'
     b.   qol rən-nin,   ənan   təm-nen   rərkə
           once HAVE-3SG.SUBJ>3SG.OBJ he.ERG kill-3SG.SUBJ>3SG.OBJ walrus.ABS
           'Once, he killed a walrus'

6.4   Pronominal clitics

In this section we examine a number of aspects of the syntax of pronominal clitics, examining three topics that have all generated a good deal of debate amongst syntacticians. The first of these is that of subject clitics in the Romance languages, and in particular in the dialects of northern Italy. The second topic is that of clitic doubling, in which the clitic shows behaviour that aligns it with agreement morphology. The third topic is that of clitic climbing, in which the clitic (or clitic cluster) appears in a higher clause than the verb whose arguments the clitics realize. This behaviour is akin to that of the 'long-distance agreement'.

6.4.1   Subject clitics

In Section 2.5 we mentioned that a number of languages have subject clitics. In general, we should not be surprised to find that a language has subject clitics. However, the history of the development of the study of clitics within Derivational models of syntax originally skewed attention towards standard varieties of the Romance languages Italian and Spanish, and these lack subject clitics. Subsequent research within that paradigm noted that the dialects of northern Italy are unlike the standard language in having a rich variety of subject clitic types, and, moreover, different from the more familiar subject clitics of standard French (an important early reference here is Rizzi 1986). The Italian and the French types of subject clitic are all similar to the object clitics in Romance in the sense that they take a verb as host, whether an auxiliary verb or the lexical verb. In this respect they differ significantly from, say, the subject clitics of Luiseño, Lummi, Udi, Warlpiri, or many of the other languages with subject clitics. A useful survey of the Romance subject clitics within the context of a general approach to clitics can be found in Everett (1996, chapter 4).

A major survey of the literature on the northern Italian dialects is provided by Poletto (2000). Anderson (2005, 252–5) gives a very useful overview of her basic typology and Roberts (2010, 3–22) provides a very succinct and clear review of the rather complex issues arising from the northern Italian varieties (and including discussion of non-subject clitics), including a brief summary of Poletto's monograph. A useful survey of pronominals in the Italian dialects is provided by Vanelli and Renzi (1997) and by Poletto (1997). Poletto (2000) distinguishes four types of subject clitic on the basis of (i) their behaviour with respect to negation, (ii) their behaviour with coordinate phrases, and (iii) their behaviour with elements associated with the complementizer position, that is, subordinating conjunctions and wh-phrases. The first type is what she calls 'invariable' clitics because they fail to cross-reference any person/number features of the subject. As Anderson (2005, 252–3) observes, it's difficult to see why such elements should be labelled as 'subject clitics' rather than, say, discourse markers. Poletto's second class, the 'deictic' subject clitics, only distinguishes 3rd person and non-3rd person. These can co-occur with other subject clitics, so it's unclear again why these are not treated as discourse markers that happen to co-vary with 3rd/non-3rd person subjects. Poletto (2000, 23) cites Paola Benincà as making the observation that "the deictic clitics are found in sentences that convey new information or in exclamative contexts", and in particular, that they may signal that the whole utterance constitutes new information:

(28) a. **A**   piove!
          SUBJ.CL rains
          'Look, it's raining!'   [Padua]
     b. **E**   **vvu**   venite!
          SUBJ.CL   2PL.SUBJ.CL[8]   come

The other two classes of subject clitic are called 'person clitic' and 'number clitic'. The person clitic is typologically rather unusual: in the dialects that have it, it takes the form *t* and cross-references just 2sg subjects. In some dialects a further form is found, *l* for 3sg subjects. The fourth type, 'number clitic', also realizes an unusual ensemble of properties. The clitic takes the forms *la, (l)i, le*, realizing respectively 3sg feminine, 3pl masculine and 3pl feminine.

Poletto notes that the type 1 and 2 subject clitics (what she calls the 'vocalic clitics') are always first in the cluster, but those in types 3 and 4 ('person clitic' and 'number clitic') come after the negation element if present. Placement with respect to coordinated phrases is the next test. Poletto examines three types of coordination. type 1 is coordination of full verb phrases, type 2 is coordination of just two distinct verbs taking a shared complement/object, and type 3 is coordination of two verb forms related inflectionally or by derivation. These are illustrated in (29) for standard Italian:

(29) a. Mangio patate   e   bevo caffé
          eat   potatoes and drink coffee
          'I eat potatoes and drink coffee' [VP coordination, 'Type 1']
     b. Uso e   sciupo sempre troppa   acqua
          use and waste always too.much water
          'I always use and waste too much water' [V coordination, 'Type 2']

    c.   Leggo e   rileggo sempre lo   stesso libro
                read   and reread always the same book
                'I'm always reading and rereading the same book' [Same-V coordination,
                    'Type 3']
    d.   Leggo e   leggerò sempre lo   stesso libro
                read   and will.read always the same book
                'I read and will always read the same book' [Same-V coordination, 'Type 3']

The 'number' and 'person' subject clitics fail to scope over coordinated VPs (Poletto 2000, 27):

(30)   *La   magna patate   e   beve   vin
                SUBJ.CL eats   potatoes and drinks wine
                (Intended: 'She eats potatoes and drinks wine') [Venice]

In this respect they differ from subject clitics in French, as shown by the example cited by Poletto (2000, 16) from Kayne (1975):

(31)   Il mangera de la viande et   boira   du   bon vin
                he will.eat of the meat   and will.drink of.the good wine
                'He will eat some meat and drink some good wine' [Standard French]

Poletto states that the same is true of coordination over single verbs (Type 2 coordination). With Type 3 coordination, in which two forms of the same verb are coordinated, we see a contrast in the behaviour of the two types: 'number' clitics can take wide scope (34) while 'person' clitics have to be repeated on each conjunct (32):

(32) a.   * **Ti**   lesi e   rilesi sempre el   stesso libro
                SUBJ.CL read and reread always the same book
    b.   **Ti**   lesi e   **ti**   rilesi sempre el   stesso libro
                SUBJ.CL read and SUBJ.CL reread always the same book
                'You always read and reread the same book' [Venice]

(33) a.   * Nisun **l'ha**   e   avarà   vist la Maria ...
                nobody SUBJ.CL.has and will.have seen the Maria
    b.   Nisun **l'ha**   e   **l'avarà**   vist la Maria ...
                nobody SUBJ.CL.has and SUBJ.CL.will.have seen the Maria
                'Nobody has seen and will see Maria ...' [Cornuda (northern Veneto)]

(34)   **La**   lese e   rilese sempre el   stesso libro
                SUBJ.CL reads and rereads always the same book
                'She always reads and rereads the same book' [Venice]

However, in Paduan the 'person' clitic can take wide scope:

(35)   **Te**   lesi e   rilesi sempre el   stesso libro
                SUBJ.CL read and reread always the same book
                'You always read and reread the same book' [Padua]

Placement with respect to the complementizer (usually *che* 'that') is the final test. Again, the 'vocalic clitics', the invariable and the deictic type 'interact' with certain complementizers. For instance, they may be compatible or incompatible with certain sorts of wh-item. The Type 3 and 4 clitics don't interact with complementizers.

Poletto's syntactic framework makes it necessary for her to provide structural positions in a syntactic representation such that dominance corresponds to left-to-right linear order (broadly speaking). For this reason, her principal focus is on word order and on which elements in the sentence appear to be adjacent. However, much of the material she reports could equally well be studied profitably by students of discourse markers and conversational particles (whether or not from the perspective of clitic systems), since that is what her 'invariable' and 'deictic subject' clitics appear to be.

Poletto (2000, chapter 4) also discusses Rhaetoromance (Romansh), one of the four official languages of Switzerland. This language has retained much of the verb-second syntax of earlier stages of the Romance languages and this interacts in complex ways with the appearance and placement of subject clitics. Romansh is also examined by Anderson (2005, 204–12), who discusses the Surmiran variety in some detail. Romansh is not a null-subject ('pro-drop') language and its basic word order is SVO. However, there are certain constructions in which the subject follows the verb, for instance, when an object or adverb is topicalized and appears in initial position. Optionally, the subject in such inversion constructions can be doubled by a subject pronominal encliticized to the verb, giving rise to a mildly emphatic variant. When the verb bears such a clitic subject the overt subject noun phrase can be elided, but in no other circumstances. At first blush this sounds like a description of non-canonical agreement. Anderson (2005, 250–1) outlines a number of ways in which the subject clitics differ from agreement markers. For instance, the subject clitics are not compatible with non-referential subject noun phrases, such as the negative pronouns *nign* 'none, no-one'. In addition, the 2sg clitic =*t* fails to trigger a lexical phonological alternation of [s] with [ʃ], suggesting that the =*t* element is not a true affix. Finally, recall that the clitics are optional.

6.4.2   Clitic doubling

The agreement affix vs clitic contrast fails in the other direction, too. There are elements that are generally referred to as clitics and which have many of the properties of the familiar pronominal clitics of French, Spanish or Italian but which permit doubling. In the case of some languages, an overt NP argument may optionally be doubled by a clitic (usually depending on factors such as animacy, specificity or information structure) while in other cases an overt NP argument is obligatorily doubled by a clitic. Working within the earlier generative framework, Jaeggli (1982), Jaeggli (1986) provided examples of this phenomenon from South American varieties of Spanish, where it is more common than in Castilian. De Bruyne (1995, 161) provides the examples in (36):

(36)   Díga=**le**   usted al   señor Yarza que ...
        tell=3SG.M you to.the Mr. Yarza that
        'Tell Señor Yarza that ...'

        Escribo   para avisar=**les** a los amigos que ...
        I.am.writing to   tell=3PL   to the friends that ...
        'I am writing to tell my friends that ...' [Standard Spanish]

However, in a number of languages of the Balkans we find that pronominal elements, which are in many respects just like the pronominal clitics of (Western) Romance languages, are freely permitted or even required as doubles to overt arguments. An extremely clear description of the relevant facts as they relate to Bulgarian, Macedonian and Albanian is presented by Friedman (1994). Much like their Romance counterparts, the pronominal clitics of Macedonian and Albanian cluster around the finite verb or auxiliary, or around the non-finite verb form if there is no finite auxiliary. As we have seen (Section 3.3), the pronominal clitics of Bulgarian enter into a cluster that includes auxiliaries and other elements and which exhibits traces of the Tobler–Mussafia Law. In (37) and (38) we see examples from Macedonian and Albanian (notice that the Albanian clitic *ia* is a portmanteau of dative and accusative clitics):

(37)   Na momče-to **mu**   **ja**   davam   kniga-ta
        to boy-DEF   3SG.DAT.M 3SG.ACC.F give.1SG.PRES book(F)-DEF
        'I give the book to the boy' [Macedonian]

(38)   Djalit   **ia**   jap   librin
        boy.DEF.DAT 3SG.DAT/3SG.ACC give.1SG-PRES book.DEF-ACC
        'I give the boy the book' [Albanian]

Friedman additionally contrasts the behaviour of the otherwise very similar constructions in Albanian and Macedonian. The standard story is that direct objects require doubling if and only if they are definite, while indirect objects (marked by the preposition *na* in Macedonian and by the dative case in Albanian) require doubling whatever their definiteness status. However, Friedman points out that actually, in ordinary speech, the notion of specificity is important.

  Now, a definite marked phrase, broadly speaking, is one in which the referent is either unique (inclusiveness reading) or uniquely identifiable (identifiablity reading) or both (for a wide-ranging review of the nature of definiteness, see Lyons 1999). An indefinite noun phrase, by contrast, bears neither of these properties. In the case of a true indefinite the referent of the noun phrase is actually unidentifiable. This is seen with so-called intensional verbs such as 'look for'. In the sentence *Harriet is looking for a Vietnamese translation of 'Oliver Twist'* there is no guarantee that such a translation exists, so the phrase *a Vietnamese translation of 'Oliver Twist'* is a true indefinite. On the other hand, in *Harriet is looking for a copy of 'Oliver Twist', which she thinks she left in the library*, the indefinite phrase *a copy of 'Oliver Twist'* refers to a specific book (namely her lost copy). This is therefore a specific indefinite. In such a case, in English we can often replace the indefinite article with the definite article.

In (39) we see a Macedonian sentence with an indefinite direct object *edna marka* (the numeral *edna* 'one' in Bulgarian and Macedonian is often used with a weakened meaning as, effectively, an indefinite article) that lacks a doubling clitic because the direct object is a true indefinite:

(39)   Barav edna marka no ne   najdov
              search one   stamp but NEG find
              'I was looking for a stamp but didn't find one' (true indefinite) [Macedonian]

In (40), by contrast, the indefinite is specific and so clitic doubling is obligatory:

(40)   **Ja**   barav edna marka no ne   **ja**   najdov
              3SG.F search one   stamp but NEG 3SG.F find
              'I was looking for a (specific) stamp but didn't find it' (specific indefinite) [Macedonian]

In (41) we see that in Albanian the specific indefinite *unë një cigarë* (marked by both the numeral *unë* and the indefinite article *një*) requires a doubling clitic, just as in Macedonian:

(41)   Atëherë po   **e**   dredh unë një   cigarë
              then   PROG 3SG roll   one INDEF cigarette
              'Then I'm rolling a cigarette, too' [Albanian]

In the light of the Bantu examples cited a little earlier in this chapter, it's intriguing to note that Friedman cites Buchholz and Fiedler (1987, 443) as saying that doubling of a definite direct object in Albanian is actually optional if the clause has the canonical SVO word order (42a) "especially if there is lexical emphasis on that object as in [(43a)]" (Friedman 1994, 96), though with indirect objects the doubling is obligatory (44a). In standard Macedonian, by contrast, doubling is obligatory in all cases where the object is definite (see (42b), (43b), (44b)):

(42) a.   Agimi   **po**   Ø/**e** vështron   hënën
              Agim.DEF PROG Ø/it watch.3SG.PRES moon.ACC.DEF
              'Agim is watching the moon' [Albanian]
     b.   Zoran *Ø/**ja** gleda   mesečina-ta
              Zoran Ø/it   watches moon-DEF
              'Zoran is watching the moon' [Macedonian]

(43) a.   Në mbledhje   Ø/**e**   kritikuan   sidomos   drejtorin
              At the.meeting Ø/him criticized-3PL.AOR especially director-ACC.DEF
              'At the meeting they especially criticized the director' [Albanian]
     b.   Na sostanokot *Ø/**go** kritikuvaa   osobeno   direktor-ot
              at   the.meeting Ø/him criticized.3PL.IMPF especially director-DEF
              'At the meeting they especially criticized the director' [Macedonian]

(44) a.   Çfaqja   *Ø/i pëlqeu   Agimit
           the.show Ø/him pleased.3SG.AOR Agim.DAT.DEF
           'The show pleased Agim (= Agim liked the show)' [Albanian]
     b.   Pretstavata *Ø/mu se   bendisa na Zoran
           the.show   Ø/him INTRANS please to Zoran
           'The show pleased Zoran (= Zoran liked the show)' [Macedonian]

Friedman also points out that clauses can trigger clitic doubling in Albanian, though not in Macedonian.

The situation with Bulgarian is somewhat different from that found in Macedonian and Albanian (even though Bulgarian and Macedonian are mutually intelligible for the most part). Clitic doubling is essentially optional for direct and indirect objects, and seems to depend on poorly understood discourse factors. A detailed summary of the factors affecting doubling in Bulgarian and Macedonian is provided by Franks and King (2000, chapter 7). They argue that the crucial factors required for doubling are specificity of the complement (for Macedonian) and specificity together with topicality for Bulgarian. A fortiori a definite noun phrase is also specific. Following Rudin (1997) they note that a fronted phrase is topicalized in Bulgarian, while a phrase that receives sentence accent and is placed in immediately preverbal position is focussed. Thus, in (45a) the indirect object phrase *na Ivan* and the direct object *knigata* are both topics and both definite (Franks and King 2000, 252). In this position the two phrases require clitic doubling, as can be seen from the ungrammatical examples (45b, c), which lack one or other of the clitics:

(45) a.   Na Ivan knigata   az **mu**   **ja**   dadox
             to Ivan the.book(F) I   3SG.M.DAT 3SG.F.ACC gave
             'I gave the book to Ivan' [Bulgarian]
     b.   * Na Ivan knigata   az **mu**   dadox
             to Ivan the.book(F) I   3SG.M.DAT gave
     c.   * Na Ivan knigata   az **ja**   dadox
             to Ivan the.book(F) I   3SG.F.ACC gave

However, in (46a) the direct object is in preverbal position and bears sentence accent (visualized as capitalization), and so it is focussed. This means it cannot be doubled by a clitic. Moreover, the indirect object is no longer in the position of a topic and so that, too, cannot license a clitic:

(46) a.   KNIGATA dadox na Ivan, a   ne ...
             the.book   I.gave to Ivan and not ...
             'It was the book I gave to Ivan, and not ...' [Bulgarian]
     b.   * KNIGATA mu   **ja**   dadox na Ivan, a   ne ...
             the.book   3SG.M.DAT 3SG.F.ACC I.gave to Ivan and not ...
     c.   * KNIGATA **ja**   dadox na Ivan, a   ne ...
             the.book   3SG.F.ACC I.gave to Ivan and not ...
     d.   * KNIGATA **mu**   dadox na Ivan, a   ne ...
             the.book   3SG.M.DAT I.gave to Ivan and not ...

What we see in Albanian, Bulgarian and Macedonian is a patterning of variation that is typical for agreement morphosyntax. Such micro-variation is simply not to be expected if we were dealing with the syntactic distribution of true pronouns, and it defies sensible description in terms of a maximally general model of syntax. The conclusion is that the pronominal clitics in these languages have acquired essentially the properties of agreement markers, even though they may not yet be fully integrated into morphological structure as typical affixes.

Slavkov points to examples such as (47a), which, he claims, show the properties of a double object construction (reflected in the translation), in contrast to (47b), which has a single object and a prepositional phrase complement:

(47) a.   Ivan ì   izprati pismo na Marija
           Ivan 3.F.SG.DAT sent   letter to Maria
           'Ivan sent Maria a letter'
    b.   Ivan izprati pismo na Marija
           Ivan sent   letter to Maria
           'Ivan sent a letter to Maria' [Bulgarian]

Outside of the South Slavic languages it is not uncommon to find clitic doubling morphosyntax. A well-known case is that of a group of Pama-Nyungan Australian languages exemplified by Warlpiri, discussed in Section 3.4. Recall that in these languages clauses typically have completely free word order, except that there is usually an auxiliary element which almost always appears in second position. This auxiliary element generally realizes features of finiteness or mood, but typically it forms a clitic cluster along with pronominal clitic elements cross-referencing subjects, objects and sometimes noun phrases bearing other grammatical relations. Now, the pronominal clitics, expressing separately person/case in some positions and number in others, are, in fact, obligatory double overt noun phrase arguments (including full-form pronouns), as discussed in detail by Simpson (1991, 148–52). A telling example is (48):

(48)   Ngaju-rna wangkaja
        I-1SG.SUBJ spoke
        'I spoke'

Example (48) illustrates two things. First, there is no overt auxiliary base to which the 1SG.SUBJ clitic -*rna* can cliticize, so it cliticizes to the first word of the clause, showing that we are dealing with a (promiscuous) clitic and not a true affix. Second, the clitic doubles the very element it attaches to, which itself is a pronoun.

However, in part the presence of clitic doubling in Warlpiri is obscured by the fact that full-form pronouns are only used for emphasis, and by the fact that 3rd person clitic pronominals are null. It is therefore very interesting to note a further type of clitic doubling in a Slavic language which is not normally associated with doubling, Slovene.

Marušič and Žaucer (2010 a, b) describe a very interesting type of clitic doubling in the Gorica variety of Slovene. The authors demonstrate that it is clitic doubling that is at stake and not some form of dislocation. The facts are interesting for several reasons. First, clitic doubling is possible only when the overt argument is a pronominal (49).

(49) a.   Js **se** **ga**   njega   spomnem še   iz   šole
              I   REFL him.ACC him.ACC remember already from school
              'I remember him already from school'

      b.   * Js **se** **ga**   Petra   spomnem še   iz   šole
              I   REFL him.ACC Peter.ACC remember already from school
              (Intended: 'I remember Peter already from school' <gloss corrected>)

Second, any pronominal form, in any case/number/person, can get doubled (the accent on the pronominal forms *nám*, *vám* in (51) is to indicate that they are the stressed full forms):

(50) a.   **Mi**   lahko   daste   kar   meni?
              Me.DAT possible give.2.PL PTCL me.DAT
              'Can you give it to me?'

      b.   Ma kaj tebe   **te**   ne zanima, kako bo   šlo koncat?
              but Q   you.GEN you.GEN not interest how   will go end
              'Don't you want to know how it will end?'

      c.   Js   **bi**   **ga**   njega   peljala domov prej
              I.NOM would him.ACC him.ACC drive   home   first
              'I would first take him home'

(51) a.   Peter **nam**   nám   ni   tou   prnest neč   za pit
              Peter us.DAT us.DAT not-is want bring   nothing for drink
              'Peter didn't want to bring us anything to drink'

      b.   Tko da   **vam**   ni   treba vám   skrbet.
              so   COMP you.DAT not-is need you.DAT care
              'So that you don't have to worry about this'

      c.   Lahko   **jih**   pa   njih   vpraša
              possible them.ACC PTCL them.ACC ask
              'He can ask them'

It even appears that it is possible to have two doubled pronouns in one clause:

(52)   Meni   **mi**   **ga**   njega   niso teli predstavit
              Me.DAT me.DAT him.ACC him.ACC not   want introduce
              'They didn't want to introduce him to me'

This patterning is unusual, in the sense that doubling normally doesn't distinguish between pronominal arguments and full-form NP arguments.

    The other point of interest about Gorica Slovene clitic doubling is that the clitics are clearly Wackernagel clitics; compare (53) with (54):

(53) a.   Js   **se**   **ga**   njega   dobro spomnim še iz   šole
              I.NOM REFL him.ACC him.ACC well   remember still from school
              'I remember him well already from school'

b.   Lahko **jih**   pa   njih   vpraša
     possible them.ACC PTCL them.ACC ask
     'He can ask them'

c.   Zato   **me**   mene   to   moti
     because me.ACC me.ACC this bothers
     'That is why this bothers me'

d.   Kdo **me**   **je**   mene   udaru?
     who me.ACC AUX me.ACC hit
     'Who hit me?'

(54) a.   * Js   njega   dobro **se**   **ga**   spomnim še iz   šole
            I.NOM him.ACC well   REFL him.ACC remember still from school
            (Intended: 'I remember him well already from school')

      b.   * Js   dobro **se**   **ga**   njega   spomnim še iz   šole
            I.NOM well   REFL him.ACC him.ACC remember still from school
            (Intended: 'I remember him well already from school')

      c.   * Zato   mene   to zelo **me**   moti
            because me.ACC this very me.ACC bothers
            (Intended: 'That is why this bothers me a lot')

From these examples we can see that Gorica Slovene is similar to Australian
languages such as Warlpiri which have doubling Wackernagel clitics, except
that the clitic doubling construction in Gorica Slovene is limited to pronominal
arguments. Thus, Gorica Slovene represents the Wackernagel clitic equivalent of
Welsh subject agreement.[9]

   Finally, we look at clitic doubling in Yagua, which we saw earlier in Chapter 3
in connection with 'ditropic' clitic placement. Yagua has two sets of cross-
referencing markers referred to as 'clitics' in the literature, one set for subjects,
possessors and objects of postpositions and the other set for direct objects of
verbs. The subject/possessor/postposition markers are more tightly bound morphophonologically than the object markers, and generally behave as affixes.
For instance, when there is no overt subject expressed, the subject marker is
obligatory on the verb. However, the object markers behave more like typical
clitics.

   Everett (1996, 100–5) provides a conveniently succinct summary of the basic
facts of Yagua clitic doubling. He notes that intransitive clauses show the
word order VS if and only if the subject is doubled, otherwise we see the
order SV:

(55) a.   SV, subject not doubled
           Pauro$_i$ púúchu-níí$_j$
           Paul   carry-3SG.OBJ
           'Paul carries her'

      b.   VS, subject doubled
           sa$_i$-púúchu   Pauro$_i$-níí$_j$
           3SG.SUBJ-carry Paul-3SG.OBJ
           'Paul carries her'

    c.   VS, subject not doubled
           *púúchu Pauro$_i$-níí$_j$
            carry   Paul-3SG.OBJ
    d.   SV, subject doubled
           *Pauro$_i$ sa$_i$-púúchu-níí$_j$
            Paul   3SG.SUBJ-carry-3SG.OBJ

Similarly, a possessor NP is doubled by a cross-referencing proclitic on the possessed noun, otherwise we find the order possessor + possessed without doubling. (Postpositions likewise are marked with a proclitic from the same set as that used for verbs and possessor marking.)

    With all clitics, proclitic or enclitic, the host must immediately precede the double. With the enclitic object markers this entails the ditropic property: the host of the direct object is necessarily a word of a different category from the direct object noun phrase itself. Thus, while the marker is attached to the verb in (55a), in (55b) and (56) it is attached to the subject noun phrase:

(56) a.   Rospita suuta-**níí**$_j$ Anita$_j$
          Rospita washes-3SG.OBJ Anita
          'Rospita washes Anita'
    b.   **sa**$_i$-suuta   Rospita$_i$-**níí**$_j$ Anita$_j$
          3SG.SUBJ-washes Rospita-3SG.OBJ Anita
          'Rospita washes Anita'

    Payne and Payne (1990, 255) provide further examples to illustrate this patterning:

(57) a.   siimyiñíí   quiivạ
          sa-jimyiy-**níí** quiivạ
          3SG-eat-3SG fish
          'He is eating the fish'
    b.   siimyiy   Alchíconíí   quiivạ
          sa-jimyiy Alchíco-**níí**   quiivạ
          3SG-eat   Alchico-3SG fish
          'Alchico is eating the fish'
    c.   siimyiy   sinumuníí   quiivạ
          sa-jimyiy sinu-mu-**níí**   quiivạ
          3SG-eat   land-LOC-3SG fish
          'He is eating the fish on land'
(58)   quiivạ siimyiy   Alchíco
        quiivạ **sa**-jimyiy Alchíco
        fish   3SG-eat   Alchico
        'Alchico is eating (the) fish'

    The verb *sạạy* 'give' is ditransitive, and both or either of its objects can be doubled by a clitic. This is illustrated in (59) Payne and Payne 1990, 256:

(59) a.   **sa**-sạạy Alchíco pạ́ạ-**níí**   sa-dee-tu
          3SG-give Alchíco bread-3SG 3SG-child-FEM
          'Alchico gives bread to his daughter'

b. **sa**-sąąy Alchíco-rà páą-**níí**   sa-dee-tu
3SG-give Alchíco-INAN bread-3SG 3SG-child-FEM
'Alchico gives the bread to his daughter'

c. **sa**-sąąy Alchíco-**níí** sa-dee-tu-rà   páą
3SG-give Alchíco-3SG 3SG-child-FEM-INAN bread
'Alchico gives his daughter the bread'

d. **sa**-sąąy Alchíco-**níí** sa-dee-tu-níí
3SG-give Alchíco-3SG 3SG-child-FEM-3SG
'Alchico gives his₍ⱼ₎ daughter to him₍ₖ₎'

(60) a. siimyaasiy-níí Moquɨɨ sųųsíyų
siiy-maasiy-**níí** Moquɨɨ **sa**-jųsiy-jų̀
run.go.out-3SG Moquɨɨ 3SG-behind-ADLAT
'Moquɨɨ runs out behind him'

b. siimyaasiy sųųsíyųníí
siiy-maasiy **sa**-jųsiy-jų̀-**níí**
run.go.out 3SG-behind-ADLAT-3SG
'He runs out behind him'

It is possible for a word to host more than one object clitic. Yagua has a productive causative suffix *-tániy* which can derive ditransitive verbs from monotransitives (Payne and Payne 1990, 284–7):

(61) a. ráchuutatánñíí   Anítara   sújay
ray-suuta-tániy-**níí**   Aaníta-**rà** sújay
1SG-wash-CAUSE-3SG Anita-INAN cloth
'I make Anita wash (the) clothes'

b. siimyityánñííra
sa-jimyiy-taniy-**níí**-**rà**
3SG-eat-CAUSE-3SG-INAN
'S/he makes him/her eat it'

Payne and Payne (1990, 299–308) describe the pragmatic effects of different types of clause structure, including those with clitic doubling. Essentially, clitic doubling gives a definite/given information reading to an object phrase, whilst bare noun phrases refer to new information and/or indefinites. Cross-linguistically, this is a common pattern, both with clitic doubling constructions and with affixal agreement patterns, as we have already seen in reference to the work of Bresnan and Mchombo (1986).

Yagua thus provides a good example of a pronominal cross-referencing system whose morphosyntax is to some extent independent of the clitic–affix distinction. As Everett (1996) argues, such systems undermine attempts at drawing a clear distinction between affixal morphosyntax which realizes agreement relations and pronominal clitic systems which realize pronominal forms of verb arguments. As we have seen repeatedly in this chapter, we can easily find affixal agreement systems with properties reminiscent of pronominal systems and clitic pronominal systems that are, for all intents and purposes, agreement systems.

6.4.3   Clitic climbing

The basic phenomenon

The term clitic climbing refers to constructions in which the clitic is associated with a verb complex in a subordinate clause but is actually pronounced in construction with a higher predicate (for instance, the matrix verb which selects that subordinate clause), even though it may have no obvious semantic or syntactic connection to that verb. A popular way of thinking about such constructions is to regard the two predicates as forming a single, complex predicate at some level of representation. Now, complex predicate formation of this kind is very frequently found in the case of causative constructions and related phenomena. A verb of causation, permission, coercion or whatever together with its complement will often display some of the syntactic properties of a single clause rather than a matrix clause + subordinate clause. This phenomenon is often referred to as 'clause union', following the analysis given within the framework of Relational Grammar in Aissen (1974).[10]

A simple illustration of clause union is provided by reflexive pronouns. In most languages a reflexive pronoun such as *himself/herself/itself* can only refer back to the subject of the clause in which the pronoun is found. This is often known as the 'clause mate condition'. This is not generally true of ordinary, non-reflexive personal pronouns. For instance, *himself* in (62a) can only refer to *lion*, while *him* in (62b) has to refer to some other unnamed participant, and cannot take *lion* as its antecedent:

(62) a.   The lion_i tickled himself_i
      b.   The lion_i tickled him_{*i}

On the other hand in (63) the reflexive has to refer to the hyena and can't refer to the lion.

(63)   The lion_i made the hyena_j tickle $\text{himself}_{*i,j}$

This is because [*the hyena tickle himself*] is a subordinate clause dependent on the matrix verb *made*, and *hyena* is the subject of that clause and hence is the only possible antecedent for the reflexive pronoun.

There is a very considerable literature on causative constructions and their kindred. One clear conclusion is that causative constructions can behave like single predicates (indeed, can be single word forms) in phrasal syntax yet behave as though they were two clauses with respect to grammatical processes such as reflexivization. This is found with a number of Bantu languages, such as ChiMwi:ni, for instance. At the same time, in other languages a causative may appear to consist of two clauses in the phrasal syntax and yet behave as though it were monoclausal with respect to processes targeting grammatical relations. The causatives of the Romance languages based on reflexes of the Latin FACERE 'do, make' are of this kind. A particularly elegant illustration of the separability of phrasal syntax and grammatical relations is provided by Butt's (1995) analysis of complex predicates in Urdu.[11]

When the subordinate clause verb takes a clitic pronominal object, we might observe the alternation or process known as clitic climbing, in which the object of the subordinate clause verb is expressed on the matrix verb:

(64) a.   The lion made [the hyena tickle=him] ⇒
    b.   The lion made=him [the hyena tickle]

In these two schematic representations both sentences are intended to mean *The lion made the hyena tickle him*, where the pronoun refers to some third party. It isn't just causatives that create complex predicates. We often find that clitic climbing is triggered by essentially the same kinds of predicates that are associated with long-distance agreement. For instance, we might see constructions of the type (65) with a verb corresponding to 'want', where the examples correspond to the English *Tom wanted to give it to Fido*:

(65) a.   Tom want [give it Fido] ⇒
    b.   Tom it=want [give Fido]

Example (65b) is intended to be synonymous with (65a). In (66b) we see a real Italian example (essentially following Monachesi 1999, 135f.):

(66) a.   Martina vuole leggere il   libro
          Martina wants read.INF the book
          'Martina wants to read the book'
    b.   Martina **lo**=vuole   leggere
          Martina it.CL=wants read.INF
          'Martina wants to read it (e.g. the book)'
    c.   Martina **lo**=[ComplexPred vuole leggere]

In (66) the clitic *lo* is the argument of the lower predicate *leggere* 'read', but its host is the higher predicate *vuole* 'wants'.

There are several different kinds of construction in which clitics appear to 'climb' out of the domain of the lexical verb. The first, and perhaps the least interesting, is found with constructions consisting of a finite auxiliary verb in construction with a non-finite lexical verb. Here we regularly find that the clitic cluster is associated with the finite auxiliary, as in the French examples (67):

(67) a.   Je **le**= **lui**=   montre quelque fois
          I it to.him show   several times
          'I show it to him several times'
    b.   Je **le**= **lui**= ai   déjà   montré
          I it   to.him have already shown
          'I have already shown it to him'

Notice that the finite auxiliary form *ai* can be separated from the verb by an adverb *déjà*. This shows that the auxiliary and the verb are distinct syntactic terminals (words) and the auxiliary *ai* is not itself a clitic or affixal tense/aspect marker. In some grammatical models the auxiliary might be said to form its own clausal domain, in which case we have a case of raising out of a lower clause.

However, there is no need to treat auxiliaries as matrix raising verbs in this way. Nonetheless, examples such as (67b) show that the clitics are not forced to be associated with lexical verbs in the way that pronominal affixes generally are.

In many languages the climbing phenomenon extends to other classes of verbs that don't have the special morphosyntax characteristic of auxiliary verbs. These are generally the same sort of verb classes that give rise to the long-distance agreement phenomena discussed in Section 6.3, specifically (adapted from Monachesi 1999, 136 and Monachesi 2005, 222, based on Rizzi 1982b, 4–5):

- modal verbs
- phasal/aspectual verbs
- motion verbs
- causative verbs[12]

These are all verb types that are associated with grammaticalization processes, and which often become morphologized. 'Modal verb' refers to a semantically heterogeneous class of verbs with meanings such as possibility/probability/necessity, obligation/prohibition, physical (in)ability, apparent truth (*seem*), desire. Phasal/aspectual verbs are those predicates that specify features of the time course of an event, such as beginning/ending, continuing, iterating/repeating and so on. Causative verbs include direct causation (such as causing a plant to die by cutting it down), indirect causation (such as causing a plant to die by forgetting to water it), giving explicit permission (*I let the cat in by unlocking its catflap*), permitting by default (that is, by failing to prohibit: *I (accidentally) let the cat in by leaving the door open*), persuading/cajoling/ordering and so on. Motion verbs, which often give rise to serial verb constructions, include notions such as come, go, return. Typically, the complex predicate formation is not driven purely by semantics, in the sense that near-synonymous verbs may differ in their ability to give rise to Restructuring. Thus, the Italian verb *volere* 'want' is a Restructuring verb, but not *desidere* 'desire'.

Languages differ as to whether clitic climbing is an obligatory phenomenon or an optional one, and if optional whether there are tangible differences between the two constructions.[13] In Italian, for instance, in addition to (66b), repeated here as (68a), we can also have (68b):[14]

(68) a.   Martina **lo**=vuole   leggere
           Martina it.CL=wants read.INF
     b.   Martina vuole legger=**lo**
           Martina wants read.INF=it.CL
           'Martina wants to read it'

Maiden and Robustelli (2000, 100) report that there is "no clearly identifiable difference in meaning" between the two constructions. They also note that the construction is sometimes obligatory. Italian verbs take one of two auxiliaries to form the perfect series of tenses, AVERE 'have' (as in English) and ESSERE 'be'. The 'have' auxiliary is generally used for transitive verbs and the 'be' for intransitives, but this depends in part on semantic factors. The point is that there is a potential mismatch in Restructuring constructions when the lower predicate takes one auxiliary and the higher predicate takes the other. For instance, the verbs DOVERE, POTERE, VOLERE 'must, can, want' take the 'have' auxiliary whereas ANDARE 'go' takes the 'be' auxiliary. In such cases either auxiliary can be selected by the complex predicate. But if a higher predicate selects AVERE then the clitic must remain on the infinitive:

(69) a.   Avevo   dovuto andar=**ci**
             HAVE.AUX must   go.INF=there.CL
             'I had had to go there'
     b.   * **Ci**   avevo   dovuto andare
             there.CL HAVE.AUX must   go.INF

On the other hand, if the complex predicate as a whole selects the ESSERE that the lower predicate selects then clitic climbing is obligatory:

(70) a.   **C'**=ero   dovuto andare
             there.CL= BE.AUX must   go.INF
             'I had had to go there'
     b.   * Ero   dovuto andar=**ci**
             BE.AUX must   go.INF=there.CL

The impression is that a reading of the verb combination as a complex predicate structure is forced when the higher predicate seems to select the 'wrong' auxiliary. Conversely, when the higher predicate selects the 'right' auxiliary, complex predicate formation would result in a clash of selection requirements, so that the only structure available is one in which the two predicates are treated as independent.

Clitic climbing in Serbian/Croatian and other Slavic languages

We now consider the phenomenon of clitic climbing in languages with 2P clitics. In Serbian/Croatian, as in other Slavic languages with second-position clitics, the clitic cluster of certain types of subordinate clause is hosted by the matrix verb and not by the verb with which the clitics are associated. The most typical examples involve non-finite, and especially infinitival clauses, as in (71):

(71) a.   Želim **mu**   **ga** dati
             I.want to.him it   give.INF
             'I want to give it to him' [Serbian/Croatian]
     b.   * Želim dati   **mu**   **ga**
             I.want give.INF to.him it

In (71) the clitic climbing is obligatory, as shown by (71b), where the clitic cluster remains in situ in the subordinate clause. Recall that the verbs which trigger such climbing in any given language are always limited in number and generally have the kind of meaning that tends to get grammaticalized cross-linguistically. Depending on the language, this includes (i) phasic verbs such as 'begin', 'finish', 'keep on (doing)', (ii) verbs of desire/belief such as 'want', 'believe', (iii) modals of various types such as 'must', 'may', 'ought', 'seem'. In the Romance languages the periphrastic causative (comparable to English 'make someone do something') also triggers clitic climbing. We mentioned that in Derivational-transformational grammar such predicates have been called Restructuring predicates (after Rizzi's 1982a analysis of Italian).

The clitic cluster in Serbian/Croatian still occupies the Wackernagel position after it has climbed out of its own clause, as can be seen in (72), in which the (non-clitic) subject pronoun serves as the host for the cluster:

(72)   Ja **mu   ga** želim dati
          I   to.him it I.want give.INF
          'I want to give it to him' [Serbian/Croatian]

The phenomenon of clitic climbing exhibits considerable uniformity across Slavic languages with Wackernagel clitics (and, indeed, obeys very similar principles to those governing clitic climbing in Romance languages), yet there are also extremely interesting divergences, even between closely related languages or dialect groups. Indeed, clitic climbing illustrates very well the extent to which clitic-related constructions can show micro-variation from one language variety to another. We will illustrate this variation in Slavic basing ourselves on the very useful discussion in Franks and King (2000, 241–8).[15]

In Czech, as in Serbian/Croatian, clitic climbing is obligatory out of infinitival complements to verbs with a modal meaning (Franks and King 2000, 117):

(73)   Včera   **mu   to** musel/chtěl dát
          yesterday to.him it must/wanted give.INF
          'Yesterday he needed/wanted to give it to him' [Czech]

Serbian/Croatian is perhaps unusual in allowing the clitic cluster to be split when it climbs, under certain circumstances, at least (Franks and King 2000, 243):[16]

(74) a.   Marija želi   da **mu   ga** predstavi
            Marija wants that to.him him introduces
            'Marija wants to introduce him to him' [Serbian/Croatian]

     b.   ?Marija **mu ga** želi da predstavi
     c.   ?Marija **mu** želi da **ga** predstavi
     d.   * Marija **ga** želi da **mu** predstavi

In (74a) we see the normal construction in which the clitic cluster *mu ga* remains associated with its verb *predstavi* in the subordinate clause. In (74b) we see that it is possible for the clitics to climb out of the finite clause, and in (74c) we see the rather unusual situation in which the cluster is split, with the dative clitic *mu* climbing and the accusative clitic *ga* remaining in situ. Example (74d) shows that it is not possible for the accusative clitic to climb on its own. It should be said, however, that judgements on examples such as these vary from speaker to speaker.

The constructions in (74) are also unusual for Slavic (and for Romance) in that the clitics have climbed out of a finite subordinate clause. In a number of languages, only non-finite clauses permit climbing. However, Serbian/Croatian is different from most other Slavic languages (and from Romance languages) in that a number of its 'modal' verbs take finite *da*-clauses as well as infinitival clauses (the two constructions are interchangeable in many cases), whereas in other languages it is rather rare for a verb that allows climbing to take a finite complement. The generalization therefore seems to be that it is more likely that a verb with the appropriate semantics will induce clitic climbing if it takes a non-finite complement, reflecting an overall tendency cross-linguistically for finite clauses to be more resistant to extraction generally than non-finite clauses.

When the subordinate clause verb is in the infinitive then the entire cluster must climb: it cannot be left in situ (75b), and it cannot be split (75c, d) (Franks and King 2000, 244):

(75) a.   Milan **mu**   **ga** želi   predstaviti
Milan to.him him wants introduce.INF
'Milan wants to introduce him to him' [Serbian/Croatian]

b.   * Milan želi **mu ga** predstaviti
c.   * Milan **mu** želi **ga** predstaviti
d.   * Milan **ga** želi **mu** predstaviti

These Serbian/Croatian examples present an interesting contrast with another South Slavic language, Slovene (Franks and King 2000, 246–7):

(76)   Milan **mu**   **ga** želi   predstaviti
Milan to.him him wants introduce.INF
'Milan wants to introduce him to him' [Slovene]

Milan želi **mu ga** predstaviti
Milan želi predstaviti **mu ga**

Milan **mu** želi **ga** predstaviti
Milan **mu** želi predstaviti **ga**

?*Milan **ga** želi predstaviti **mu**
?*Milan **ga** želi **mu** predstaviti

Franks and King (2000, 119) cite Czech examples from Avgustinova and Oliva (1995) in which there are several clauses headed by predicates which permit climbing:

(77)   Jana bude muset   začít   chtít   **se**   usmívat
Jana will must.INF begin.INF want.INF REFL smile.INF
'Jana will have to start wanting to smile' [Czech]

> Jana bude muset začít **se** chtít usmívat
> Jana bude muset **se** začít chtít usmívat
> Jana **se** bude muset začít chtít usmívat

Those authors provide examples in which two of the clauses concerned host reflexive clitics. In this case, either each remains in situ, or we can observe climbing so that the two reflexive pronominals, either accusative or dative, apparently end up in the same clause. However, when this happens only one of the clitics is pronounced, an instance of the familiar phenomenon of haplology in the clitic cluster:

(78) a.   Jan **se**   snažil **se**   elegantně obléci
           Jan REFL.ACC tried   REFL.ACC elegantly dress.INF
           'Jan tried to dress elegantly'
     b.   Jan **se**   snažil elegantně obléci
           Jan REFL.ACC tried   elegantly dress.INF [Czech]

(79) a.   Jan **si**   netroufá **si**   koupit nové auto
           Jan REFL.DAT NEG.dare REFL.DAT buy.INF new   car
           'Jan does not dare buy himself a new car'
     b.   Jan **si**   netroufá koupit nové auto
           Jan REFL.DAT NEG.dare buy.INF new   car   [Czech]

If, however, the two clauses contain clitics of different case, then such climbing isn't possible:

(80)   Stále   **se**   snažím získat   **si**   její přízeň
           constantly REFL.ACC I.try   win.INF REFL.DAT her affection [Czech]
(81)   Stále   **se**   snažím **si**   získat její přízeň
           constantly REFL.ACC I.try   REFL.DAT win.INF her affection
           'I am constantly trying to win her affection' [Czech]
           *Stále **se si** snažím získat její přízeň
           *Stále **si se** snažím získat její přízeň

Franks and King (2000, 248) observe that such haplology with reflexive clitics is widespread throughout Slavic clitic systems (and indeed in Romance). Such examples illustrate yet again the close relation between a clitic cluster and an affix cluster, since haplology of this sort is particularly associated with affixes rather than with true words (Sections 5.4, 8.5).

In earlier discussion of clitic climbing, such behaviour was taken to be a good sign that we are dealing with a pronominal element that is represented in the syntax and that has to be moved by a syntactic rule. However, this conclusion is undermined by our earlier observation that essentially the same phenomenon is exhibited by morphological agreement systems (or at least pronominal affixes). Clitic climbing in languages such as Czech and Serbian/Croatian has been studied in some detail (see, for instance, the references in Franks and King 2000).

In the Romance languages there has been even greater research devoted to the phenomenon.

6.4.4   Ethical Datives

There is one type of pronominal clitic that is very widespread amongst languages with pronominal clitics, but which has been discussed only sporadically in the literature. This is what we will call the Ethical Dative. By this we mean a pronoun, prototypically in the dative case, which expresses a subjective modal or attitudinal pragmatic function, sometimes positive ('for my benefit') and sometimes negative ('to my disadvantage/annoyance'). Very often such elements are entirely untranslatable. If a language lacks a dative case (or cases generally) then the Ethical Dative will often be expressed in whatever way indirect objects are typically expressed. The term 'Ethical Dative' is borrowed from the terminology of the philology of classical languages (Latin, 'dativus ethicus'). A nice example of this in Latin is cited by Greenough et al. (1983, 236):

(82)   at   tibi   repente   venit mihi   Caninius
           and 2SG.DAT suddenly came 1SG.DAT Caninius
           'but, look you, of a sudden comes to me Caninius' [modern rendering: 'and
                 there you are, all of a sudden Caninius comes to me']

Here the 2nd person pronoun *tibi* is used effectively as a discourse marker. It has no argumental status (unlike the 1st person dative pronoun *mihi* later in the sentence). In English, Ethical Datives are often expressed using the preposition *on*: *My computer's crashed on me*.

A very interesting discussion of this kind of construction in (Modern) Hebrew is provided by Borer and Grodzinsky (1986). They point out that there are three distinct dative pronominal constructions apparent in Hebrew, what they call the Possessive Dative, the Reflexive Dative and the Ethical Dative. The Possessive and Reflexive Datives are illustrated in (83) and (84):

(83)   ha-yalda 'axla **li**   'et ha-tapu'ax
           the-girl   ate   to.me OBJ the-apple
           'The girl ate my apple' [Possessive Dative]
(84)   ha-yalda$_i$ 'axla la$_i$ 'et ha-tapu'ax
           the-girl   ate   to.her(self) OBJ the-apple
           'The girl ate the apple' [Reflexive Dative]

In (83) the girl eats someone else's apple. Borer and Grodzinsky (1986, 180) describe (84) as indicating that "the girl is understood as engaging in an activity of apple-eating for her own pleasure".

Borer and Grodzinsky (1986, 179) provide examples (85), (86) and (87) as instances of the Ethical Dative:

(85)   hem kol ha-zman mitxatnim **li**
           they all the-time marry   to.me
           'They are getting married on me all the time (and it bothers me)'

(86)   lama hu yorek **li**   pit'om?
  why he spits to.me suddenly
  'Why is he spitting all of a sudden "on me"?'
(87)   be-'emca   ha-seret   hem nixnasim **li**
  in-the.middle the-movie they enter   to.me
  'They enter in the middle of the movie (aggravating me)'

Unlike Reflexive Datives, Ethical Datives cannot be coreferential to any other participant in the clause, and they don't express a possessor relationship (unlike Possessive Datives). Moreover, they have to be expressed as true clitics: no other dative-marked expression can substitute for the clitic pronominal form of *l-*, they must be adjacent to the verb and they cannot be questioned (Borer and Grodzinsky 1986, 180–1).

Borer and Grodzinsky (1986, 202) show that the Ethical Datives and the Reflexive Datives behave very much like each other morphosyntactically and contrast with the Possessive Datives, which show much more syntactic autonomy. They therefore argue that both Ethical Datives and Reflexive Datives are essentially affixes, but 'syntactic affixes', that is, morphological objects that are introduced into word structure by syntactic rules.

Ethical Dative constructions, whether they involve clitic pronominals or not, are very interesting from the point of view of discourse organization, but it would be beyond the scope of our discussion to examine that aspect. The main reason for drawing attention to these constructions in the context of pronominal clitics is the way that they interact, or rather fail to interact, with other pronominals. As we have mentioned (Chapter 5), there is a strong tendency cross-linguistically for clitics denoting direct and indirect objects to be linearized in very specific ways depending on their person/number features. However, by and large, the Ethical Datives do not behave like dative clitics with respect to these restrictions (Simpson and Withgott 1986, 160–1). Although they often form part of the normal clitic cluster, they don't obey common restrictions on combinability. Indeed, they often show the unique property of combining with another clitic expressing the same case, dative (just as we saw in the Latin example (82) above). For example, Franks and King (2000, 105) cite example (88) from Czech, in which the Ethical Dative clitic *ti* occurs alongside the dative-case marked pronominal argument *jí* of the verb *help*:

(88)   On **ti**   **jí**   nepomůže
  he you.DAT her.DAT he.won't.help
  'He won't help her (I tell you)'[17]

They also cite two different authors (Fried 1994 and Veselovská 1995), who provide different orders of the Czech Ethical Dative with respect to the reflexive accusative clitic *se* in clusters:[18]

(89)   On **ti**   **se**   **mi**   ani   neomluvil
  he you.DAT REFL.ACC me.DAT not.even apologized
  '(I'm telling you) he didn't even apologize to me' (Fried 1994, 173)

(90)   Já jsem **se**   **ti**   **mu**   **to**   neodvážila říci
         I   AUX REFL.ACC you.DAT him.DAT it.ACC not.dared   to.say
         '(I am telling you) I didn't dare to say it to him' (Veselovská 1995, 332)

6.5   Syntactic constraints – Tagalog clitic distribution

We conclude our discussion of clitics and syntax with a survey of the complex pattern of interaction between syntactic structure and the various types of discourse clitics of Tagalog. Schachter and Otanes (1972, 429–37) divide the eighteen enclitic discourse particles of Tagalog into four groups:[19]

Group A: *ba* 'interrogative' (*kasi, kaya, man*)
Group B: *din/rin* 'too' (*daw/raw, ho, nama, nga, pala, po, sana, tuloy,*
              yata)
Group C: *lamang/lang* 'just', *muna* 'first'
Group D: *na* 'soon', *pa* 'some more'

We will only illustrate those we have glossed in the list.[20] These groups are differentiated by their distributional privileges of occurrence. To understand how, we need to consider a little Tagalog syntax. Tagalog clauses are generally of the form VSO (although there is considerable debate about the appropriateness of labels 'subject' and 'object' for the arguments of Tagalog predicates). Non-clitic arguments of verbs are marked with what we will gloss as 'articles' (ART, mainly *ang, ng* in these examples) depending on the voice of the verb and other factors.

(91)   Tinanggap ko ang sulat kahapon
         received   I   ART letter yesterday
         'I received a letter yesterday' (Schachter and Otanes 1972, 486)

In the Inverted Topic construction an argument is preposed and connected to the predication with *ay*:

(92)   Ang sulat ay tinanggap ko kahapon
         ART letter AY received   I   yesterday
         'I received the letter yesterday' (Schachter and Otanes 1972, 488)

Adverbs, too, can be topicalized (Schachter and Otanes 1972, 486):

(93) a. Ipinagbili niya ang kalabaw   niya noong   Lunes
         sold   he   ART calabaw[21] his Monday
     b. Noong Lunes ay ipinagbili niya ang kalabaw niya
         Monday   AY sold   he   ART calabaw his
         'He sold his calabaw on Monday'

Inversion can give rise to contrastive constructions, which do not involve the marker AY, but in which the inverted phrase is followed by a pause (i.e. it forms its own intonational unit) (Schachter and Otanes 1972, 493):

(94)   Kami, magpapahinga. Kayo, magtatrabaho
            we   will.rest   you   will.work
            'We will rest. You will work' [contrastive inversion]

The final construction to consider is what Schachter and Otanes call a 'nominal-ized verbal'. This is essentially a type of equational clause structure consisting of a nominal argument followed by the particle *ang* (ANG) and the rest of the verb phrase, as illustrated by (95) (Schachter and Otanes 1972, 62):

(95)   Artista ang nagluto ng   pagkain
            actress ANG cooked ART food
            'The one who cooked some food is an actress' [nominalized verbal]

We are now in a position to see how the particles are arranged with respect to these grammatical constructions.

    The particles of Group A (*ba, kasi, kaya, man*) occur in second position in a complete clause (CP domain). This means they may follow immediately after the predicate, after an Inverted Topic, or after an Inverted Adverb. In (96) below we see that the interrogative particle *ba* can appear either after the entire adverbial phrase *bukas ng gabi* 'tomorrow night' (96c) or after the first word of that phrase (96d) (Schachter and Otanes 1972, 429-30):

(96)   (Kung pakikiusapan ko sila,)
            'If I ask them to,'
    a.   sasayaw   **ba** sila ng   pandanggo bukas   ng   gabi?
            will.dance Q   they ART fandango   tomorrow ART night
            [post-predicate]

    b.   sila **ba**'-y sasayaw   ng   pandanggo bukas   ng   gabi?
            they Q-AY will.dance ART fandango   tomorrow ART night
            [internal to Inverted Topic + *ay*]

    c.   bukas   **ba** ng gabi'-y sasayaw sila ng pandanggo?
            tomorrow Q   ART night-AY will.dance they ART fandango
            [internal to Inverted Adverbial + *ay*]

    d.   bukas   ng gabi **ba**'-y sasayaw   sila ng pandanggo?
            tomorrow ART night Q- AY will.dance they ART fandango
            [after Inverted Adverbial + *ay*]

            '. . . will they dance a fandango tomorrow night?'

    Particles of Group B usually occur in the same places as Group A particles, but in addition they can appear in other, non-clause-initial, positions, including positions other than second in any type of clause. In (97a) we see the Group B particle *din/rin* 'too' in position after an Inverted Predicate + *ay*, and in (97b) we see the particle inside the Inverted Predicate (Schachter and Otanes 1972, 430).[22] Example (97c) illustrates the particle inside and after the Inverted Adverbial:

(97) a.   Sila-'y sasayaw **din** ng pandanggo bukas   ng gabi
           they-AY will.dance DIN ART fandango   tomorrow ART night
           'They will dance a fandango tomorrow night too'
           [Inverted Predicate]

b.   Sila **rin** ay sasayaw   ng pandanggo bukas   ng gabi
      they DIN AY will.dance ART fandango   tomorrow ART night
      'Tomorrow night too they will dance a fandango'
      [Inverted Topic + *ay*]

c.
Bukas	**din**	ng	gabi-	'y		sasayaw	sila	ng	pandanggo
tomorrow	DIN	ART	night-	AY		will.dance	they	ART	fandango
Bukas	ng	gabi	**rin**	ay					
tomorrow	ART	night	DIN	AY					

   'They too will dance a fandango tomorrow night'

In (98) we see the clitic particle *din* respectively after and inside a nominalized verb constituent:

(98) a.   Sila ang sasayaw   **din** ng pandanggo
           they ANG will.dance DIN ART fandango   [Inverted Predicate after
           nominalized verbal]
b.   Sila **rin** ang sasayaw   ng pandanggo
      they DIN ANG will.dance ART fandango   [nominalized verbal]

Group B particles can also occur inside adverbials (Schachter and Otanes 1972, 431):

(99)   Ito ang binili   ko para **rin** sa   iyo
           this ANG bought I   for DIN ART you
           'This is the one I bought for you too'

This example illustrates a further feature of these particles, namely, that their domain can be a phrase within the clause itself, in this case the 'prepositional phrase' introduced by *para* 'for'.

   The particles of Group C are similar to those of Group B except that they can't appear inside an Inverted Adverbial + *ay*. Thus, while example (100) with *lamang* 'just' or *muna* 'first' is possible, example (101) is not:

(100)   Bukas ng gabi ay sasayaw   **lamang/muna** sila ng pandanggo
           tomorrow night AY will.dance just/first   they ART fandango
           'They will just/first dance a fandango tonight' [Inverted Predicate]
(101)   *Bukas   **lamang/muna** ng gabi ay sasayaw   sila ng pandanggo
           tomorrow just/first   ANG night AY will.dance they ART fandango
                                         *[internal to Inverted Adverbial + *ay*]

However, Group C particles can appear inside an Inverted Topic followed by *ay*, or after an Inverted Predicate + *ay*:

(102) a. Sila **lamang/muna** ay sasayaw   ng pandanggo bukas ng gabi
          they just/first   AY will.dance ART fandango   tomorrow night
          [internal to Inverted Topic + *ay*]

      b. Sila'y   sasayaw   **lamang/muna** ng   pandanggo bukas ng   gabi
          they AY will.dance just/first   ART fandango tomorrow night
           [after Inverted Predicate]

          'They will just/first dance a fandango tomorrow night'

      c. Sila ang sasayaw   **lamang/muna** ng   pandanggo
          they ANG will.dance just/first   ART   fandango
          'They're the ones who will just/first dance a fandango' [nominalized verbal]

The Group D particles are like those of Group B. In (103) and (104) respectively we see the particles *na* 'soon' and *pa* 'some more' appearing after an Inverted Topic/Adverbial (Schachter and Otanes 1972, 431–3):

(103)   Sila'y   sasayaw   **na/pa** ng pandanggo bukas ng   gabi
          they AY will.dance NA/PA ART fandango tomorrow night
          [after Inverted Topic + *ay*]

(104)   Bukas ng gabi'y   sasayaw   **na/pa**   sila ng pandanggo
          tomorrow night AY will.dance NA/PA   they ART fandango
          'They will dance a fandango soon/some more tomorrow night' [after
              Inverted Adverbial + *ay*]

However, the Group D clitics can't occur inside an Inverted Topic or Adverbial + *ay*:

(105) a. *Sila **na**'y/**pa**'y sasayaw   ng pandanggo bukas ng   gabi
           they NA AY/PA AY will.dance ART fandango tomorrow   night
           *[internal to Inverted Topic + *ay*]

      b. *Bukas   **na/pa** ng gabi'y   sasayaw   sila ng pandanggo
          tomorrow NA/PA ART night AY will.dance they ART fandango
           *[internal to Inverted Adverbial]

Finally, like the Group B, C clitics, but unlike the Group A clitics, the Group D clitics can appear inside a nominalized verbal:

(106)   Sila ang sasayaw   **na/pa** ng   pandanggo
          they ANG will.dance NA/PA ART fandango
          'They're the ones who will now dance/go dancing a fandango'
          [nominalized verbal]

This patterning is summarized in (107):

(107)   Distribution of clitic particles by syntactic construction

	A	B	C	D
Inverted predicate + *ay*	✗	✓	✓	✓
After Inverted Topic + *ay*	✓	✓	✓	✓
Internal to Inverted Topic + *ay*	✓	✓	✓	✗
Contrastive topic + pause	✗	✓	✓	✓
After Inverted Adverbial + *ay*	✓	✓	✓	✓
Internal to Inverted Adverbial + *ay*	✓	✓	✗	✗
Nominalized verb	✗	✓	✓	✓
Non-Inverted Adverbial	✗	✓	✓	✓

Schachter and Otanes label any word that an enclitic can take as a host as a pre-enclitic word. Any word which can precede a Pre-enclitic word is a Non-pre-enclitic word. There is a finite list of Non-pre-enclitic words (though the list for enclitic pronouns is slightly different from that for discourse particles). Some of the Non-pre-enclitic words can never host a clitic (Obligatory non-pre-enclitic words), whilst others may or may not function as hosts (Optional non-pre-enclitic words). The list is somewhat long (seven pages (!), Schachter and Otanes 1972, 187–93) so we will just summarize some of the characteristic elements that fail to act as clitic hosts.

Non-pre-enclitics (for pronouns):

1.   Various nominal markers, including the plural *mga*, the inversion marker *ay/'y*, the existential *may* 'there is/are', and most subordinating and coordinating conjunctions (this marks a significant difference from languages such as Warlpiri, or Serbian/Croatian, where complementizers regularly serve as clitic hosts).

2.   Various 'small constructions', which are like phrases only more tightly cohesive, cannot be interrupted by clitics because the non-final component of such phrases is always non-pre-enclitic. These include compound proper names such as *Juan (Cruz)*, compound numbers such as *sampung (libo)* 'ten (thousand)', phrases involving reduplication such as *mabait na mabait* 'very kind' or *pagkarating ng pagkarating* 'as soon as ... had arrived', and various other types.

Optional non-pre-enclitics
The Optional non-pre-enclitics include:

1.   A variety of words with meanings such as 'like, similar to', 'for', 'from', 'facing', 'why', 'maybe', 'it seems', and certain types of subordinating and coordinating conjunctions.

2.   A variety of 'small constructions' such as adjective + noun, and adjective + complement constructions, as well as a variety of

one-word adverbials linked to the predication by the linker *na/-ng*. To illustrate the latter see (108) (Schachter and Otanes 1972, 193):

(108)   Madalas na   naririnig **ko**   iyon
          often   LINKER heard   I.CLITIC that

          Madalas **ko**-ng   naririnig iyon
          often   I.CLITIC-LINKER heard   that
          'I've often heard that'

This gives a flavour of the great complexity of the factors that govern the overall distribution of clitics in what seems at first sight to be a straightforward instance of a language with a Wackernagel clitic cluster. Such variability and complexity, however, is the norm amongst clitic systems, once they are examined in proper detail, as is apparent from the earliest work on Indo-European clitic systems, such as Wackernagel (1892) or more specialist studies of Ancient Greek by Denniston (2002). Systems such as the Tagalog discourse clitic system illustrate particularly well how clitic placement and clitic behaviour in general is the result of a complex interaction of factors and can rarely be reduced to a single grammatical property. The abiding impression is that Tagalog clitics are sensitive to very specific aspects of specific grammatical constructions. It may well be, of course, that with sufficient ingenuity we might unearth a small set of simple, abstract principles governing such behaviour, but it is rather more likely that systems such as this are irreducibly idiosyncratic and require direct reference to specific constructions or to a relatively unstructured list of component grammatical properties.

6.6   Summary

There are a number of ways in which clitics appear to behave like syntactically represented words. However, we must be cautious in drawing too many conclusions from this. We began this chapter by pointing out that the boundaries between non-clitic function words and clitics is often blurred, and that on occasions a function word may even have properties that are more commonly associated with affixes, such as taking narrow scope over coordinated phrases. For this reason it is often difficult to say that a given clitic construction provides evidence of purely syntactic patterning, since it's generally possible to find a corresponding affixal construction that has similar properties. Thus, clitic climbing doesn't necessarily provide evidence that we are dealing with syntactic elements because we observe very similar patterns of long-distance agreement. Likewise, complementarity between clitics and noun phrase arguments doesn't necessarily prove that the clitics themselves are arguments. First, even pronominal affixes aren't arguments according to some linguists, and second there are languages with pronominal affixes that can't co-occur with overt noun phrases.

Our aim in this chapter hasn't been just to show how blurred the linguistic boundaries are, however. Even if we conceive of clitics as essentially morphological objects, we still need to understand how they interact with syntactic structures. Unlike affixes, clitics often show considerable sensitivity to syntax. For instance, in many cases their positioning is at least partly determined by syntactic structure. The Tagalog case study illustrates just how complex this dependence can be.

We have focussed on pronominal clitics in illustrating this, for the simple reason that this is where most of the research has been conducted and because there are ample instances in the world's languages, but we could presumably have reached similar conclusions with respect to auxiliary verb clitics, for instance. The reasons why it's so difficult to tease apart affixal systems from pronominal clitics is obvious: affixal morphology generally arises from clitics and morphologization is almost always gradual, with different constructions undergoing greater degrees of morphologization than others. This simple fact of linguistic life often confounds attempts at finding neatly uniform analyses of clitic phenomena.

7   Clitics, affixes and words

7.1   Introduction

In this chapter we bring together a number of points raised in earlier chapters and ask to what extent we can draw a clear dividing line between clitics, words and affixes. We will show that the search for clear dividing lines is an arduous one. On the one hand we'll see a variety of ways in which elements that we would normally wish to call affixes may exhibit properties typical of clitics. We'll conclude the chapter with instances in which the divide between clitic and (inflecting) lexeme is blurred. Between those two types of situation we'll examine instances in which one and the same set of elements in a language can behave sometimes like affixes and sometimes like clitics (what we call 'mixed systems'). In effect, then, we will start by examining elements that are fairly clear instances of clitics and progressively move towards elements that increasingly show properties of words.

However, we set the scene with three case studies of elements that might be considered clitics (or even weak function words) but which are certainly (German infinitive marker, Finnish possessor inflections), or almost certainly (Greek verbal 'clitics'), affixes. The purpose of these case studies is to alert us to the fact that things aren't always as they seem, and that traditional perspectives, or analyses that initially look very promising, can be misleading.

The next set of case studies considers the extent to which affixes can show clitic-like properties while still remaining affixes. We begin by looking at the clitic-like phonology of English 'Class II' affixes. Inflectional affixes are supposed to conform to strict ordering constraints, but in a number of languages the syntactic past history of the clitics has left vestiges in the form of ordering variation. Sometimes the order is significant, as when identical pronominal clitics in Bantu languages occupy one position or the other within the affix string depending on whether they express the subject or the object argument. Sometimes the ordering is free, as in the remarkable case of the prefix system of the Kiranti language, Chintang. We mentioned in Chapter 1 that function words take wide scope over conjoined phrases, while affixes have to be repeated on each conjunct. Needless to say, this is no more than a general tendency. There are numerous cases in which elements that behave in most respects like affixes can take wide scope, and we survey some of these in this chapter. We will even see an affix that occupies the second position in an affix string, the prototypical position for a so-called Wackernagel clitic.

Next, we survey the properties of pronominal clitics in European Portuguese and Udi. In both these languages we encounter elements that seem to be prototypical affixes in some grammatical contexts and prototypical clitics in others.

Clitics are generally taken to be elements that realize a single morphosyntactic property, but partial grammaticalization of inflecting function words such as auxiliary verbs or case-marked pronouns means that we sometimes find clitics that appear to undergo inflectional morphology themselves. The existence of such clitics is important for morphologically based theories of clitics, especially those that adopt the 'a-morphous' approach to morphology. If a clitic is just a kind of affix, and if affixes are just phonological strings with no morphological properties of their own, then we wouldn't expect a clitic to enter into the morphological system and inflect as though it were a lexeme. We discuss a typical example of an inflecting clitic from the Czech Wackernagel clitic system. We conclude by comparing clitics with particles (non-projecting words), looking specifically at a grammatical particle in Russian that has pretty complete freedom of placement within the clause and which is the principal exponent of the conditional mood in that language.

7.2   'Clitics' which aren't

In this section we discuss a number of cases that have frequently been labelled as clitic phenomena but which are clearly instances of affixation. We will find it instructive to look at such cases, because the reasons why earlier investigators have labelled phenomena as clitics are quite varied, and illustrate some of the pitfalls of the clitic concept that can trap the unwary.

7.2.1   German *zu*

We begin with a simple and straightforward case illustrating how orthographic convention can sometimes fail to keep pace with linguistic change.

German verbs inflect for an infinitive form in *-en*. However, in a good many constructions requiring the infinitive, the bare infinitive form has to be supplemented by an element *zu*. Like its English cognate, the infinitive particle *to*, this element is homophonous with, and historically related to, a preposition *zu* 'to'.

Complements to verbs such as *versuchen* 'try' require the *zu*-infinitive:

(1)   Sie versucht, das Buch zu lesen
         She tries   the book to read
         'She tries to read the book'

This *zu* element is usually written separately from the verb, as in example (1) above. However, this orthographic convention is misleading. While the English 'to' particle seems to behave like an independent syntactic terminal the German *zu* is clearly a prefix in all its uses. This point is made explicitly, for instance, in the standard descriptive grammar of German (Der Grosse Duden, 2006, 446).

Unlike English 'to', *zu* can never be split from its host verb. While in English it is possible to say 'to boldly go' in German the equivalent has to be *tapfer zu gehen*, literally, 'boldly to go'. An alternative with the *zu* 'split', *zu tapfer gehen is completely ungrammatical, not just stylistically marked as it is in English. German verbs often have preverbs often called 'separable prefixes'. In citation forms, and when the verb is clause final the preverb appears immediately before the verb form as a kind of prefix (and can receive primary word stress in that position). In certain morphosyntactic environments, for instance, when the lexical verb is in clause-second position the preverb shifts to a different position in the sentence. These options are illustrated for the verb *hinaus=gehen* 'out-go, to go out':

(2) a.   Sie ging sofort   hinaus
            She went immediately out
            'She immediately went out'

    b.   Er sagte, dass sie sofort   hináusging
            He said   that she immediately out.went
            'He said that she went out immediately'

We indicate the position of word stress on the preverb in *hináusging*.

In the *zu*-infinitive form the *zu* element always appears between the preverb and the lexical verb root:

(3)   Sie versuchte, hinaus-zu-gehen
            She tried   out-to-go
            'She tried to go out'

(With lexical non-separable prefixes such as *ver-* in *versuchen* the *zu* element is prefixed after the lexical prefix: *zu versuchen*. However, it still cannot be split from the verb.)

Finally, *zu* fails to exhibit wide scope over coordinated phrases (Der Grosse Duden 2006, 446):

(4) a.   * Ich muss Ihnen davon   abraten, täglich zu rauchen und Alkohol
            I   must you therefrom dissuade daily   to smoke and alcohol
               trinken
               drink

    b.   Ich muss Ihnen davon   abraten, täglich zu rauchen und Alkohol zu
            I   must you therefrom dissuade daily   to smoke and alcohol to
               trinken
               drink
               'I must discourage you from smoking and drinking alcohol every day'

We next turn to an almost equally clear case of an affix, though one that has sometimes been misanalysed in the literature.

7.2.2   Finnish possessor agreement

Traditionally, possessor agreement markers in Finnish have been treated as inflectional suffixes (albeit with special properties). However, in the 1980s a number of linguists started treating them as clitics (Pierrehumbert 1980, Nevis 1986). We will briefly summarize their arguments and the counter-arguments of Kanerva (1987).

Finnish nouns bear relatively agglutinative inflectional suffixes expressing number (singular/plural, with singular unmarked), case (a dozen case suffixes are found) and possessor agreement (the noun agreeing with a possessor for the pronominal properties of person/number).

The number marker takes the form *-t* in the nominative case and *-i-* with other cases (it alternates phonologically with the glide /j/ between vowels). These and the various case suffixes behave like cohering affixes, triggering and undergoing various types of allomorphy, particularly consonant gradation (see below).

Many (though by no means all) Finnish nouns can be inflected with the possessive suffixes, cross-referencing the possessor in person/number. These take the form shown in (5) (after a case suffix ending in a vowel, *V*, the 3rd person suffix often takes the form *-Vn*):

(5)   Finnish possessor suffixes

	Singular		Plural
1st	-ni		-mme
2nd	-si		-nne
3rd		-nsa/nsä	

The 3rd person form has two vowel-harmony variants, a back vowel alternant *-nsa* and a front vowel alternant *-nsä* (IPA [nsæ]).

Pierrehumbert (1980) argued that the possessive markers are clitics on the basis principally of their syntactic behaviour. Possessive markers in all three person forms are able to cross-reference an overt possessor, provided it takes the form of a personal pronoun. The paradigm in (6) is taken from Nelson (1998, 187):

(6) a.   Poika   myi   marsu-nsa
            boy.NOM sell.PAST guinea pig-PX3
            'The boy sold his guinea pig'
    b.   Poika   myi   hänen   marsu-nsa
            boy.NOM sell.PAST his.GEN guinea pig-PX3
            'The boy sold his guinea pig'
    c.   Poika   myi   marsu-ni
            boy.NOM sell.PAST guinea pig-PX1SG
            'The boy sold my guinea pig'
    d.   Poika   myi   minun   marsu-ni
            boy.NOM sell.PAST my.GEN guinea pig-PX1SG
            'The boy sold my guinea pig'

Examples (6c, d) are semantically equivalent except that (6d) puts some emphasis on the pronoun. Similar examples could be constructed with the 1pl forms and
the second person forms. The possessor suffixes for those person/number forms
therefore behave like 'pro-drop' inflections, in that they don't need to co-occur
with an overt pronoun, but they are allowed to. The significant fact is that (6a, b)
are not synonymous: (6a) means that the boy sold his own guinea pig, a reflexive interpretation, while (6b), with an overt possessive pronoun, can only mean
that he sold someone else's guinea pig, a non-reflexive interpretation. Although
it isn't obvious from these example (6a, b) illustrate another point about 3rd person possessed forms: the possessor suffix has to have an overt antecedent of some
sort in its domain.

Pierrehumbert argues that data such as (6a, b) show that the pronominal
suffix and the overt pronoun are in complementary distribution. She therefore
argues that the suffix itself is actually an incorporated pronominal. For theory-
internal reasons, to do with the kind of incorporation rule she proposes and the
kinds of syntactic structures she assumes, from this it follows (or at least it is
plausible to assume) that the pronominal is in fact a clitic. A further morphosyntactic property concerns the agreement patterns shown by attributive adjectives.
These agree with their head noun in number and case, but not in possessor
agreement.

Pierrehumbert mentions an important anomaly from allomorphy/morphopho-
nology to back up her claim that possessive markers are clitics: consonant
gradation. Nevis (1986) takes this point and expands on it, to justify an analysis
of possessive markers as clitics. We now turn to consonant gradation.

In consonant gradation environments the geminate stops /pp tt kk/ alternate
with singleton stops /p t k/ while the singleton stops /p t k/ alternate with /v d Ø/.
After a sonorant the singleton stops alternate as shown in (7):

(7)   Finnish consonant gradation
           mp   ~   mm
           nt   ~   nn
           nk   ~   ng (= /ŋŋ/)
           lt   ~   ll
           rt   ~   rr

Consonant gradation is found when the stop or sonorant-stop pair is followed
by a vowel in the stem. The gradation is triggered by particular suffixes. Typical
examples are seen in (8) (Karlsson 1987, 30–1):

(8)   kaappi   'cupboard'   kaapi-ssa   'in the cupboard'
           matto   'mat'   mato-lla   'on the mat'
           kukka   'flower'   kuka-n   'of the flower'
           tupa   'hut'   tuva-ssa   'in the hut'
           katu   'street'   kadu-lla   'on the street'
           jalka   'foot'   jala-n   'of the foot'
           ranta   'shore'   ranna-lla   'on the shore'

kulta	'gold'	kulla-n	'of the gold'
parta	'beard'	parra-ssa	'in the beard'

There are complex phonological conditions governing when gradation occurs. The suffix has to close the syllable after the gradating consonant (hence, it must consist of a single consonant such as genitive case *-n* or it must begin with two consonants, such as the inessive case *-ssa*). In addition, the target consonant cannot be followed by a long vowel. However, it can be followed by a short vowel followed by the *-i* plural suffix. Examples are shown in (9) (Karlsson 1987, 32–3) from KATTO 'roof':

(9)   Gradation   No gradation

      kato-n   'of the roof'   katto-na   'as a roof'
      kato-lla   'on the roof'   katto-a   'roof
                                                 (partitive case)'
      kato-lta   'from the roof'
      kato-ksi   'to (become) a roof' katto-on   'onto the roof'
      kato-i-lla   'on the roofs'   katto-j-en   'of the roofs'
                                             (/j/ = plural 'i')
      kato-i-lta   'from the roofs'   katto-i-hin   'into the roofs'

Crucially, consonant gradation is not found with possessive suffixes. The suffixes *-mme*, *-nne*, *-nsa/nsä* have the right phonological shape to trigger consonant gradation but they fail to do so:

(10)   katto-mme (*kato-mme)   'our roof'
        katto-nne   'your roof'

This fact is particularly striking when we consider verbs. Verbs take person/number inflections (among others). Consonant gradation is also found with verb stems, patterning very much like consonant gradation in nouns. For instance, the stem *kerto-* 'tell' appears as *kerro-* before consonant-only endings:

(11)   Consonant gradation in verbs:
    a.   kerro-n   'I tell'
    b.   kerro-t   'you tell'
    c.   kerro-i-t 'you told'

In the last example, (11c), we can see that the past tense suffix *-i-* is no barrier to gradation, any more than the homophonous plural suffix. The interesting observation is found with 1pl/2pl suffixes *-mme/tte*, for both of these trigger gradation: *kerro-mme* 'we tell', *kerro-tte* 'you tell'. The contrast between *kerro-mme* with gradation and *katto-mme* with no gradation shows that the alternation is not purely phonological.

    Pierrehumbert and Nevis both argue that the failure of possessive markers to trigger consonant gradation is due to their clitic status: they are adjoined to the inflected word form 'after' all the word-internal morphophonological adjustments have taken place. In other words, possessive markers fail to trigger (one particular type of) allomorphy on their hosts, and this is behaviour associated with clitics.

However, Kanerva (1987) outlines a number of morphological and morphophonological properties of the possessive markers which show that they are suffixes (albeit not absolutely typical ones). First, the possessive markers are associated with allomorphic alternations on the stem to which they attach, it's just that consonant gradation isn't one of those alternations. For instance, a number of nouns show phonologically related stem allomorphy in the form of their final vowels. Thus, in its suffixed forms a noun such as LAPSI 'child' has the stem form *lapse-*, as in the nominative plural *lapse-t*. However, the unsuffixed allomorph of this stem ends in /i/: *lapsi*. That form also surfaces when the noun receives a true clitic, such as the interrogative clitic we saw in Section 3.5: *lapsi=ko* 'the child?' However, with a possessive suffix the *-e* final form of the stem is found: *lapse-ni* 'my child'.

A further affix-like property is that the possessive suffixes trigger truncation of the final consonant of any case ending (Karlsson 1987, 92):

(12)   tytö-n 'of the girl'   tyttö-mme 'of our girl'
         lauku-t 'bags (nominative)'   laukku-nne 'your bags'

When the suffix truncates a case ending in this way it may remove the trigger for consonant gradation, resulting in the *-tt-/-t-* and *-kk-/-k-*-alternations seen in (12) above.

One morphophonological property that is sometimes a diagnostic for morphological status is vowel harmony. In languages such as Finnish, Hungarian, Turkish and many others, vowel harmony is restricted to word units. Even highly lexicalized compounds will generally fail to show vowel harmony in these languages. Thus, in Finnish we have words such as *pääkaupunki* 'capital city' (literally, *pää* 'head', *kaupunki* 'city'), consisting of a front vowel noun compounded with a back vowel noun (the vowel /i/ is transparent to vowel harmony in Finnish). It might be thought, then, that the 3rd person possessive marker *-nsa/nsä*, at least, was an affix by this criterion. However, in Finnish there are a fair number of bona fide and uncontroversial clitics such as the sentential interrogative clitic *-ko/kö* discussed in Chapter 3. In a number of cases these have vowels that can alternate, in which case they show vowel harmony. Thus, this particular morphophonological property is insufficient to distinguish clitics from affixes.

The anomalous morphophonological behaviour of Finnish possessive suffixes in not triggering consonant gradation is one of the outstanding puzzles of the morphophonology of the language. However, researchers no longer treat this as evidence for clitic status. It is uniformly assumed that these are suffixes, though with unusual morphosyntax. Toivonen (2000) presents an LFG analysis of these affixes and argues that they are just like pronominal affixes in PRO-drop languages, in that they are polysemous and have two distinct (though related) lexical representations: when doubling personal pronouns they are agreement markers, but when they appear on their own they are incorporated pronominals with their own 'meaning' (see Section 6.4 for this distinction with respect to subject agreement markers). Because the latter representations are meaningful (they have there own 'PRED' value in Toivonen's LFG analysis) they cannot be coreferential with an overt pronoun, because there would be a clash of PRED values. For this reason, only the agreement type of possessor suffix can co-occur with an overt pronoun, and this interpretation of the possessor suffix therefore has to have the same antecedent as the overt pronoun it agrees with. It remains to be explained why it is only pronouns that trigger such agreement, though such restrictions are not uncommon in agreement systems (similar observations can be made about subject agreement morphology in Welsh, for instance, Section 6.3).

The moral to be drawn from this story is that affixal systems involving morphologized pronominals tend to retain varying degrees of pronominal morphosyntax, even after they have lost all or most of their non-affixal clitic morphology and morphophonology and have become morphophonologically integrated into the affixal system proper. The most frequent and obvious instance of this is the phenomenon often referred to as 'pro-drop', discussed in greater detail in Section 6.4. In that section we also saw that languages select different options over what kinds of nominal phrases can be the antecedent of agreement morphology. The Finnish possessive suffixes are reminiscent of the subject agreement morphology of Welsh, in that they are able to select only pronominal antecedents. However, since these are possessive markers, they can signal a semantic distinction that is difficult to reproduce with ordinary subject agreement morphosyntax, namely, stipulated non-coreference with an overt pronominal. Once we appreciate just how complex the morphosyntax of affixal agreement can be and once we appreciate that different groups of affixes can exhibit different morphophonological regularities, then there is no need to treat the Finnish possessives as anything other than a kind of affix.

In Section 6.4 we also looked at the phenomenon of 'clitic doubling' in some detail. Clitic doubling is very similar to agreement and presumably is the first stage in the historical development of many agreement systems. When we contrasted Macedonian and Albanian clitic doubling systems we tacitly assumed that we were talking about clitics. In both languages the pronominal elements concerned are written as separate words, and the descriptive and theoretical tradition uniformly refers to those elements as 'clitics'. However, as should now be obvious, it's not entirely clear whether the term 'clitic' is always appropriate for such systems. The crucial morphosyntactic fact about those systems is that the clitic cluster aggregates around the verb head and thus lacks the positional freedom normally associated with clitics. This is a conceptual worry that dates back to the earliest work on pronominal clitics in contemporary linguistics (Klavans 1982, 1985). Recall that Klavans' original typology of clitic systems included the possibility of the verb as a domain for cliticization, though she herself noted that it is a property of affixes, not clitics, to be associated with a head word rather than with a position in a phrase. In effect, the notion of a 'head-marking clitic' is at best odd and at worst incoherent.

The Romance languages were the ones that Klavans was principally concerned about, but as we have seen, the Slavic language Macedonian and the Indo-European isolate Albanian both have verb-directed pronominal clitic systems which could equally be analysed as aberrant types of affixation (say, 'Class II pronominal affixation' as opposed to 'Class I' affixation). Another language that illustrates exactly the same kind of phenomenon is Greek. Joseph (1988) argues explicitly that the so-called clitic system is really (now) an affixal system.

7.2.3   Greek verbal 'clitics'

Joseph examines the pronominal 'clitics' of Modern Greek and compares their behaviour against the checklist of clitic/affix properties developed by Zwicky (e.g. in Zwicky and Pullum 1983). He concludes that the pronominals lack most of the properties of clitics but do show a number of affixal properties.

Greek nouns distinguish nominative, genitive and accusative case. Genitive case often has the function of a dative case in other languages. The weak pronominal elements, however, only realize genitive and accusative. They are shown in (13):

(13)   Greek weak pronominals ('clitics')

		Singular		Plural	
		genitive	accusative	genitive	accusative
1st		mu	me	mas	mas
2nd		su	se	sas	sas
3rd	masculine	tu	ton	tus	tus
	feminine	tis	tin	tus	tis
	neuter	tu	to	tus	ta

The weak pronominals occur before finite verb forms but after imperatives (much like pronominal clitics in Macedonian and several Romance languages):

(14)   férte   mas   álo   uzáki
        bring.IMPERATIVE.PL us.GEN another ouzo.ACC
        'Bring us another ouzo!'
(15)   sas   to   férame
        you.GEN it.ACC.N brought.1PL.AOR
        'We brought it to you'

Joseph assumes that there are two prefixes in Greek expressing future tense, *θa*, and negation, *ðe(n)*. These elements are always immediately adjacent to the verb and cannot be separated even by short unstressed adverbials. The only elements that can intervene between *ðe(n)/θa* and the verb are the weak pronominals:

(16) a.   ðen to vlépo
             NEG it I.see
             'I don't see it'
      b.   θa   to vlépo
             FUT it I.see
             'I will see it'
      c.   ðe   θa   to vlépo
             NEG FUT it I.see
             'I won't see it'

Joseph shows that the weak pronominals are certainly not independent word forms because they are invariably positioned adjacent to the verb (and after *ðe(n)/θa*) and cannot stand alone. Moreover, they show selectivity typical of affixes in that they are found adjacent only to verbs. There are a handful of exceptions to this: some prepositions (though not all) take the pronominals as arguments: *metaksí tus* 'between them', *mazí tu* 'with him', but we don't find the pronominal affixes in, say, **apó tu* 'from him'. The pronominals can also be found with a very restricted set of adjectives, specifically, *monós* 'only': *monós tu* 'on his own'. Again, this is highly exceptional behaviour. These deviations from strict selectivity do not alter the affixal status of the pronominals, however. It is actually quite common for agreement affixes to appear both on verbs and on (specific) prepositions, as happens in Welsh, for instance.

The pronominals exhibit certain morphological idiosyncrasies that are typical of affixes but not of clitics. Joseph points out that the 2sg genitive form *su* loses its vowel when it comes before (t-initial) 3rd person accusative pronouns.

(17)   θa   su   to   ðóso ⇒ θastoðóso
         FUT 2SG.GEN it.ACC I.give
         'I will give it to you'

The weak pronominals in some of the dialects of Greek exhibit further properties typical of affixes and not typical of clitics. In certain of the northern dialects, of Thessaly and Macedonia, the 1sg accusative pronominal appears inside the imperative plural affix, as seen in (18):

(18)   1sg inside plural agreement
      a.   pé-m-ti
           tell.IMPERATIVE-me-PL
           '(You, plural) tell me!'
      b.   ð-ó-m-ti
           give.IMPERATIVE-me-PL
           '(You, plural) give (to) me!'

c.   féri-mé-ti
      bring.IMPERATIVE-me-PL
      '(You, plural) bring (to) me!'

Finally, the pronominal forms of Greek resemble affixal agreement markers in that they permit, and sometimes require, doubling by an overt noun phrase (Anagnostopoulou 1999).[1]

The contrast with, say, descriptions of the German *zu* infinitive marker is striking. In both cases we have elements that are traditionally written as separate words but which cannot ever be separated from their verb hosts. Yet in the case of German there is universal agreement that the marker is really a prefix, while for Greek, Joseph's arguments seem to have been universally ignored, even though the case he makes for affixal status seems no less strong than the case for German *zu*.

7.3   Affixes with clitic-like properties

7.3.1   Clitics and English Word-level affixation (Aronoff and Sridhar 1983)

Aronoff and Sridhar (1983)[2] take as their starting point an old debate with generative morphology about the nature of affixes in English. According to the model of Lexical Phonology (Kiparsky 1982, Siegel 1974) there are two classes of affix in English, Class I and Class II (see Spencer 1991, 79–81, 179–83 for discussion). The Class I affixes can trigger idiosyncratic allomorphy on their stems, undergo idiosyncratic allomorphy themselves and crucially, can trigger stress shift. The Class II affixes are phonologically neutral in this respect. Examples of Class I affixes are the irregular past tense inflection *-t* (as in *keep~kep-t*, /kiːp/~/kɛp-t/ and the deadjectival nominal suffix *-ity* (as in *sane~sanity*, /seːn/~/san-ɪtɪ/). Examples of Class II affixes are the regular past tense suffix *-ed* and the deadjectival nominal suffix *-ness*.

In the model that came to be known as Lexical Phonology, an important morphological claim was made about Class I vs Class II affixation, the Affix Ordering Generalization: Class I affixes always appear nearer to the root than Class II affixes. This claim was controversial from the outset (Aronoff 1976), mainly because there were obvious counterexamples to it in English. Nonetheless, it reflected the strong intuition that affixes in English come in two flavours, one of which attaches to a (possibly bound) stem (often called a Root or Stem affix) and the other of which attaches to an existing word form (often called a Word affix). The distinction remains useful as a descriptive rule of thumb for English.

One of the problems with the Affix Ordering Generalization was that it generated a series of paradoxical structures. A notorious example is that of *ungrammaticality* and its ilk. The prefix *un-* is uncontroversially Class II and it clearly selects adjective stems. The suffix *-ity* is equally uncontroversially Class I and it too clearly selects adjective stems. But the meaning of the word is (roughly) that shown in (19), and that implies that the Class I suffix *-ity* is attached peripherally to the Class II prefix *un-*, contrary to the Affix Ordering Generalization:

(19)   Classic example of a 'bracketing paradox'

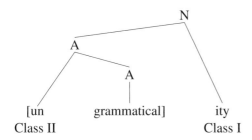

Cases such as this came to be known as 'bracketing paradoxes' (see Section 4.6). Aronoff and Sridhar, recall, reject the (already dubious) claim embodied in the Affix Ordering Generalization. But the intuition remains that a word such as *ungrammaticality* consists of the prefix *un-* added (contrary to subcategorization requirements) to the noun *grammaticality*. They resolve this 'paradox' by arguing that phonologically or prosodically the word consists of two phonological words, ($_\omega$ un)($_\omega$ grammaticality). Further, they argue that the same can be said of words with a string of suffixes, such as [[[[compartment]al]iz]ation]. This, they claim, has the prosodic structure: (compart) (mental) (ization), which they say is the same as that of the phrase *combat mental elation*.

The kind of prosodic structure they have in mind arises when a Stem suffix is attached to a word ending in a Word affix, as is the case with words of the form *Xability, Xization, Xistic* (e.g. *interpretability, organization, narcissistic*). These have the prosodic structures: ($_\omega$X)($_\omega$ ability), ($_\omega$X)($_\omega$ ization), ($_\omega$X)($_\omega$ istic), so that prosodically, *interpretability* is identical to *interpret ability*. Aronoff and Sridhar compare this situation to the kind of mismatch between syntactic structure and prosodic structure that was noted in Structuralist accounts and in early generative phonology, of the kind *(this is the cat)(that chased the rat)* or *(the book) (was in an unlikely) (place)* (see Chapter 4). They then make an important connection between Word affixation in English and the phonology of the simple clitic. When a word is affixed solely with Word-level affixes, those affixes have no effect on the stress of the word; they neither bear stress, nor do they change the stress of the word. In this respect they are prosodically very similar to those simple clitics that merely adjoin to a prosodic category, as exemplified by the pronominal clitics of Standard Italian discussed in Chapter 4. Aronoff and Sridhar describe the prosodic structure of a word such as *unrelentlessness* as containing three (phonological) clitics, *un-, -less, -ness*: ((un(relent)less)ness). In terms of the model of Peperkamp (1997) we might say that the affixes are adjoined to a phonological phrase, ϕ, in exactly the same way that an unaccented function word, for instance, the indefinite article, is adjoined to a phonological phrase containing the nominal phrase with which it combines. In other words, Class II affixes are essentially indistinguishable prosodically from unstressed function words which are phonologically cliticized to their host. Thus, prosodically, there's little difference, if any, between, say, *reader demands* and *read a demand* (or, indeed, in casual speech, *read her demands*).

7.3.2   Variation in affix ordering

We have seen at various places in this book that clitics tend to cluster in a fixed, sometimes idiosyncratic, linear order. This, of course, is also a property of affix strings. However, we also find instances in which affixes can appear in different orders.

One reason why this might occur is phonology: it has been reported for a number of languages that affixes may appear in different orders depending on the segmental phonology of the stem, as in the Cushitic language Qafar (also written 'Afar'), as described by Fulmer (1991, 1997). In that language conjugation classes appear to be defined in terms of the phonology of the stem, in that several of the inflectional affixes in the conjugation system appear as suffixes with stems that begin with a consonant or [ɑ] and as a prefix otherwise. Thus, in *t-okm-e*, '2nd-eat-PERF' 'You (sg.) ate' the stem is *okm* and the person marker *t* is a prefix, while in *rab-t-e* '2nd-die-PERF' 'You died' the stem is *rab* and the person marker is a suffix (Fulmer 1997, 10).[3] A similar claim has been made for the phonological conditioning of clitic linearization in the Australian language Yir-Yoront, which we discuss briefly in Section 8.4.

The second reason for varied order in affix systems is essentially syntactic: if a language has a set of pronominal affixes realizing subject and object arguments, and if those affixes arose from a pronoun/clitic system in which only relative order distinguished the arguments, then that linear conditioning may well remain once the clitics have been thoroughly morphologized as affixes. We discuss an example of this from the Bantu language Lingala.

A third reason why affixes might show variable ordering is semantics: we occasionally find that the meaning of a word form can depend on the order in which affixes occur. This is most likely where the affixes realize meanings corresponding to predicates or operators that can take scope over each other such as quantifiers or negation. However, it's also common with affixes realizing argument structure alternations. We'll exemplify this with argument structure alternations in Quechua.

Finally, affix order may exhibit free variation, without any particular grammatical conditioning. Sometimes such variation might be associated with dialect differences, where speakers effectively command more than one dialectal variant and switch between the two, and in other cases there may be other subtle sociolinguistic or discourse factors involved, but it would seem that such variation is often more of a tendency, so that the conditioning is statistical rather than grammaticalized. The variation in prefix order that we describe for Chintang appears to be of this sort.

Pronominal affix order in Lingala

In Section 5.4 we saw that the Uto-Aztecan language Classical Nahuatl has pronominal affixes serving as arguments on verbs. The ordering of those affixes is fixed, and, moreover, the form of the pronominal affix generally depends on its function: that is, the subject affix for a given person/number combination is usually different in form from the corresponding object affix. In clitic systems we also often find a fixed ordering of elements, as demonstrated for Italian pronominal clitics in Section 5.4.2, and for Bulgarian in Section 3.3, subsection 3.3.3, often with idiosyncratic determination of order. For instance, we have seen that the order of direct and indirect object clitics can vary depending on the person of the clitic pronominal.

However, there is one sense in which the order of pronominal affixes can be manipulated by the grammar of a language, so that it becomes impossible to say of a given formative exactly what position in the affix string it must occupy. This occurs most commonly in languages that have subject and object agreement markers, say, for person/number, derived from pronominals such that the actual form of the person/number marker remains constant but the position in the affix string depends on the grammatical function that marker realizes. We illustrate with examples from the Bantu language Lingala, a language spoken by some 10 million people in the Democratic Republic of Congo (our exposition follows Stump 2001, 144–5, after Dzokanga 1979).

Lingala verbs are inflected with a set of prefixes, including (amongst other properties), subject agreement markers (SM), object agreement markers (OM) and the tense-aspect-mood marker -*ko*- in the order: SM-*ko*-OM. Lingala nouns fall into a number of noun classes or genders, each with its own agreement marker. The forms of the SMs and OMs are given in Table 7.1 below, with the traditional numbering of the noun classes (we cite eight of the noun classes). The forms in square brackets are those in which SM and OM are differentiated. All the other forms are identical whether they realize subject or object grammatical functions. Their role is therefore only differentiated by their linear position in the prefix string.

Scope and argument structure in Quechua and Bantu

Another common source of scope effects from affix ordering is with morphology that realizes argument structure alternations such as passive, causative, applicative, and other quasi-derivational alternations such as reflexive and reciprocal morphology. The logic is very simple. Suppose we have a language in which there is, say, passive, reciprocal ('each other') and causative morphology. From a basic transitive clause such as *Mother washes the children* we can then derive the following clause types:

(20)   The children wash.PASS (by Mother)
          'The children are washed (by Mother)'   [Passive]
(21)   Mother wash.CAUSE the children Mary
          'Mother makes Mary wash the children'   [Causative]

Table 7.1 *Lingala pronominal affixes*

PERSON		SUBJECT		OBJECT	
		SG	PL	SG	PL
1st		[na-]	[to-]	n-/m-	lo-
2nd		[o-]	bo-	ko-	bo-
3rd:	CLASSES				
	1–2	[a-]	ba-	mo-	ba-
	3–4	mo-	mi-	mo-	mi-
	5–6	li-	ma-	li-	ma-
	7–8	e-	bi-	e-	bi-
	9–10	e-	i-	e-	i-
	11–10	lo-	i-	lo-	i-
	11–6	lo-	ma-	lo-	ma-
	14–6	bo-	ma-	bo-	ma-

(22)   Children wash.RECIP
        'The children wash each other'   [Reciprocal]

Given these derived forms we can derive further forms. For instance, we can take the causative and passivize it:

(23)   Children wash.CAUSE.PASS (by Mother)
        'The children are made to be washed'   [Passive of Causative]

But equally we might be able to take a passive clause and causativize it:

(24)   Mary wash.PASS.CAUSE the children
        'Mary causes the children to be washed' [Causative of Passive]

Clearly, the meaning of the complex verb form *wash.CAUSE.PASS* is distinct from the meaning of *wash.PASS.CAUSE* in these hypothetical examples. Similarly, we can take the reflexive and causativize it:

(25)   Mother wash.RECIP.CAUSE children
        'Mother made the children wash each other' [Causative of Reciprocal]

or alternatively, we can take the causative and reflexivize it:

(26)   The children wash.CAUSE.RECIP
        'The children make (someone) wash each other' [Reciprocal of Causative]

Again, the order of affixes here reflects distinct semantic/logical interpretations.

In practice the syntax of such constructions can be somewhat complex and there are often rather complex constraints on exactly how such meanings are expressed or even whether they are possible. However, a concrete example of the causative/reflexive alternation is reported for Equadorian Quechua by Muysken (1981) (see also Spencer 1991, 74). This language has a reciprocal suffix *-naku*

and a causative/permissive suffix *-chi*, which can occur in either order with
respect to each other:

(27) a.   maqa-naku-ya-chi-n
        beat-RECIP-DURATIVE-CAUSE-3
        'He is causing them to beat each other'
    b.   maqa-chi-naku-rka-n
        beat-CAUSE-RECIP-PL-3
        'They let each other be beaten'

Another language group that has productive and regular argument structure
alternations is Bantu. In many languages of this group verbs receive a suffixal
extension to create Causative, Applicative,[4] Reciprocal or Passive forms. In a
number of the Bantu languages these extensions can be combined in a variety
of orders to give different meanings, much as in the Quechua example above.
Interestingly, however, there is a very strong tendency for the affixes to appear
in the specific order Causative–Applicative–Reciprocal–Passive throughout the
languages of the group, whatever the scope relationships. Hyman (2003) refers
to this as the CARP template and provides an analysis within Optimality Theory
of the various meaning–form relationships exhibited by the extension suffixes.
The Bantu case shows clearly how affixal systems tend to shift towards a fixed
element order even where this goes against the order implied by considerations
of semantic scope.[5]

Free variation in affix order: the case of Chintang prefixes

In Chapter 3 we saw that some clitic systems permit variation in the order
of elements of a kind that is not normally found with affixal systems. Thus,
the disyllabic pronominal Wackernagel clitics of Tagalog show a good deal of
apparently free variation in order. Similarly, the discourse particles of Finnish
(Section 3.5) may show order variation unrelated to semantic scope or other
conditioning factors (Nevis 2000). It is also possible to find instances of free
variation in pronominal clitic order. Bickel et al. (2007, 70) cite the following
examples from Swiss German:

(28) a.   Hèt=er=s=em   gsait?
        has-he-it-to.him said
    b.   Hèt=er=em=s   gsait?
        has-he-to.him-it said
        'Did he tell it to him?'

Similar examples can be cited from English, of course: *Did he give him it*~*Did
he give it him?* /dɪdɪgɪvɪmɪt~dɪdɪgɪvɪtɪm/.

Given that, for many linguists at least, clitics are a kind of prosodically weak
word, and given that we often see fairly free word order, we might expect to see
free variation in some clitic clusters. And indeed, with discourse clitics this is
sometimes the case. But at the very least, even if free variation in ordering is

rather rare among clitic systems, it ought to at least serve as a diagnostic property of clitics: if a string of formatives permits free variation in ordering, then those formatives cannot be affixes, but must be either words or clitics. Unfortunately, although this is a good rule of thumb, it cannot be elevated to the status of foolproof test. For there have been a number of studies that have claimed to find free variation in the linearization of bona fide affixes. Perhaps the two clearest cases come from nominal inflection in Uralic languages, such as Mari (Luutonen 1997, Spencer 2009) and the remarkable case of prefix ordering in the Kiranti language, Chintang (Bickel et al. 2007), which we now turn to.

Chintang verbs consist of a stem (which itself is often complex, consisting of two substems) together with a set of suffixes expressing polarity, tense, subject/object agreement and other properties and a set of prefixes, expressing similar properties (often exhibiting extended exponence). Bickel et al. (2007, 44) provide the following rather spectacular examples of free ordering of three prefixes:[6]

(29) a.   a-ma-im-yokt-e
           2-NEG-sleep-NEG-PAST

     b.   ma-a-im-yokt-e
           NEG-2-sleep-NEG-PAST
           'You didn't sleep'

(30) a.   u-kha-ma-cop-yokt-e
           3NS.A-1NS.P-NEG-see-NEG-PAST

     b.   u-ma-kha-cop-yokt-e
           3NS.A-NEG-1NS.P-see-NEG-PAST

     c.   kha-u-ma-cop-yokt-e
           1NS.P-3NS.A-NEG-see-NEG-PAST

     d.   ma-u-kha-cop-yokt-e
           NEG-3NS.A-1NS.P-see-NEG-PAST

     e.   kha-ma-u-cop-yokt-e
           1NS.P-NEG-3NS.A-see-NEG-PAST

     f.   ma-kha-u-cop-yokt-e
           NEG-1NS.P-3NS.A-see-NEG-PAST
           'They didn't see us'

The examples in (30) represent the limit of possible variation because, for independent reasons, it is only possible to have a maximum of three prefixes in a word.

The authors demonstrate in detail that the prefixed forms illustrated above represent single grammatical words (rather than, say, words with proclitics), and that the various orders don't reflect semantic differences or differences of dialect, idiolect and so on.

Beginning with grammatical wordhood, Bickel et al. (2007, 52–8) show that the prefixes respect the typical affixal properties of the kind discussed by Zwicky and Pullum (1983) and others. First, all the prefixes select just verb stems and cannot appear on their own. Second, the prefixes are obligatory parts of the verbal word form.

In addition, there are dependencies between some of the prefixes and other affixes that are characteristic of affixal systems. For instance, the negation prefix *mai-* and the past tense suffix *-yokt* select each other. Bickel et al. provide the following example of extended exponence, a characteristic of affix systems (p. 54):

(31)   Extended exponence in Sambugāū
             a-mai-kha-tup-t-a-ce

             [2.A], [NEG][1DU.EX.PL] [PST]
             'You (sg/du/pl) didn't meet us (dual excl.)' (Sambugāū[7] dialect)

The argument is that such extended exponence is characteristic of affixal systems but not of syntactic systems. This argument seems to be exaggerated, however. It's easy to think of cases of periphrasis in which exactly this kind of extended exponence is found. Take the English auxiliary system, for instance. We have two auxiliary verbs (HAVE, BE) and two non-finite verb forms, the *-ing*, *-en* forms and by judicious combination of these we obtain the progressive and perfect aspects and the passive voice, as seen in (32):

(32)   Extended exponence in periphrasis
             had   be-en   eat-ing

             [PERF], [PROG], [ACT]

Again, there are descriptions of extended exponence in other languages with formatives that are clearly clitics rather than affixes. A notable example is the person/number proclitics in the Algonquian language Potawatomi, *n-* '1st person (non-inclusive)', *w-* '3rd person' and *k-* '2nd person or 1pl inclusive' (Hockett 1965). Without inspecting the verb form with which such a clitic is associated it is impossible to tell whether these clitics denote subjects (non-inverse verb forms) or objects (inverse transitive forms).

The final piece of evidence in favour of treating the preverbal formatives as prefixes comes from syntactic integrity. No word may intervene between the prefix and the stem. The sole exception to this statement is a pair of focussing clitics, *=yaŋ*, *=ta*, but these are exceptional anyway inasmuch as they are endoclitics, and are even able to split single morphemes (much in the manner of the endoclitics in Udi; Harris 2000, 2002).

The explanation for this unusual behaviour lies in the fact that the prefixes select prosodic words as their host. The Chintang verb stem is often complex and generally consists of two or more prosodic words. The prefixes show a mild degree of promiscuity, in the sense that they can align with any prosodic word boundary provided it is part of the verb stem. Since the result is itself a prosodic word, other prefixes can select that prosodic unit to which to adjoin, giving

the impression of random prefix ordering. This is illustrated by their examples
(33)–(35) (pp. 66–7):

(33) a.   a-($_\omega$ kha)($_\omega$ tube)
     b.   ($_\omega$ kha)a-($_\omega$ tube)
             Both: 'You (sg.) met us'

(34) a.   a-($_\omega$ ya)($_\omega$ cepte)
     b.   ($_\omega$ ya)a-($_\omega$ cepte)
             Both: 'You (sg.) called'

(35) a.   ($_\omega$ kos-a)-u-($_\omega$ gond-e)
             walk-PAST-3NS.S-AMB-PAST
             'They walked around'
     b.   ($_\omega$ ko-na)-a-($_\omega$ gon-no)
             walk-NA-2-AMB-NPAST
             'You (will) walk around'

Finally, Bickel et al. explicitly point out that the prefixes do not behave
like clitics. They select only a verb stem and hence fail to show promiscuous
attachment, and they do not take scope over conjoined phrases, the two most
characteristic properties of clitics (and in this respect they differ from the genuine
clitics in Chintang).

From the detailed and meticulous description provided by Bickel et al. it is
clear that the Chintang formatives are prefixes, but not prototypical ones. They
exhibit an unusual type of promiscuity, in that they attach to any appropriate
prosodic unit within their domain. However, that domain is defined morphologically, just as it is for any normal affix. But as a consequence of this promiscuity,
they exhibit a freedom of linearization found otherwise only with free word
forms or certain types of clitic.

The Chintang prefix system therefore illustrates very well the important point
that it is not so much important to ascertain whether a formative is a clitic or
an affix; rather, it is necessary to specify all the constraints on its realization,
whether phonological, morphological, syntactic or other. Whether you call the
resulting formative a clitic, an affix or something else may well be immaterial,
if the language itself doesn't draw a clear-cut distinction between two types of
formative in its grammar.

7.3.3   Affixes with wide scope

One of the prototypical properties of affixes compared with (many)
function words is that they cannot take wide scope over conjoined phrases. Thus,
while we can say *the cats and dogs* in which the definite article applies to both
cats and *dogs*, we cannot say **the [cat- and dog]-s* in an interpretation under
which *cat* is interpreted as plural as well as *dogs*. That is, the plural affix has
narrow scope and has to be repeated on each conjunct. In general, clitics pattern
along with function words with regard to scope over coordinated phrases and

show wide scope. In other words, it is not usually necessary to repeat a clitic on each conjunct.

Now, this property of wide vs narrow scope doesn't reliably distinguish affixes and clitics from function words, in the sense that there are function words that also fail to take wide scope. In Romance languages such as Portuguese monosyllabic function words such as articles and prepositions (which are often phonological clitics) generally have to be repeated on each conjunct. Thus, the equivalence between affix~narrow scope and clitic/function word~wide scope fails in the direction 'clitic/function word implies wide scope'.

However, the equivalence fails in the other direction, too: we cannot say that wide scope implies we are dealing with a clitic and not an affix, because there are well-documented cases in a good many languages in which it seems that an affix can indeed take wide scope over coordinated phrases. That is, we find cases in which an expression that has a form similar to *[[cat and dog]s]* is interpreted as *[cats and dogs]*. When it applies to inflectional morphology, the phenomenon is often referred to as group inflection. However, since the phenomenon extends beyond inflection, it is better to focus on the fact that it is a bound (affixal) ele-ment that takes wide scope. Another popular term, which focusses on the fact that this is a formal property of a bound affixal element, is suspended affixation. This is the term we will sometimes use. However, we will try to refer to the phe-nomenon using the rather cumbersome phraseology 'affix with wide scope' or 'wide scope affix'. This is because there are several distinct ways of picturing such constructions and we wish to remain as neutral as possible about the way individual cases are represented.

Remaining with our hypothetical example of *[cat and dog-s]*, we see in (36) some of the logically distinct ways of thinking about the syntax underlying this structure:

(36) a. [[cat] and [dog]]-s
     b. [[cat] and [dog-s]]
     c. [[cat-∅] and [dog-s]]
     d. [[[cat-∅] and [dog-∅]]-s]
     e. [[cat-s] and [dog-s]]

In (36a) we have an element that is attached to the coordinated phrase as a whole in much the same way that a function word might be. In (36b), by contrast, we have an inflected word coordinated with a non-inflected conjunct which, how-ever, is interpreted as though it were inflected itself. In (36c) we see a variant of (36b) in which we assume that the first conjunct bears some kind of zero inflection which is then identified with the overt inflection on the second con-junct. Crucially, the representation [cat-∅] is representationally distinct from the singular form of 'cat'. In (36d) we see an analysis in which the plural marker is taken to be a property of each conjoined word but the overt marker of that property is moved to a position outside the phrase. The zero markers could then be traces of movement in a syntactic theory that countenances such things, or they could be inserted zeros that are interpreted as identical to the externally positioned overt marker. In a copy-and-delete alternative to movement models an equivalent representation for (36d) would be [[[cat-s] and [dog-s]]-s]. Finally, in (36e) we have provided an analysis under which the first conjunct is inflected for plural at some stage but some later process (perhaps phonological in some sense) deletes the first occurrence under identity with the second occurrence.

We labour the point about representational indeterminacy somewhat because it is important to realize that just observing forms such as *cat and dogs* with the relevant interpretation doesn't necessarily tell us a great deal about the morphology or syntax of the construction or of the inflectional marking. Moreover, it is easy to imagine theoretical frameworks that would be more or less obliged to adopt one or other of these representations irrespective of how else the construction behaved or what the other properties might be of the inflectional markers concerned. It would take us too far afield to discuss the various syntactic approaches to coordination. A detailed summary of the LFG approach can be found in Dalrymple (2001, chapter 12), and natural coordination[8] in LFG is the topic of Dalrymple and Nikolaeva (2006). In Sag et al. (2003, 249) we see a formulation of coordination in HPSG which is explicitly designed to prevent such things as suspended affixation. On the other hand, that formulation prevents the description of such phenomena as Right Node Raising or (Backward) Coordinate Reduction as in *The principal suspended ____ and Sandy defended him*, so the rule is modified to allow reference to such gaps in Sag et al. (2003, 445). This, in principle, could permit wide scope affixation, provided the affixes were represented somehow in syntactic structure. In Minimalist syntax Johannessen (1998) is a standard reference.

From the perspective of the student of clitics, the point of our hypothetical example (36) is that some of these representations are better compatible with an analysis of the plural marker as a clitic and some are better compatible with an analysis as an affix. For instance, the constituent structures of (36b, c, e) seem to imply an affixal analysis, while the constituent structure of (36a) seems to imply a clitic analysis, with the remaining structure, (36d), being perhaps neutral.

The term 'suspended affixation' was introduced by Lewis (1967, 35) in his grammar of Turkish, and Turkish and other Turkic languages provide the best-known examples of the phenomenon. It has been discussed in the context of the role of morphology within HPSG by Orgun (1996a, b) and more recently by Good and Yu (2005), with a response by Kabak (2007). In suspended affixation we see what appears to be an affix taking wide scope over conjoined elements. If the wide scope markers really are affixes we thus find that what appeared to be a useful diagnostic for clitics is no longer usable.

The basic facts of suspended affixation in Turkish are summarized by Göksel and Kerslake (2005, 534–6), whom we follow here. (We follow those authors by indicating suspended affixes with (...).) In almost all cases it is the non-final suffixes that get elided. It is possible to elide affixal copular markers and person markers from what Göksel and Kerslake call Group 2 markers (the 'z-paradigm' of Good and Yu 2005, Kabak 2007). In (37) we see suspension of two suffixes, the affixal copular *ti*, found with the *-miş* perfect suffix, and the person/number desinence *-m*:

(37)   Hem sinemaya   git-miş(...) hem de biraz
              both cinema.DAT go.PERF   both also a.little

                gez-miş-ti-m
                go.around-PERF-PAST.COP-1SG
                'I had both gone to the cinema and walked around a bit'

Turkish nouns can take three types of suffix: a plural marker *lEr*,[9] possessive agreement markers cross-referencing the possessor in person/number, and one of five case markers (accusative, genitive, dative, locative, ablative; nominative case is unmarked). In noun phrases the plural suffix *lEr* can be suspended together with any subsequent suffixes:

(38)   bütün kitap(...) ve defter-ler-imiz
              all   book   and notebook-PL-1PL.POSS
              'all our books and notebooks'

It is noteworthy that what has been suspended in (38) is an abstract representation of the plural suffix, not an actual form. The plural of 'book' would be *kitaplar* with the back vowel allomorph *-lar*, whereas *defterlerimiz* has the front vowel allomorph.

Case markers and adverbial elements with case-like functions can be suspended:

(39) a.   Vapur hem Napoli(...) hem Venedik'-e uğruyormuş
            boat and Naples   and Venice-LOC stops.EVIDENTIAL
            'Apparently the boat stops at both Naples and Venice'
     b.   öğretmen-ler(...) ve öğrenci-ler-le
            teacher-PL   and student-PL-WITH
            'with (the) students and (the) teachers'

All three sets of suffix can be suspended together:[10]

(40)   köy(...), kasaba(...) ve kent-ler-imiz-den
              village   small.town and city-PL-1PL.POSS-ABL
              'from our villages, small towns and cities'

In yes-no questions it is the last suffix that is elided:

(41)   Öğretmen mi-siniz (yoksa) öğrenci mi(...)?
              teacher   BE-2SG or   student BE
              'Are you a teacher, or a student?'

These cases of elision are reminiscent of the elision of function words such as the postposition *için* 'for':

(42)   karısı(...) ve kendisi için
        wife.GEN and self.GEN for
        'for his wife and for himself'

In (43) we provide examples adapted from Wälchli (2005, 48) of variable scope
affixation in Mari, a Uralic language that exhibits a certain degree of variability
in its suffix ordering (Spencer 2009, 192–3):

(43) a.   Tide [ergy-m den üdyr-vlak-em]-lan   pölek
           this [son-my with daughter-PL-my]-DAT present
           'This is a present for my son and my daughters'
     b.   Tide [ergy-m-lan den üdyr-em-vlak-lan]   pölek
           this [son-my-DAT with daughter-my-PL-DAT] present
           'This is a present for my son and my daughters'
     c.   Tide [ergy-m den üdyr-em-vlak]-lan   pölek
           this [son-my with daughter-my-PL]-DAT present
           'This is a present for my son (one) and my daughters'
           'This is a present for my sons and my daughters (together more than two)'
     d.   Tide [ergy-m den üdyr-em-vlak-lan]   pölek
           this [son-my with daughter-my-PL-DAT] present
           'This is a present for my son (one) and my daughters'
           'This is a present for my sons and my daughters (together more than two)'

In the nominal domain especially, wide scope inflection is widespread in the
languages of Eurasia, becoming more prominent from west to east (Wälchli
2005). Wälchli discusses the phenomenon under the rubric of non-relational
marking and argues that it is often a symptom of natural coordination as opposed
to ordinary coordination. Natural coordination refers to the coordination of terms
that are associated with high frequency because of culture or because of the
natural properties of the coordinands. Thus, in Western culture it is natural to
coordinate the terms *knife* and *fork*, and in pretty well all cultures it is natural
to coordinate terms such as *father*, *mother* or *wind*, *rain*. Such coordinations are
therefore natural. Occasional coordinations, of the kind *my doctor and Harriet's
supervisor* or *The Tower of London and the Taj Mahal* are not therefore natural.
Suspended affixation effects are much more common with natural coordination.

Wide scope affixation can be found with inflectional and derivational morphology in a number of languages, and it is often a symptom of recent and not
quite complete morphologization. For instance, the Romance languages inno-
vated a deadjectival adverbial suffix from the ablative singular form of the Latin
feminine gender lexeme MĒNS 'mind', *mente*. This formed a phrase with the
adjective, which agreed with *mente* in number/gender. In French and Italian
the combination fused into a single word form, though we can still detect the
feminine singular form of the adjective ending in *-a* (which has now become
the stem form to which the suffix *-ment(e)* attaches): *rapido* 'quick', *rapida* ⇒
rapidamente. In Portuguese and Spanish (though not, for instance, in modern
French or Italian), this *-mente* element can take scope over conjoined adjectives;

indeed, this is the norm in the written language: *rápida e facilmente* 'quickly and easily'.

The discussion so far treats suspended affixation as arising from the attachment of an affix to the edge of a coordinated phrase and taking wide scope over that coordination. However, there is another way of looking at such cases. We can think of the wide scope as resulting from the reduction of a coordination that includes a repeated suffix, so-called Coordination Reduction. Booij (1985) proposes a deletion analysis of such cases in Dutch (see also Booij 2007, 164). Thus, the non-cohering affix *-achtig* '-like, -ish' permits Coordination Reduction:

(44)   storm- en   regen-achtig
              storm   and rain-ACHTIG
              'stormy and rainy'

He treats this as resulting from the deletion of the suffix on the first conjunct under identity with the suffix on the second conjunct: *storm-~~achtig~~ en regenachtig*. Booij argues that the reduction process is only possible when the remnant of reduction is a prosodic word. The process is rather similar to what we see with certain loosely cohering suffixes in English, as in *cat- or dog-like (behaviour)*.

A very similar phenomenon is found with compounds:

(45)   wespen- en   bijen-steken
              wasp-   and bee-stings
              'wasp- and bee-stings'

We may ask why we don't treat these cases as instances of a single element taking scope over a coordinated host. In the case of the compounds we can motivate a semantic justification for the reduction analysis: the expression *wasp- and bee-stings* doesn't denote a set of stings that simultaneously are associated with a wasp and a bee, but rather a set of wasp-stings and a set of bee-stings. At some level of semantic analysis, therefore, we have to accept that *wasp- and bee-stings* means WASP-STINGS1 and BEE-STINGS2, for distinct sets of stings.

Kenesei (2007) discusses a number of instances of Coordination Reduction in Hungarian, involving what he calls affixoids, namely, the case suffix *-ként* 'in the capacity of', and the derivational suffixes *-szor* 'times (multiplied by)' and *-talan* 'without':[11]

(46)   feleség- és   anya-ként
              wife-   and mother-AS
              'as a wife and mother'

(47)   hat- vagy nyolc-szor
              six- or   eight-TIMES
              'six or eight times'

(48)   ajtó- és   ablak-talan
              door- and window-LESS
              'door- and window-less'

Kenesei notes that there are other affixes, such as -szerű 'like', that permit suspended affixation and which in addition can be themselves conjoined (in his
terms, permit Forward Coordinate Reduction, that is, elision of the second host):

(49) a.   telefon-   és autó-szerű (dolgok)
            telephone- and car-like   (things)
            'telephone- and car-like (things)'
     b.   telefon-féle   vagy -szerű (dolgok)
            telephone-kind or   -like (things)
            'things like or resembling telephones'

There seem to be no elements that permit Forward Coordinate Reduction but not
Backward Coordinate Reduction. Elements such as -szerű Kenesei calls semiwords.

      To summarize, the phenomenon of elements that take wide scope over
coordinated expressions is found with compounding, and with certain types
of derivation-like affixes in a number of languages. How does this relate to
suspended affixation in Turkish? In particular, would we need to assume a
Coordination Reduction analysis for suspended affixes?

      The first point to bear in mind is that the Turkish suspendable affixes for the
most part appear to be inflectional. Now, since it is so difficult to draw a clear
line between inflection and derivation, this may not be helpful to us. However,
the meanings associated with the Turkish suspended affixes are clearly func-
tional/inflectional, and this means that we lose the main motivation for proposing
a Coordination Reduction analysis. On the contrary, we occasionally find constructions in which there is a potential semantic distinction between a wide scope
construction and a construction in which the affix is repeated on each conjunct.
We saw this in example (22) in Chapter 2, where with wide scope the possession
is interpreted as extending over both brothers simultaneously (so that they are
brothers to each other) while with repetition of the possessive marker the two
men needn't be brothers.

      We conclude, therefore, that there are instances in which we should treat an
affix-like element as attaching to the word at the edge of a conjoined phrase and
having wide scope over the whole coordinate phrase. If we have every reason
for saying that such an element is an affix (and not a clitic, say) then we have
cases of bona fide suspended affixation, and we have lost a potential diagnostic
for distinguishing clitics from affixes.

      The suffixes of Turkish have the affix property of attaching to a specific kind
of head; that is, they do not exhibit promiscuous attachment. Nonetheless, on
the grounds of the wide scope property alone we can ask whether we are dealing with genuine affixes or with clitics. For cases such as Turkish the issue is
clouded by the fact that the affixes are suffixes and the syntax of the language
is predominantly (indeed, overwhelmingly) head final. This means that it is very
difficult to know whether an element is an affix attached to a head, which is
therefore at the right edge of its phrase, or whether that element is a clitic/phrasal

affix/edge inflection attached to the right edge of the phrase and hence hosted by the head of that phrase. What is the behaviour of elements that, on other grounds, we take to be clitics?

We have seen that the Bulgarian noun phrase has a Wackernagel definite article, which behaves morphophonologically like an affix (Section 5.5). We have also seen that it has a Wackernagel pronominal clitic possessor marker (Section 3.4, Franks and King 2000, 55–8, Mišeska Tomić 2006, 101–5). Wälchli (2005, 63) cites example (50) (from the Bulgarian translation of the Universal Declaration of Human Rights):

(50)   v lični-ja   mu   život,   semejstvo-to,
           in personal-DEF.FEM 3SG.POSS life(FEM) family(NEUT)-DEF.NEUT
           žilište-to   i   korespondencija-ta
           home(NEUT)-DEF.NEUT or correspondence(FEM)-DEF.FEM
           '<to arbitrary interference> with his privacy, family, home or
              correspondence'

In this example the definite article is repeated on each conjunct (no doubt because it agrees in number/gender with its host) while the (invariable) possessive pronominal takes wide scope (even though it is not positioned at the edge of the phrase).

Recall the Polish floating/mobile inflections discussed in Chapter 4. Here, the person/number markers used with past tense verbs in Polish trigger idiosyncratic allomorphic alternations on their hosts, a property that we can usually take to be a clear sign that we are dealing with an affix. Thus, the mobile inflections present conflicting properties with respect to the affix/clitic distinction. However, they show the wide scope property typical of clitics (Franks and King 2000, 144f.):

(51)   Ale=m poszła i   zobaczyła
           but=1SG [went and saw]
           'But I went and saw it'
           Narrow scope is also possible: *poszła=m i zobzczyła=m*
(52)   W kawiarni=śmy jedli lody,   albo pili   kawę
           in cafe=1PL   [ate ice-cream or   drank coffee]
           'In the cafe we ate ice-cream or drank coffee'
           Narrow scope is also possible: *jedli=śmy lody, albo pili=śmy kawę*

These examples are especially interesting because the wide scope clitic is phonologically attached to a word that has no syntactic relationship to the elements of the conjoined phrase that the clitic itself applies to. Thus, in (51) the verbal clitic is attached to a sentential coordinating conjunction *ale* 'but', and in (52) it is attached to the edge of an adjunct phrase 'in the cafe'.

7.3.4   A Wackernagel affix in Lithuanian

A particularly interesting example of an affix that preserves clitic properties is the Lithuanian reflexive prefix *s(i)*, as described by Nevis and

Joseph (1993). Verbs in this language often have preverbs, prefix-like elements that change the lexical or aspectual semantics of the verb root. They generally have a default spatial semantics, though in most cases they have no meaning as such, much like the *under* of English *understand*, *undergo* etc. Examples are *at-* 'towards', *iš-* 'out of', *pa-* 'completion', as in *at-sãkė* 'answer' (from *sãkė* 'say'), *iš-laikaù* 'withstand' (from *laikaũ* 'maintain'). A verb may have more than one preverb, as in *pri-pa-žìnti* 'acknowledge'. There are no purely inflectional prefixes in Lithuanian.

The Lithuanian reflexive marker generally appears at the end of the verb form: *matýti* 'to see (infinitive)', *matýti-s* 'to see each other, meet (infinitive)', *keliù* 'I raise, lift up', *keliúo-si* 'I get up, arise'. However, when the verb has a preverb the reflexive marker appears between that preverb and the verb root:

(53) a.   iš-laikaũ 'I preserve, withstand'
             iš-si-laikaũ 'I hold my stand'
      b.   at-sãkė 'answered (3sg)'
             at-si-sãkė 'refused (3sg)'
      c.   pér-keliu 'I move, transfer'
             pér-si-keliu 'I move, remove' (cf. keliúo-si above)

When the verb has two preverbs, *-si-* comes after the first of them:

(54)   pri-pa-žìnti 'to acknowledge'
             pri-si-pa-žìnti 'to confess, avow'

From the distribution of *-si-* it would appear that this is an affix that obeys Wackernagel's Law: it must appear in second position in the word. However, this presupposes that the reflexive marker really is an affix (and that the preverbs are prefixes). Nevis and Joseph demonstrate the affixhood of *-si-* in various ways, adducing the Zwicky–Pullum criteria for distinguishing clitics and affixes. First, the reflexive is selective with respect to word category. It attaches only to verbs or to deverbal nominalizations: *pa-si-mãtymas* 'meeting, date (nom.sg.)'. Second, there are gaps in the paradigms of some lexemes taking *-si-*. Deverbal nouns in the suffix *-mas* lack dative, accusative, instrumental and locative case forms in the plural (they have regular nominative and genitive plural forms and regular oblique forms in the singular). Third, the *-si-* formative triggers idiosyncratic allomorphy on its host. For instance, the low front vowel æ (written 'e') is raised to a mid vowel (written 'ė'): *mãtome* 'we see' ~ *mãtomė-s* 'we see each other'. Moreover, this alternation is morpholexically conditioned: the preverb *be-* fails to alternate before *-si-*, for instance.

7.4   Mixed clitic systems

In this section we look at languages in which pronominal forms behave like typical clitics in one context but like affixes in other contexts.

This situation often arises when grammaticalization or morphologization of a clitic system has not reached completion in an even manner. In some instances, recently morphologized affixes have integrated into affixal morphology only in certain morphosyntactic contexts. In Chapter 4 we discussed Polish clitics, which attach to words of any lexical class, like clitics, but which trigger idiosyncratic allomorphy on their hosts, just like affixes. These clitics are mixed in the sense that they are simultaneously like prototypical clitics and like prototypical affixes wherever they occur. In European Portuguese and Udi, however, we'll see clitics that appear to have all the typical properties of clitics in one construction and all the typical properties of affixes in slightly different constructions. The existence of such constructions should come as no surprise, since English auxiliary clitics have exactly this mixed property. When the host of the reduced auxiliary is a subject pronoun the 'clitic' triggers completely idiosyncratic allomorphy on some of those pronouns, as we saw in Section 4.5.5. This means that, while in most instances the reduced auxiliary behaves like a (simple) clitic, in construction with a subject pronoun it behaves like an affix, indeed, like a root/stem level affix, and not even like a word-level (Class II) affix. In the next two sections we'll see that exactly the same kind of phenomenon can be observed with special clitics.

7.4.1   European Portuguese and mesoclisis

European Portuguese has a system of pronominal object clitics similar in most respects to that of other Romance languages. It distinguishes two types of object, which we will label 'accusative' and 'dative' (without claiming, of course, that Portuguese has a case system). The basic forms are shown in (55):

(55)   European Portuguese pronominal clitics

Reflexive	Dat/Acc, Dat 3rd	Acc 3rd
se	me 1sg	o(s) m.sg/pl
	te 2sg	a(s) f.sg/pl
	nos 1pl	
	vos 2pl	
	lhe(s) 3sg/pl	

It is possible for two clitics to combine into a cluster. This frequently gives rise to suppletive or portmanteau forms. These are illustrated in (56):

(56)   Combinations with *o(s)*, *a(s)*

plain	cl-o(s)	cl-a(s)
me	mo(s),	ma(s)
te	to(s)	ta(s)
lhe(s)	lho(s)	lha(s)
nos	no-lo(s)	no-la(s)
vos	vo-lo(s)	vo-la(s)

A convenient way of thinking of the cluster is in terms of three 'virtual' slots, as shown in (57):

(57)   Attested positions – three slots analysis

REFL	DAT	ACC
me	me	me
te	te	te
nos	nos	nos
vos	vos	vos
se	lhe(s)	o(s), a(s)

There are several respects in which the cluster behaves like a string of affixal elements rather than syntactically represented words. First, the cluster cannot be split up and it is therefore placed as a unit, either as an enclitic string, immediately after the (usually finite) verb host, or as a proclitic string immediately to the left of the verb group. Second, a variety of idiosyncratic allomorphic alternations are found with specific combinations of clitics. For instance, the clitics *nos/vos* trigger allomorphy of the 1pl form (e.g. *mostramos* 'we show') by deleting the final *-s* (as in *mostramo-nos* 'we show ourselves'). Such truncation is limited to just these person/number verb forms. A more general final consonant truncation is found with the 3rd person non-reflexive clitics, *o/os/a/as*, which deletes all word-final occurrences of *-s* and *-r*. These clitics then acquire an initial consonant /l/ (or /n/ after a nasalized vowel): *mostramos* + *o* ⇒ *mostramo-lo* 'we show it', *lav[ãw]* + *o* ⇒ *lav[ãw]-no* 'they wash him'.

Regardless of whether the clause is finite or non-finite, the clitic cluster attaches by default to the right edge of the verb. This is the lexical verb, as shown in (58a, b), unless the clause expresses one of the compound tenses with the auxiliary verbs SER 'be' or TENER 'have', in which case it is the auxiliary that serves as the host or anchor, (58c, d).

(58) a.   mostramos 'we show'
      b.   mostramos-**lho** 'we show it to him'
      c.   temos mostrado 'we have shown'
      d.   temos-**lho** mostrado 'we have shown it to him'

An interesting fact about cliticized verbs in European Portuguese is illustrated in (59), where the cluster attaches verb-internally to future and conditional verb stems, before person and number agreement. These verb forms, also known as mesoclitic verb forms, carry two lexical stresses (indicated in (59) by capitalization). This stress pattern is not found elsewhere in the Portuguese verb system. We return to it in Section 8.5.

(59) a.   mostrAr-**lho**-Emos 'we will show it to him'
      b.   mostr-Ar-**lho**-Iamos 'we would show it to him'
      c.   tEr-**lho**-Emos mostrado 'we will have shown it to him'
      d.   tEr-**lho**-Iamos mostrado 'we would have shown it to him'

Where European Portuguese differs markedly and interestingly from other Romance languages (including Brazilian Portuguese) is that the proclitic placement of the cluster is triggered by specific morphosyntactic and semantic contexts in preverbal position. Some of the proclisis triggering words and phrases include complementizers, relative pronouns, fronted focus phrases, operator-like adverbs, wh-phrases, quantified subjects and the negation marker.

Essentially, the facts are as follows: in postverbal position the pronominal cluster has all the hallmarks of a string of affixes, while in preverbal position the self-same cluster has all the properties of a clitic string. For instance, the enclitic cluster is unable to scope over conjoined verb phrases:

(60) a.   Eu sei   que a Maria **me**   escreve cartas e   envia postais
            I   know that the Maria 1SG.DAT writes   letters and sends postcards
            'I know that Maria writes me letters and sends me postcards'
     b.   *A Maria escreve-**me**   cartas e   envia postais
            the Maria writes-1SG.DAT letters and sends postcards
     c.   *A Maria escreve cartas e   envia-**me**   postais
            the Maria writes   letters and sends-1SG.DAT postcards

However, a proclitic cluster can take wide scope over coordinated hosts, as in (60a). Example (61) illustrates how even a portmanteau cluster, *lho*, can take wide scope as a proclitic cluster (here triggered by being in a subordinate clause):

(61)   Nós sabemos que a   Maria
            we   know   that the Maria

            lho   comprou de manhã e   ofereceu à   noite
            3SG.DAT.3SG.MASC.ACC bought   of morning and gave   in.the evening

            'We know that Maria bought it for him/her in the morning and gave it (to him/her) in the evening'

The salient facts, then, are the following:

- There are two sets of pronominal forms for cliticized verbs: suffixes (postverbally) and proclitics (preverbally).
- The default cluster placement is suffixation to the verb.
- The cluster placement for a verb in the future/conditional is suffixation to a special future/conditional stem (mesoclisis).
- In the presence of proclitic triggers, the alternative cluster placement is (syntactically) aligned to the left edge of a projection of a syntactic V^0 category.
- This is valid for all tense/aspect forms, including compound (Perfect) tenses and future/conditional tenses.

A similar patterning can be seen in certain varieties of Greek. While the standard language has a clitic system that is more or less morphologized into an affix system, as we've seen (Joseph 1988), in earlier varieties and in a number of extant dialects we see a picture comparable to that of European Portuguese, in which preverbally we have proclitics and postverbally we have affixes. Very interesting discussion of these dialects can be found in Condoravdi and Kiparsky (2001, 2004).

7.4.2   Udi subject Person Markers

Finally, we come to a particularly spectacular instance of elements that can behave as prototypical clitics in some contexts and as highly idiosyncratic affixes in others. Udi, a North East Caucasian language, has a set of person markers (henceforth PM) that cross-reference subjects. Their behaviour and the historical origins of the constructions they enter into has been meticulously documented by Harris (2000, 2002). Harris' monograph in particular is an exemplary presentation and analysis of these fascinating elements, in which she not only gives a clear and comprehensive description of the complex array of facts, but also provides an explicit analysis (within Optimality Theory, briefly discussed in Chapter 8) as well as a detailed survey of the unique confluence of historical changes that gave rise to the system.[12]

Harris explicitly presents the Udi data as disconfirming the Lexical Integrity Hypothesis. The PMs are clitics when they attach as phrasal affixes to focussed phrases, therefore when they appear inside verb stem morphemes they must be endoclitics, the clitic equivalent of infixes. This logic is unimpeachable, of course. However, we include discussion of her analysis in this section under the rubric of mixed systems, because from a superficial vantage point what we have is a single formative that behaves as a prototypical clitic in some contexts and as an affix in other contexts, much like the European Portuguese system. In Chapter 8 we will outline a slightly different perspective from that of Harris, under which the PMs (like the Portuguese pronominal clitics) are not syntactic elements that can break up words, but rather are aberrant morphological objects that can be 'liberated' (in the words of Crysmann 2002) and can select phrasal rather than lexical hosts.

There are three sets of PM,[13] namely, the Inversion set, the Possession set and the General set, as shown in (62):

(62)   Person markers in Udi

	General	Inversion	Possession
1sg	-zu, -z	-za	-bez, -bes
2sg	-nu, -n, -ru, -lu	-va	-vi
3sg	-ne, -le, -re	-t'u	-t'a
1pl	-yan	-ya	-beš
2pl	-nan, -ran, -lan	-va, -vạn	-ef̣
3Pl	-q'un	-q'o	-q'o

For the most part they are obligatory, and co-occur with overt subject noun phrases; hence, they are effectively agreement markers. Which set is selected in a given clause depends on the verb's category. The Inversion set is selected by verbs belonging to the inversion category (*buq'* 'love, want', *ak'-* 'see', *ababak-* 'know'); the set labelled Possession is used mainly with verbs denoting possession, while the General set occurs with all other verbs.

Depending on a variety of grammatical conditions, they can appear in any one of the following positions: at the right edge of a focussed constituent, verb-finally, inside complex verb stems (63a) or even inside monomorphemic verb stems (63b). In the latter two positions they constitute not just affixes but infixes; in other words, the PMs conceived of as clitics appear as endoclitics in certain positions.

(63) a.   lašk'oq'unbesa
        lašk'o   **q'un** b esa
        marriage 3PL.PM LV PRES
        'They get married'
    b.   azq'e
        a **z**   q' e
        take 1SG.PM take AORII
        'I received'

Harris shows in detail that the enclitic uses of the PMs pass the standard Zwicky–Pullum tests for clitics. The claim that the verb form in (63) contains an endoclitic necessarily entails the assumption that words can break up other words or, paraphrasing somewhat, that the syntax can see inside words, in clear violation of the Lexical Integrity Hypothesis (Lapointe 1980), under which only affixes can appear word-internally. For this reason alone the Udi clitics are of great theoretical interest.

The minimal verb form in Udi comprises a verb stem and a tense-mood-aspect suffix. In (64) the verb form *aq'o* consists of the verb stem *aq'* and the future suffix *-o*.

(64)   aq' -o
        take -FUTI
        '(someone) will take'

An important property of Udi is that verb stems can either be simplex or complex. Simplex stems are monomorphemic and constitute the minority pattern in this language:

(65)   aq'-   bi-   ef-   buq'- baq'-
        'take' 'die' 'keep' 'love' 'hold'

Complex verb stems, on the contrary, combine a verb or light verb with an incorporated element, as in (66):

(66)   a. lašk'o-b-   b. kala-bak   c. oc'-k'
          wedding-LV   big-BECOME   wash-LV
          'marry'   'grow up'   'wash'

There are six light verbs in Udi, *b* 'do', *bak* 'be, become', *p* 'say', *eg* 'come', *d* (no meaning), *k* (no meaning), the first three of which can also be used as independent meaningful verb stems. For the most part, however, we should regard the light verbs as meaningless forms (cranberry morph(emes)) and we gloss them simply as 'LV'. Incorporated elements can be nouns (66a), adjectives (66b), intransitive simplex verb stems (66c), borrowed verbs, adverbs, or an assortment of unidentifiable elements (p. 65).

As we have seen, there are two basic types of placement patterns for Udi PM: phrasal and verbal. We discuss each in turn. If there is a focussed constituent in the clause (italicized in the examples below), the PM encliticizes to it. Negative particles and question words are obligatorily in focus in Udi (cf. (67) and (68)). If both a negative particle and a question word co-occur, then the PM attaches to the negative particle (p. 119):

(67)　　　nana-n　　　*te=**ne***　　　buɣa-b-e　　　(*te=**ne***)　　　p'ạ ačik'alšey
　　　　　mother-ERG NEG-3SG.PM find-LV-AORII (NEG-3SG.PM) two toy.ABS
　　　　　'Mother did not find two toys'

(68)　　　*manu muz-in=**nu***　　　　　ayt-exa?
　　　　　which language-INST-2SG.PM word-LV.PRES
　　　　　'WHAT LANGUAGE are you speaking?'

PMs can also attach to other focussed arguments, as in (69), but if a negative particle or a question word is present, then the negative particle or the wh-word take precedence, as seen in the contrast between (70a) and (70b),[14] while negation takes precedence over question words, as seen in (71) (pp. 120–1):

(69) a.　　*yaq'-a=**ne***　　　ba-st'a
　　　　　road-DAT-3SG.PM in-LV.PRES
　　　　　'ON THE ROAD he opens it'

　　　b.　　merab-en　*ayt=**ne***　　　　　ef-sa
　　　　　Merab-ERG word.ABS-3SG.PM keep-PRES
　　　　　'Merab keeps his WORD'　　　Harris (2002, 3)

(70) a.　　äyelen　　　k'uč'an-**ne**　　　beɣ-sa
　　　　　child.ERG puppy-3SG.PM watch-PRES
　　　　　'The child is watching a puppy'

　　　b.　　äyelen　　　k'uč'an te-**ne**　　　　　beɣ-sa
　　　　　child.ERG puppy　NEG-3SG.PM watch-PRES
　　　　　'The child isn't watching a puppy'

　　　c.　　*äyelen　k'uč'an-**ne**　　　te　beɣ-sa
　　　　　child.ERG puppy-3SG.PM NEG watch-PRES
　　　　　(Intended: 'The child isn't watching a puppy')

(71)　　　ek'alu te-**n**　　　　　mạɣ-exa?
　　　　　why　NEG-2SG.PM song-SAY.PRES
　　　　　'Why aren't you singing?'

Finally, in clauses with zero copulas, the PM is hosted by the predicate nominal, unless the subject is in focus:

(72)   nana   k'wa=**ne**
          mother.ABS house.DAT-3SG.PM
          'Mother is at the house' Harris (2002, 121)

The PMs can thus attach to four hosts: a negative particle, a wh-word, other focussed arguments and a nominal predicate.

In contexts in which information structure is neutral, or in which the main verb itself is in focus we find attachment of the PM to the verb. The first observation to make is that PMs are final in the verb stem if the verb is in the future II, the subjunctive I, the subjunctive II, or the imperative.[15] These TAM categories override the general principle of focus-driven placement and position the PM in verb-final position, regardless of whether there is a negative particle or a wh-word (pp. 116–19):[16]

(73) a.   q'ačaɣ-ɣ-on bez tänginax   bašq'-al-*q'un*
            thief-PL-ERG my money.DAT steal-FUTII-3PL.PM
            'Thieves will steal my money'
      b.   eɣ-a-*q'un*?
            come-SUBJUNCTII-3PL.PM
            'will they come?'
      c.   besp'-a-*nan*
            kill-IMPER-2PL.PM
            'You kill [her]'   (Harris 2002, 117)

Next we consider verbs with complex stems. The PM can break up the components of the complex stem, appearing between the incorporated element and the light verb or verb root. In these cases the PM occurs between morpheme boundaries:

(74) a.   eč-es-*ne*-st'a
            bring-INF-3SG.PM-CAUSE.PRES
            '(he) brought'   (adapted from Harris 2002, 122, ex. (32))
      b.   zer-ev-*ne*-k'sa
            decorate-CAUSE-3SG.PM-LV-PRES
            'S/he arranges [the house]'   (Harris 2002, 122)

The placement patterns seen in (74) are not observed if the verb form is in one of the TAM categories that trigger verb-final placement, future II, the subjunctive I, the subjunctive II, or imperative. In that case, the more general verb-final placement rule applies:

(75)   bez vičen   aš-b-al-*ne*   zavoda
          my brother work-DO-FUTII-3SG.PM in.factory
          'My brother will work in a factory' (Harris 2002, 123)

The PMs can also appear immediately before the final consonant in monomorphemic verb roots. In (76), various examples of intramorphemic placement are given.[17]

(76) a. be-*ne*-ɣ-sa   (verb stem *beɣ-*)
          look₁-3SG.PM-look₂-PRES
          'look at'

   b. a-*z*-q'-e   (verb stem *aq'-*)
          receive₁-1SG.PM-receive₂-AORII
          'received'

   c. baš-*q'un*-q'-e   (verb stem *bašq'-*)
          steal₁-3PL.PM-steal₂-AORII
          'stole'

   d. ba-*ne*-k-sa   (verb stem *bak-*)
          be₁-3SG.PM-be₂-PRES
          'is'

To summarize, phrasal attachment occurs if there is a focussed constituent in the clause other than the verb itself. Verb-final placement is triggered by specific TMA properties of the verb. Verb-internal placement constitutes the default position, found in focus-neutral contexts, when neither the factors triggering verb-final nor those triggering phrasal attachment are operative.

7.5   Inflecting clitics

We have seen examples of systems that are sometimes described as clitic systems but where we could with equal or better justification label them as affixal systems. In this section we look at a subtly different type of situation. Here we have a reputable clitic system (in our case it will be a typical Wackernagel clitic cluster) but where some of the elements appear to be inflecting word forms. If a clitic is a highly weakened function word that has lost its syntactic integrity and has undergone partial morphologization then we don't expect it to undergo standard inflectional morphology. This is a serious conceptual problem for certain types of approach to realizational morphology which see clitic systems as an extension of affixal systems. In realizational morphology an affix is just a mark on an inflected word which helps to indicate what morphosyntactic properties the inflecting word bears. If a clitic is just like an affix but with different privileges of placement then it's hard to see how it itself can bear inflections.

Klavans (1979) argued that there are clitics in Ngiyambaa that inflect. She proposed this because otherwise it would be necessary to accept the possibility of a clitic appearing inside a string of inflectional affixes (endoclisis), which at the time was regarded as a theoretically undesirable consequence. However, it is clear that there are many languages with clitic systems in which the clitics take on forms that are homologous to the inflected forms of full-form words. These include auxiliary verb clitics with finite or non-finite inflections, and pronominal clitics that inflect for person/number/case. For instance, Erschler (2009) reports the second-position clitic system of the Indo-Iranian language, Ossetic, in which

Table 7.2 *Czech pronominal clitics*

	1Sg	2Sg	Refl	1Pl	2Pl
Nom	já	ty	—	my	vy
Acc	mnje	tebe~**tje**	sebe~**se**	na:s	va:s
Gen	mnje	tebe~**tje**	sebe~**se**	na:s	va:s
Dat	mnje~**mi**	tobje~**ti**	sobje~**si**	na:m	va:m
(Instr	mnou	tebou	sebou	na:mi	va:mi)

	3SgMasc/Neut	3SgFem	Pl
Nom	on/ono	ona	oni/ony/ona
Acc	jej~**ho**	ji	je
Gen	jeho~**ho**	ji:	jich
Dat	jemu~**mu**	ji:	jim
(Instr	ji:m	ji:	jimi)

Table 7.3 *Czech auxiliary* BÝT *'be' compared with* JÍT *'go'*

	BÝT 'be'				JÍT 'go'
	Pres	Cond	Negated	Future	
1Sg	**sem**	bych	nejsem	budu	du
2Sg	**si**	bys	nejsi	budeš	deš
3Sg	**je**	by	neni:	bude	de
1Pl	**sme**	bychom	nejsme	budeme	deme
2Pl	**ste**	byste	nejste	budete	dete
3Pl	**sou**	by	nejsou	budou	dou

pronominals inflect for six cases as well as for person/number. Essentially, what we often find is that even special clitics are morphophonologically little more than unaccented or phonologically weakened forms of fully inflecting lexemes and that they therefore share much if not all of the morphology of full-form pronouns, auxiliary verbs or whatever.

A typical example of this situation is presented by Czech. In Table 7.2 (Short 1993, 471) we see full and cliticized forms of the personal pronouns, while in Table 7.3 (Short, 1993, 491) we see full and cliticized forms of the auxiliary verb BÝT 'be', compared with lexical verb JÍT 'go' (the examples are given in a pseudo-phonological transcription). The unambiguous clitic forms are in bold-face in these tables. The clitic forms are just those of the Present Tense, in the first column of the table.

As we know from Chapter 3 the Czech clitics represent a pretty standard kind of Wackernagel system, with the clitic cluster having the form (77) (Short 1993, 494–5):

(77)   Czech clitic cluster

	I	II	III	IV	V	VI	
	Q	Aux	Refl	Dat	Acc/Gen	particles	host
nemělo	-li	by	se	mu	to	tedy	říct

'whether he ought not then to be told'

One way of interpreting these paradigms is to say that even the shortened, clitic forms of the auxiliary and of the pronominals are inflected (if somewhat idiosyncratically in some cases).

Spencer (2005a) provides an analysis of the Czech inflecting clitics within a variant of Stump's Paradigm Function Morphology, in which the clitic forms are derived from full forms by means of a correspondence function, which at the very least defines the clitic forms as atonic, and in other cases defines a more drastic phonological weakening of the form. In that way we preserve the analysis of these forms as clitics while still relating them to inflecting forms. Interestingly, that analysis only works on the assumption that inflecting clitics have identifiable corresponding lexical, non-clitic forms which inflect in the same way as the clitics. In other words, it only works if the inflecting clitics are effectively like simple clitics. However, unlike most simple clitics, the inflecting clitics on Spencer's model can be subject to highly idiosyncratic placement principles, such as Wackernagel positioning.

The use of a correspondence function can be warranted here by the fact that the inflecting clitic forms really do correspond to full-word forms. If that were not the case then there would be little reason to suppose that the clitic forms belonged to some inflectional paradigm in the first place. For instance, the pronominal clitics of most Romance languages, and of Bulgarian and Macedonian, retain what are usually described as 'case forms', usually accusative and dative, yet those languages have lost their case system. For such languages it is actually a conceptual error to speak of 'case-marked clitics': case-marking only makes sense if it is a property of noun phrases, not of highly morphologized pronominal elements. Such clitics are therefore more properly given some other label, reflecting their grammatical function (for instance 'OBJ1/OBJ2 clitic') or, perhaps better, a completely arbitrary label.

As far as we can tell, very little attention has been paid to the problem of clitics that have their own inflectional paradigms whilst realizing particular sets of morphosyntactic properties. The problem is intimately connected with the problem of periphrastic constructions, another understudied area. We will not comment further on these questions, therefore.[18]

7.6   Words with affix-like properties: shape conditions

The converse of affixes that behave like clitics or fully fledged function words is seen when function words, or even lexical words, show behaviour normally only associated with affixes, namely, idiosyncratic allomorphy triggered by the phonological environment. In English, for instance, the indefinite article has the form *a* before a consonant and *an* before a vowel. In French the adjective *beau* /boː/ has a suppletive feminine singular form *belle* /bɛl/. This form (in the spelling *bel*) is found when the adjective comes immediately before a word beginning in a vowel: *bel ami* 'good friend'. Alternations of this kind are generally ignored in formal grammatical descriptions, though attention is repeatedly drawn to them, notably by Arnold Zwicky (for instance, in Zwicky 1986). In some cases the results are remarkably similar to the effects of an affix triggering allomorphy on a stem. Well-known cases from Romance and German concern combinations of preposition and definite article. In French, for instance, the definite article takes three forms, *le* /lə/ masculine singular, *la* /la/ feminine singular and *les* /le/ plural. However, after the prepositions *de* /də/ 'of, from' and *à* /a/ 'to' we find fused or portmanteau forms: while *de* + *la* is pronounced /dəla/ as expected, the other two forms of the article trigger the changes *de* + *le* ⇒ *du* /dy/, *de* + *les* ⇒ *des* /de/. Similarly, with *à* we see the changes *à* + *le* ⇒ *au* /o/, *à* + *les* ⇒ *aux* /o/. In different Romance languages and in German a variety of other prepositions show similar behaviour. Thus, in German we have examples such as *zu* + *der* 'to + the.fem.dat.sg' ⇒ *zur*, *an* + *dem* 'at + the.masc.dat.sg' ⇒ *am* and so on. In Czech, as in a number of Slavic languages, a combination of a preposition with a 3rd person pronoun causes the pronoun to alternate with an *n*-initial allomorph: *na* + *jich* /na/,/jix/ ⇒ *na nich* /naɲix/ 'on them'. However, with the 3sg masculine pronoun *jeho* /jefio/ in combination with the prepositions *na* 'on', *za* 'behind' and *pro* 'for', the two word forms fuse to give the portmanteau forms *naň* /naɲ/, *zaň* /zaɲ/, *proň* /proɲ/ (Short 1993, 470). Other cases of portmanteau forms arise in Slavic and other languages when a negation particle such as Czech *ne* is in construction with the present tense forms of the auxiliary/copular verb *být* 'be'. The basic forms are pronounced with initial /s/, /sem, si, …/ 'I am, thou art, …' but the negated forms are pronounced /nejsem, nejsi, …/ with epenthetic /j/. The 3sg form *je* has a suppletive negated form *není*.

Cases such as these arise when highly frequent words occur next to each other with high frequency. The result is what we might think of as a morphological idiom, in which the word structure goes entirely against the syntactic structure. Under normal circumstances a preposition and a following definite article don't form any kind of syntactic constituent in French or German. Therefore, there is no syntactic unit that a portmanteau form such as *du* is a portmanteau of. The situation is very reminiscent of that found with English auxiliary clitics in combination with subject pronoun forms, for example *you* + *are* ⇒ *you're* (/juː + ɑː/ ⇒ /jɔː/). Wescoat (2002) explicitly draws this comparison and analyses both phenomena in terms of a model of 'lexical sharing' (discussed briefly in Section 8.7).

7.7   Clitics and particles: the Russian Conditional Marker *by*

In this section we look at a number of elements that are often labelled 'particles' and which in principle might be regarded as types of clitic. We will suggest that such elements are only clitics in the weak sense of being phonologicals, that is, phonologically weak elements that are prosodically integrated with some host.

The distinction between clitics and particles is discussed in detail by Zwicky (1985a). He comes to the conclusion that, while there are clitics, there are no particles. Those elements that are labelled particles in the descriptive and theoretical literature are in reality either misanalysed affixes, misanalysed clitics, or just words whose category is difficult to specify (but which nonetheless belong to some kind of bona fide lexical category rather than the waste bin of 'particle').

We will illustrate Zwicky's point with a brief discussion of the Russian Conditional Mood 'particle' *by*. The particle *by* (/bi/) is used to construct the Conditional/Subjunctive Mood, that is, irrealis or hypothetical conditional clauses. It has a conversational vowelless allomorph /b/. It combines with the l-participle of the verb or, less commonly, with the infinitive:

(78)   Ja by čital etu knigu
         I BY read this book
         'I would read this book'

(79) a.   Mne   by počitat′   takuju knigu!
           me.DAT BY read   such   book
     b.   Mne počitat′ by takuju knigu!
           'If only I could read such a book!'

It generally appears immediately after the l-participle/infinitive, or immediately before it. The protasis of a conditional clause is generally introduced by the word *esli* 'if'. In a hypothetical conditional *esli* is usually followed immediately by *by*, but not necessarily:

(80) a.   Esli by ty   dejstvitel′no ne xotela ...
           If   BY you really   not wanted
           'If you really didn't want ...'
     b.   Esli ty by dejstvitel′no ne xotela...
     c.   Esli ty dejstvitel′no ne xotela by...

There are restrictions on where in the clause the *by* particle can appear. It rarely occurs after any constituent that itself follows the main verb:

(81)   *Ja čital etu knigu by

One position that is completely excluded for *by* is clause-initial position:

(82) a.   *By mne čitat′ takie knigi!
      b.   *By ja čital etu knigu
      c.   *By čital ja etu knigu

In the colloquial language we occasionally hear the particle repeated:

(83)   Esli by ona xotela by
             if   BY she wanted BY
             '...if she wanted to ...'

In summary, the positioning of the *by* particle is relatively free but restricted to non-initial positions. That restriction makes the particle resemble a clitic. However, we can account for that restriction by the simple observation that phonologically the particle is an enclitic and therefore requires a prosodic host to its left (in its own clause – the cliticization cannot take place across a clause boundary).

Is *by* a clitic? It is not a special clitic. It is a grammatical particle that could be thought of categorially as a kind of adverb, though one with somewhat restricted placement. The principal restriction is phonological: it requires a host to its left. Effectively, then, we are dealing with a word that has broadly speaking the same distribution as a phonologically weak adverbial discourse marker, such as *-to* (see Section 2.6.3). The interesting feature of the Russian conditional is that the particle is the partial exponent of a grammatical category of Mood, rather than an adverbial meaning or discourse function.

The *by* particle also occurs in fused form in the subordinating conjunction *čtoby* (allomorph *čtob*). Historically, this is a combination of the conjunction *čto* with *by*. However, we must consider *čtoby* a single word, not a free combination, because the *by* element cannot be moved:

(84) a.   Ja vyexal rano, čtoby   ne opozdat′
             I left   early in.order not to.be.late
             'I left early so as not to be late'
      b.   Ja vyexal rano, čtoby   ja ne opozdal
             I left   early in.order I not be.late
             'I left early so as not to be late'

(85) a.   *Ja vyexal rano, čto ne opozdat′ by
      b.   *Ja vyexal rano, čto ja ne opozdal by

There is thus a clear distinction between the *-by* suffix of *čtoby* and the free-standing element *by*.

In the next chapter we will discuss proposals by Toivonen (2003) for how to treat 'particles' such as Russian *by*. Anticipating that discussion, the suggestion is that there are words that are syntactically represented as terminals in syntactic structure but that can't license fully fledged phrases (what Toivonen calls non-projecting words). A grammatical particle such as the Russian *by* has the hallmarks of such a non-projecting word.

7.8   Summary

In Chapters 5 and 6 we concentrated specifically on morphology and syntactic aspects of clitic systems and saw that it can be very difficult to characterize just what we mean by 'morphology' and, especially, by 'syntax' in this context. There are pronominal affix systems that show complementary distribution with overt arguments, just like clitics (in Breton, Hebrew, Chamorro and other languages), and conversely there are clitic systems that subserve obligatory agreement (e.g. Macedonian, Udi). In this chapter we've looked at the same kinds of mixed properties but from the perspective of the clitics and affixes themselves, so to speak. Affixes can display a variety of clitic-like properties, while still, apparently, remaining affixes (at least according to standard descriptions). As we will argue in the next chapter, the existence of 'mixed systems', particularly those shown by European Portuguese and Udi, make it more or less impossible to propose a model of grammar in which there is a lexicon of clitics that remain clitics in all respects, whatever construction they are part of. This strongly suggests that linguistic theory shouldn't actually draw a clear distinction between clitics and affixes. Given the preponderance of affix-like properties that special clitics exhibit, the obvious conclusion is that special clitics are in fact special affixes, special in the sense that their placement is defined in terms of syntactic and prosodic constituents and not just in terms of classes of stems. This is the phrasal affix thesis of Anderson, of course. However, that thesis, and Anderson's implementation of it in particular, is not without its own problems. We elaborate on some of these in the next chapter. Two of them have been illustrated in this chapter. Some clitics ('inflecting clitics') behave like inflecting lexemes, contrary to the claim that clitics (qua affixes) are just pieces of phonology added to the edges of phrases. And some elements, such as the Russian particle *by*, have many of the properties of clitics, including that of realizing a morphosyntactic ('inflectional') property without showing any signs of attaching to the edges of specifically defined phrases, a property shared by the floating inflections of Polish discussed in Section 4.4.

8   Approaches to clitics

8.1   Introduction

In this chapter we briefly survey a number of theoretical approaches
to clitics. As we mentioned in our Introduction to the book, we will not discuss
any specific model of morphosyntax in any detail. Rather, we will sketch the
kinds of issues that the most popular theoretical approaches address and outline
the ways in which those models deal with those issues in the form of a highly
selective annotated bibliography.[1]

We should point out that it is a little difficult to provide an exhaustive or completely coherent 'typology' of theoretical approaches to the problem of clitics. In
part this is because different authors sometimes mean different things by 'clitic',
so that the empirical bases are not always comparable. In part the difficulty is that
a number of approaches adopt several different perspectives on clitics, treating
them as properties of the interface between phonology, morphology and syntax (what Franks and King 2000 refer to as 'mixed approaches'). Finally, it is
not entirely straightforward to identify a particular kind of approach with a particular theoretical model of grammar. This is particularly true where theorists
deploy the machinery of Optimality Theory (OT). The OT approach can, in principle, be integrated with any of the major theoretical models of grammar, and it
has particularly been applied to the Principles and Parameters model (Grimshaw
1997, 2001) and to the Lexical Functional Grammar model (Kuhn 2001, Bresnan
1998, 2001a), though not to Head Driven Phrase Structure Grammar (HPSG). In
the context of clitics, however, it has also been used to model an essentially
morphological approach to clitics (Legendre 1996, 2000a, b, Legendre 2001).
However, it's fair to say that for any of the three models of formal syntax that
have had most to say about clitic systems, practitioners of a given model will
tend to show a reasonable amount of agreement amongst themselves as to how
best to approach clitics. For this reason we will treat those models individually.

A number of authors have made theoretical proposals that rely on clitics falling
into discrete types, so we return to the question of what a typology of clitics
might look like. We then briefly consider very general models of clitics as interface phenomena before looking in more detail at the way that clitics systems
have been handled in morphological theory and in the three principal models of
syntax.

8.2   The typology of clitics revisited

Before we turn to look at the way that various grammatical models have approached clitic systems, we can take stock of the discussion so far to revisit the question of clitic typology: what kinds of clitic system are there and what are the different types of clitics. To some extent this is an enterprise that we believe cannot be successful. We shall take the view that ultimately there are no clitics. There are clitic-associated properties that tend to cluster together in typical cases, but these properties are in principle independent of each other and in principle can combine in more or less any fashion. Nonetheless, it will be helpful at this point to see how various investigators have tried to make sense of the 'clitic space' provided by the world's languages.

The typology of clitics that informs all current work on the topic, that of Arnold Zwicky (1977), originally distinguished simple clitics, special clitics and bound words. The distinction between bound words and other sorts of clitic is generally agreed to be arbitrary and of no interest to linguistic theory (Anderson 2005, Zwicky 1985a). However, the simple/special clitic distinction is still widely accepted. At the same time, however, there is no generally agreed set of criteria that will reliably distinguish clitics from affixes, and a number of linguists, working in different theoretical frameworks, have concluded that there is no principled way of drawing the distinction (Börjars 1998, Embick and Noyer 2001, Luís and Spencer 2005). In general it seems to be assumed that it is the special clitics that grammaticalize or morphologize and become affixes. However, this doesn't seem to be a tenable assumption. The English auxiliary clitic is generally taken to be a standard example of a simple clitic, and yet when its host is a personal pronoun it has the morphological properties of an affix (Spencer 1991, 383).

When we consider the simple/special clitic distinction, it turns out to be difficult to find a set of clear-cut criteria that will reliably differentiate the two types. The problem is with the notion of syntactic distribution. The distribution of a simple clitic is typically determined in part by phonological factors such as sentence prosody (phrasal stress and emphasis) and pragmatic factors such as topic/focus articulation (itself often expressed in terms of prosody). At the same time, clitics often have phonological attachment properties of their own. In particular, we often find that a set of clitics is exclusively suffixing (enclitic) or prefixing (proclitic).

More often than not clitics are enclitic. It's extremely hard to find good examples of pure proclitics. Anderson's (2005) survey of clitics only mentions proclitics twice, for instance, and he gives no examples of pure proclisis. But this means that the set of linear positions open to any clitic, even a simple one, is likely to be different from the set of positions open to a full-form corresponding word. An obvious example of this is provided again by the English auxiliary clitics. These are exclusively enclitic. However, English has an auxiliary verb fronting process which puts a finite auxiliary at the very beginning of a clause, in order to form questions and so on: *Is Harriet a linguist? Are you joking?* As we've seen (Chapter 4), these fronted auxiliaries can't be replaced by clitics because the clitic would have no leftward host. Actually, we've also seen that matters are more complex than this, since even when there is a potential host, a fronted auxiliary has to be in its full form: **But's Harriet a linguist?* This means that we will sometimes find that a given clitic is impossible in certain syntactic contexts simply because there's no way to realize the clitic prosodically.

Before we discuss the problems identified in the overview, we will summarize a set of proposals for a typology of pronominal elements, which includes pronominal clitics, offered by Cardinaletti and Starke (1999). We next summarize Toivonen's (2003) proposals that there are words that are syntactically represented but that fail to project full phrases. Some of these non-projecting words have certain of the characteristics of prototypical clitics. We then examine the typological distinction proposed by Anderson between 'inflectional' clitics and 'derivational' clitics, arguing that Anderson's specific proposals don't hold up well, even though the distinction he draws is a very important one. We finally briefly introduce the notion of 'canonical clitic' from an approach to typology known as Canonical Typology (Spencer and Luís 2012).

8.2.1   Three types of pronoun

Cardinaletti and Starke (1999) present an interesting view of pronominals, arguing that there are exactly three distinct types. The first is the Strong pronominal, which can be referential and which can occupy much the same syntactic positions as any other noun phrase (or determiner phrase). Contrasted to this type are two 'deficient' types. These show varying degrees of grammaticalization which prevent them from enjoying the full privileges of occurrence that full noun phrases or Strong pronouns enjoy. Cardinaletti and Starke make a number of strong claims about which phonological, morphological, syntactic and semantic properties cluster together in the three types.

The idea that a clitic pronominal is structurally deficient and hence approaches an inflectional agreement marker is generally agreed, and different frameworks have different ways of reflecting such an analysis. Cardinaletti and Starke capture the idea by proposing a very rich syntactic structure for the individual word types themselves. As pronominals become more deficient, so they lose 'layers' of this syntactic structure. Allegedly universal properties of Strong pronouns are that they can be coordinated (like ordinary noun phrases) but that unlike, say, demonstrative pronouns, they only refer to humans. To illustrate this they contrast the behaviour of the Italian pronominals *loro* and *esse*. The pronoun *loro* is Strong, and as a result it can be coordinated with other phrases, but it only denotes people. On the other hand, *esse* is Weak and therefore cannot be coordinated, though it can denote non-humans as well as humans.

(1) a.   Loro   (e   quelle accanto) sono troppo alte
             3PL.NOM.FEM.HUM and those beside   are too   tall
             'They (girls/women) (and those at their side) are too tall'

     b.   Esse   (*e quelle accanto) sono troppo alte
             3PL.NOM.FEM.HUM/NON-HUM and those beside   are too   tall/high
             'They (and those at the side of them) are too tall'

In (1b) *esse* can refer to inanimate things of feminine gender, but this is not
possible for *loro* in (1). In French both types of pronominal are expressed by
the same form in the feminine plural, *elles*, but when coordinated *elles* gains the
ability to refer to non-humans, suggesting that the single form is homophonous
between a Strong and a Weak reading.

   Amongst the properties that distinguish deficient from Strong pronouns are
the following. Deficient pronouns cannot occur in argumental (theta) positions,
nor in 'peripheral' positions associated with syntactic constructions such as
clefts or left/right dislocation. Similarly, the deficient pronouns cannot occur
in isolation, say, as one-word answers to questions. Modifiers that modify
the whole noun phrase, such as *really, only, and so on*, may equally modify
Strong pronouns, but not deficient pronouns. Thus, in French we can have
(vraiment, seulement ...) lui, '(truly, only, ...) him, (Strong), *lui seul, aussi, ...*
'him (Strong) only, too, ... ', but these constructions are not possible with the
corresponding Weak pronoun 3SG.MASC pronoun *il*. Strong pronouns can be
contrastively stressed and can have their referent defined by a pointing gesture
(ostension), while deficient pronouns allow these constructions only if they refer
to an already prominent discourse item. As Cardinaletti and Starke put it (1999,
154), "[d]eficient personal pronouns must have an antecedent prominent in the
discourse". On the other hand, only deficient pronouns and not Strong pronouns
can be expletives. An expletive is an element such as the meaningless *it* or *there*
in *It is raining* or *There is cat on the mat*. Likewise, what Cardinaletti and Starke
call 'impersonals' can only be deficient, while 'generics' have to be Strong. An
impersonal use of *they* is illustrated in (2a), while a generic use is illustrated in
(2b) (see Cardinaletti and Starke 1999, 154–9 for discussion of this rather subtle
difference):

(2) a.   They've sent me the wrong book
     b.   They usually send books at parcel rate in this country

   Bringing these properties together is the crucial property of 'range': this is
some property or description that serves to limit or restrict the denotation of
the element. Full lexical items come with their own predefined range as part
of their meaning. Pronouns lack such semantic specification. Generic pronouns
require some specification of range (for instance, *in this country* in (2b)). Expletive pronouns are completely meaningless and therefore cannot have a range by
definition. Impersonal pronouns cannot have a range either (otherwise they will
be interpreted as generics). Thus, Cardinaletti and Starke conclude that a Strong

pronoun has a range, while a deficient pronoun doesn't. This is enshrined in their Semantic Asymmetry #2 (p. 159):

(3)   Semantic Asymmetry #2
   a.   Deficient pronouns are incapable of bearing their own range restriction (and are therefore either rangeless (expletives, impersonals, non-referential datives), or associated with the range-restriction of an element prominent in the discourse).
   b.   Strong pronouns always bear their own range-restriction.

Cardinaletti and Starke argue that phonological and morphological deficiency correlate with this typology (though they point out, §2.8, pp. 161–5, that deficiency cannot be reduced to mere prosodic weakness). They then argue for a tripartite division dividing the non-Strong pronouns into Weak pronouns and clitics. For instance, in Italian we have the notorious 3pl indirect object pronominal *loro*. This fails to have the full privileges of occurrence of the corresponding full phrase *a lui/a lei* 'to him/to her', but equally it does not behave as a true pronominal clitic, and for this reason it is often referred to as a 'semi-clitic' (Maiden and Robustelli 2000, 102–3). Cardinaletti and Starke therefore treat it as a Weak pronoun, distinct from both Strong pronouns and clitics (p. 165):[2]

(4)

a. (i)	Non	*a lui		dirò	mai	*a lui	tutto	a lui
(ii)	Non	*loro		dirò	mai	loro	tutto	*loro
(iii)	Non	gli		dirò	mai	*gli	tutto	*gli
	no	to.him/to.them		(I).will.say	never		everything	
	'I will never say everything to him/them'							
b. (i)	✓Non			dirò	mai	tutto	a lui e a lei	
(ii)	*Non			dirò	mai	loro e loro	tutto	
(iii)	*Non	gli e le		dirò	mai			
	no	to.him and to.her		(I).will.say	never		everything	
	'I will never say everything to him and her'							

In (4a(i)) the phrase *a lui* 'to him' can only appear after *tutto* 'everything', just as though it were a phrase such as *ai bambini* 'to the children'. In (4c(i)) we have a clitic that is constrained to appear in preverbal position and nowhere else. In (4b(i)) we see that the phrase *a lui* can be conjoined but the clitic *gli* cannot (4b(iii)). The semi-clitic *loro*, however, differs from the Strong pronominal in that it cannot occur with the preposition *a*; it has to appear before the object *tutto* (4a(ii)) and it cannot be conjoined (4b(ii)). However, *loro* differs from the clitic in that it cannot occur in the usual preverbal position for clitics (4a(ii)).

Based on examples such as these from a variety of languages, Cardinaletti and Starke propose a three-way division of pronominals into Strong > Weak > Clitic. They then reach what they call an "unavoidable" conclusion (p. 178):

> A more deficient pronoun is morphologically lighter than stronger pronouns *because* it contains less [sic] (underlying) morphemes <. . . > and it contains less [sic] morphemes *because* it realises less [sic] syntactic heads (79b–c) [emphasis original]:

(79) a.   clitic ≤ Weak ≤ Strong
     b.   morph(clitic) < morph(Weak) < morph(Strong)
     c.   struct (clitic) < struct (Weak) < struct (Strong)

In other words, deficiency is a progressive lack of syntactic functional heads. They illustrate this with the diagrams in (5) (p. 195):

(5)   a.   Strong pronouns
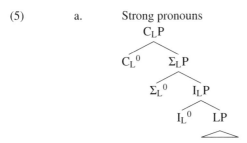

           b.   Weak pronouns
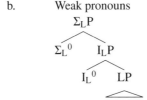

           c.   clitics
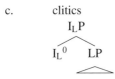

The heads C and I are meant to be reminiscent of the clausal heads familiar from sentence syntax. The C head accommodates features relating to referentiality. The I head locates features relating to agreement (pronominal features of person, number and so on, or 'phi features' in the terminology of PPT). The Σ is a special 'nominal support morpheme', related to affirmation/negation. When its default value is overtly present we obtain a contrastive reading. L stands for any lexical category. The features missing from (5b, c) must be recoverable from the context in which the deficient pronoun is used (p. 186). Hence, a Strong pronoun can occur in positions in which the referential range of the pronoun is not given elsewhere in the utterance or discourse, while Weak pronouns and clitics require some element to specify their range.

   The findings of Cardinaletti and Starke, though based on a very small sample of languages (for the most part areally linked) is fairly robust. However, Testelets (2003) argues that some of their key conclusions are falsified by Russian pronouns, so we cannot necessarily conclude that the typology will stand up to more detailed scrutiny. The main point of the typology is that even something as unassuming as a clitic pronoun can be imbued with considerable structure if all conceivable properties of a word or formative are coded in terms of binary branching syntactic structures. Of course, if you reject that hypothesis in the first place then the Cardinaletti/Starke analysis is irrelevant to you. Nonetheless, their proposals cast traditional views about grammaticalization and 'semantic bleaching' with respect to pronominals in an interesting light.

8.2.2   Non-projecting words

Toivonen (2003) discusses Swedish postverbal particles, arguing that they are not clitics or affixes, but fully-fledged words. The difference between these particles and other words is that they are unable to project a full phrase, that is, they are non-projecting words. An example of such a particle construction is (6):

(6)   Vi släppte ut   hunden
           we let   out.PRT dog.DEF
           'We let the dog out'   (Toivonen 2003, 159)

As can be seen in (7), the particle has to remain adjacent to the verb (unlike corresponding elements in English, for instance):

(7)   * Vi släppte hunden ut
           we let dog.DEF out.PRT
           'We let the dog out'

A particle verb can take two objects, as in (8):

(8)   Maria satte på   pojken   kläderna
           Maria put   on.PRT boy.DEF clothes.DEF
           'Maria put the clothes on the boy'   (Toivonen 2003, 92)

The string *på pojken* is not a prepositional phrase. If it were it would be expected to appear after the direct object (given neutral intonation). In fact, it is possible with this verb for the first object *pojken* to alternate with a genuine prepositional phrase, in which case *på* is still retained as a postverbal particle:

(9)   Maria satte på   kläderna   på pojken
           Maria put   on.PRT clothes.DEF on boy.DEF
           'Maria put the clothes on the boy'   (Toivonen 2003, 92)

Toivonen (chapter 4) argues at length that the particle is a non-projecting word which is head-adjoined to the V^0 (the notation '$\hat{P}$' represents a non-projecting word, that is, a word that cannot project a phrase):

(10) V^0

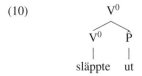

For this reason it cannot appear to the right of the direct object. Particles are still words in Swedish. A sign of this is the fact that they remain in the position of a verb phrase even when the verb itself is displaced. This occurs in a variety of 'verb-second' constructions in Swedish, for instance with negation:

(11) a.   Jan åt upp   kakorna
           Jan ate up.PRT cookies.DEF
           'Jan ate up the cookies'
     b.   Jan åt inte upp   kakorna
           Jan ate not up.PRT cookies.DEF
           'Jan did not eat up the cookies' (Toivonen 2003, 13)

(12) a.   Han slängde bort   boken
           he   threw away.PRT book.DEF
     b.   Boken   slängde han bort
           book.DEF threw he   away.PRT
           'He threw the book away' (Toivonen 2003, 43)

It is also found in conjoined verb phrases when the second verb is 'gapped':

(13)   Han ville   kasta   in   kläderna   och ut   skorna
           He   wanted to.throw in.PRT clothes.DEF and out.PRT shoes.DEF
           'He wanted to throw the clothes in and the shoes out' (Toivonen 2003, 169)

Interestingly, there are occasions when the particle becomes a prefix. Thus, in addition to its particle use in (14) (cf. (6)), we can see *ut-* as a verb prefix in (15):

(14)   Karin lånada ut   bökerna
           Karin lent   out.PRT books.DEF
           'Karin lent the books out' (Toivonen 2003, 38)

(15) a.   Bökerna   blev   ut-lånada
           books.DEF remained out-lent
           'The books got lent out'
     b.   * Bökerna   blev   lånada ut
           books.DEF remained lent   out
     c.   Ut-låningen av böcker har ökat
           out-lending of books has increased
           'The lending of books has increased'
     d.   * Låningen   ut av böcker har ökat
           out-lending out of books has increased (Toivonen 2003, 38)

Danish shows the opposite patterning to Swedish. While Swedish particles are prohibited from coming after the verb's object, in Danish this is the only place they can appear:

(16)   Danish particle verbs
     a.   Vi slap hunden ud
           we let dog.DEF out
           'We let the dog out'

b.   * Vi slap ud hunden
          we let   out dog.DEF (Toivonen 2003, 160)

Toivonen takes this to mean that Danish particles are actually intransitive prepositions (rather like English *before* in *I've never done this before*). This means that they are projecting words, not non-projecting. In support of that contention, she shows that the Danish equivalents of the Swedish particles can be modified, something that is not possible in Swedish:

(17)   De sendte ham langt ud på landet
           they sent   him far   out on countryside.DEF
           'They sent him far out into the countryside' (Toivonen 2003, 162)

   Toivonen notes the well-known fact that English particles can appear either immediately after the verb or after the direct object.

(18) a.   Tom turned the light on
     b.   Tom turned on the light

When it follows the verb, the particle is very tightly connected to it. For instance, the verb can't be gapped:

(19)   * Tom turned off the radio and on the light

On the other hand, when it comes after the direct object the particle has fewer restrictions. For instance, verb gapping is possible:

(20)   Tom turned the radio off and the light on

It's also possible to conjoin post-object particles, but not postverbal particles:

(21) a.   Tom turned the light on and off
     b.   * Tom turned on and off the light

An example such as (21b) would only be possible if we had a 'heavy' direct object which had been extraposed to the end of the sentence:

(22)   Tom turned on and off the expensive halogen light that had been
           malfunctioning

   Toivonen concludes that the postverbal particles cohere more closely with their verb host than do the corresponding Swedish postverbal particles. She therefore proposes that those instances are actually suffixes. (She actually speaks about the verb and particle being 'lexically combined' and notates this with the hash symbol #: *throw#out*. This leaves open the possibility that the combination is actually a kind of compound, though it's difficult to see what the difference could be between a compound and a suffix analysis.) On the other hand, the post-object particles can be treated exactly as their Danish counterparts, that is, as projecting words.

Toivonen (2003, 41–52) compares and contrasts in some detail the Swedish particles and familiar instances of clitics. She argues for a four-way typology of words in which the term 'clitic' is superseded and the different types of clitic treated as types of words that are either phonologically dependent, non-projecting or both. True clitics are described as being those that are phonologically dependent and at the same time non-projecting (Toivonen 2003, 194):

(23)   Toivonen's typology of words

	NON-PROJECTING	PROJECTING
PHON DEP	French 'clitic' pronouns Serbo-Croatian pronouns and auxiliaries	Kwak'wala and Yagua determiners[3] English reduced auxiliaries Swedish genitive marker Finnish, Russian and Bulgarian question particles
PHON INDEP	Swedish verbal particles Yoruba Weak pronouns	English verbs Yoruba Strong pronouns Estonian question particles

The 'Weak pronouns' of Cardinaletti and Starke (1999) are then treated as phonologically independent, non-projecting words.

8.2.3   'Inflectional' and 'derivational' clitics

We noted in Chapter 2 that Tagalog has a set of pronominal clitics and a set of discourse clitics (which we discussed in some detail in Chapter 6). Since Zwicky's (1977) original discussion it has been noted that the Tagalog system poses a very intriguing problem: the pronominal cluster is split up by the discourse clitics, apparently on phonological grounds: monosyllabic pronominals come to the left of the discourse clitics while disyllabic pronominals come to their right. Basing himself on his analysis in Anderson (1992), Anderson (2005, 165–76) argues that the Tagalog facts can be handled by appealing to ranked OT constraints which favour leftmost alignment of monosyllabic pronominal clitics, but which otherwise favour left alignment of non-pronominals. (We discuss the details of Anderson's OT implementations later in the chapter.) The disyllabic pronominal clitics will then be left 'stranded', so to speak, at the right edge of the cluster. However, he then argues for a semantically based distinction between the pronominal types and the particles. We now evaluate that proposal. Our discussion will be critical, but we should point out that Anderson is one of the few to raise this very important and potentially very challenging set of issues.

Pursuing the idea that clitics are essentially phrasal affixes Anderson points out that in affixal systems we generally find that derivational affixes appear closer to the root than inflectional affixes. He further suggests (Anderson 2005, 169):

> [W]e could say the ordering of particles before pronouns reflects the same
> regularity: particles have various semantic and pragmatic content, and are thus
> 'derivational', as opposed to pronouns, which are (on this analysis) agreement
> markers, and thus 'inflectional'. It would be natural for pronominal elements to
> be suffixed outside of particle, then, and thus to follow them.

The crucial idea here seems to be 'meaning-bearing' derivation-like clitics as opposed to non-meaning-bearing inflection-like clitics. Anderson's use of the 'inflection/derivation' terminology for this distinction is perhaps a little idiosyncratic, and it might be better to speak of 'grammatical clitics' as opposed to 'semantic/pragmatic clitics'.

Unfortunately, it proves difficult to draw a clear distinction in general. Inflection, to be sure, usually realizes a set of morphosyntactic features on Anderson's model, but according to Booij (1996b, 2007) it's necessary to distinguish two sorts of inflection: contextual inflection and inherent inflection. Contextual inflection is found when a word inflects solely to respect some sort of grammatical (syntactic) dependency, as when a word agrees with a head or when a governee takes a specific form determined by its governor. Inherent inflection is inflection that represents a choice at the level of the lexeme. Booij cites the case of singular/plural number for nouns or present/past tense for verbs. The choice here is made on the basis of the meaning associated with the inflected forms. This entails that inherent inflection is, at some level, ultimately cashed out in terms of a semantic interpretation of the inflected form, whereas this is not (necessarily) true of contextual inflection.

In the case of number or tense inflection, it isn't clear that we have to say that the inflections themselves are Saussurean signs so that the inflectional elements themselves are paired with semantic representations of number or tense (though this is the common way of representing such inflection in all the dominant syntactic models). There are very good grounds for saying that the number or tense features on English nouns and verbs are merely features at the level of word forms or even syntactic heads and that those features are not interpreted semantically until we get to the level of phrases. For instance, we don't want to say that the form *were* actually bears the meaning 'past time reference' in a sentence with sequence-of-tense like *I thought you were coming tomorrow*. Rather, we need to say that semantic interpretation is postponed until the clause level, at which point the semantics can be instructed to suppress the default 'past time reference' in sequence-of-tense contexts such as these (see Spencer 2000 for discussion). However, there are clear instances of inflection in which it would be perverse to deny that the inflection itself bore meaning. Innumerable languages have elaborated case systems in which the case morphology realizes concrete spatial or other concepts on a par with English prepositions, and in which there is little or no grammaticalization of those meanings (Spencer 2008). Similarly, there are numerous languages with argument–structure alternations such as causatives that introduce a semantic predicate into the verb's representation. Admittedly, such alternations are often referred to as 'derivational' for that reason, but in many cases the alternations are part of a system that includes alternations that are far less like derivational, such as passives or applicatives.

For these reasons, it is simply not possible to say with any certainty that we can partition morphological processes into a non-meaning-bearing 'inflectional' set and a meaning-bearing 'derivational' set under any coherent characterization of any of these terms. However, even if we could, we would find that there are serious empirical difficulties when we confront Anderson's proposals for Tagalog with the clitic systems of other languages. In Standard Italian the locative clitic *ci* occupies position II out of six while the partitive *ne* occupies position VI. Thus, Italian poses serious problems for any analysis that tries to separate 'inflectional' pronominal clitics from 'derivational' locative/partitive clitics. The difficulty is compounded when we compare Sardinian, a Romance language closely related to Italian. Jones (1993, 213–39) describes the clitic system of Sardinian. The pronominal clitics distinguish 'accusative' and 'dative' forms in 3rd person forms, as in several other Romance languages, as shown in (24):

(24)   Sardinian pronominal clitics

	Singular		Plural	
	Acc	Dat	Acc	Dat
1st	mi	mi	nos	nos
2nd	ti	ti	bos	bos
3rd masculine	lu	li	los	lis
feminine	la	li	las	lis
reflexive		si		

Additionally, Sardinian distinguishes three clitics which Jones describes as 'adverbial'. The clitics *bi*, *nke* translate roughly as locational adverbs, 'there, at/to/from that place', while *nde* is a 'partitive' proform for phrases introduced by the preposition *de* 'of' (Jones 1993, 218). The cluster template is shown in (25):

(25)   The Sardinian clitic template

I	II	III	IV	V	VI
mi					lu
ti				li	la
si	bi	nke	nde		los
nos				lis	las
bos					

Here, the equivalent of Italian *ne* occupies a position in the middle of the cluster, separating the slot containing the 1st/2nd person and reflexive clitics from the slots housing the 3rd person clitics. It's difficult to see how the 'derivational clitics' notion can be reconciled with both Italian and Sardinian placement facts.

Now, it might be open to us (though not to Anderson) to claim that the Romance clitic sequences are really affix strings and hence not comparable to second-position clitic clusters. However, that would not answer the most damaging objection, which comes from the behaviour of lexical reflexive verbs in many languages. All the Romance and Slavic languages have verbs that are reflexive in form but that are not semantically related to their non-reflexive bases.[4] In some cases there is no non-reflexive base. This is true of the Slavic languages with Wackernagel clitics. Thus, in Czech we have the verb *bát se* 'fear', as in:

(26)   Já jsem   se   ho   bál
         I   AUX.1SG.CL REFL.CL him.CL feared
         'I was afraid of him'

This is a reflexivum tantum verb: there is no verb *bát*. The reflexive is expressed by means of a clitic pronominal in exactly the manner of a true reflexive verb and the reflexive clitic occupies the same place it would occupy with such a verb. On the other hand, the reflexive verb *brát se* is ambiguous. On the one hand, it represents a perfectly regular reflexive (imperfective) passive form of the verb *brát* 'take', on the other hand, it is a derived verb with the entirely idiomatic, non-compositional meaning 'take care of (a problem), concern oneself with'. Again, the reflexive occupies the same position in the clitic cluster that it always occupies:

(27)   Brál jsem   se   o   to,   aby   ...
         took AUX.1SG.CL REFL.CL about that, in.order.to ...
         'I took steps to ensure that ...'

Examples such as this can easily be multiplied. They demonstrate that one and the same clitic can sometimes play the role of a pronominal, and hence be 'inflectional' in Anderson's terms, and can sometimes serve to create a lexeme that is entirely distinct from the base lexeme, and that is hence 'derivational' in Anderson's sense. Yet the position of the reflexive clitic is the same in both cases. We conclude that Anderson's explanation for the placement conditions on Tagalog clitics at the very least fails to generalize beyond the dataset it was originally designed for.

In an important sense, our criticism of Anderson's proposals are unfair: Anderson has raised serious issues that must be addressed by any theory of clitics, especially the realizational models discussed below in Section 8.5.1. Morphologically oriented theories have to offer some kind of explanation for the way that clitic systems can freely mix inflectional properties with entirely different types of property (notably adverbs and discourse markers). Syntactically oriented theories have to provide an explanation for the blatant disparity between the placement conditions operating over non-inflectional clitics and the normal principles of syntax that govern the placement of adverbials. Our own predilections are towards the morphological approach to clitics, but we have no particularly convincing story to replace Anderson's. What does seem clear, though, is that grammatical theory has to have some way of accommodating the fact that some clitics are exponents just of morphosyntactic properties while other clitics are exponents of representations with more semantic content, possibly even full-blown semantic predicates.

8.2.4   Clitics in Canonical Typology

Until recently typological relationships have been defined in one of two ways: either in terms of Chomskyan universals, abstract statements meant to be (potentially) true of all languages, or in terms of Greenbergian universals, that is, statements that are true of a large percentage of the world's languages or a large percentage of some subclass of languages. Recently, however, a logically distinct approach to typological description has been proposed by G. Corbett (Corbett 2006, 2007) under which typological relationships are defined in terms of a logical space defined by canonical properties. Canonical properties of a category or construction type are properties that we can all agree characterize good instances of that category or construction. However, canonical properties don't have to be prototypical properties. A prototype is some existing entity, such as a sparrow or eagle (prototypical bird) or a red or blue square on a colour chart (prototypical colour) that somehow encapsulates what people think is a typical exemplar of that category. Whatever the value of prototypes in cognitive psychology, they are not very valuable in linguistics because (most of) linguistics deals with abstract structures. It is therefore more difficult to imagine what a prototypical noun would be. However, we can imagine what sorts of abstract properties we expect a noun to have. For instance, we expect it to denote a physical, countable object, and we expect the expression to be able to serve particular grammatical functions, such as being the object of a verb. Depending on other aspects of grammar we might also expect it to have number/case forms or possessed/possessor forms and so on. It is less likely to show a tense distinction (though this is far from rare). We can therefore enumerate a series of properties that are canonical for nouns and ask to what extent real nouns in a language match the canonical set.

The canonical approach has been applied to a number of linguistic categories, including agreement (Corbett 2006), suppletion (Corbett 2007), passive constructions (Siewierska 2012), finiteness (Nikolaeva 2012) and others. In Spencer and Luís (2012) we apply the canonical method to the question of the nature of clitics. We take as our starting point the idea that, canonically speaking, clitics are like prosodically weak function words in terms of their syntactic distribution but like affixes in terms of the formal properties. Thus, like (canonical) function words, canonical clitics do not show selection of the word classes they are in immediate construction with (in other words, they show promiscuous attachment) and like function words they take wide scope over conjoined phrases. However, like (canonical) affixes they are prosodically dependent, and like affixes they have a form that is less than the minimal, syntactically independent, word form. In effect, then, a canonical clitic is something like a canonical phrasal affix; that is, an element with the distribution of a (function) word but the form and prosodic properties of an affix.

Of course, in practice we see plenty of entities that have some but not all of these properties, or that have canonical properties but only to a limited degree, in circumscribed contexts. One clear case of this would be the Polish floating inflections. These have the properties of prototypical (not canonical!) affixes in that they trigger allomorphy on their hosts, just like affixes, but they also have the properties of prototypical clitics in taking wide scope and showing highly promiscuous attachment. Such clitics are not canonical as either clitics or affixes and to a large extent it is immaterial what we actually call them. But however we label them, we need to be able to characterize their behaviour in various grammatical contexts, and for the most part this means simply listing those properties, because few if any of them are entailments of other properties.

8.3   General approaches to clitics

In this section we summarize some of the theoretical positions that have been adopted by linguists seeking a single general account of clitics, either cross-linguistically or (more commonly) for the clitics, or a subset of clitics, in a single language. We will divide these approaches broadly into phonological/prosodic approaches, morphological approaches and syntactic approaches. However, in a number of cases we see a mixed approach, especially where phonological factors are concerned.

In purely phonological/prosodic approaches clitics are regarded as phonologically aberrant words, and clitic placement is defined in terms of phonological phrasing. There is often a complex interaction between prosodic conditioning and information structure (topic/focus articulation). For instance, in defining 'second position' with respect to a prosodic phrase, we may wish to ignore a clause-initial topicalized phrase in computing the domain for second-position placement.

In syntactic approaches, clitics are treated as a kind of function word (often as 'functional heads'). In transformational models, such as the Principles and Parameters model, they are moved from canonical argument/adverb positions in the syntax to their eventual resting places. Clitic positions therefore have to be defined in terms of syntactic positions.

A further set of approaches to clitics can be identified, which we will call 'mapping approaches'. In such models a set of independent principles are established for morphology and for syntax, and clitics are regarded as representing a mismatch between the two. The mismatch is then handled by a set of 'mapping principles' that regulate the morphology–syntax interface. Examples of such proposals are Marantz (1988) and Sadock (1991) (see also Sproat 1998 for a general discussion of mapping principle models). For instance, Sadock (1991, 163), in his model of Autolexical Syntax, proposes the following set of constraints for mapping syntactic (Level 1) and morphological (Level 2) structures:

(28)   Linearity Constraints (LC)
  a.   Strong: The associated elements of Level 1 and Level 2 representations must occur in the same linear order.
  b.   Weak: The associated elements of Level 1 and Level 2 representations must occur in as close to the same linear order except where the Level 2 requirement of lexemes make this impossible.

(29)   Constructional Integrity Constraints (CIC)
  a.   Strong: If a lexeme combines with a phrase P at Level 1 and with a host at Level 2, then the Level 2 host must be associated with the head of the Level 1 phrase P.
  b.   Weak: If a lexeme combines with an expression P at Level 1 and with a host at Level 2, then the morphological host must be associated with some element of the Level 1 expression P.

The Weak Linearity Constraint permits morphological principles to override syntactic principles. For instance, a language may place determiners initially in a noun phrase, but an enclitic determiner will be placed after its host, and therefore could not appear initially in the phrase. The Strong Constructional Integrity Constraint requires inflection-like marking to be head-marking, but the Weak Constructional Integrity Constraint effectively permits phrasal affixation. The permitted variation in clitic placement cross-linguistically is then said to be the result of the Cliticization Principle (Sadock 1991, 105):

(30)   Cliticization Principle
         If a lexeme combines with an inflected word in the morphology and with a phrase in the syntax, its morphosyntactic association will conform to at least the weak Linearity Constraint.

As Spencer (1993) observes, Sadock devotes rather little attention to the problem of Wackernagel placement and it is not entirely clear how 2W systems, in which the second-position host is a word rather than a phrase, can be incorporated into his system.

For many types of clitic system some aspects of phonology, morphology and syntax will all play a role in determining clitic placement (and in some cases, semantic or discourse factors may also be relevant). However, we will begin our survey by looking at approaches that focus on just one aspect of the problem.

8.4   Prosodic approaches

There are a number of senses in which we may speak of a 'prosodic' or 'phonological' approach to the study of clitic systems. In the first place, we can ask what phonological properties clitics have in any given language. The answer we give will depend on the assumptions we make about phonological structure and the nature of prosodic categories such as prosodic words and prosodic phrases, as outlined in Chapter 4. These issues are largely independent of other views we may have about clitics, and any approach to clitics needs to take a stance on those issues if it lays claim to being complete. However, there is another sense of 'phonological approach' under which we might seek to analyse all of the important behaviour of clitics in terms of phonological properties. In effect, this is to abandon the notion of 'special clitic' in favour of treating all clitics as 'simple/phonological' clitics. It is fair to say that this is by far the minority view, but it nonetheless has had its advocates, for a number of theorists have taken up Wackernagel's baton (so to speak) and sought a purely prosodic motivation for clitic behaviour.

For Serbian/Croatian this has been argued for particularly by Radanović-Kocić (1996), though most observers reject the idea that a purely phonological analysis of that language is possible. Taylor (1996, and references cited there) argues for an essentially phonological analysis of Ancient Greek, extending the database of Wackernagel's original study in various ways, though without claiming that phonology is the sole determinant of clitic placement. For Sanskrit, Hock (1996) has argued for a purely phonological account (though the possibility of this is disputed by Hale 1996 and Schäufele 1996). Anderson (2005, 126) mentions unpublished observations by his colleague, the Sanskritologist Stanley Insler, according to which the Sanskrit clitics are arranged in the order 'V-intial before C-initial', and 'high vowel before low vowel'.[5] Anderson points out that there are a variety of clitic systems in which phonological structure seems to play a role in cluster ordering, citing remarks by Alpher (1991, 42) on the Pama-Nyungan (Australian) language Yir-Yoront. Alpher notes that subject and object clitics can be hosted by separate elements in the clause, but that when they come together they are ordered according to the principles in (31):[6]

(31)   Clitic ordering in Yir-Yoront
  1.   1st person < 2nd/3rd person: *nginh uwl* '2DUAL.SUBJ 1SG.OBJ (ye two < me)', *nginh ewl* '2PL.SUBJ 1SG.OBJ (you-all < me)', *ngeynuwn 'r* '2SG.SUBJ 1EXCL.PL.OBJ (thou < us.exclusive)' etc.; *nginh 'l* '3SG.SUBJ 1SG.OBJ (s/he < me)', *nginh pul* '3DUAL.SUBJ 1SG.OBJ (they-two < me)', *nginh pinn* '3PL.SUBJ 1SG.OBJ (they-many < me)', etc.; *'y un* '1SG.SUBJ 2SG.OBJ (I < thee)', *ngenn un* '1EXCL.DUAL.SUBJ 2SG.OBJ (we-two(exclusive) < thee)', *ngeyn inh* '1EXCL.PL.SUBJ 2SG.OBJ(we-many(exclusive) < thee)', *'y ungnh* '1SG.SUBJ 3SG.OBJ (I < him/her)'.
  2.   'Lighter' precedes 'heavier' (for combinations of 2nd and 3rd person pronominals): *'l un* or *'l inh* 's/he < thee', *(nh)un(h) pinn* 'they(plural) < thee'.
  3.   exceptional ordering in certain fixed combinations in which the first element is a full pronoun rather than a clitic.

However, given that the pronominals can be separated from each other, it's not clear to what extent we are seeing phonological constraints on weak pronoun ordering as opposed to phonological constraints on the ordering of more canonical types of clitic.

This is not to say that there cannot be languages whose clitic placement principles are largely or entirely phonological, of course. In Chapter 4 we looked at the placement of the Pashto clitic cluster and at the placement of the *li* interrogative marker in Bulgarian. In both cases it was argued that the principal determinant of clitic placement was stress. Another, particularly clear, instance of a phonologically determined clitic system is that of the Austronesian language Chamorro, as described by Chung (2003).[7] Chung argues that the pronominals are special clitics, indeed, Wackernagel clitics whose positioning is defined purely in terms of prosodic structure. In (32) we see the weak and full pronominal forms (Chung 2003, 550):[8]

(32)   Chamorro pronouns

	Weak	Independent
1sg	yu'	guahu
2sg	hao	hagu
3sg anim	gui'	guiya
1 incl pl	hit	hita
1 excl pl	häm	hämi
2pl	hämyu	hämyu
3pl anim	siha	siha

Because of various morphosyntactic constraints, only one pronominal clitic per clause is found, usually functioning as a direct object, but sometimes appearing as an intransitive subject. The pronominal clitics co-occur with discourse marker clitics. The pronominals appear to the right of the first predicate in the clause. However, where the predicate is a verb or adjective with a complement phrase, the pronoun appears after the verb or adjective head, not after the complement (Chung 2003, 556):

(33) a.   Malägu' **gui'** neubu na   kareta
             AGR.want she   new   LINKER car
             'She wants a new car'

      b.   ?? [Malägu' neubu na   kareta] **gui'**
             AGR.want new   LINKER car   she

(34) a.   Metgot-ña   **hao** ki   guahu
             AGR.strong-COMPARATIVE you than me
             'You are stronger than me'

      b.   * [Metgot-ña   ki   guahu] **hao**
             AGR.strong-COMPARATIVE than me   you

With possessed noun phrases the pronoun must appear after the head noun and not after the (postnominal) possessor phrase (pp. 557–8):

(35) a.   * [Ma'estro-nña si   Carmen] **gui'**
             teacher-AGR   ART Carmen he

      b.   Ma'estro-nña **gui'** si   Carmen
             teacher-AGR   he   ART Carmen
             'He is Carmen's teacher'

A similar pattern is observed with other postnominal modifiers.

With prenominal modifiers the clitic can occur after the head noun or further to the left, hosted by the modifier (pp. 554–9):

(36) a. [Más yä-hu   na   taotao] **hao**
         most WH[OBJ].like-AGR LINKER person you

   b. [Más yä-hu   **hao** na   taotao]
       most WH[OBJ].like-AGR you LINKER person

       'You're the person I like most'

Chung points out that some prenominal modifiers that can host the clitic are not constituents and could not have been placed in clause-initial position by any kind of movement transformation. In general, there is no way of characterizing the possible hosts of the clitic in syntactic terms.[9]

Chung (p. 574) proposes that the positioning of the clitics can be understood in purely prosodic terms. She argues that the clitic pronouns bear a subcategorization frame as in (37):

(37)   [i[p[p   ] —]

She describes and motivates an algorithm for computing prosodic structure from syntactic structure. The algorithm will assign the structure shown in (38a) to a sentence such as (33a), where the arrow marks the point of adjunction for the clitic, giving us the structure shown in (38b) (modifying Chung's representations from p. 575 somewhat for clarity of exposition):

(38)   Prosodic phrasing and clitic placement for (33a)

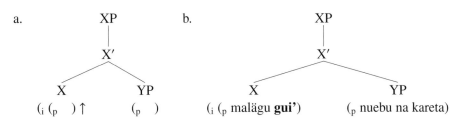

As an example of the difficulty a purely syntactic analysis would face, Chung mentions (p. 553) that the clitic occurs in third position in subordinate clauses, citing (39):

(39)   Man-maleffa na   [mansiudadanu-n Amerikanu] **hit** lokkui'
          AGR-forget   COMP citizens-LINKER American   we also

          'They've forgotten that we are also American citizens'

As far as we can tell, this falls neatly out of her analysis on the reasonable assumption that the subordinate clause initiates its own intonation group (Chung doesn't seem to return to this example in her paper). The example is potentially of interest because in this respect Chamorro contrasts with, say, Serbian/Croatian, in which the clitic cluster would immediately follow the complementizer.

8.5   Morphological approaches

As with phonological approaches, there are several senses in which we can speak of morphological approaches to clitic systems. The strongest sense of morphological approach is that in which all or a substantial number of clitics systems are treated as morphological phenomena, to be handled by the morphological component. This is the notion of clitics as 'phrasal affixes', as advocated most consistently by Stephen Anderson. We will call this the 'phrasal affix' class of models. In a phrasal affix model clitics are regarded as aberrant affixes whose placement is determined with respect to non-morphological hosts (fully inflected words, edges of phrases, edges of prosodic categories). The details and specifics of such approaches depend on the approach to morphology generally. The dominant approach to inflectional morphology within morphology as a subdiscipline is probably the inferential-realizational approach as advocated by Anderson (1992), Aronoff (1994), Corbett and Fraser (1993), Stump (2001), Zwicky (1985b) and many others.

Morphological approaches take a clitic system and re-analyse that system as affixational. In this section we survey a number of such approaches, focusing in particular on analyses within inferential-realizational morphology. The analyses we will look at have been implemented within OT (Section 8.5.2), within an HPSG-inspired formalization of Paradigm Function Morphology (PFM) (Section 8.5.3), within an extended version of PFM (Section 8.5.4) and within Anderson's A-Morphous Morphology model (Section 8.5.3). Many linguists working within the Minimalist Program have addressed the question of clitics in a variety of languages, and those that address the problem of the morphology of clitics do so within the framework of Distributed Morphology. We survey one such approach in Section 8.5.5.

The model of morphology impacts considerably on how we look at clitics, so it will be necessary to devote a little attention to models of morphology.

8.5.1   Realizational models of morphology

There are essentially two ways of thinking of inflected word forms such as, say, {cat, cats}. The classical morphemic approach holds that there is a list of morphemes. Each morpheme is a lexical entry pairing a form with a meaning, just as in an ordinary dictionary. The morphemes required to inflect CAT are (with very crude semantic specifications):

(40) a.   </kat/, [CAT(x)]>
      b.   </z/, [PLURAL(NOUN)]>
      c.   </∅/, [SINGULAR(NOUN)]>

The entry for singular number in (40c) is required because otherwise we would not know whether the form *cat* denoted just the concept 'cat' (as in the compound *catfood*) or the concept 'cat-in-the-singular' (as in *There is a cat on the mat*). In this approach there is no real difference in type between a content morpheme such as *cat* and a functional morpheme such as /z/ or /∅/.

In an inferential-realizational approach inflectional affixes are not conceived of as Saussurean signs, that is, as combinations of form and meaning, like content words. Rather, an inflection is simply a morphophonological way of marking that certain features or feature combinations are realized on that inflected word form. Hence, there is no lexical entry for an inflectional morpheme and no list of morphemes-as-signs. Instead, we work with a notion of lexeme and paradigm.

A lexeme can be thought of very approximately as a lexical entry for a content word, containing a specification of unpredictable information about the word, namely, the pronunciation of the basic form(s) of the word (for instance, the root), the meaning, and perhaps the syntactic category as well as any idiosyncratic information such as morphological irregularities. In addition, there is a morphological grammar which specifies the form of inflectional paradigms for each class of lexemes. The grammar of English, for instance, specifies that all count nouns must be inflected for the values {singular, plural} of the feature [NUMBER]. This feature declaration effectively defines for us the paradigm of the noun lexeme. The principle of the paradigm (often referred to as 'Word-and-Paradigm' morphology) dictates that each cell defined by the feature set for that class of lexemes must be filled by some word form. In other words, the grammar of English stipulates that count nouns must have a singular form and a plural form.

The grammar also has to include a specification of what the actual inflected word forms are. In a model such as that of Stump (2001) this is achieved by means of a set of functions that tell us how to deduce the inflected form of a word given its root form and given the set of inflectional (morphosyntactic) properties that it realizes. For instance, English grammar will include the rule (41). This should be read as a function, f, which maps the root form, X, of a lexeme, and a set of features to an inflected form:

(41) $f<X,\{[NUM:plural]\}>= Xz$

This is a 'Block I' rule, which means it applies after the rule selecting appropriate stem forms have applied. The appeal to rules blocks is essential where we have strings of affixes in a fixed linear order, that is, for the vast majority of morphological systems. To see how the notion of rule block works, consider a hypothetical language with up to three inflectional suffixes per word (think of Hungarian nouns for concreteness, if you will). A word form such as (42) will be defined by means of rules ordered in three blocks, I, II, III as in (43), where the symbol σ denotes a set of morphosyntactic properties (features):

(42)   stem-a-b-c

(43) a.   Block I
            $f<X, \sigma_1> = $ X-a
     b.   Block II
            $f<X, \sigma_2> = $ X-b

    c.   Block III

           $f<X, \sigma_3> = X\text{-}c$

The input of each block of rules is the output of the previous block. Thus, the 'X' in (43c) is the form *Xab*. These rules therefore define the form *Xabc*.

    We may well find that a given affix appears to straddle two position classes. In that case Stump's model defines a portmanteau position class; for instance, we might find that there is a suffix *d* which is in paradigmatic opposition both to *b* and *c*, and therefore pre-empts the appearance of either. Stump notates such a portmanteau slot as Block [III,II]. A special rule (44) will introduce the *d* suffix:

(44)   Block [III,II]

             $f<X, \sigma_4> = Xd$

The introduction of the d suffix is triggered by a specific set of properties, σ_4. For other sets of features, the composite Block [III,II] reverts to the sequence <Block II, Block III>, as for (43b–c) above.

    Such models presuppose a universal default rule of the form (45):

(45) $f<X,\{[ANY\!:\!any]\}> = X$

The rule (45) states that for any value of any feature the default realization of a form is that form itself. In other words, all else being equal, the default morphology is zero morphology. (This is what Stump 2001 calls the Identity Function Default: by default the function defining any inflected form is the identity function.) Wherever this rule is in competition with a more specific rule (which in practice means any rule whatever), it will be overridden by that more specific rule. This is a consequence of a general principle of default inheritance, originating in Panini's famous grammar of Sanskrit. The principle goes by a variety of names; the Elsewhere Condition (Kiparsky 1982), the Proper Inclusion Principle (Koutsoudas et al. 1974) or, giving due credit to its originator, Paninian Determinism (Stump 2001).[10]

    The principle of default inheritance is crucial to many varieties of morphological theory and serves as a principle governing the way all morphological rules interact: where two rules are in competition, the more specific is applied in preference to the more general. Thus, we might have a minority plural or past tense ending for one class of verbs in competition with the more general ending. In that case, a lexeme indexed so as to belong to the minority class will undergo the more specific rule, while a lexeme lacking any such index will undergo the default plural/past tense rule. Completely irregular lexemes (for instance, those showing suppletion) will have their irregular forms listed by means of a rule that is maximally specific (i.e. applying to just one lexeme) which will therefore override any other rule whatsoever.

    The immediate consequence of having a general default function of the type (45), together with the definition of 'paradigm' in terms of obligatory feature values, is that we no longer need to define default forms in terms of zero morphemes. The rules of English together with the lexical entry for 'cat' tell us that (i) the noun 'cat' has a singular and a plural form, (ii) the root of 'cat' is /kat/,

(iii) the plural of 'cat' is /katz/. There is no rule telling us what the singular form is, so we must assume the general default rule in (45). From this general principle together with information in (i–iii) we can infer that the remaining singular form must bc identical to the lexeme's root form /kat/. In other words we capture the notion that the root form is the default realization for the singular (or, indeed, for the form that is not specified at all for number which appears in compounds such as *catfood*).

Because we are able to infer that /kat/ is the realization of the singular, rather than having this specified directly by means of a zero morpheme, we refer to such models as inferential. They are to be contrasted with lexical models, in which an element bearing the meaning 'singular' has to be added to the representation of the 'cat' morpheme in order to define the form /kat/ as representing singular number.

At the same time, our morphological rules serve to realize the complete set of feature values that characterize the inflected word form. They do not alter the content of that set of features, either by adding or removing values or features. For this reason, such a class of models is referred to as realizational. These are contrasted with incremental models, in which a rule or morpheme enriches (or depletes) the feature content. For instance, in the classical morpheme-based model, the plural morpheme adds the property 'plural number' to the representation of the 'cat' morpheme.[11]

The set of cells defined by the feature system and the set of forms occupying those cells go to make up the inflectional paradigm associated with a lexeme or class of lexemes. One of the important features of inferential-realizational models of inflection is that they are able to state even arbitrary dependencies between parts of a paradigm. Specifically, in more complex systems in which a given lexeme may be associated with paradigms that have dozens or hundreds of distinct cells, we almost always encounter the phenomenon of syncretism. This refers to a situation in which one cell in the paradigm is systematically identical to some other cell. Sometimes a situation looking like syncretism may arise because the paradigm is not as symmetrical and exhaustive as we expect. For instance, in many languages there is a distinction of gender in singular forms of nouns, adjectives and perhaps even verbs, but in the plural there is no distinction of gender. This is the situation in Russian, for instance, which has masculine, feminine and neuter gender in the singular. In the plural there is one set of forms for adjectives and past tense forms of verbs (the two categories that show gender agreement in the singular) irrespective of the gender of the noun. The best way of thinking of such cases is to say that the feature systems defining gender and number forms are not independent. Rather, there is a feature co-occurrence restriction or some equivalent formal statement that records the fact that the property [GENDER] is defined only for those elements that are also specified for the feature value [NUMBER:singular].

Another type of inflectional homonymy can be illustrated by Russian.[12] In (46) we see partial paradigms for two Russian nouns, the Class I noun ZAKON 'law' and the Class II noun KOMNATA 'room'.

(46)   Partial paradigms for Russian ZAKON, KOMNATA

Singular		
Nom	zakon	komnat-a
Acc	zakon	komnat-u
Gen	zakon-a	komnat-i
Dat	zakon-u	komnat-e
Plural		
Nom	zakon-i	komnat-i
Acc	zakon-i	komnat-i
Gen	zakon-ov	komnat

The two lexemes share the same endings for different word forms in different cells of the paradigm. Specifically, ZAKON and KOMNATA have identical forms respectively for nom/acc.sg~gen.pl, gen.sg~nom.sg, dat.sg~acc.sg, nom/acc.pl~gen.sg. Now, it turns out that it is impossible to find any sensible explanation for this coincidence of forms. The forms are identical by accident (it is not an accident that the endings are all either zero or single consonants – it is precisely in such cases that we can expect accidents of historical change to give rise to accidental homophony of this sort).[13]

However, there are many other cases in which the inflectional homonymy is systematic and not accidental, but it can't be straightforwardly reduced to the neutralization of one property in the context of another. A typical example is that of what Carstairs (1987) calls a 'take-over'. Latin verbs have indicative and subjunctive mood paradigms as well as active and passive voice paradigms. For both moods and both voices there are various tense forms including a present tense for the indicative and subjunctive and a future tense for the indicative. Finally, verbs fall into a variety of inflectional classes that determine exactly what endings they take when inflected. One clear take-over can be seen when we consider verbs of the third conjugation (Class III). The present and future tense forms of the indicative and subjunctive are shown in (47):

(47)   Partial paradigm of REGO

	Present Indicative		Present Subjunctive		Future Indicative	
	Active	Passive	Active	Passive	Active	Passive
1sg	rego:	regor	*regam*	*regar*	**regam**	**regar**
2sg	regis	regeris	rega:s	rega:ris	rege:s	rege:ris
3sg	regit	regitur	regat	rega:tur	reget	rege:tur
1pl	regimus	regimur	rega:mus	rega:mur	rege:mus	rege:mur
2pl	regitis	regimini:	rega:tis	rega:mini:	rege:tis	rege:mini:
3pl	regunt	reguntur	regant	regantur	regent	regentur

Given the rest of the paradigm for verbs of this class we would expect the future forms to be *regem*, *reger*. Although these are perfectly well-formed words phonologically (indeed, *regem* is an existing word form, the accusative singular of the word REX 'king'), they are usurped by the italicized present subjunctive forms for the 1sg. From the tables and from the fact that this homonymy extends to the passive as well as the active, we can conclude that this is a systematic fact about verbs of this class.

Systematic dependencies of this sort between distinct cells in a paradigm are often handled by rules of referral. A rule of referral is no more than a direct statement of a syncretic relationship. In the case of the Latin future~subjunctive syncretism, the grammar would provide a rule stating 'the form of the 1sg future indicative is computed/defined/inferred by taking the form defined for the 1sg present subjunctive', in other words to deduce the 1sg future indicative we are referred to the 1sg present subjunctive. Different formal models achieve this in various ways. In Stump's Paradigm Function model a particular type of function is defined which has the effect of a rule of referral and which is integrated into the rest of the rule system. In the very closely related model of Network Morphology (Corbett and Fraser 1993) inflectional paradigms are defined in terms of the default~override relations between parts of the paradigm, so that, in a sense, the whole architecture is built on the notion of referral: to deduce an inflected form first deduce a more general form, until you reach a feature set that has to be expressed by some stipulated rule of exponence. Each type of model can readily handle the rich variety of syncretic relationship explored in Baerman et al. (2005) and other such research. Moreover, it is important that the descriptive apparatus be very powerful: in principle, diachronic serendipity could give rise to more-or-less any kind of systematic syncretic relationship.

In sum, we contrast the two main models of morphology. The classical morpheme-based model of American Structuralism is a lexical-incremental model: morphemes are lexical entries pairing a form with a meaning/property content, and the content of a morphologically complex word is defined by combining the meanings of its pieces. The dominant contemporary model of inflection is an inferential-realizational model in which a complete set of properties is realized by a set of rules with inferential relationships (for instance, those defined by Paninian Determinism). The morpheme-based model is, of course, what underlies those approaches that take clitics to be syntactically represented objects, in that clitics on such models are a type of lexeme. The models of interest to us are therefore those that apply the inferential-realizational approach. In the context of the Minimalist Program for syntax, the principal model of morphology is Distributed Morphology (Halle and Marantz 1993). For discussion of clitics in the context of this model, see Embick and Noyer (2001). This is a mixed model, in the sense that it operates with realization rules defined over feature sets, but it requires that morphology insert lexically stored morphemes into syntactic terminals, and is therefore a lexical model. We will not discuss this model in detail since its application is restricted entirely to research within the Minimalist Program of syntax, and the main differences between Minimalist approaches (and PPT approaches generally) and other approaches lies in the syntactic assumptions rather than assumptions about morphology.[14] However, we present a brief summary of Noyer's (2001) analysis of the pronominal prefix/clitic sequences of Nunggubuyu as an example of the way Distributed Morphology has been deployed.

The morphological approaches that have been recently proposed have been implemented within Optimality Theory (Legendre 1996 2000a, b, Legendre 2001, Anderson 2005), within the model of HPSG (Miller 1992, Miller and Sag 1997, Monachesi 1999, 2005), within Anderson's (1992) A-Morphous Morphology realizational model (Klamer 1997), and within Stump's (2001) Paradigm Function Morphology (Bonami and Boyé 2007) or a variant thereof (Spencer 2001, Luís and Spencer 2005). We first briefly survey Anderson's OT approach. We then survey the very interesting system of the Austronesian language Kambera, as described by Klamer (1997, 1998a), a language that may pose interesting challenges for phrasal affixation approaches to clitics. Next we look at two implementations of the Paradigm Function Morphology model, one based on the 'classical' model of Stump (2001), the other based on a modification of that model specifically designed to handle typical clitic systems (Luís and Spencer 2005). We conclude with a brief survey of a Distributed Morphology analysis of the clitic system of the Australian language Nunggubuyu.

8.5.2   OT approaches

In Optimality Theory, grammatical generalizations are stated in the form of constraints on surface form. A battery of constraints dictate what kinds of forms are permitted and what kinds are excluded. However, the constraints are 'soft' in the sense that any form is allowed to violate (more or less) any constraint. This is because the constraints are ranked: an output or representation is permissible if it violates less highly ranked constraints than any conceivable competitor. For a survey of Optimality Theory, see Kager (1999) (mainly phonology) and McCarthy (2002).

From the point of view of clitic systems, the most important type of constraint in such models is the alignment constraint. An element is constrained to appear at the edge of some constituent or domain. Constraints generally take one of two forms, which we can think of as 'imperative' and 'prohibitive'. An imperative constraint compels an element to appear in a certain position, to adopt a certain form or whatever. For instance, we might have a constraint of the form 'element X should be a disyllabic word' or 'element X should appear at the left edge of domain D'. A prohibitive constraint excludes forms of a certain type of positioning in a particular place. Such constraints are usually notated using an asterisk '*'. For instance, we might have a constraint of the form 'element X may not contain a stressed syllable ('***Stress**')' or 'element X may not appear initially in domain D ('***Initial**')'.

For instance, the Wackernagel position can be defined using two OT constraints, one imperative, one prohibitive:

AlignLeft: A clitic must be the left-most element in its domain

*Initial: A clitic may not be the first element in its domain

Clearly, these constraints conflict with each other: **AlignLeft** demands that the clitic appear in initial position, but ***Initial** rules this out. If **AlignLeft** is ranked more highly than ***Initial** then the clitic will be forced to appear initially despite the demands of ***Initial** (and that constraint will effectively be invisible or 'occluded'). However, if we have the opposite ranking then we obtain an interesting effect. **AlignLeft** will require the clitic to be initial, but that is ruled out by ***Initial**. Now, in the case of alignment constraints, the further an element is from its constrained position the worse the violation. Thus, in a phrase with, say, three constituents, X-Y-Z, if a clitic is placed to the right of Y this is a worse violation than being placed to the right of X (and the position to the right of Z at the right edge of the domain is even worse). What this means is that the position to the right of X is the least severe violation of **AlignLeft** compatible with the more highly ranked constraint ***Initial**. This is illustrated in the schematic tableau below:

(48)

/input/	*INITIAL	ALIGNLEFT
a. cl=X-Y-Z	*!	
☞ b. X=cl-Y-Z		*
c. X-Y=cl-Z		*!*
d. X-Y-Z=cl		*!**

We freely generate all possible combinations of X, Y, Z and clitic (only four of the infinite set of possibilities are illustrated here) and submit each to the evaluation of the constraint set. In the tableau every occurrence of the symbol * indicates a single violation of the constraint while the exclamation mark ! after a violation mark indicates that that violation is fatal (*!). The symbol ☞ picks out the optimal candidate (i.e. the grammatical string). In this case both the optimal candidate (b) and the losing candidate (a) violate one constraint, once. However, candidate (a) violates a higher ranking constraint than (b) and so is less optimal than (b). The other two candidates violate the lower ranking constraint, but not the higher ranking constraint. However, each violates that constraint more often than the optimal candidate.

A system of this sort can easily be enriched to account for a standard clitic cluster with fixed ordering. All that is needed is to set up a constraint for each 'slot' in the cluster and rank the constraints according to the order in which the clitics come in the cluster. For instance, if we have a language in which dative clitics appear to the left of accusative clitics we set up the constraints **AlignLeft(Dat)** and **AlignLeft(Acc)** and rank them **AlignLeft(Dat)** ≫ **Align-Left(Acc)**. That way, both types of clitic will incur violations if they are not the leftmost element in their domain. If there are both types of clitic in the input to be evaluated the optimal candidate will be that which shows the order Dat–Acc. Indeed, even rather aberrant clusters such as those of South Slavic languages can be accommodated very easily in this way. For those languages (Serbian/Croatian, Bulgarian, Macedonian) the auxiliary clitic comes to the left of the pronominal clitics except in the case of the 3sg (or 3sg/pl for Macedonian), in which case that clitic appears rightmost in the cluster. Clearly, such templatic ordering facts can easily be captured by ranking **AlignLeft(Aux)** high but **AlignLeft(Aux3sg)** low, given the convention that 'Aux' refers to any auxiliary except 3sg. Further refinements are possible by specifying different domains for different clitics, and by introducing, say, prosodic or other phonological conditions into the constraints system.

Given these preliminaries we are now in a position to look at the way that Optimality Theory has been deployed to account for clitics. A number of works have employed OT to throw light on clitics. However, it should be borne in mind that OT is not, in and of itself, a theory of anything (least of all, clitics). Rather, it is a technology that can be integrated with a whole host of morphological and syntactic frameworks, to a greater or lesser extent. For instance, the work of Grimshaw (1997, 2001) deploys an essentially PPT view of syntax but implemented in OT. On the other hand, Gerlach (2002) implements the morpheme-based model of Minimalist Morphology (Wunderlich and Fabri 1995) within an essentially PPT model of syntax in her OT analysis of Romance clitic systems. In this subsection, however, we will look briefly at the proposals of Anderson, rooted in a realizational model of morphology.

Anderson (1992) adopts what in Stump's typology would be an inferential-realizational model of morphology. In his 'a-morphous' model of morphology, affixation is a purely phonological operation, in the sense that the addition of a prefix or suffix is conceived of as the addition of purely phonological material to the phonological form of a (partially inflected) word. He extends this by treating clitics as phrasal affixes, that is, as morphophonological operations applied to (edges of) phrases rather than to roots, stems or words. This means that clitics, like affixes, serve to realize morphosyntactic properties. In effect, Anderson is arguing that phrases, and not just lexemes, fall into inflectional paradigms. Here we will follow the exposition in Anderson (2005), especially chapters 6 and 8.

As we saw in Chapter 3, Wackernagel's original characterization of clitic placement was stated in terms of words: the clitic (cluster) occupies the position after the first word of the domain, or 2W position. However, in many languages the relevant 'anchor' or host for the clitics is the first constituent or phrase (2D). Anderson accounts for this by proposing that in some languages there is a highly ranked constraint **Integrity(XP)** which prohibits a phrase from being broken up. In languages such as Serbian/Croatian, in which both 2W and 2D are possible placements, Anderson proposes (along with many others; for discussion, see Bošković 2001) that the 2W placements result from free reordering of words in the syntax. Thus, when a clitic cluster seems to have been placed inside a subject noun phrase, say, this is because the first word of that phrase has been fronted further to the left (to a 'higher' position in a syntactic tree) and so forms a kind of degenerate one-word phrase which then hosts the clitic.

To account for Romance pronominal clitics, which cluster around a verb form, Anderson proposes that a possible anchor for clitics is a syntactic head (2005, 146). Thus, the constraints compel the clitics to appear to the right/left of the verb rather than being aligned with respect to a sentence constituent or phrase edge. Anderson proposes that the Tobler–Mussafia effects found in earlier varieties of Romance and in modern Bulgarian can be accounted for by treating the clitics as anchored to the V head, but with the possibility of V-fronting. He assumes a constraint **NonInitial(cl_i, CP)** which prohibits a clitic from being initial in the clause ('Complementizer Phrase', CP) and an alignment constraint forcing clitics to come to the immediate left of a verb head, **LeftMost(cl_i, V)**. These are ranked **NonInitial(cl_i, CP) $\gg$ LeftMost(cl_i, V)**. As a result, the clitics will come before the verb in all cases, except where the verb itself is initial, in which case the clitics will occupy the Wackernagel position.

Anderson discusses in some detail the way his machinery might account for a variety of the clitics systems we have illustrated in this book: Tagalog second-position clitics, Pashto 'endoclitics' and (genuine) endoclitics in Udi, and he proposes a variety of ways in which prosodic structure can interact with clitic placement in order to obtain the kinds of effects we have discussed in Chapter 4. (We should mention that he does not deploy the notion of Clitic Group in his phonological descriptions.) In particular, he argues that considerations of prosodic structure can account for clitic ordering in a language such as Taga-log, where we seen that there is a great deal of variation in ordering, and an important factor seems to be whether the clitic is monosyllabic or disyllabic. His chapter 8 is devoted to pronominal clitics and agreement systems of the kind we have surveyed in our Chapter 6.

Anderson also ties in his views on clitics with the syntax of verb-second lan-guages (that is, languages with relatively free word order but in which the finite verb is constrained to appear in second position in the clause, reminiscent of Wackernagel clitics), as well as developing a theory of noun incorporation. We leave it to the reader to explore those ideas. It should be said that Anderson's actual analyses are largely free of detailed technical exposition (there are hardly any OT tableaux in his book or related publications).[15]

Anderson provides an outline analysis of Udi Person Markers. Here is a brief sketch of Harris' own highly detailed and carefully worked out OT analysis. We saw in Section 7.4.2 that the Udi subject person markers (PMs) attach either as enclitics to the right edge of the focussed phrase or as suffixes/infixes to the verb. Harris (2000, 2002) derives the positioning of the PMs through specific alignment constraints of the following kind:

a.   Enclisis to a verb is derived through the alignment constraint which aligns the left edge of the PM with the right edge of the inflected verb form (in the future II, subjunctive I and II, and imperative).

b.   Enclisis to a focussed constituent follows from an alignment constraint which states that the left edge of the PM is aligned with the right edge of that constituent.

c.   Intermorphemic placement (between the incorporated element and the light verb) is captured through an alignment constraint which aligns the left edge of the PM with the right edge of the incorporated element.

d.   Intramorphemic placement is derived as infixation, incorporating the idea that a constraint that is very highly ranked, and hence normally not violated, might still yet be violated by forms which respect an even more highly ranked constraint. In this case, the alignment constraint requires that the right edge of the PM be aligned with the *right* edge of the verb stem. Since this entails overlapping segments the constraint will always be violated to some degree. The least violation is incurred when there is a mismatch of only one segment, which effectively means that the PM is moved to the left of the rightmost consonant. This is illustrated in Harris' Tableau 7.5 (p. 153), adapted here as (49), where '|' indicates the right edge of the verb stem and '+' the right edge of the PM:

(49)   Endoclisis in a simplex verbstem, {beɣ-, -e, ne}

Candidates	ALIGN-PM-VERBSTEM
a. ne+beɣ|-e	beɣ!
b. b-ne+eɣ|-e	eɣ!
☞ c. be-ne+ɣ|	ɣ
d. beɣ-ne+e	ne!

This alignment constraint can be ranked above whatever constraints together guarantee lexical integrity, thereby letting in endoclisis.

    Before we leave the OT models we must raise some questions. The constraints that Anderson and others propose generally make explicit reference to clitics themselves. And yet Anderson's model, in particular, is 'a-morphous': phrasal affixes, just like word affixes, are mere phonological accretions without any morphological presence. It is therefore not entirely clear how the constraints recognize a piece of phonology as a clitic in the first place. This is a question that is raised by all OT-inspired analyses that do not recognize clitics as instances of classical morphemes.

    To what extent is an OT-implementation motivated in preference to other types of implementations, for instance, in terms of re-writing rules? Anderson argues that the OT implementation has two main advantages over a rules-based approach. The first concerns what we might call 'clairvoyant allomorphy'. Recall that in Serbian/Croatian the 3sg auxiliary clitic and the 3sg feminine accusative clitic are homophonous: *je*. When they are adjacent the pronominal alternates with the form *ju* (Anderson 2005, 127):

(50) a. Oni =**su** =**je/*ju** zaboravili
          they AUX her   forgotten
          'They forgot her'
     b. On =**ju/*je je**   zaboravio
          he her   AUX forgotten
          'He forgot her'

Anderson argues that this poses a problem if we assume that the 3sg feminine accusative clitic is introduced before the auxiliary clitic because the wrong form, *je*, will already have been introduced. We confess that we don't fully understand the force of this argument, since it depends on exactly how the *je* ⇒ *ju* alternation is defined by the morphophonological component of the grammar. However, assuming that this is a genuine problem, we might suggest that this simply argues against the view that clitics (or affixes for that matter) are mere pieces of phonology. Instead, we might propose that morphological formatives are morphs, that is, morphological objects with morphological properties as well as phonological properties. One such property would be allomorphic variants. We could then propose that the rules introducing the pronominal clitic introduce a complex element {*je, ju*} whose base form or default form is *je*, but which reverts to the *ju* form if the *je* form would induce a morphophonological violation (a model of affixational morphology along these lines is proposed in Spencer 1989).

Anderson also points out a more serious problem for models of pronominal cliticization that presuppose that clitics are added one at a time, like layers of affixes. In many languages a clitic cluster will sometimes appear to the left of a verb (e.g. when the verb is finite) and sometimes to the right of the verb (e.g. when the verb is non-finite or imperative), but in each case the relative linear ordering is always the same. However, if the clitics were added 'from the inside outwards', then we would expect the clitics to appear in mirror-image order in the two conditions, as illustrated in (51):

(51)   mirror-image ordering of clitics
     a. V ⇒ [V=cl$_1$] ⇒ [[V=cl$_1$]=cl$_2$]   b.   V ⇒ [cl$_1$=V] ⇒ [cl$_2$=[cl$_1$=V]]
          cl$_1$ < cl$_2$ cl$_2$ < cl$_1$

However, this is not found. But, if the relative ordering is defined by a set of invariant OT constraints, this invariance of ordering is what we would expect.

This observation is crucial to the model of clitic placement we have developed for Bulgarian (Spencer 2001) and especially for European Portuguese (Luís 2004, Luís and Spencer 2005) and so we will return to it when we discuss that work.

8.5.3   Realizational approaches to clitics

In this section we consider a number of proposals that adopt a realizational approach to clitics. We begin with Klamer's 1997 treatment of the very interesting system of Kambera. Klamer presupposes an analysis in the spirit of Anderson (1992) (though this is not actually formalized as such), but the main interest of her paper is the complex patterning of data she describes. We then turn to a fully explicit analysis of French clitics as affixes within a version of Stump's 2001 Paradigm Function Morphology implemented in HPSG by Bonami and Boyé (2007). In addition to the detailed formal analysis, we see here important empirical claims about a familiar system. We close the section by looking at the way that Luís and Spencer (2005) extend the Paradigm Function model to account for the system of European Portuguese, in which the clitics have all the properties of affixes when they come after the verb and most of the properties of true clitics when they come before the verb.

Kambera

Klamer (1997) has provided an analysis of the clitic system of the Austronesian language Kambera, which, she claims, should be analysed within a realizational model of inflectional morphology such as that proposed by Anderson (1992). We will sketch her arguments in some detail, partly because hers is one of the few discussions of clitics that explicitly argue for treating them as morphological phenomena (despite the fact that a good many morphologists would argue that clitic systems are essentially morphological) and partly because the data she adduces are typologically very interesting and raise serious questions as to how best to treat clitic systems.

The Kambera clitic cluster comprises up to nine slots bearing clitics with various modal and aspectual functions as well as pronominal clitics realizing verbal arguments (subjects and direct/indirect objects). The modal markers fall into two groups, A and B (Klamer 1997, 897):

(52)   Mood: A.   *bia* 'just', *mbu* 'also/too', *wa* 'hortative', *àru* 'hortative (polite)'
                        B.   *ma* 'emphasis', *du/di* 'emphasis',
                                ki 'diminutive: just a bit/only a while', *a* 'just, no more than'
        Aspect: *ka* 'perfective', *pa* 'imperfective', *i* 'iterative: again/also'

The pronominal clitics are shown in (53):

(53)   Kambera pronominal clitics

	NOM	ACC	DAT	GEN
1sg	ku=	=ka	=ngga	=nggu
2sg	(m)u=	=kau	=nggau	=mu
3sg	na=	=ya	=nya	=na
1pl incl	ta=	=ta	=nda	=nda
1pl excl	ma=	=kama	=nggama	=ma
2pl	(m)i=	=ka(m)i	=ngga(m)i	=mi
3pl	da=	=ha	=nja	=da

There are two types of anchor for the clitics, the nominal phrase (for possessive pronominal clitics) and what Klamer refers to as the verbal projection, the verb head and its adverbial modifiers. Example (54) contains six clitics (p. 901):[16]

(54)   Njàpu =ma   =du   =a   =na   =nya   =i
         finished =MOOD =MOOD =MOOD =3SG.GEN.CL =3SG.DAT.CL =ITER.CL

         nú,   na ngara ngia uhu
         DEICTIC ART way place rice

         'Thus it is finished, (the story about) the way to grow rice'

Most of the clitics are enclitics; however, there is also a set of subject proclitics, two of which are illustrated in (55) (Klamer 1997, 898):[17]

(55) a.   [Na=   [mài]]_S na sopir
          3SG.NOM.CL= come   ART driver

          'The driver comes (here)'
     b.   [Ku=   [hili mài]]_S
          1SG.NOM.CL= again come

          'I come again/I'll come again'

Recall the example (56) repeated here from Section 3.5 (example (80)), in which we see both proclitics and enclitics in the same clause (Klamer 1997, 899):

(56)   Napa [ku=   [hili beli pàku] =nya_j]_S   [na umbuk
         later 1SG.NOM.CL= again return first   =3SG.DAT.CL ART grandson

         =nggu]_j
         =1SG.GEN.CL

         'I'll first have to go back to my grandson again'

We said that this example demonstrates that both the proclitic *ku* and the enclitic *nya* are phrasal affixes, showing promiscuous attachment (to the adverbs *hili* 'again' and *páku* 'first' respectively). The phrases labelled 'S' represent what Klamer calls a 'nuclear clause', the minimal sequence that can serve as an independent sentence. She argues that this constituent plays an important role in Kambera syntax.

In (57) we see possessive clitics attached to a nominal phrase (as we also saw in (56), *na umbuk=nggu* 'my grandson'):[18]

(57) a.   [Na uma =nggu]_{NP}
          ART house =1SG.GEN.CL

          'My house'
     b.   [Na uma bàkul =nggu]_{NP}
          ART house be.big =1SG.GEN.CL

          'My big house'

In (58) the nominal is the clause's predicate (there is no copular verb in Kambera). The accusative clitics *ya*, *kai* are the standard way of marking the argument of a clausal predicate that is not a verb.

(58) a.   [[Uma [bàkul ai lulu]]_{NP} =ya]_S
            house be.big very   =3SG.ACC.CL

          'It's a very big house'

b.   [[Tau   mayila]_{NP} =**mbu** =**kai**]_S   nyimi ná
      person be.poor   =also =2PL.ACC.CL you(PL) there
      '...(moreover) you (are) also poor people'

In (59) we see the clitics attached to a locative prepositional phrase:

(59) a.   La uma
           LOC house
           'At home'
     b.   [La uma]_{PP} =**ya**
           LOC house =3SG.ACC.CL
           'S/he (is) at home'
     c.   [Mbu ndàba =**na**]_j   [[la   uma =**na**]_{PP}   =**nya**_j]_S
           everything =3SG.GEN.CL   LOC house =3SG.GEN.CL =3SG.DAT.CL
           'Everything is at/in his/her house'

Again we see the accusative clitic *ya*, marking the non-verbal predicate phrase in (59b). However, in (59c) this accusative is replaced by a dative clitic. This is because the previous clitic in the cluster is a genitive clitic. We return to this alternation in due course.

Adapting somewhat Klamer's analysis we can say that the basic clitic template is as follows:

(60)   Mood B1 > Mood B2 > Mood B3 > Mood B4 > Gen > Dat1 > Dat2 >
           Asp1 > Asp2

Aspect clitics may co-occur, their relative order being decided by semantic scope.

However, there are two types of variant. First, when the nominative case subject proclitic is present there is no genitive enclitic. However, the Dat1 clitic position can be replaced with an accusative clitic. Second, independently of the presence of a subject proclitic, a Mood A clitic can appear at the left edge of the enclitic cluster, supplanting any Mood B clitics.

These variants are of theoretical interest. First, we can see that we require a more articulated notion of position class to account for the paradigmatic relationship between Mood A clitics and the set of Mood B clitics. What is required is for a single Mood A slot 1 to be segmented into four subslots to accommodate the Mood B set. Second, we need to account for the dependencies between the nominative proclitic and the genitive/dative/accusative enclitic set.

The combinatorial possibilities are illustrated in (61) (p. 902):

(61)   Kambera enclitic sequences

	Mood	Pronominal	Clausal aspect
B	ma, ki	gen, dat/acc	pa/ka/i
	du, a	DAT	I/ka
A	bia		
	mbu		
	wa		
	àru		

Although the pronominal clitics are given traditional case labels, their relation
to grammatical functions is complex. The subject function may be realized by
nominative, genitive or accusative clitics depending on complex semantic factors
(Klamer 1998a, chapter 5, Klamer 1998b). For instance, in (55) we see nominative proclitic subjects, while in (62) and (63) below we see a genitive marked
subject. The direct object can be expressed by either an accusative or a dative
clitic. In case there is also an indirect object, we may have two datives in the
order indirect < direct, as illustrated in (62) (p. 901):

(62)   Daingu [wua =**na**   =**nggau**   =**nya**]s   haromu,   jàka
         surely give =3SG.GEN.CL =2SG.DAT.CL =3SG.DAT.CL tomorrow when
         [**u**=   laku]s
         2SG.NOM.CL= go
         'I'll surely give it to you when you go'[19]

A particularly intriguing construction with pronominal clitics is the continuative
aspect construction (Klamer 1998a, 67–8, 152–61). This is formed by adding a
formative that is homophonous with the 3sg dative clitic after the subject enclitic,
as seen in (63) (Klamer 1998a, 153):

(63)   Lodu hau   tàka =**nggu**   =**nya**   =**ka**   la
         day   one.CLASSIFIER arrive =1SG.GEN.CL =3SG.DAT.CL =PERF.CL LOC
         tana Humba
         land Sumba
         'On Monday I'll arrive on Sumba'

Examples (64) and (65) (Klamer 1998a, 155, 153) illustrate neatly the difference between genuine occurrences of a dative clitic and the aspectual use
(where the aspectual dative clitic is represented as fused with the genitive subject
clitic):[20]

(64) a. Mbàda kanabu =**na**   =**ka**
         already fall   =3SG.GEN.CL =PERF.CL
         'It has already fallen (e.g. coconut)'
    b.   Mbàda kanabu =**na**$_j$ =**nya**$_k$ =**ka**
         already fall   =3SG.GEN.CL =3SG.DAT.CL =PERF.CL
         'It has already fallen on him (e.g. coconut from tree)'
    c.   Kanabu =**na+nya**   =**ka**
         fall   =3SG.GEN.CL+3SG.DAT.CL =PERF.CL
         'It is falling'
(65)   Kambu =**na**   =**nya**   una   dá,
         stomach =3SG.GEN.CL =3SG.DAT.CL EMPH.3SG inside

         ba   wundu   =**na+nya**   na kambu =**na**
         CONJ be.swollen =3SG.GEN.CL+3SG.DAT.CL ART stomach =3SG.GEN.CL

         'It is his stomach (that makes the noise), inside, because his stomach
         is swollen'

Klamer notes that the continuative aspect construction is formally very similar to the way that subjects are marked in predicative noun phrases, suggesting a historical relationship (Klamer 1998a, 153):

(66)   Nda mbapa **=a**   **=nggu**   **=nya**,   balu
         NEG husband =MOOD =1SG.GEN.CL =3SG.DAT.CL husband's.brother

         =nggu   **=nya**
         =1SG.GEN.CL =3SG.DAT.CL
         'He is not my husband, he is my husband's brother'

We can identify the sequencing restrictions itemized in (67) (Klamer 1997, 903):

(67) •   A genitive subject clitic occurs closer to the verb than an object clitic.
     •   Only a dative clitic may follow a genitive.
     •   The order for clitics realizing the arguments of a ditransitive predicate is indirect < direct.
     •   Such a double object sequence is only permissible when the first clitic is non-3rd person and the second clitic is 3rd person.

The restriction (67) is typical of pronominal clitic sequences as we have seen, though it is not identical to corresponding restrictions, say, in French or Italian. For instance, we have seen that in French it is possible to have co-occurring 3rd person direct and indirect objects, with the clitic order accusative < dative (*le lui*), the opposite of that with non-3rd person combinations (*me le*) (Section 5.4). It is, however, possible to express the missing person/number combinations syntactically with full pronouns.

Klamer (1997, 916) discusses interesting aspects of the morphosyntax of the pronominal clitics. First we must distinguish the behaviour of subjects and objects. Definite subjects show obligatory clitic doubling (except that contextually given subjects can be dropped entirely and not expressed either by an overt noun phrase or a clitic). Indefinite subjects are optionally expressed by clitics, in which case that clitic may optionally be doubled (though indefinite subjects are themselves rare and are usually expressed just by an indefinite noun phrase). However, definite direct objects are obligatorily expressed by clitics, which then effectively act as agreement markers to any overt noun phrase object. Indefinite direct objects cannot be realized by clitics and must be expressed by an overt noun phrase. Thus, with respect to (in)definiteness, Kambera objects are similar to those of Macedonian.

Klamer argues that the Kambera system can't be handled by syntactic means and proposes that the best way to analyse the Kambera clitic system is as phrasal affixation, suggesting that this can be implemented using the framework of Anderson (1992). She doesn't, however, propose a rule system as such. In fact, there is one construction that makes it difficult to apply a purely realizational analysis such as that of Anderson (1992) or Stump (2001). Any clitic realizing an object function that (immediately) follows a genitive case pronominal clitic must be a dative clitic, not accusative (Klamer 1997, 918, Klamer 1998a, 76–7).

In (68a) the object is realized by the accusative clitic *ya* because the subject clitic is nominative, and hence to the left of the verb. However, in (68b) the subject clitic is genitive and hence comes after the verb root. However, the object clitic now appears immediately after this genitive subject clitic, so the object clitic must now appear in the dative and not accusative (68c):

(68) a.   Hi   **ku**=   rongu =**ya**
            CONJ 1SG.NOM= hear   =3SG.ACC
            'So I'll hear it'

     b.   Mbàda rongu =**nggu**   =**nya**
            already hear   =1SG.GEN =3SG.DAT
            'I (have) heard it already'

     c.   * Mbàda rongu =**nggu**   =**ya**
            already hear   =1SG.GEN =3SG.ACC

Klamer suggests that the alternation requires an idiosyncratic surface restriction on the relevant clitic sequences (p. 919). However, such a restriction can only be stated over clitics as signs (classical morphemes), since any formal process that accomplishes the alternation would seem to have to have access to the fact that there is a sequence of Gen-clitic + Acc-clitic. But this contradicts the assumption that the clitics are phrasal affixes, because it implies that the rule introducing *nya* has to have access to the fact that the *na* on *uma=na* is a pronominal clitic bearing the Case feature [Gen]. If *na* were truly just a spell out of features, how could the copular clitic have access to that information across a PP boundary?

The crucial determinant of this Acc ⇒ Dat alternation is that the accusative clitic be linearly adjacent to the genitive clitic. This is seen very clearly in one specific instance of the alternation. In copular constructions the predicative noun/locative phrase is usually marked by the accusative case clitic, as seen in (69), where the subject function is expressed by the accusative clitic, and the coreferential NP is optional.

(69)   La   uma =**ya**   (nyuna)
           LOC house =3SG.ACC.CL (s)he
           '(S)he is at the house'

Given this we would expect to see the construction seen in (70) to translate '(S)he is at my house':

(70)   *la uma =**nggu**   =**ya**   nyuna
           LOC house =3SG.GEN =3SG.ACC.CL (s)he

However, as shown, this is ungrammatical because the Acc ⇒ Dat alternation is triggered by this construction, too (Marian Klamer, personal communication). The correct variant is:

(71)   la uma =**nggu**   =**nya**   nyuna
        LOC house =1SG.GEN.CL =3SG.DAT.CL (s)he
        '(S)he is at my house'

The examples in (72) further demonstrate that we are dealing with an alternation that is sensitive to linear adjacency. In (72a) the two clitics are not linearly adjacent, since the accusative clitic encliticizes to the 1st person full pronominal. Hence, the Acc ⇒ Dat alternation is not triggered. However, in (72b) the clitics are adjacent and so the alternation takes place. Yet, here the genitive clitic is part of a possessed noun phrase, and isn't functioning as a subject clitic.

(72) a.   Nda mbapa =**nggu**   nyungga =**ya**
           NEG husband =1SG.GEN.CL I   =3SG.ACC.CL
           'He is not my husband'
      b.   Nda mbapa =**nggu**   =**nya**
           NEG husband =1SG.GEN.CL =3SG.DAT.CL
           'He is not my husband'

These examples, then, suggest that whatever the rules are that govern the selection of accusative and dative direct object marking clitics, they are sensitive to the featural context of the genitive subject/possessor clitic, even across phrase boundaries. This represents quite a tough challenge to realizational approaches to clitics.

Paradigm Function Morphology approach to French clitics

In addition to Optimality Theoretic morphological analyses of clitic systems, we can imagine rule-based analyses that make no appeal to the principles of Optimality Theory. One such analysis, of the French clitic system, has been provided by Bonami and Boyé (2007). They present a very clear overview of the crucial facts, and we will summarize their empirical observations before turning to the analysis itself.

In examples (73)–(76) we see some by now familiar restrictions at work. In (73) and (74) we see that dative clitics precede accusative clitics except where both are 3rd person, in which case we get the order accusative before dative. In (76a, b, c) we see that a combination of the reflexive with a non-reflexive clitic is impossible, so that the non-reflexive has to be expressed as a full pronoun (76d, e):

(73) a.   Paul **me**   **la**   présentera
           Paul CL.DAT.1SG CL.3SG.FEM.ACC present-FUT.3SG
           'Paul will present her to me'
      b.   * Paul **la**   **me**   présentera
           Paul CL.3SG.FEM.ACC CL.DAT.1SG present-FUT.3SG

(74) a.   Paul **la**   **lui**   présentera
           Paul 3SG.FEM.ACC CL.DAT.3SG present-FUT.3SG
           'Paul will present her to him'

b.   * Paul **lui**   **la**   présentera
           Paul CL.DAT.3SG CL.3SG.FEM.ACC present-FUT.3SG

(75) a.   Paul **te**   présentera   Jean
           Paul CL.2SG.DAT present-FUT.3SG Jean
           'Paul will present Jean to you'
    b.   Paul **se**   présentera   à Marie
           Paul CL.3.REFL present-FUT.3SG to Marie
           'Paul will present himself to Marie'

(76) a.   * Paul **se**   **te**   présentera
           Paul CL.3.REFL CL.2SG.DAT present-FUT.3SG
    b.   * Paul **te**   **se**   présentera
           Paul CL.2SG.DAT CL.3.REFL present-FUT.3SG
    c.   * Paul **se**   **lui**   présentera
           Paul CL.3.REFL CL.DAT.3SG present-FUT.3SG
    d.   Paul **se**   présentera   à toi
           Paul CL.3.REFL present-FUT.3SG to PRO.2SG
           'Paul will present himself to you'
    e.   Paul **se**   présentera   à elle
           Paul CL.3.REFL present-FUT.3SG to PRO.3FEM.SG
           'Paul will present himself to her'

These restrictions need to be built into the morphological rules by imposing restrictions on which sets of features can combine with each other. This effectively means that we build 'paradigm gaps' into the system by means of feature co-occurrence restrictions.

In Table 8.1 we see the standard description of the French clitic system.[21] Clearly, we will need to account for seven position classes, and hence the rules will be arranged into seven blocks.

Bonami and Boyé (2007) note a number of morphophonological idiosyncrasies in the clitic sequences which are found solely with clitics, and not with other (possibly homophonous) combinations. For instance, the 1sg subject clitic

Table 8.1 *The traditional description of the French proclitic system*

7	6	5	4	3	2	1
[1s,nom] *je*	negation: *ne*	[1s,acc/dat]: *me*	[3ms,acc,nonrefl]: *le*	[3s,dat,nonrefl]: *lui*	[loc]: *y*	[de]: *en*
[2s,nom] *tu*		[2s,acc/dat]: *te*	[predicative]: *le*	[3p,dat,nonrefl]: *leur*		
[3ms,nom] *il*		[3,acc/dat,refl]: *se*	[3fs,acc,nonrefl]: *la*			
[3fs,nom] *elle*		[1p,acc/dat]: *nous*	[3p,acc,nonrefl]: *les*			
…		[2p,acc/dat]: *vous*				

can fuse morphophonologically with the present tense form of the verb ÊTRE 'be', though not with any other verb, for instance SUIVRE 'follow', whose 1sg present form is homophonous:

(77)   Clitic-verb fusion

a.   ʒəsɥiynfij
       Je suis une fille
       'I am a girl'/'I follow a girl'

b.   ʃɥiynfij with fusion [ʒəs] ⇒ [ʃ]
       'I am a girl' / *'I follow a girl'

Similarly, we observe morphophonological fusion of two adjacent clitics in some cases. In (78a) the two clitics can fuse from [ʒəlɥi] to [ʒɥi] or even [ʒi], but this is excluded for the homophonous sequence with the verb form *luis* [lɥi], from LUIRE 'to glow' (78b):

(78)   Clitic-clitic fusion

a.   **Je**   **lui**   dirai
       CL.NOM.1SG CL.DAT.3SG tell-FUT.1SG
       'I will tell him' [ʒlɥidiʁɛ]/[ʒɥidiʁɛ]/[ʒidiʁɛ]

b.   **Je**   luis   dans le   noir
       CL.NOM.1SG glow-PRES.1SG in   the dark
       'I glow in the dark' [ʒlɥidɑ̃lnwaʁ]/*[ʒɥidɑ̃lnwaʁ]/*[ʒidɑ̃lnwaʁ]

A related phenomenon is observed in (79), where we see that the clitic can be dropped entirely in certain circumstances. In (79b) the object clitic has been dropped but (79b) can still be interpreted as synonymous with (79a):

(79)   Clitic drop

a.   Paul **la**   **lui**   apportera
       Paul CL.3SG.FEM.ACC CL.DAT.3SG bring-FUT.3SG
       'Paul will bring it to her'

b.   Paul **lui**   apportera
       Paul CL.DAT.3SG bring-FUT.3SG
       'Paul will bring it to her'

We might imagine that this is simply because the verb requires a direct object and that it can therefore remain 'understood' in such contexts, but example (80b) shows that the presence of the dative clitic is crucial. When the indirect object is expressed by an overt noun phrase and not by the clitic, dropping of the object clitic is impossible:

(80) a.   Paul **l'**   apportera   à Marie
           Paul CL.3SG.FEM.ACC bring-FUT.3SG to Marie
           'Paul will bring it to Marie'

b.   * Paul apportera   à Marie
           Paul bring-FUT.3SG to Marie

We mention below the HPSG analysis of French clitics by Miller and Sag (1997) and the analyses of Italian and Romanian clitic systems that Monachesi

(1999, 2005) proposes. We don't actually specify how these authors account for clitic cluster ordering. In fact, their approach is maximally simple, in that they simply list the possible combinations and then allow the grammar to call up members of that list as required. For Italian, this is a reasonable analytic solution, since there are only some 56 clitic combinations possible. We have not computed the possible clitic combinations of Romanian, but judging from the appendices in Gerlach (2002), for instance, there are rather more possibilities than this because the object clitics combine with auxiliary clitics in the cluster. From Gerlach's data there are 84 such combinations and 28 combinations of direct and indirect object. However, Bonami and Boyé calculate that there are 1,909 possible clitic combinations in French, which makes it more reasonable to seek an analysis that reduces the burden of listing and captures the regularities that can be observed in the system, just as with a complex inflectional paradigm. Bonami and Boyé propose a PFM analysis of this system, building on the analysis of Miller and Sag (1997) but incorporating a battery of realization rules to describe the paradigm space occupied by the clitic sequences.

Bonami and Boyé follow Monachesi in providing verbs with a feature CLTS which lists the clitics a verb form can be associated with. The rules they propose then spell out the form of the clitic corresponding to various morpholexical, morphosyntactic or even (in principle) discourse level features.[22]

(81)   Block 1:
          $f\langle V,\{CLTS \langle \ldots ,\{de\},\ldots \rangle \}\rangle \to \tilde{a}(n) \oplus X$
(82)   Block 2:
          $f\langle V,\{CLTS \langle \ldots ,\{loc\},\ldots \rangle \}\rangle \to i \oplus X$
(83)   Block 3:
     a. $f\langle V,\{CLTS \langle \ldots ,\{dat,3sg,nonrefl\},\ldots \rangle \}\rangle \to l\mu i \oplus X$
     b. $f\langle V,\{CLTS \langle \ldots ,\{dat,3pl,nonrefl\},\ldots \rangle \}\rangle \to l\oe \varkappa \oplus X$
(84)   Block 4:
     a. $f\langle V,\{CLTS \langle \ldots ,\{acc,3masc.sg,nonrefl\},\ldots \rangle \}\rangle \to l\vartheta \oplus X$
     b. $f\langle V,\{CLTS \langle \ldots ,\{acc,3fem.sg,nonrefl\},\ldots \rangle \}\rangle \to l(a) \oplus X$
     c. $f\langle V,\{CLTS \langle \ldots ,\{acc,3pl,nonrefl\},\ldots \rangle \}\rangle \to le(z) \oplus X$
     d. $f\langle V,\{CLTS \langle \ldots ,\{PRED +\},\ldots \rangle \}\rangle \to l\vartheta \oplus X$
(85)   Block 5:
     a. $f\langle V,\{CLTS \langle \ldots ,\{obj,1sg\},\ldots \rangle \}\rangle \to m\vartheta \oplus X$
     b. $f\langle V,\{CLTS \langle \ldots ,\{obj,2sg\},\ldots \rangle \}\rangle \to t\vartheta \oplus X$
     c. $f\langle V,\{CLTS \langle \ldots ,\{obj,3sg,refl\},\ldots \rangle \}\rangle \to s\vartheta \oplus X$
     d. $f\langle V,\{CLTS \langle \ldots ,\{obj,1pl\},\ldots \rangle \}\rangle \to nu(z) \oplus X$
     e. $f\langle V,\{CLTS \langle \ldots ,\{obj,2pl\},\ldots \rangle \}\rangle \to vu(z) \oplus X$
(86)   Block 6:
          $f\langle V,\{NE +\}\rangle \to n\vartheta \oplus X$
(87)   Block 7:
     a. $f\langle V,\{INV -, CLTS \langle \ldots ,\{nom,1sg\},\ldots \rangle \}\rangle \to 3\vartheta \oplus X$
     b. $f\langle V,\{INV -, CLTS \langle \ldots ,\{nom,2sg\},\ldots \rangle \}\rangle \to ty \oplus X$
     c. $f\langle V,\{INV -, CLTS \langle \ldots ,\{nom,3masc.sg\},\ldots \rangle \}\rangle \to il \oplus X$
     d.   etc.

The rules are largely transparent. The rule for negation expresses the assumption that the *ne* particle is essentially a scope marker in modern French and not the exponent of negation as such, and hence it realizes an abstract morphosyntactic property. The feature [INV −] refers to a sentence type in which the subject and verb are not inverted, that is, the standard declarative construction.

The rules overgenerate in the sense that they predict non-existent sequence *se lui*. Bonami and Boyé cash in on the fact that they are working within a paradigm-based theory of morphology, in which the feature system defines the paradigm space for a lexeme. They therefore propose a feature co-occurrence restriction to rule out the systematically absent forms:

(88)   Feature co-occurrence restriction {CLTS ⟨..., x : {obj},...,{dat},...⟩} ⇒
            x : {3,nonrefl}

Rule (88) states that only 3rd person non-reflexive clitics are allowed to co-occur with dative clitics. This rules out not only (76c) but also (89a), which can only be expressed as (89b):

(89) a.   * Présente   lui   moi!
            present-IMPERATIVE.2SG DAT.SG OBJ.1SG

     b.   Présente   moi   à elle/lui!
            present-IMPERATIVE.2SG OBJ.1SG to 3SG.FEM/MASC
            'Present me to her!'

To account for the data seen in examples such as (77b) and (78a) they propose rules (90) and (91), and to account for the clitic drop example (79b) they propose rule (92):

(90)   Portmanteau Block1–Block7 rule
            f⟨ÊTRE,{INV, CLTS ⟨{nom,1sg}⟩,MODE indic, TENSE pres} → ʃɥi
(91)   Portmanteau Block3–Block7 rule
            f⟨X,{INV, CLTS ⟨...,{nom,1sg},...,{dat,3sg,nonrefl},...⟩} → ʒɥi ⊕ X
(92)   Portmanteau Block3–Block4 rule
            f⟨X,{CLTS ⟨...,{acc,3sg,nonrefl},{dat,3sg,nonrefl},...⟩} → X

One interesting aspect of this rule system is that it integrates the 'genitive' and 'locative' clitics *en* and *y* into the pronominal system. Bonami and Boyé don't distinguish between inflectional and 'derivational' clitics in the manner of Anderson (2005). In HPSG it is possible to collect all the information needed to specify the clitic systems, whether inflectional, semantic or pragmatic, in a single feature system.

Another important aspect of Bonami and Boyé's analysis is the fact that a single morphosyntactic property set (feature set) has to correspond to more than one output. In this respect the system fails to describe a standardly paradigmatic pattern of organization: the cells in a normal paradigm are occupied by at most one word form. From a formal point of view this means that the rule system is no longer based on (mathematical) functions but on relations. A function is defined as a relationship between two sets, X and Y, which associates each element of X with precisely one element of Y. Different members of X can be associated with the same element of Y. An example of a function is the arithmetic relationship SQ(x) of being the square of a number. Here, the sets X and Y are the same set, namely, the set of (real) numbers. For instance, SQ(5) = 25 and also SQ(−5) = 25. The SQ function can be contrasted with the inverse relationship of square root, SQRT(x). This is because there are always two square roots for any given (positive) number: SQRT(25) = {5, −5}. Because SQRT doesn't deliver a unique value, it isn't a function; rather, it's a relation. The paradigm 'function' rules of Bonami and Boyé likewise don't deliver unique values, so they argue for a relational model of morphology. One important reason why Stump originally cast his rule system as a set of functions is because in that way he can define a simple notion of 'Pāṇinian Determinism' on the basis of specificity of rule. In fact, given the way Stump formalizes Paradigm Function Morphology, he is effectively able to define 'more specific' as 'containing more symbols'. However, if the rules are not functions and don't deliver unique outputs then it becomes impossible to formalize the notion of default override by a more specific rule in this way, as Bonami and Boyé observe. They therefore argue that the effects of default override have to be written into the rule system (much as is done in constraints-based models of syntax).

Before we leave the French clitic system it's worth noting another respect in which the system isn't strictly paradigmatic. In the imperative mood we find considerable variation in the way that clitic pronominals are expressed. We summarize the discussion provided in Jones (1996, 255). The set of forms found in the standard (written) language is seen in (93) (where 'ProPP' stands for 'Prepositional Phrase pro-form'):[23]

(93)   Standard positive imperative

I	II	III
ACC	DAT	ProPP
le	lui	y
la	leur	en
les	ACC/DAT	
	m' (moi)	
	t' (toi)	
	nous	
	vous	

In (94) we see the types of forms mandated in the standard language:

(94)   Formal style imperatives
    a.   Donnez-**le-moi**
        give-3SG.MASC.ACC-1SG.DAT
        'Give it to me'

    b.   Donnez-**m'en**
             give-1SG.DAT-PARTITIVE.CL
             'Give me some'

    c.   Donnez-**lui-en**
             give-3SG.DAT-PARTITIVE.CL
             'Give him/her some'

    d.   Donnez-**les-lui**
             give-3PL.ACC-3SG.DAT
             'Give them to him/her'

    e.   Mettez-**les-y**
             put-3PL.ACC-LOC.CL
             'Put them there'

    f.   Parlez-**leur-en**
             speak-3PL.DAT-PARTITIVE.CL
             'Speak to them about it'

    g.   Occupe-**t'en**
             busy-2SG.REFL.ACC-PARTITIVE.CL
             'Deal with it'

In (95) we see the kinds of forms that speakers are more likely to use (the z represents an epenthetic consonant introduced to break the vowel hiatus):

(95)   Informal style imperatives

    a.   Donnez-**moi-z-en**
             give-1SG.DAT-Z-PARTITIVE.CL
             'Give me some'

    b.   Occupe-**toi-z-en**
             busy-2SG.REFL.ACC-Z-PARTITIVE.CL
             'Deal with it'

In a number of cases it seems that combinations are excluded because they would require two clitics from the same slot of the table in (93):

(96) a.   * Présentez-**vous-moi**
              present-2PL.REFL.ACC-1SG.DAT

    b.   * Présentez-**moi-leur**
              present-1SG.ACC-3PL.DAT

    c.   * Présentez-nous-lui
              present-1PL.ACC-3SG.DAT

As we have seen, in non-imperatives, corresponding sequences such as *Il me leur présentera* have to be excluded by a special restriction such as feature co-occurrence rule (88), because there's no slot competition in that case. This means that the unattested forms are unrealized for two reasons in the imperative.

    Finally, Jones notes that there are variations in order in ordinary conversation, so that for 1st/2nd person combinations we sometimes find the order Dat < Acc just as in declaratives:

(97)   Donnez-**moi-le**
            give-1SG.DAT-3SG.ACC
            'Give it to me'

As Bonami and Boyé observe, variation of this sort makes it necessary to account for as much of the systematicity in terms of some kind of principled grammatical statement (e.g. a rule system), but at the same time it makes the system look far less canonically paradigmatic, and therefore makes it less plausible to deploy rules in the form of functions rather than relations. There are other ways of handling the problem of multiple outputs of rules, however. In the cases discussed by Bonami and Boyé, as well as a good many other cases found in inflectional systems, there are sociolinguistic or other register features associated with the different variants. Thus, some of the clitic combinations, especially for imperative sentences, are informal, dialectal, and may even be rejected as 'substandard' forms by some speakers and by some linguistic authorities. In such cases we may not necessarily be dealing with truly equivalent outputs. However, that leaves the question of what kind of a paradigm we have when some of its members (but by no means all) are differentiated by distinct sociolinguistic or register labels. How are such labels to be integrated into the system of morphosyntactic properties? In addition, it's far from clear that all such cases can be dealt with in such a way. In English inflection, for instance, we find doublets such as the past tense forms *spelled/spelt* from *spell*. We ourselves have no idea how these are used throughout the English-speaking world generally, but for one of us these are absolutely identical in acceptability and his use vacillates (in much the same way that the pronunciation of the words *(n)either* vacillates between [niːðə] and [naɪðə]). The question of whether there are true perfect doublets in inflection or clitic systems is ultimately an empirical one rather than one that can be decided on a priori theoretical grounds. If, as seems likely, doublets do exist, then the function-based model will have to be modified to accommodate that fact.

8.5.4   Clitics in Extended Paradigm Function Morphology

We noted above a potential problem with inferential-realizational approaches to clitic clusters in languages such as Romance or Macedonian, in which the cluster may appear either as a set of proclitics to the verb or a set of enclitics. In general, the pattern is very simple: the clitics form the same linear order whether they are placed before or after the verb. However, in a model such as Paradigm Function Morphology, and other models that add affixes progressively outwards from the root, we have to have some way of ensuring that the linear order is preserved and that we avoid the unattested mirror-image ordering. In the case of French the problem is not particularly acute because this is a language in which the postverbal clitic set is rather different from the preverbal set. Different clitic forms are found and a given set doesn't necessarily appear in the same order as its partner set on the other side of the verb. However, for other languages with verb-oriented clitics the mirror-image difficulty is a real problem.

Now, in a model such as PFM it is, in fact, perfectly possible to separate off the linear ordering of affixes from their rules of exponence. Stump (2001) does this, in fact, in order to account for the way that pronominal affixes in some languages metathesize when expressing certain person/number combinations (essentially just like the clitics of Romance). In principle, therefore, it would be possible to deploy such devices to subvert the natural tendency towards mirror-image ordering. However, the result would be highly counter-intuitive: we would need to define functions that established a linear order for one of the placement types (say, the proclitics) and that then redefined the rule block labels successively for each block when the cluster was placed as enclitics.

Spencer (2001) proposes a solution to this problem, taking as his point of departure explicit proposals by Stump (1993, 174–5) for treating the affixal system of Swahili. In that language most of the TAM affixes and pronominal affixes are prefixes. However, there is one set of Relative forms in which a special relative pronominal affix appears postverbally (Stump 1993, 141):

(98) a.   mtu   a-na-ye-soma
            person AGR.SUBJ-PRES-REL-read
            'a person who is reading'

    b.   mtu   a-si-ye-soma
            person AGR.SUBJ-NEG-REL-read
            'a person who doesn't read'

    c.   mtu   a-soma-ye
            person AGR.SUBJ-read-REL
            'a person who reads'

    d.   kitabu a-na-cho-ki-soma   Hamisi
            book   AGR.SUBJ-PRES-REL-AGR.OBJ-read Hamisi
            'the book which Hamisi is reading'

    e.   kitabu a-si-cho-ki-taka   Hamisi
            book   AGR.SUBJ-NEG-REL-AGR.OBJ-want Hamisi
            'the book which Hamisi doesn't want'

    f.   kitabu a-ki-taka-cho   Hamisi
            book   AGR.SUBJ-AGR.OBJ-want-REL Hamisi
            'the book which Hamisi wants'

The suffixal placement of the Relative marker is found whenever the verb is overtly marked neither for tense nor for negative polarity. Stump (1993, 146) proposes a metarule to handle this situation, that is, a rule defined over (sets of) rules. Essentially what this rule says is that for Slot II (that is, the prefix position where the Relative marker is placed) the order of root and affix is reversed provided the verb bears the feature specifications [TENSE:none, POLARITY:positive]. However, Stump (1993, 174–5) later entertains a different possibility, under which the morphological rules of exponence (the rules that define the form of an affix) are separated from rules of linearization.[24] It is this suggestion that Spencer (2001) takes up for extending the PFM model to the clitic system of Bulgarian. In Luís (2004) and Luís and Spencer (2005) the idea is developed further to account for clitic placement in European Portuguese.

The idea effectively combines Stump's proposals for linearizing affixes with Klavans' proposals for placing clitics, essentially in the manner suggested by Anderson (1992, 210). Recall that in PFM the affixed word forms are defined by means of sets of realization rules applying in blocks. Each rule is indexed for the block in which it applies. The input of a realization rule is the output of the previous block, and each rule performs some morphophonological operation on that output. The rules of the first block operate over the root form or some specially defined stem form. In schematic and simplified form, then, a realization rule takes the form (99):

(99) a. $RR_{\text{Block index, features, lexeme class}}(X, \sigma) = \text{<X-suffix}, \sigma\text{>}$
     b. $RR_{\text{Block index, features, lexeme class}}(X) = \text{<prefix-X}, \sigma\text{>}$

In rules of this sort the linear placement (as prefix/suffix) is conflated with the exponence. We can decouple them by allowing the Block index to effectively become a property of the affix, and removing reference to the stem to which the affix is attached:

(100) $RR_{\text{features, lexeme class}}(\sigma) = \text{<affix, index>}$

The affix's index can be defined conventionally to be positive for suffixes and negative for prefixes. Using integers automatically defines for us a default linearization. However, that linearization can easily be overridden by special linearization statements. We then finally add the specification of the stem to which the affixes attach. For the irregular noun *house*, for instance, we define a special plural stem <hauz, pl.stem> which is called up by the Paradigm Function defining the plural for this noun:

(101) $PF(\text{HOUSE}, \{\text{plural}\}) =$
     a.   Host: pl.stem(HOUSE) = <hauz, pl.stem>
     b.   Exponence: $RR_{\text{plural, HOUSE}} = \text{<z, slot-I>}$
     c.   Linearization: <stem, z> (by default)
     d.   Output: hauz⊕əz

For the more complex system of European Portuguese clitics we need to distinguish two 'layers' of morphology, one for the standard verb suffixes and the other for the clitic sequences. For instance, to define the form *mostramos-to* 'we show it to you' we need to define two sets of morphosyntactic properties which we label ι (ordinary inflectional properties) and κ (clitic property sets). For instance, using obvious abbreviations, *mostramos-to* realizes the inflectional properties $\iota = \{[\text{pres}, 1\text{pl}]\}$, and the clitic properties $\kappa = \{[3\text{sg.acc}, 2\text{sg.dat}]\}$. We treat a form such as *mostramos-to* as an inflected word form realizing the morphosyntactic property set $\sigma = \iota \cup \kappa$. What is special about this word form is that the set of suffixes realizing the κ properties, that is, the clitic cluster, is added to an independently well-formed inflected word *mostramos*.

We can reflect this bipartite structuring by defining the Paradigm Function in two parts:

(102)   For $\sigma = \iota \cup \kappa$, $\iota = \{[\text{pres, 1pl}]\}$, $\kappa = \{[\text{3sg.acc, 2sg.dat}]\}$

$$\text{PF}(\text{MOSTRAR}, \sigma) =_{\text{def}} \begin{cases} \text{a.} & \text{stem} \qquad\qquad \text{PF}(\text{MOSTRAR}, \iota) \\ \text{b.} & \text{exponence:} \quad R_{\text{clitics}}(\sigma) \end{cases}$$

The function $R_{\text{clitics}}(\sigma)$ is a shorthand for the function that defines the clitic cluster. When we discussed the Portuguese clitics earlier we said that it was easier to describe the cluster as having three slots, with conventional labels 'refl', 'dat', 'acc'. In the original PFM model these slots might correspond to three functions R_{refl}, R_{dat}, R_{acc}, which define the following set of clitics:

(103) ia. $R_{\text{refl, \{3, Refl\}}}(\sigma) = \text{se}$
       iia. $R_{\text{dat, \{1sg, dat\}}}(\sigma) = \text{me}$
       iib. $R_{\text{dat, \{2sg, dat\}}}(\sigma) = \text{te}$

               . . .

       iif. $R_{\text{dat, \{3pl, dat\}}}(\sigma) = \text{lhes}$

       iiia. $R_{\text{acc, \{masc, sg, non-refl\}}}(\sigma) = \text{o}$
       iiib. $R_{\text{acc, \{masc, pl, non-refl\}}}(\sigma) = \text{a}$

       iiic. $R_{\text{acc, \{fem, sg, non-refl\}}}(\sigma) = \text{os}$
       iiid. $R_{\text{acc, \{fem, pl, non-refl\}}}(\sigma) = \text{as}$

By making the block (slot) index a property of each clitic and by defining the functions solely in terms of the properties they realize we obtain the functions shown in (104):

(104) ia. $R(3 \text{ Refl}) = \text{<se, refl>}$

       iia. $R(1\text{sg dat}) = \text{<me, dat>}$
       iib. $R(2\text{sg dat}) = \text{<te, dat>}$

               . . .

       iif. $R(3\text{pl dat}) = \text{<lhes, dat>}$

       iiia. $R(\text{masc sg non-refl}) = \text{<o, acc>}$
       iiib. $R(\text{masc pl non-refl}) = \text{<a, acc>}$

       iiic. $R(\text{fem sg non-refl}) = \text{<os, acc>}$
       iiid. $R(\text{fem pl non-refl}) = \text{<as, acc>}$

For the portmanteau forms we can define composite clusters, such as *to* 'to thee, it' (2sg dat, masc 3sg acc):

(105) $R(2\text{sg dat}) \circ R(\text{masc sg non-refl}) = \text{<to, dat} \circ \text{acc>}$

The cluster *to* will now be linearized in the same way as a sequence of dative + accusative clitics, but as a single element.

We now have a set of inflectional rules that define strings of affixes and stems and linearize them appropriately, and which define strings of clitics. We now have to ensure that the clitics are linearized appropriately. When the clitics attach as (effectively) suffixes to the inflected word form, we simply have a second layer of affixation, but when the clitics appear as proclitics, they are no longer (necessarily) attached morphophonologically to the verb whose properties they realize. Thus, we have a kind of 'discontinuous word form'. How exactly the clitic cluster is positioned depends on the model of syntax we adopt, so we will provide a generic description of the kind that could be fairly easily implemented in a constraints-based model such as HPSG, or in LFG, as in Luís and Sadler (2003), Luís and Otoguro (2004, 2011) and Luís and Spencer (2005).

The proclitic/enclitic environment triggers effectively define two subconjugations for Portuguese verbs. The simplest way to reflect this is with a feature [RESTRICTED:{yes,no}], which partitions the conjugation system appropriately. The proclitic contexts are reflected in the feature specification [RESTRICTED:yes] and the morphosyntax ensures that appropriate syntactic contexts are matched with verbs bearing the correct feature specification for [RESTRICTED]. A verb marked [RESTRICTED:yes] will have exactly the same host/exponence specifications, but the linearization specification will state something along the lines of (106):

(106)   R(clitics)=[$_{VP}$

Statement (106) places the output of the clitics rules to the left edge of the verb phrase projected by the main verb.

Given this machinery we can turn to the question of mesoclisis. Recall that enclitic pronominals appear between the verb stem and the person/number endings for the future/conditional forms: *mostrar=to=emos/íamos* 'we will/would show it to you'. Constructions of this sort raise very intriguing questions about the nature of linguistic primes such as 'affix' and 'clitic'. Specifically, should we regard the pronominal mesoclitic cluster as essentially clitics or as essentially affixes (or as something else)?

Our argument will be that the question is not well formed, and indeed constructions such as European Portuguese mesoclisis show very clearly why we have to be careful about assuming that notions such as 'clitic' or 'affix' are well understood and universally accepted primitives of linguistic theory. First, observe that the mesoclitics are not typical affixes. As emphasized by Vigário (2003) they exhibit a host of phonological properties that distinguish them from normal suffixes in Portuguese. However, Vigário's meticulous study of the Prosodic Phonology of Portuguese demonstrates what we already know from the Prosodic Phonology of many other languages: there are often mismatches between morphosyntactic definitions of wordhood and phonological/prosodic definitions. Vigário presents a wealth of evidence to show that the pronominal clitic cluster has prosodic and phonological properties that distinguish it from a lexical affix string. She draws from this the conclusion that it is inappropriate to regard the pronominal cluster as a type of inflectional affix. But that conclusion is hasty. The correct conclusion to draw is that pronominal clitics are not the same as lexical affixes, and no more (Bermúdez-Otero and Luís 2009a, b,

Luís 2009). This doesn't prevent us from concluding that, in its enclitic instantiation at least, the pronominal cluster is a less highly integrated or morphologized
species of affix (akin, say, to the English Class II affixes). Now, as we saw in
Section 8.4, there is a sense in which the English Class II affix is 'really' a clitic.
In most respects, the Portuguese enclitic cluster behaves rather like an English
Class II affix. We can conclude, if we wish, that the Portuguese enclitics are
'really' affixes and that the English affixes are 'really' clitics. But this entirely
misses the point, of course. What we really need to do is to establish the specific properties of each class of elements and the way they relate to the rest of
the grammar. Then we need to apportion the various properties to appropriate
modules of grammar, bearing in mind continually the ever-present possibility
of mismatches between the behaviour in one aspect (say, phonological) and the
behaviour in another aspect (say, morphosyntactic or semantic).

Given this caveat, we can now re-examine the mesoclitics to ascertain just
what properties they actually have. First, recall that the mesoclitic + stem combination *mostrar=to* constitutes a separate prosodic word, so that the whole is
two prosodic words, each having its own stress, *mostrAr=to=Emos* (with the
first stress being secondary and the second stress the primary, main stress of the
word). This would normally lead us to conclude that we have two morphological words and two syntactic words, but this is only the default situation. As
Luís and Spencer (2005, 206–7) observe, the double stress in mesoclitic forms
doesn't force us to propose a two-word (syntactic) analysis of those forms. They
point out that compound words such as *pós-clássico* also have two stresses, and
Vigário (2003, 243) makes the point that acronyms such as *PCP*[25] have three
stresses (the main stress falling on the final syllable/letter, ω_s):

(107)

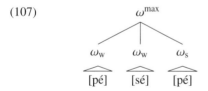

Whereas a normally inflected word consists of a single prosodic word, the mesoclisis examples contain two prosodic words, with the clitic cluster adjoined to the
first of these: $(_\omega(_\omega(_\omega \text{mostrar})=\text{to} (_\omega \text{iamos})))$, as diagrammed in (108). Clearly,
then, one of the idiosyncrasies that has to be written into the grammar of meso-
clisis is the unexpected prosodic structure (cf. also Anderson 2005, 157–61).
We will show how to do this when we have considered the morphology of the
construction in a little more detail.

(108)

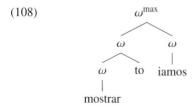

Thus far the grammar provides a set of clitic clusters which are attached as proclitics to the verb phrase if the verb is marked 'Restricted' and by default suffixed to the output of the first 'layer' of inflection. When the feature set of the verb includes specifications for future tense or conditional mood, however, the suffixation linearization statement is overridden. First, consider how the future/conditional forms are defined in the absence of pronominal clitics. The endings shown in (109) are added to a special stem which we will call 'stem-r'. A handful of verbs have an irregular stem-r form, but in the majority of cases the stem-r form is the form to which the infinitive defaults (reflecting the fact that this stem form arose from encliticizing an auxiliary verb to the infinitive).

(109)   Portuguese Future/Conditional endings

	Future	Conditional
1sg	-ei	-ía
2sg	-ás	-ías
3sg	-á	-ía
1pl	-emos	-íamos
2pl	-eis	-íeis
3pl	-ão	-íam

The inflectional rules defining the future/conditional forms define the stem-r as the host for the suffixation of the endings in (109) (we simplify the statement of the rules for the endings for the sake of exposition):

(110)   Definition of inflected form of <MOSTRAR, σ>, where σ = {1pl, cond}
          a. Host: stem-r(MOSTRAR)   =   <mostrar, stem-r>
          b. Exponence: R(1pl, conditional)   =   <íamos, slot-I>
          c. Linearization: <stem-r, íamos> (by default)
          d. Output: muʃtrar⊕íamuʃ

Now consider what happens when σ = {1pl, cond} ∪ {2sg dat, masc 3sg acc}. The normal rules of exponence apply, defining the sequences íamos and to. The default rules of linearization would put these in the order íamos to but a special linearization statement is triggered by the property {conditional}, as shown in (111):

(111)   Definition of inflected form of <MOSTRAR, σ>, where σ = {1pl, cond}
          a.   Host: stem-r(MOSTRAR)   =   <mostrar, stem-r>
          b1. Exponence: R(1pl, conditional)   =   <íamos, slot-I>
          b2. Exponence: R(2sg dat, masc 3sg acc)   =   <to, dat∘acc>
          c.   Linearization: <($_\omega$stem-r), dat∘acc)$_\omega$, slot-I>
          d.   Output: muʃ‚trar⊕tu⊕'íamuʃ

The stem and clitic sequence are annotated with prosodic word labels, thus guaranteeing the required stress pattern.

In this fashion we can treat the simple enclisis as (almost) normal suffixation, the mesoclisis as highly specific, prosodically marked suffixation and proclisis as phrasal affixation, but in each case defined over a clitic cluster that remains the same morphological object no matter where it is placed. Additionally, we treat the future/conditional endings as essentially the same with and without mesoclisis. In this way we don't need to propose two entirely separate future/conditional constructions just to handle the mesoclisis examples (as is proposed, for instance, by Vigário 2003, 152).

8.5.5   Clitics in Distributed Morphology

Noyer (2001, 768–78) provides a very detailed and intricate Distributed Morphology analysis of the clitic sequences[26] of Nunggubuyu, a Australian language of the Gunwinyguan family.[27] He links two sets of phenomena. Some feature combinations are not expressed by unique clitic sequences, but rather several sets of feature combinations may be expressed by one and the same sequence. This is syncretism. Second, the clitics appear in a set order. Noyer appeals to two notions to account for these facts, Impoverishment and Morphological Merger.

The leading idea behind Impoverishment is that some feature combinations are simplified by deleting certain feature values. The deleted values are then filled in by default specifications which operate according to a markedness hierarchy. The idea was first introduced into PPT-type models by Bonet's (1991, 1995) analysis of Catalan clitic clusters, which show much the same types of idiosyncrasy as other Romance clusters, including a type of 'Spurious-*se*' process. Noyer adduces the common instance of a language that distinguishes singular, dual and plural number for subjects and objects, but in which a combination of, say, dual subject acting on dual object is neutralized morphologically and expressed with the same affix or clitic set as (say) plural subject acting on dual object. First we assume the markedness hierarchy in (112), where 'u:' denotes an unmarked value and 'm:' a marked value:

(112)

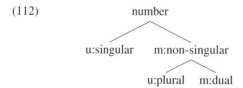

If we erase a [Number:dual] feature valuation from a feature set, the markedness hierarchy will specify the feature for the 'nearest' unmarked value, in this case 'plural'. This is the essence of Impoverishment. It is intended to account for all types of systematic syncretism.[28]

Noyer introduces another factor into the discussion. He proposes that Impoverishment is motivated by a notion of complexity. Certain combinations of features or feature values are treated by some grammars (of languages or of dialects of languages) as 'too complex'. They are therefore subject to co-occurrence restrictions ruling them out, of the form *[[dual][dual]], which rules out two distinct sets of dual number specifications. He argues (2001, 770) that neutralizations and syncretisms expressed by such co-occurrence restrictions "present a puzzle for learnability theory". The problem is, apparently, to prevent children from overgeneralizing and creating the forms that are banned by the neutralization process. The argument rests on assumptions about child language acquisition that are controversial amongst child language specialists, to say the least. Noyer proposes a formal way of capturing the idea that children are conservative learners: the assumption is that neutralization is the default situation, and that for the acquisition of more complex systems the learner requires positive evidence that neutralization has not occurred.

Nunggubuyu shows a set of feature contrasts that are typical of non-Pama-Nyungan languages. There are eight genders, including three genders referring to humans, masculine, feminine and 'plural', a type of collective. There are four person values: 1st, 1st inclusive ('I + addressee'), 2nd and 3rd. Nunggubuyu also has an augmented number system, which increases the default number by (at least) one. For instance, the augmented form of 1sg is 1st person exclusive dual or plural, while the augmented form of 1st inclusive plural (which minimally denotes 'I and thou') is minimally a trial form. As a result there are a good many possible combinations of feature values, but by no means all of these are attested in the clitic sequence paradigms. In addition, there is a clitic *wan* which gives rise to clusters called 'B' series, for expressing negative past, negative present, past potential and non-negative future.

In the case of Nunggubuyu, a principal neutralization of interest to Noyer is that of gender in the presence of number. For instance, while the sequence in (113a) is fine, the sequence corresponding to 'he ... her' is neutralized, removing the clitic that would normally express the masculine 3sg subject, so that the expected sequence in (113b) is replaced by the single clitic for 'her', as in (113c):

(113) a.   ŋi   nu   . . .
            3SG.FEM.SUBJ 3SG.MASC.OBJ
            'she ... him'

      b.   (*ni)   ŋu   . . .
            3SG.MASC.SUBJ 3SG.FEM.OBJ

      c.   ŋu   . . .
            3SG.FEM.OBJ
            'he ... her'

Noyer outlines a number of such cases, involving various types of feature combination, and argues for a set of impoverishment rules: Object Gender Impoverishment (for the case just illustrated), Person Gender Impoverishment and Subject Gender Impoverishment. The first of these is exemplified in (114)

(114)   Object Gender Impoverishment (OGI)
            $[_\alpha$ gender$] \rightarrow \emptyset/[+\text{aug}\_\_ \text{object}]$

He then goes on to investigate their relationships, arguing for feeding and bleeding interactions.

Noyer also addresses the question of clitic ordering in Nunggubuyu. In intransitive clauses we find that person, number and gender may, in principle, be expressed by separate clitics in that order:

(115)   Alignment by Type
          Person » Number » Gender

Thus, the form *ni:ni* '2nd augmented masculine' is segmented as *nV-wu-ni* (where 'V' stands for an underspecified vowel), analysed as 2nd-AUG-MASC. For transitive clauses a further principle applies:

(116)   Subject clitics precede object clitics

However, the two principles are often in conflict, of course, in which case Alignment-by-Type often prevails. Where that principle fails to apply, principle (116) operates. Moreover, whenever an object clitic precedes a subject clitic a special 'inverse affix', notated 'N', follows the object clitic. Finally, clitics expressing neuter gender always appear at the end of the cluster. As a result of these various restrictions, clitic sequences respect principle (117) (Noyer 2001, 786, citing Heath 1984, 366):

(117)   Inviolable Output Condition on Clitic order
          Person » B » Number » Gender » Neuter

Noyer adopts the assumptions of Distributed Morphology under which syntactic principles provide a structure that implies a basic linear ordering, but that ordering can be altered by rules deriving a Morphological Structure (MS) from syntactic structure.[29] He argues that the re-orderings required respect a principle of locality. Thus, while the re-orderings in (118) are permitted, that in (119) is not:

(118) a. $x \wedge [_y \ y \wedge w]$
            $\rightarrow [[_y \ y + x] \wedge w]$
      b. $x \wedge [_y \ y \wedge w]$
            $\rightarrow [[_y \ x + y] \wedge w]$
(119) $[z \wedge x \wedge [_y \ y]] \nrightarrow [z \wedge [_y \ y + x]]$

The re-orderings in (118) preserve the adjacency (in a technical sense) between $y \wedge w$, but that in (119) prevents 'z' and 'x' from being adjacent. The Merger operation can re-order the 'B' clitic, which Noyer takes to be a complementizer originating at the left periphery of the clause. It can also re-order some of the remaining clitics but not all. Where a clitic sequence would violate (117) and no Merger can save the sequence, then deletion in the form of Impoverishment is invoked as a 'last resort' strategy.

One of the virtues of the Distributed Morphology approach advocated by Noyer is that it doesn't commit the analyst to an artificial division between weak function word–clitic–affix. The clitic properties emerge from the inter-action with other properties. The other virtue of the approach is that it is syntax driven, so that it is possible to bring together generalizations about clitic placement that overlap with other syntactic properties that don't involve cli-tics (we have also seen that this is a feature of the way that Warlpiri auxiliary clitics interact with complementizers in that language (Legate 2008)). In fair-ness, however, it should be said that Noyer's analysis has not gone without criticism.

Baerman et al. (2005, chapter 4) discuss critically a variety of formal models aimed at providing a principled restrictive theory of syncretism (the mod-els relate to inflectional paradigms but the reasoning extends equally to clitic systems, especially with respect to a model such as Distributed Morphology which doesn't draw a distinction between the two). Their discussion includes an explicit critique of one set of claims made for the Impoverishment approach (Baerman et al. 2005, 160–3). In their summary to that chapter they include a section on 'predictions and counter-examples' (Baerman et al. 2005, 166–9). They emphasize an important point about syncretism, which we alluded to earlier in the chapter: there is often a tension between treating surface iden-tity/homophony as the result of some systematic, principled fact about the paradigm structure, or treating it is accidental. They observe (Baerman et al. 2005, 166, fn.13) that Noyer's analysis "forces systematic syncretism to be treated as the concatenation of separate instances of accidental homophony". They point out that for one of the two sets of prefixes/clitics, Nunggubuyu shows systematic person/number syncretism as well as the gender/number syn-cretism discussed in detail by Noyer: 1st exclusive forms are syncretic with 2nd non-singular forms. As Baerman et al. detail, Noyer's analysis treats this patterning as the result of a series of accidents, no doubt because it would be a clear counter-example to the Impoverishment analysis if it were treated as systematic.

In addition to Whitman's (1991) brief treatment of some of the Nunggubuyu facts, there are alternative, morphologically based, approaches to very similar morphological paradigms in other Gunwinyguan languages. Evans et al. (2001) provide an analysis of syncretisms in the pronominal paradigms of Dalabon within the framework of Network Morphology (a model that is very similar to the Paradigm Function Morphology of Stump) and Wunderlich (2001) analyses similar data within his model of Minimalist Morphology.

8.6   Syntactic approaches

We will divide the syntactic theoretical approaches into two types:[30]

1   Two closely related constraints-based models: Lexical Functional Grammar (LFG) and Head-Driven Phrase Structure Grammar;

2   'Principles-and-Parameters' (PPT) models, which include Chomsky's
            Government-Binding framework (Chomsky 1981) and his Minimal-
            ist Program (Chomsky 1995b, 2001, 2008).

Constraints-based approaches: LFG

There has been relatively little work conducted on clitics systems as such within
the Lexical Functional Grammar framework. An important contribution is that
of Toivonen (2003) reviewed above. In LFG, morphology has generally been
handled in terms of classical morphemes, so that affixes are given lexical entries
and contribute featural and other information to the word form as a whole by a
process of unification. This kind of approach is difficult to reconcile with realizational models of morphology (for an attempt, in the context of Kayardild multiple
case marking, see Nordlinger and Sadler 2006). Clitic systems are therefore
generally treated as a kind of unusual syntax.

   The principal theoretical issue surrounding clitic systems that LFG has
addressed concerns the relation between pronominal clitic systems, 'pronoun
incorporation' and agreement, discussed in Section 6.3. Those pronouns which
are described as clitics in the descriptive literature are generally treated as
idiosyncratic pronominals with their own pronominal semantics (a 'PRED' value
in the terminology of LFG). When the pronominal loses this PRED value and
comes simply to realize features, it functions as an agreement marker. Agreement
morphology in PRO-drop systems is often systematically ambiguous between
this PRED-bearing lexical entry and the non-PRED lexical entry, as we saw
in Toivonen's analysis of Finnish possessive suffixes (Section 7.2.2). The question of incorporation of a pronominal complete with its PRED value as opposed
to the agreement function of pronominal affixes is the subject of chapter 8 of
Bresnan (2001b). Bresnan (2001b, 146–8) discusses clitic doubling in the context of pronominal incorporation vs agreement, and she provides clitic doubling
data in Problem Set 2 of that book. Dalrymple (2001) discusses clitics in various
places within her survey of LFG. In her discussion of clitic doubling in Bulgarian, Dalrymple places a (single) object clitic pronominal under the I position,
adjoined to the I position that houses the lexical verb in her representation for the
sentence:

(120)

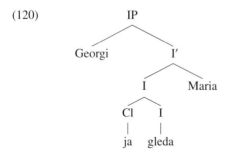

(121)   Georgi ja   gleda   Maria
               Georgi 3SG.ACC.FEM watches Maria
               'Georgi is watching Maria' [Bulgarian]

In this representation the PRED value for the clitic pronoun is optional, which permits the doubling by the overt object *Maria* (Dalrymple 2001, 139). On the other hand, clitic doubling is disallowed in Serbo-Croat because the clitic pronominals (like the full-form pronominals) bear an obligatory PRED value, and this cannot be combined with any other PRED value, even that of a full-form pronominal bearing the same features (Dalrymple 2001, 106).

One of the few detailed LFG studies devoted specifically to clitics is that of Sadler (1997), which we will summarize below, along with a brief discussion of Luís and Sadler's (2003) analysis of mesoclisis in European Portuguese.

Constraints-based approaches: HPSG

There has been an assumption within HPSG that morphology is best handled in terms of a realizational model (see, for instance, Sag et al. 2003). Relatively few explicit analyses along these lines have been provided for complex morphological systems, however. Nonetheless, the realizational bias in HPSG makes it easier for theorists working in that framework to propose analyses that effectively treat clitic systems as a kind of unusual morphology. Early studies in this vein include Miller (1992) and Halpern (1995). An influential contribution was the Miller and Sag (1997) analysis of French pronominal clitics as affixation. Monachesi (1999, 2000, 2005) adopts a similar approach to the study of other Romance clitic systems, particularly Italian and Romanian (see our discussion of clitic cluster templates in Chapter 5). This HPSG lexicalist tradition has been extended by Bonami and Boyé (2007), who, as we have seen, have implemented a Paradigm Function Morphology analysis of French clitics in HPSG in a way that allows them to integrate their analysis with a standard HPSG implementation of French morphosyntax.

One important question that a morphological approach to pronominal clitics must address is the fact that clitics are generally in complementary distribution with overt noun phrase (or DP) complements (including full forms of pronouns). That is, a subject or object clitic functions as the subject or object of the predicate (i.e. the verb, or sometimes the preposition) and this is what motivated the original movement analysis. Now, as we have seen, uncontroversial cases of affixed agreement inflections can, and usually do, function as arguments to predicates. This is the so-called 'pro-drop' phenomenon. In earlier versions of PPT it was assumed that there was a special empty pronominal *pro* (called 'little pro' colloquially) which served as the real argument of the verb/preposition and which carried the pronominal features expressed by the agreement morphology. The agreement inflections then agree with that 'little pro'. Essentially, this analysis is carried over to the base-generated analysis of pronominal clitics, as proposed by Jaeggli (1982), Jaeggli (1986) and Borer (1984) among others.

In HPSG the relationship between a verb and its arguments is coded in a rather different way from PPT models. The lexical entry for a verb has a subcategorization frame, which lists the complements it takes. The full set of complements that an expression can take in a clause is its valency, coded by means of a feature VAL which takes as its value a list of complements (itself a feature, COMPS). Monachesi (2005, 78) proposes the following lexical rule to relate verbs without clitic arguments to verb forms that are associated with a clitic:

(122)   Monachesi's Complement Cliticization Lexical Rule (CCLR)

$$
\begin{bmatrix} word \\ \text{HEAD} & verb \\ \text{VAL} \mid \text{COMPS} & \boxed{1} \bigcirc \boxed{2} \\ \text{CLTS} & elist \end{bmatrix} \mapsto \begin{bmatrix} \text{VAL} \mid \text{COMPS} & \boxed{1} \\ \text{CLTS} & \boxed{2} \text{ list } (cl\text{-}ss) \end{bmatrix}
$$

What this rule does is to replace one of the complements on the valency list of the verb (in this case, complement $\boxed{2}$, the direct object) and replace it with a clitic.[31]

Given a rule of this sort it is not possible for the clitic to be doubled by an overt noun phrase argument. Monachesi therefore proposes a slightly different rule to account for instances of clitic doubling of the kind found in Balkan languages. She considers (2005, 84) the Romanian example of indirect object clitic doubling illustrated in (123), an example that is largely parallel to the indirect clitic doubling we've already seen for Bulgarian, Macedonian, Albanian and other languages.[32]

(123)   Martina îi   dă   preşedentelui o carte
          Martina CL.DAT gives president.the a book
          'Martina gives the president a book' [Romanian]

Here, the indirect object *preşedentelui*, marked with an oblique form of the postpositive definite article suffix, *lui*, is doubled by the dative clitic *îi*.

To account for such cases, Monachesi proposes a slight modification to the Complement Clitic Lexical Rule, namely, a Clitic Doubling Lexical Rule:

(124)   Monachesi's Clitic Doubling Lexical Rule (CDLR)

$$
\begin{bmatrix} word \\ \text{HEAD} & verb \\ \text{VAL} \mid \text{COMPS} & \boxed{1} \bigcirc \boxed{2} \text{NP}[dat] \\ \text{CLTS} & elist \end{bmatrix} \mapsto \begin{bmatrix} \text{VAL} \mid \text{COMPS} & \boxed{1} \bigcirc \boxed{2} [dat] \\ \text{CLTS} & \boxed{2} \end{bmatrix}
$$

Rule (124) differs from rule (122) in that the complements of the verb remain on the COMPS list and are not 'saturated' by the clitic. The clitic, however, bears the tag '$\boxed{2}$', showing that it shares all its features with the second complement of the verb (including its case). Formally speaking, within the HPSG architecture this means that the clitic agrees with the indirect object. A rule such as this has to be supplemented by various additional pieces of information about the semantics and pragmatics of the indirect object. The HPSG model provides ample formal machinery for stating such conditions in a single (rather large!) feature structure, including rather subtle pragmatic conditions to do with topicality, information structure and so forth, of a kind we know to be implicated in clitic doubling constructions (and inflectional agreement systems, for that matter).

The mixed cases of European Portuguese and Udi (amongst others) have been analysed using the notion of order domains by Berthold Crysmann (2000, 2002). He proposes an analysis of the clitics under which the placement of such clitics is handled by rules that have access equally to syntactic and morphological structure. The analysis is extremely technical and beyond the scope of a general survey such as this. Kupść and Tseng (2005) have treated the Polish floating inflections as a kind of inflection. Avgustinova (1997) devotes much of her analysis of Bulgarian to auxiliary and pronominal clitics, presenting an essentially syntactic analysis of clitic placement, which contrasts with the morphological analyses we find for Romance languages. This is no doubt motivated by the Tobler–Mussafia syntactic structures we find in Bulgarian compared with (modern) Romance languages, in which the clitics generally cluster around the verbal head.

One area in which HPSG has been deployed in detail is a phenomenon that has suffered relative neglect in formally oriented studies, namely, edge inflection. We will therefore summarize Samvelian's (2007) analysis of the Persian ezafe construction to illustrate how HPSG can be used to formalize that notion.

PPT approaches

In the PPT class of models, morphology is generally treated as a species of syntax. Affixes, clitics and function words alike are analysed as syntactic functional heads. There is, therefore, no principled difference between clitics and any other functional element (Embick and Noyer 2001, 2007). For approaches such as these, some of the properties of clitics are expected whilst others pose problems. For instance, pronominal clitics are treated as syntactic pronouns that have unusual placement properties. This makes it easy to handle the complementarity between pronominal clitics that realize arguments and overt arguments. However, it raises difficulties in languages that show clitic doubling. For a number of models the existence of subject clitics in Romance languages has posed technical problems. Other models, particularly constraints-based models, don't generally share the crucial structural and architectural assumptions and so such subject clitics don't pose the same kinds of problem. For this reason we will not discuss the theoretical issues surrounding subject clitics in PPT but simply redirect the reader to the literature cited in Section 6.4.1.

In the PPT approaches placement is generally the result of syntactic movement processes. Such syntactic movement requires an appropriate 'landing site'. In principle this can be some dedicated clitic head position, unique to clitics, but in general analysts prefer to collapse clitic placement with other aspects of syntactic structure and engineer clitic movement so that the clitics land in, or adjoin to, already motivated syntactic positions. For instance, Wackernagel clitics might be analysed as clustering in the COMP position, or in the AgrS position (the function head position that canonically houses subject DPs) or some other structure position that is to the left periphery of the clause but not actually the leftmost position. This position is often the same position as that occupied by the finite verb in analyses of 'verb second' syntax (Cardinaletti and Roberts 2002).

There are two ways we can conceive of pronominal clitic systems within the PPT framework. One approach (for instance, Borer 1984) takes the clitics to be generated in their final position ('base-generated'). The other, earlier, approach takes the clitics to be placed like any other complement to the verb and then moved into the special clitic position by a syntactic rule.[33]

There are two main motivations for adopting the movement approach. First, many clitic systems disallow doubling of a pronominal clitic with an overt noun phrase. This is largely true of the clitic systems of the Romance languages. This behaviour can be understood if we take the clitic to be a genuine argument of the verb that has been moved to its clitic position. Thus, a simple account of the French example in (125) would take the structure in (126a) as underlying and derive the structure in (126b) by shifting the clitic:

(125)   **Je le** vois
          I   it see
          'I see it'

(126) a.   Je   vois le $\Rightarrow$
      b.   Je le$_i$ vois ___$_i$

The second phenomenon that readily lends itself to syntactic analysis is clitic climbing. As we saw in Chapter 6, in Italian we have examples such as (127):

(127)   Martina **lo** vuole leggere
          Martina it wants to.read
          'Martina wants to read it'

The clitic *lo* in (127), serves as the direct object of the subordinate clause verb *leggere* 'to read', and yet (in this example) the pronominal procliticizes to the matrix verb *vuole* 'wants'. Again, a natural way to describe this situation is to say that the clitic originates as the direct object in the subordinate clause and is then raised to a higher position in the syntactic structure, associating itself with the matrix verb, as in (128):

(128) a.   Martina vuole [$_S$ leggere lo]
      b.   Martina lo$_i$=vuole [$_S$ leggere ___$_i$]

Since at least the work of Kayne (1975), the fact that Romance clitics are generally in complementary distribution with overt NPs has been taken by many syntacticians as clear proof that clitics are syntactically represented words and that they are moved from their base position by a transformation of some kind. Of course, there are other systems regularly described as clitic systems in which

doubling is either an optional possibility or is even obligatory. It is impossible
to apply any argument from complementary distribution in such cases and very
difficult to see how a principled movement analysis of clitic placement is even
possible. Moreover, the argument from complementary distribution is seriously
undermined by the facts discussed in Chapter 6, in which we saw that affixal
pronominal markers can sometimes be in complementary distribution with overt
argument phrases, or with certain classes of such phrases. We will therefore
briefly summarize the way that PPT syntacticians have risen to such challenges.
To begin with, however, we look at two specific proposals for handling two rather
different construction types, the first an LFG analysis of Welsh clitics and the
second an HPSG analysis of Persian ezafe as edge inflection.

8.7   Clitics in LFG

8.7.1   Welsh

One clitic system that has been examined in some detail from an LFG
perspective is that of Welsh. Here we discuss Sadler's (1997) analysis of Welsh
pronominal clitics and then briefly survey an analysis of European Portuguese
pronominal clitics (Luís and Sadler 2003).

We have seen examples of the agreement system of Welsh, but we have yet to
see how the clitic system works. Welsh is interesting because of the way its clitic
system has developed since the Middle Ages and because essentially the same
clitic system can be found with both nouns and verbs. With nouns the clitics
express possessive relations. With verbs exactly the same clitics express direct
object properties. Historically, this situation has arisen because the transitive verb
was treated as a nominal (and in many descriptions it is still referred to as a
verbal noun, even though it is in reality the head of a finite verb construction; see
Borsley 1993).[34]

Welsh is a language that exhibits considerable diglossia, in that the spoken
variety differs considerably from the written, literary variety. Here we describe
mainly the spoken variety, following Borsley et al. (2007), but supplemented
by examples from Rhys Jones (1977), which deals specifically with the spoken language. We will refer to this variety as 'Spoken Welsh', or simply as
'Welsh'.

Welsh has developed a system of pronominal possessive marking in which
the possessed noun is flanked by two distinct pronominal elements. The
prenominal element triggers initial consonant mutation, a widespread morphophonological set of alternations in Welsh and Celtic generally.[35] In Welsh
there are three principal types of initial consonant mutation. The commonest
is soft mutation, found in a host of morphological and syntactic contexts. The
other two are the nasal mutation and the aspirate mutation. The effects are
shown in (129):[36]

(129)   Welsh initial consonant mutations

Mutation:	Soft	Nasal	Aspirate
Basic consonant			
p	b	mh	ph
t	d	nh	th
c	g	ngh	ch
b	f	m	—
d	dd	n	—
g	∅	ng	—
m	f	—	—
ll	l	—	—
rh	r	—	—

Examples of possessive constructions in Spoken Welsh are given in (130) (Rhys Jones 1977, 325):

(130)   Mutations in possessive constructions

	'his' Soft Mutation	'my' Nasal Mutation	'her' Aspirate Mutation
car 'car'	ei gar e	'y nghar i	ei char hi
pen 'hen'	ei ben e	'y mhen i	ei phen hi
teulu 'family'	ei deulu e	'y nheulu i	ei theulu hi
gardd 'garden'	ei ardd e	'y ngardd i	ei gardd hi
bag 'bag'	ei fag e	'y mag i	ei bag hi
desg 'desk'	ei ddesg e	'y nesg i	ei desg hi
mam 'mother'	ei fam e	'y mam i	ei mam hi
llaw 'hand'	ei law e	'yn llaw i	ei llaw hi
rhestr 'list'	ei restr e	'yn rhestr i	ei rhestr hi

In (131)–(133) we see the possessive pronominals used as direct object markers (Rhys Jones 1977, 116):

(131)   Rydw i   yn ei   nabod e
          be.1SG 1SG.SUBJ PRT 3SG.POSS know 3SG.M.POSS
          'I know him'

(132)   Mae   e   yn 'yn   nabod i
          be.3SG 3SG.SUBJ PRT 1SG.POSS know 1SG.POSS
          'He knows me'

(133)   Ydich chi   yn ei   nabod hi
          be.1SG 1SG.SUBJ PRT 3SG.POSS know 3SG.FEM.POSS
          'Do you know her?'

Rhys Jones (1977, 117–18) provides neat examples illustrating the way that pronominal object marking parallels possessor marking, using the noun *car* 'car' and the verb *cario* 'carry'. *Mae* is a 3sg auxiliary used in the progressive present construction.

(134)   Mae 'nghar   i   yn 'y   nghario   i
          AUX car(NasMut) 1SG.POSS PRT 1SG.POSS carry(NasMut) 1SG.POSS
          'My car carries/is carrying me'
(135)   Mae ei   gar   e   yn ei   gario
          AUX 3SG car(SoftMut) 3SG.M.POSS PRT 3SG.POSS carry(SoftMut)
          fe[37]
          3SG.M.POSS
          'His car carries/is carrying him'
(136)   Mae ei   char   hi   yn ei   chario
          AUX 3SG car(AspMut) 3SG.FEM.POSS PRT 3SG.POSS carry(SoftMut)
          ei
          3SG.FEM.POSS
          'Her car carries/is carrying her'
(137)   Mae 'n   car ni   yn ein   cario ni
          AUX 1PL car 1PL.POSS PRT 1PL.POSS carry 1PL.POSS
          'Our car carries/is carrying us'
(138)   Mae 'ch car chi   yn eich   cario chi
          AUX 2PL car 2PL.POSS PRT 2PL.POSS carry 2PL.POSS
          'Your car carries/is carrying you'
(139)   Mae eu   car nhw   yn eu   cario nhw
          AUX 3PL car 3PL.POSS PRT 3PL.POSS carry 3PL.POSS
          'Their car carries/is carrying them'

Given these descriptive preliminaries we can ask how to represent the possessed nouns and the pronominal direct objects.

As Borsley et al. (2007) point out, in traditional (i.e. native Welsh) accounts of Welsh grammar the principal exponent of the possessive features is the prenominal pronoun form. The postnominal element is then regarded as an 'auxiliary'. However, in the generative tradition of description, particularly that established by Awbery (1976) and Sadler (1988), it has become standard to treat the postnominal pronoun as a self-standing pronoun that is obligatorily 'doubled' by the prenominal clitic. If this clitic were a standard affix we would then speak of an agreement prefix. However, Sadler (1997) points out that the pronominal elements show a number of the typical properties of clitics (though not all such properties). Properties arguing in favour of clitic status for the prenominal elements are:[38]

- No idiosyncratic gaps: all words capable of accepting prehead pronominals do so.
- Separability: the prehead pronominal can be separated from the noun/verb head by various adjectives and numerals.

On the other hand, there are more restricted ways in which the prehead pronominals behave more like affixes:

- Order: Welsh syntax is head-initial, but the host of the pronominals is final.

- Narrow scope over coordinate phrases: the pronominals have to be repeated on each conjunct.

It's worth noting that the pervasive system of consonant mutation is not evidence of affix status over clitic, because mutations of this sort can be triggered by purely syntactic environments (for instance, an adjective following a feminine singular noun). On the other hand, the prehead pronominals don't trigger other types of idiosyncratic allomorphy on their hosts.

We should also note that non-canonical word order and failure to take wide scope are widespread with unaccented function words generally, whether clitics or not. The evidence thus favours a clitic analysis of the prehead pronominals. Sadler goes on to argue that further syntactic evidence, together with theoretical considerations internal to LFG, mean that the clitics have to be represented as syntactic terminals. We thus have syntactically represented clitics that function, essentially, as agreement markers.

In LFG, syntactic structure receives two distinct representations. The first is c-structure, the familiar constituent structure/phrase structure representation of many contemporary models of syntax. The second is functional structure (f-structure). This is a set of features that express the grammatical relations between phrases (such as SUBJECT, OBJECT, ADJUNCT) together with other morphosyntactic properties (such as TENSE, PERSON/NUMBER, GENDER). The two levels of representation are linked by mapping functions of the kind that say 'the first NP in c-structure after the verb maps to the f-structure feature SUB-JECT', or 'a verb in c-structure which bears the [TENSE:PAST] property maps to the f-structure feature [TENSE:PAST]'.

Sadler takes the prenominal possessive clitics to be of category D ('determiner'), adjoined to the head noun. The postnominal pronominals are taken to be full determiner phrases (DP). The c-structure for *ei gi mawr hi* 'her big dog' will therefore be:

(140)

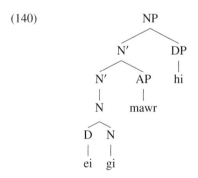

The adjunction construction of the form [$_N$ [$_D$ ei] [$_N$ gi]] is an instance of a 'small construction', that is, a multiword construction that fails to respect the normal principles of syntax, namely, that a head projects a phrase.[39]

Sadler notes that a prenominal clitic is frequently doubled by a postnominal pronoun but is never doubled by a lexical noun phrase. This is exactly the pattern we have observed with subject–verb agreement in Welsh, Section 6.3. This is the property of mutual exclusion. In addition, the pronominal argument hardly ever appears in the position of a canonical argument of the predicate; rather, a pronominal argument has to be expressed by means of the clitic construction (pre-emption). Sadler adopts the notion of 'blocking' developed by Andrews (1990) to explain similar (though not identical!) phenomena in Irish agreement. Normally, in LFG pronominal agreement features are introduced directly into f-structure representations in the form of feature values. There is no sense in which such properties are considered properties of a pronominal 'lexeme'. However, Sadler, following Andrews, argues that the Welsh clitic pronominal has its own 'PRED' value and thus behaves as though it were a lexeme in its own right. But in LFG it is impossible for two distinct elements with distinct PRED values to map to a single grammatical function. Therefore, the clitic will never be doubled by a lexical noun. Sadler takes the prenominal clitic to introduce an obliga-tory PRED value, while the postnominal pronoun does so optionally. When the postnominal pronoun is not furnished with its own PRED value it can serve as the double of the prenominal clitic, because there will be no extraneous PRED value.

The lexical representations proposed by Sadler are:

(141)   Lexical entries for 3sg clitics/pronouns

        ei: D   hi: D

        ($\uparrow$PRED) = 'PRO'   (($\uparrow$PRED) = 'PRO')
        ($\uparrow$PERS) = 3   ($\uparrow$PERS) = 3
        ($\uparrow$NUM) = SG   ($\uparrow$NUM) = SG
        ($\uparrow$GEN) = FEM   ($\uparrow$GEN) = FEM

These representations account for the mutual exclusion property. The pre-emption property is derived from Andrews' Principle of Morphological Block-ing, which states, in simple terms, that where there is a morphological form that is in competition with a syntactic form expressing exactly the same meaning, the morphological form is favoured.

Consider example (142):

(142) a.   Mae Emrys wedi **ei**   weld (hi)
          AUX Emrys PERF 3SG.FEM see   (3SG.FEM)
          'Emrys has seen her'
    b.   * Mae Emrys wedi weld (hi)
          AUX Emrys PERF see   (3SG.FEM)

To account for the relative grammaticality of these examples, Sadler requires the Blocking Principle to apply to a clitic + host combination such as (143a) to pre-empt the purely syntactic representation in (143b):

(143)   a.   V   b. V

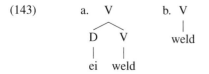

(144)   (↑PRED) = 'PRO'
             (↑PERS) = 3
             (↑NUM) = SG
             (↑GEN) = FEM

Sadler argues that (143a) represents a 'small construction' and that it is a property of such constructions that they count as 'morphological' for the purposes of blocking. Thus, structure (143a) is favoured over (143b).

In structure (143a) the feature values associated with the *ei* clitic shown in (144) are passed by general convention to the D node, then to the dominating V node. As a result the [D + V] complex comes to supply these features to the OBJ of that verb. This means that the partial f-structure in (145) will be created:

(145)
$$
\begin{bmatrix}
\text{PRED} & \text{'see}\langle\text{SUBJ, OBJ}\rangle\text{'} \\
\text{SUBJ} & \\
\text{OBJ} & \begin{bmatrix} \text{PRED 'PRO'} \\ \text{PERS 3} \\ \text{NUM SG} \\ \text{GEN FEM} \end{bmatrix}
\end{bmatrix}
$$

This will then combine with information from other nodes in the tree to give the complete f-structure in (146):

(146)
$$
\begin{bmatrix}
\text{PRED} & \text{'see}\langle\text{SUBJ, OBJ}\rangle\text{'} \\
\text{SUBJ} & \text{PRED 'Emrys'} \\
\text{OBJ} & \begin{bmatrix} \text{PRED 'PRO'} \\ \text{PERS 3} \\ \text{NUM SG} \\ \text{GEN FEM} \end{bmatrix} \\
\text{ASP} & \text{PERF}
\end{bmatrix}
$$

As an interesting postscript to this analysis, Sadler notes that the proclitic pronominals will often appear as enclitics, attached to the previous word if that is vowel-final (an example of a ditropic clitic). She suggests that this can be treated as a purely phonological phenomenon, while noting (1997, p. 15, n.15) that in some cases the enclitic seems to behave more like an affix morphophonologically than a clitic. In this respect, the clitics behave somewhat like English auxiliary clitics when attached to subject pronouns.[40]

8.7.2   European Portuguese

In Section 7.4 we discussed the unusual patterning of pronominal clitics in European Portuguese. This system is analysed in the LFG framework by Luís and Sadler (2003). Recall that in postverbal position the clitics are actually suffixes, while in preverbal position they behave more like proclitics. One symptom of this status is that as suffixes the pronominals take only narrow scope over conjoined verbs, while as proclitics they can take either narrow scope (as in (147b)) or wide scope (as in (147a)):

(147) a.   Apenas a   minha mãe   me   ajudou e   incentivou
               only   the my   mother 1.SG.ACC helped and encouraged

       b.   Apenas a   minha mãe   me   ajudou e   me   incentivou
               only   the my   mother 1.SG.ACC helped and 1.SG.ACC encouraged
               'Only my mother helped me and encouraged me'

On the other hand the proclitics don't behave as though they were syntactic terminals. For instance, they fail to coordinate with each other and they cannot be modified.

     Luís and Sadler account for the behaviour of the proclitics by assuming that the feature values they contribute to f-structure can be associated with two distinct syntactic nodes in c-structure, either the terminal verb node or the higher VP node:

(148) a.

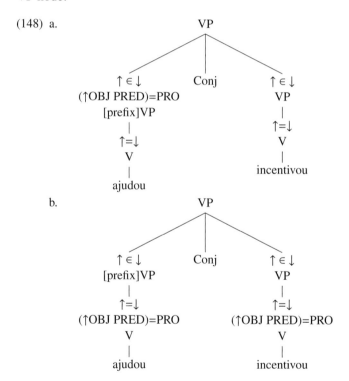

In (148b) it is the V nodes that bear the object pronominal features, and this corresponds to the narrow scope interpretation of (147b). In (148a), however, those features are associated with the VP. They are therefore interpreted as properties of the conjoined phrase of which the first VP is a joint head. This means that they are taken to be properties of both VPs even though they are formally marked only on the first. In this way we obtain the wide scope reading.

A very interesting model of morphosyntax is developed within the LFG framework by Wescoat (2002). Wescoat proposes a way of accounting for the intuition
that English reduced auxiliaries are simultaneously parts of morphological words
and two distinct syntactic words, by the simple ploy of allowing two distinct
syntactic terminal nodes to dominate the single word form.

The obvious way of doing this would be to draw a diagram such as (149)
(Wescoat 2002, 12):

(149)

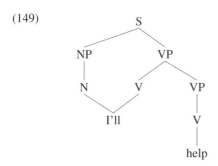

In standard accounts of phrase structure grammar this is not allowable, however. Wescoat therefore refines the notion 'word' in the context of phrase
structure representations. He distinguishes between the abstract 'slots' in terminal positions in syntactic trees and the morphosyntactic word forms that
are associated with those slots. He then introduces a function λ which maps
a collection of contiguous syntactic terminals (actually, either one or two terminals) to a single morphosyntactic word form. We can picture the effect
as in (150) (where 'V*' means a terminal that maps to a single word
form):

(150)

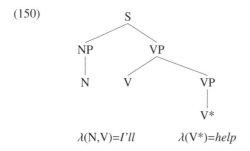

Wescoat provides extensive formal justification for this way of analysing English
auxiliary clitics, as well as portmanteau (fused) preposition + determiner
sequences as found in Romance languages and German. For example, the French
portmanteau form *du* from the preposition *de* 'of' and the masculine sg. definite article, as in the expression *du garçon* 'of the boy', can be represented
as in (151):

(151)

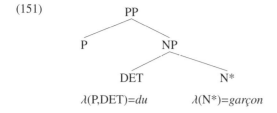

$\lambda(P,DET)=du$ $\lambda(N^*)=garçon$

A crucial feature of lexical sharing is that it can only be defined over terminals that are linearly adjacent. This means that the phrase structure representation must include both immediate domination information and linear precedence information (in distinction to a number of proposals in various syntactic frameworks).

Wescoat deploys the lexical sharing idea to handle a number of phenomena, not all of them involving clitics. In Wescoat (2009) he applies the technique to the Subject Marker clitics of Udi. He cashes in on two facts about the construction: Subject Markers are attracted to the rightmost element of a focussed phrase and the focussed phrase is always immediately to the left of the main verb (a common pattern, cross-linguistically). This means he is able to treat the Subject Marker as an essentially verbal affix/clitic that is 'shared' by the element to its left under certain circumstances.

Other recent discussion of the (endo)clitics of Pashto in LFG can be found in Bögel (2010), who argues that prosodic constraints can override the otherwise inviolable LFG condition, Lexical Integrity.

8.8   Edge inflection in HPSG

8.8.1   Overview

The analyses of clitics commonly found in the HPSG framework generally take clitics to be essentially morphological phenomena, following the influential proposals of Miller (1992) and Miller and Sag (1997). In this subsection we take the opportunity to see how HPSG deals with a somewhat controversial phenomenon, namely, edge inflection. This phenomenon is the most affix-like behaviour we find defined in terms of phrases, and for some the notion is synonymous with 'phrasal affixation'. However, it appears that there are phenomena which cannot easily be accounted for unless we assume that inflectional morphology can target lexemes that just happen to be situated at the edge of a phrase rather than targeting the head lexeme of a syntactic construction. Precise and detailed studies of edge inflection are therefore important for understanding the limits on clitic phenomena. We will first introduce the analysis of edge inflection first presented by Halpern and colleagues. This is an analysis of the English 'Saxon genitive' or 'group' construction. In fact, the analysis of the

group genitive as an edge inflection is very controversial, but since the facts
are widely known and since this construction has played an important role in
the development of the notion of edge inflection, we will present the original
analysis, before commenting on some of its flaws. Then we will briefly describe
a more convincing case of edge inflection, the Persian ezafe construction, in the
HPSG analysis proposed by Samvelian (2007). As usual, we will try to keep
technicalities to a bare minimum.

8.8.2   Analysing edge inflection

In some respects the problem of edge inflections is reminiscent of
the problems posed by the Polish floating inflections, except that the Polish
elements are not strictly speaking phrasal affixes in any of the senses discussed here. But in both cases we have an example of formatives that are
clitics by syntactic criteria (by virtue of showing promiscuous attachment) but
affixes by morphological (especially morphophonological) criteria. Nonetheless, a number of authors (Lapointe 1990, 1992, Miller 1992, Nevis 1986,
Poser 1985, Zwicky 1987, and following them Halpern 1995) have argued
that we must analyse edge inflection in a different way from that in which
we analyse ordinary phrasal affixation. For such authors, phrasal affixation
by clitics involves placing a clitic with respect to a host in a phrase, while
edge inflection involves selecting a inflected form of a word in a given syntactic context. We will briefly summarize the key theoretical issues that this
raises.

The existence of edge inflection as a phenomenon has been somewhat
controversial until recently. Anderson (2005, 89–101) discusses two possible
cases of edge inflection in detail: the English possessive 's, and the 'definitive accent' construction in Tongan and other Polynesian languages which we
discussed in Section 5.5.1. There he argues that there is no need to treat the
phenomenon as an instance of edge inflection. Rather, we can regard this as
an instance of phrasal affixation. The affixation process adjoins an element (the
clitic) to the right/left edge of a phrase. The implication is that all instances of
edge inflection can be treated in this fashion. However, this style of explanation
encounters serious difficulties in cases in which the host of the phrasal affixation
can undergo idiosyncratic morphological variation of a kind normally associated with irregular inflection. If that happens, then we can't simply say that a
clitic/affix has been adjoined to some part of a phrase, because the grammar has
to be able to retrieve the irregular inflected form of the word. This seems to be
the case with the Bulgarian and Macedonian definite articles. The three cases
discussed in Anderson et al. (2006) establish very clearly that edge inflection has
to be acknowledged.

How can grammatical theory capture the notion of edge inflection, and distinguish it from phrasal affixation? The answer to this depends very largely on

details of syntactic theory which differ from one model to the next. Consider the example *the larger of the two cats' paws*. This phrase means the paws of the larger of the two cats, in which the possessive /z/ applies to the expression *(the) larger (cat)*. On an edge inflection account we need to be able to say that *cats'* is inflected for [Number:Plural] and also for a feature [Possessor:Yes]. That [Possessor] feature applies to the entire phrase *the larger of the two cats*, as seen in the tree diagram in (152):

(152)

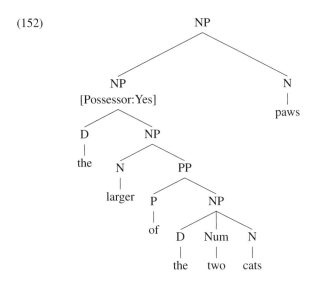

Structurally speaking, (152) is now equivalent to (153):

(153)

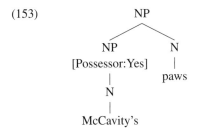

If we were dealing with ordinary head-oriented inflection it would be the word *larger* which would get marked morphologically to express the [Possessor:Yes] feature. However, since we have a case of edge inflection the [Possessor:Yes] property has to be realized on the rightmost element of the phrase bearing the [Possessor:Yes] feature. There are several possible ways of doing this, depend-

ing on other theoretical assumptions. In the account proposed originally by
Zwicky (1987) each rightmost node in the tree was additionally marked with
the same [Possessor:Yes] feature value, until we reach the rightmost word, as
shown in (154):

(154)

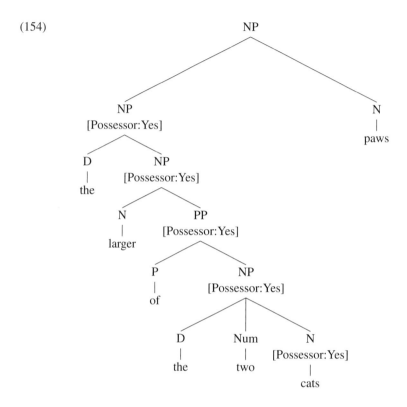

Depending on exactly what assumptions we make about the structure of the
grammar and the nature of feature copying of this sort, this type of solution
may give rise to technical problems with coordinated constructions such as
[John and Mary]'s children (where John and Mary are parents of the same
children). The problem is that under certain assumptions the feature copying
mechanism would have to treat the words *John* and *Mary* as independent right
edges and would therefore predict that only *John's and Mary's children* is
grammatical.

We may ask why exactly it's necessary to mark each of the right edges of the
syntactic structure. In fact, this is a theory-internal assumption in the work of
authors working within a phrase-structure grammar approach (such as Lapointe
1990, Miller 1992 and, effectively, Halpern 1995). In principle we could imagine
a theoretical framework that permitted us to relate the feature marking of the
phrase as a whole with feature marking on a peripheral element without reference
to any intermediate levels of structure. The representation of (154) would then
look more like (155):

(155)

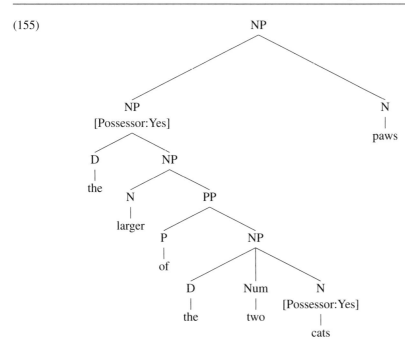

In effect this is the proposal of Anderson et al. (2006) (though they don't claim that the English possessive should be analysed as edge inflection). They argue for an analysis within Optimality Theory. Applied, for the sake of illustration, to the English possessive this analysis would essentially include one constraint that says that a possessor phrase has to be marked somewhere for [Possessor:Yes], but penalizing any phrase marked more than once for this value. There would then be an alignment constraint, stating that the right edge of the phrase should be aligned with the right edge of a word bearing the [Possessor:Yes] feature marking. Inspecting the representation in (155) we can see that this structure would meet these constraints. Optimality Theoretic analyses generally include an additional set of constraints that forbid extraneous marking (multiple exponence). Such a constraint would, in fact, reject a multiply marked structure such as (154).[41]

Before leaving the English group genitive, we should ask whether it really is an instance of inflection, rather than straightforward cliticization. The main problem with analysing it as a species of inflection is posed by personal pronouns. These have special forms when they appear as possessive modifiers: *my, your, his, her, our, their*.[42] When used as 'fused' pronouns, or as modifiers of null noun heads they have the forms: *mine, yours, his, hers, its, ours, theirs, (one's)*. However, a personal pronoun that just happens to appear at the end of a possessive phrase can take its normal form with *'s*.

(156) a.   my friend
       b.   your friend and mine
       c.   the girl standing next to me's friend
       d.   a friend of mine's name

The problem posed by these forms is that they all instantiate the same collection of features [Person/Number:1sg, Possessor:Yes], so why are they different?

There are two alternatives that have been explored in the recent literature. The solution of *The Cambridge Grammar of the English Language* (CGEL, Payne and Huddleston 2002, 479–81, see also Payne 2009) is to divide possessive constructions into two types. In head genitives the *'s* is effectively a suffix attaching to a noun, while in phrasal genitives it is a suffix attaching to a phrase. In both cases it is an inflection, so in the case of the phrasal genitive it is an edge inflection. Some morphological support for this comes from possessive forms of plural nouns. When the possessive *-s* marks a head noun with regular plural inflection we have haplology: *the ducks'* ([dʌks], *[dʌksəs]) eggs*. With irregular plurals, even those ending in /s/, we get the regular inflection: *the geese's* ([giːsəz], *[giːs]) eggs*. This indicates that we're dealing with an affix, hence, inflection. With the phrasal genitive there is some evidence for a similar type of haplology: *one of my students' assignment* may be pronounced with either *[stjuːdənts]* or *[stjuːdəntsəz]*, though both variants sound rather odd to some speakers, including one of the authors.[43] On the other hand, *one of my geese's egg* (if it's acceptable at all) has to be pronounced with *[giːsəz]*, not with *[giːs]*. This, too, suggests that we are dealing with morphological affixation (though it must be admitted that this is very weak evidence). In the case of (156a, b) we have head inflection, but of a personal pronoun. The pronouns have suppletive possessive forms, again indicating that we are dealing with inflection. With the forms *me's* and *mine's* in (156c, d) we have double inflection, a very unusual situation for English, but then this is an unusual construction.

The other alternative, favoured by Anderson (2005, 90–4) is to treat all cases of the possessive construction as instances of phrasal affixation, so that the *'s* element is throughout a special clitic, not an affix. His reasons for treating the formative as a clitic and not an affix are essentially that there is rather little morphological idiosyncrasy in the construction, and the uncontroversial instances of it reside in the pronominal system. It must be conceded that pronouns often have special morphosyntax. In English, for instance, it is only pronouns that have special objective/subjective ('accusative/nominative') forms, a fairly typical picture with languages that have lost an earlier nominal case marking system. Like Payne and Huddleston, therefore, Anderson argues that we simply have to accept that the possessive pronouns are suppletive forms. Although he doesn't state the case in this way, we could liken the situation (for Anderson, though not for Payne and Huddleston) to instances of 'anti-periphrasis' noted by Haspelmath (2000), in which a construction that is normally expressed by a multiword expression is exceptionally expressed by an inflected form for a restricted class of words. The portmanteau preposition + determiner combinations of many European languages are a case in point, for instance, the French *de + le* 'of + the.DEF.MASC.SG' ⇒ *du*. One could also draw a comparison with the English reduced auxiliaries. As we have seen (Section 4.5.5) with pronominal hosts, these often appear not as clitics but as affixes triggering idiosyncratic allomorphy on their host: *you are* ⇒ *you're* ([jɔː]).

Anderson's approach rather than that of Payne and Huddleston seems closer to our analysis of European Portuguese pronominal clitics (Luís and Spencer 2005). The point of that analysis is that one and the same string of formatives can function now as a clitic string and now as an affix string depending on exactly what the host is.

An important point that emerges from this rather technical discussion is that it isn't possible to provide a proper account of the nature of edge inflection without a thoroughly explicit model of syntactic representations and an equally explicit model of the interface between morphological and syntactic representations. Unfortunately, linguists are far from agreed on relatively basic aspects of syntactic representation, and there is virtually no agreement on the morphology–syntax interface. It's therefore impossible for us to say anything definitive about these issues here. However, if it can be shown that there are clear-cut cases of edge inflection, then this ought to persuade syntacticians of the need to develop models that can accommodate it.

8.8.3   Edge inflection, phrasal affixation, head inflection

We conclude this discussion by reviewing and making explicit the conceptual issues that surround the notions of edge inflection and phrasal affixation. This is an area that still engenders a fair deal of confusion in the literature, irrespective of the technical details of specific grammatical frameworks.

First, we must distinguish edge inflection and phrasal affixation on the one hand from head affixation/inflection on the other hand. In head inflection it is the head of the phrase that undergoes some morphological process to realize a value of a particular feature. That feature value is then associated with the whole phrase. For instance, in the Russian example in (157) the head noun *girl* in the phrase *the girl in the black dress* is inflected for genitive case:

(157)   imja [devušk-i v čornom platje]
         name girl-GEN in black   dress
         'the name of the girl in the black dress'

Because the head of the phrase bears the possessive (genitive) feature, the whole phrase is also associated with the possessive property. Different syntactic theories have different ways of representing this fact.

It's important to realize that the role of the inflected head noun in the head inflection construction is to define the whole noun phrase as a possessor. The fact that it is the head of the phrase that is marked morphologically, as opposed to the first word, the last word or the edge of the first constituent of that noun phrase, is irrelevant to the rest of the syntax. This means that edge inflection/phrasal affixation differs from head inflection simply in the locus of the marked constituent within the phrase.

On the kind of analysis just presented, edge inflection differs from phrasal affixation in certain important respects. Phrasal affixation consists of applying some morphological process to the edge of a phrase. Typically, the process is that of adjoining some morphological element, the clitic. However, if we accept that 'morphological process' can include non-affixal processes such as changing a consonant or shifting an accent, then we can include constructions that alter the phonological make-up of the first/last word of a phrase. This is the position taken by Anderson (2005). On his view, the English possessive 's is an element added to the right edge of a noun phrase. This element then marks the whole phrase as expressing the feature [Possessor:Yes].

Edge inflection conceptualizes such constructions in a subtly different way. Any word in the language that is capable of ending a phrase of the relevant kind is assumed to inflect for the features expressed by the clitic. On this view, it isn't the noun phrase that inflects for possession, but rather the last word of any noun phrase. The [Possessor:Yes] feature value is then applied to the whole noun phrase. The difference between edge inflection and phrasal affixation therefore boils down to this. In phrasal affixation the whole phrase is regarded as the target of a morphological process. In edge inflection a designated word (e.g. the first/last word of the phrase) is inflected and the value of the inflectional feature is then associated with the phrase as a whole, in much the same way as with head inflection. In a sense, then, head inflection and edge inflection both specify a phrase for a feature value in an indirect way, through the inflectional properties of one of its constituent words. In phrasal affixation this specification is done directly.[44]

8.8.4   Persian ezafe as edge inflection

We turn now to the analysis of the Persian ezafe presented in Samvelian (2007) (page references are to that work unless otherwise noted). The ezafe marker -e/ye in Persian is an invariable marker attached to the right edge of the noun phrase. It marks any noun that is modified by an adjective or a possessor phrase. In (158) we see the head noun ketâb marked with ezafe so that it can be modified by the possessor phrase that man:

(158)   ketâb-e an mard
         book-EZ that man
         'that man's book'

The ezafe construction marks attributive modifiers, too (p. 608):

(159) a.   lebâs-e arusi
            dress-EZ wedding
            'wedding dress'

b.   lebâs-e   sefid
      dress-EZ white
      'white dress'

c.   lebâs-e   bi   âstin
      dress-EZ without sleeves
      'a sleeveless dress'

It is possible to have a sequence of such ezafe-marked modifiers:

(160)   lebâs-e   arusi-e   sefid-e   bi   âstin-e   maryam
           dress-EZ wedding-EZ white-EZ without sleeve-EZ Maryam
           'Maryam's white sleeveless wedding dress'

In some cases we obtain fairly complex dependency structures, as in (161)
(Ghomeshi 1997, 736):

(161)   otâq-e   kuchik-e zir-e   shirvuni-e ali
           room-EZ small-EZ under-EZ roof-EZ   Ali
           'Ali's small room under the roof'

The constituent structure implicit in example (161) is shown in (162). Note in
particular that the rightmost ezafe marker (on *shirvuni*) actually serves to link *ali*
'Ali' to *otâq* 'room'.

(162)   [[otâq-e   kuchik]-e [zir-e   shirvuni]]-e ali
           [[room-EZ small]-EZ [under-EZ roof]]-EZ   ali

   Samvelian discusses three edge inflections: the indefinite suffix *-i*, the possessor suffixes and the ezafe. The indefinite suffix *-i* is illustrated in (163):

(163)   lebâs-e   qermez-e bi   âstin-i
           dress-EZ red-EZ   without sleeve-INDEF
           'a red dress without sleeves' (p. 622)

The possessor agreements (PAF) are shown in (164):

(164)   Persian possessor agreements

	Singular	Plural
1	-am	-emân
2	-at	-etân
3	-aš	-ešân

Possessor agreement is illustrated in (165):

(165)   lebâs-e   sefid-e   bi   âstin-am
           dress-EZ white-EZ without sleeve-PAF.1SG
           'my white dress without sleeves' (p. 621)

These examples show that the possessor marker is found on the right edge of the
noun phrase, not on its noun head.

In many respects these behave like clitics rather than affixes. For instance, they show relatively few morphological or morphophonological idiosyncrasies and they take wide scope over conjoined phrases, as seen in (166) (p. 630):

(166) a.   [kolâh-e sefid(-aš)   va lebâs-e zard]-aš
            [hat-EZ white-(PAF.3SG) and dress-EZ yellow]-PAF.3SG
            'her/his white hat and yellow dress'

       b.   [kolâh-e sefid(-i)   va lebâs-e zard]-i
            [hat-EZ white-(INDEF) and dress-EZ yellow]-INDEF
            'a white hat and a yellow dress'

       c.   [kolâh-e sefid(*-e) va lebâs-e zard]-e   maryam
            [hat-EZ white-(EZ) and dress-EZ yellow]-EZ Maryam
            'Maryam's white hat and yellow dress'

(Intriguingly, the ezafe marker can take wide scope as in (166c) but it can't be repeated on conjuncts.)

However, each of the three affixes compete for a single slot on whatever word they are attached to, even if they would take different scopes. Samvelian (2007, 627) refers to this as 'haplology', though a better term for it would be 'position class competition'. Instead of stacking up in the way expected of (agglutinative) clitics, the edge inflections are in paradigmatic opposition occupying a single slot. She provides the paradigm in (167) (pp. 627–8):

(167) a.   xâne-ye digar-i
            house-EZ another-INDEF
            'another house'

       b.   xâne-i   digar
            house-INDEF another
            'another house'

       c.   * xâne-i-e/-e-i   digar
            house-INDEF-EZ/EZ-INDEF another
            (Intended: 'another house')

       d.   * xâne digari-i
            house another-INDEF
            (Intended: 'another house')

In (167a) we see a doubly marked phrase with the ezafe marker indicating that the head noun is modified and the indefinite marker appearing phrase-finally. In (167b) we see that the indefinite marker can appear on the head noun, in which case it excludes the ezafe marker, even though the head noun is still modified. Example (167c) shows that it is impossible to include both indefinite and ezafe markers on the head noun (in any order), while (167d) demonstrates that the ezafe is required on 'house' if its place isn't taken by the indefinite marker. This kind of slot competition is behaviour we expect of affixal systems, not clitic systems. Another telling minimal pair is illustrated by the behaviour of the two variant phrases with reduced relative clause (RRC) modifier in (168) (p. 629):

(168) a.   qahremân-e [_{RRC} az   mihan-aš   rânde šode]
           hero-EZ   from homeland-PAF.3SG driven AUX

    b.   qahremân-e [_{RRC} rânde šode az   mihan-aš]
           hero-EZ   driven AUX from homeland-PAF.3SG
           'the hero driven away from his homeland'

The relative clause in (168b) ends in a word that is marked with the possessor suffix, and this is sufficient to prevent that phrase as a whole from receiving the ezafe marker (169b). However, as we can see from (169a), the variant ending with an auxiliary participle can take the ezafe and thus the phrase in that form can serve as a modifier to *in roman* 'this novel':

(169) a.   qahremân-e [_{RRC} az   mihan-aš   rânde šode]-ye in roman
           hero-EZ   from homeland-PAF.3SG driven AUX-EZ this novel
           'the hero of this novel, (who is) driven away from his homeland'

    b.   * qahremân-e [_{RRC} rânde šode az   mihan-aš]-e   in roman
           hero-EZ   driven AUX from homeland-PAF.3SG-EZ this novel

    To see how Samvelian encodes edge inflection in HPSG, consider her example (170) (p. 635):

(170)   mojgân-e   az rimel   sangin-e maryam
        eyelid.PL-EZ of mascara heavy-EZ Maryam
        'Maryam's mascara-laden eyelids'

The analysis is illustrated in the tree shown in (171):

(171)

The feature DEP indicates that the constituent must be followed by some other (non-verbal) constituent. This feature is reminiscent of the DEP feature which

Sells (1995) appeals to in his HPSG analysis of Korean syntax. A set of syn-tactic constraints (pp. 642–3) require that a modified noun or a noun with a possessor complement is marked [DEP +] and that this feature value is inher-ited by higher projections of that head (the node marked N′[−EZ, +DEP] in (171)).

The effects of inserting lexical items into the syntactic structures made avail-able by the syntactic rules is indicated in (171) by the upwards arrows. Initially, all lexemes are taken to be negatively specified for the [EZ] feature. Two distinct ezafe marking rules come into play depending on whether we have head-marking ezafe or phrasal marking. When a head noun is in a modification relation in the syntax, ezafe rule (1) triggers ezafe inflection on that head noun. When a word is at the edge of a phrase that modifies a head noun (*az rimel sangin*), ezafe rule (2) applies to specify ezafe marking on the right edge of that phrase. The phrasal node labelled N′[−EZ, +DEP] in (171) has to end in an ezafe-marked word in order for all the syntactic constraints related to the [+DEP] specification to be satisfied.

In addition to the two ezafe suffixation rules, Samvelian assumes a morpho-logical function, F_{EZ}, which defines the form of the ezafe marker:

(172)   Morphophonological definition of ezafe marker

X	$F_{EZ}(X)$
X ending with vowel ≠ [i]	X-*ye*
Otherwise	X-*e*

The first ezafe suffixation rule, (173), defines the result of adding the ezafe suffix to a lexical head, as in examples (158) and (159):

(173)   ezafe suffixation rule (1)

$$
\begin{bmatrix} pl\text{-}nom\text{-}wd \\ \text{PHON}\,\boxed{1} \\ \text{CAT[DEP }-] \end{bmatrix}
\;\mapsto\;
\begin{bmatrix} ph\text{-}af\text{-}nom\text{-}wd \\ \text{PHON}\;F_{EZ}\!\left(\boxed{1}\right) \\ \text{CAT[DEP }+] \end{bmatrix}
$$

In (173) the type label *pl-nom-wd* means 'plain nominal word', while the type label *ph-af-nom-wd* means 'nominal word containing a phrasal affix'. The rule takes a word that has no phrasal affix and delivers the form defined by the F_{EZ} rule, while at the same time switching the value of the [DEP] feature, with the result that the ezafe-marked phrase is now defined syntactically as the kind of phrase that has to serve as a dependent of a modified noun.

The second ezafe rule is more complex. It defines the edge inflection function of ezafe when it is added to a non-head that happens to be at the right edge of the phrase:

(174)   ezafe suffixation rule (2)

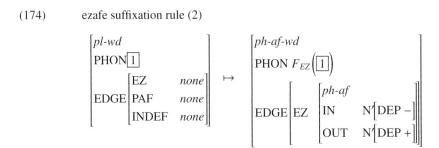

For the second ezafe rule, which applies within noun phrases, we see an additional attribute, EDGE, which takes as values the three types of edge inflection, ezafe (EZ), possessor agreement (PAF) and the indefinite marker (INDEF). This feature is propagated up the tree by means of a special feature-passing mechanism, the Edge Feature Principle (p. 638) which simply allows EDGE features to be propagated in much the same manner that head features are propagated up a tree. The two attributes IN, OUT refer to the input and output phrases: the input phrase has to be marked [DEP −] and the output phrase is marked [DEP +].

To summarize in oversimplified terms, what this analysis does is the following: for heads marked by ezafe the syntactic configuration merely requires that the ezafe rule (1) be applied to that head, to ensure that the constraints on [+DEP] marking on that head are satisfied. For the marking of edge inflection an EDGE feature is invoked, with three competing values, EZ, PAF, INDEF, each of which are themselves features. The positive value for the EZ feature is now a complex object which is satisfied by applying the F_{EZ} function to the rightmost word of a [−DEP] marked phrase to deliver a phrase marked [+DEP], which can therefore license an appropriate modifier or possessor complement.

8.9   Approaches to 2P clitics

We have seen that Optimality Theoretic approaches to 2P clitic placement account for Wackernagel positioning by postulating sets of conflicting alignment constraints, whose ranking determines the Wackernagel position to be the optimal position. In a morphological approach which does not deploy the machinery of OT there are various ways in which second position effects can be obtained, depending on what actually defines the anchor point for hosting the clitics. In principle, this could be a syntactically defined position, a prosodic unit or some combination of factors.

In this section we are looking principally at syntactic approaches to clitics. In general, we see that syntacticians propose either a purely syntactic definition of second position or propose a mixed system in which prosodic units play a role. In such a mixed system we have to be able to explain how the phonological and syntactic factors can interact with each other. There is a general assumption that phonology and syntax are distinct levels of representation and don't interface directly with each other. Rather, the interface is achieved by means of rules or principles that map syntactic structure onto prosodic structure (see the discussion of Prosodic Phonology in Chapter 4). But even when we have a way of defining prosodic structure and its relation to syntactic structure, we still need a way of ensuring that the prosodic structure can regulate clitic placement.

We will discuss two influential proposals for dealing with this problem. The first is a rule of Prosodic Inversion, proposed by Halpern (1995). The second is a response to those proposals from Bošković (2001).

8.9.1   Syntactic approaches to 2P

In a typical syntactic approach, 2P clitics are fronted and adjoined to some syntactic position containing phonologically overt material, such as the complementizer (Progovac 1996) position or the Specifier of the complementizer position (Spec, CP).

(175)

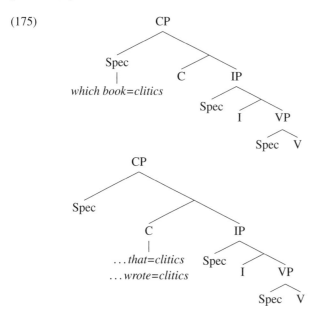

The main problem faced by such approaches is to find a principled way to account for the ordering of the clitics within the cluster, given that this ordering is generally entirely different from what we would expect given the rest of the syntax of the language. To a large extent this is a problem that is internal to the PPT class of models. We will return to some of the empirical difficulties with the purely syntactic approach when we discuss the arguments of Bošković in the next section.

8.9.2   Prosodically based approaches to 2P

Under the rubric of 'prosodic approaches' we will consider two rather different ways of looking at 2P clitics. In the first type of approach the claim is very simply that there is some kind of prosodic constituent at the beginning of the clause and this constituent serves as the (leftward) host for the clitic cluster. The challenge here is to find empirical (phonetic and phonological) evidence that the prosodic phrases do indeed exist and that the clitic cluster does indeed attach to just the first of them.

We have summarized the 'pure' version of the phonological approach to 2P placement above. This approach has not found wide favour with those who have looked at 2P positioning in detail. The problems of this approach can be illustrated with the case of Serbian/Croatian. Recall that 'second position' in this language can refer to either the first full syntactic phrase (other than a verb phrase) or to the first accented word. This leads to the suggestion that the clitic host can be defined in two ways: either the first phonological phrase (however that is best defined in Serbian/Croatian) or the first phonological word (which means the first word with an accented syllable that can in principle bear a tone). One problem with this formulation concerns prepositions. As might be expected a monosyllabic preposition such as *na* 'on' or *u* 'in' cannot be separated from its complement by the clitic cluster (Progovac 1996, 416):

(176) a.   Na sto=**ga** ostavi
              on table=it leave
              'Leave it on the table'

     b.   * Na=**ga** sto   ostavi
              on=it   table leave

This is easy to understand if we treat monosyllabic prepositions in these constructions as inherently accentless and hence unsuitable prosodic hosts for the clitic. However, there are prepositions that consist of two syllables, which cannot be regarded as unaccented. These are etymologically often derived from compound expressions (like the English 'beside' or 'against') but in the contemporary language they are clearly single words. However, even when contrastively stressed, as *prema* 'toward (+ dative case)' in (177), such a preposition is unable to host a clitic cluster (Progovac 1996, 417):

(177)   * Prema=**ga**=**je** Milanu   Marija bacila,
          toward=it=is Milan.DAT Marija threw
          a   ne od njega
          and not from him
          (Intended: 'Mary threw it toward Milan, not away from him')

The second sense in which prosody has been implicated in 2P placement relates to a proposal by Halpern (1995, chapter 2). Halpern argues that second-position clitics such as those of Serbian/Croatian are originally placed initially in their domain, that is, at the beginning of the clause, but that they then move minimally to the right until they are adjacent to a prosodically suitable host. This minimal movement is called Prosodic Inversion.

Halpern illustrates Prosodic Inversion for sentence (178), in which the first lexical word of the subject noun phrase *taj čovek* 'that man' serves as the host for the clitic *je*:

(178)   Taj=**je** čovek voleo Mariju
             that=is man   loved Marija
             'That man loved Marija'

Halpern proposes that the initial structure underlying (178) is (179):

(179)

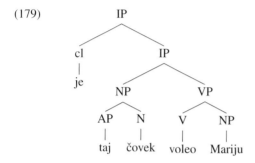

After Prosodic Inversion we obtain (180):

(180)

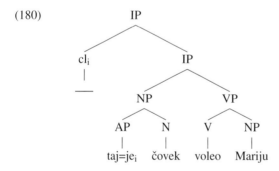

This accounts for 2W constructions. The explanation for the 2P construction, as seen in (181), is somewhat different.

(181)   Taj čovek=**je** voleo Mariju
             that man=is   loved Marija
             'That man loved Marija'

For the 2P type Halpern assumes that the phrase preceding the clitic cluster is placed by the syntax in sentence-initial position (in fact, in the position of Spec, CP) and that there is therefore no need for the cluster to move anywhere. The resulting structure is shown in (182):

(182)

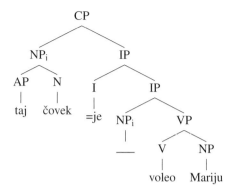

There are various problems with this way of looking at 2P phenomena, and Prosodic Inversion is not generally accepted as the neatest way of handling these facts. However, Halpern's proposal is descriptively useful in highlighting the problem and the essential features of the construction type.

A detailed set of alternative proposals is presented by Bošković (2001). Bošković examines a variety of theoretical approaches to the question of clitic placement in South Slavic languages, specifically Serbian/Croatian and Bulgarian/Macedonian. (His main focus in looking at Bulgarian/Macedonian is the positioning of the *li* interrogative clitic.)[45]

The main issues surrounding the Serbian/Croatian clitics are the following:

- Granted that the clitics tend to cluster in 'second position' in their clause, how do we define 'second position'?
- Granted that clitics tend to cluster together in a set order and without being separated, how do we account for this inseparability and this fixed order?

In addressing these issues Bošković argues that there are basically four different types of approach possible to such second-position clitics. In principle this typology is valid whatever syntactic model we presuppose, though Bošković only discusses their implications for the Minimalist Program. The approaches are summarized here:

- Strong Syntax: clitic placement is determined entirely by principles of syntax (most Minimalist approaches to clitics).
- Strong Phonology: clitic placement is determined entirely by principles of phonology (e.g. Radanović-Kocić 1996, Hock 1996).
- Weak Syntax: Wackernagel clitics are placed in domain-initial position and then moved after the first word/phrase in the phonology by Prosodic Inversion (Halpern 1995).
- Weak Phonology: clitics are placed by syntactic principles but some outputs correspond to phonological forms that violate phonological well-formedness conditions. Thus, the phonology has passive, filtering function over those outputs.

It is the last type of model that Bošković opts for. He argues that the Strong
Syntax models are unable to account for the full variety of patterns of clitic
placement and that they are unable to account for the demonstrable fashion in
which prosodic phrasing affects the acceptability of clitic placement. The argumentation is subtle and worth considering in some detail (see Bošković 1995 for
the basic argument and Anderson 2005, 120 for a brief summary).

Like many languages, Serbian/Croatian has adverbs that get different interpretations depending on whether they are taken to modify just the verb phrase or the
whole clause. In some cases, just as in English, we can construct sentences that
are ambiguous with respect to the two readings, as in (183) (Bošković 1995, 40):

(183)   Jovan **je**   pravilno odgovorio   Mileni
            Jovan 3SG.AUX correctly answered.LPART Milena

            a. 'Jovan gave Milena a correct answer (= [Jovan [answered Milena cor-
            rectly]])'

            b. 'Jovan did the right thing in answering Milena (= [correctly [Jovan
            [answered Milena]]])'

In the (a) interpretation the adverb has VP scope while in the (b) interpretation it
has sentence-scope.

Following Slavicist tradition, we have labelled the main verb form *odgovorio*
as 'l-participle', because the final *-o* alternates with *-l* in feminine and plural
forms. The relative positioning of the l-participle form and the adverb is crucial
for interpretation. In (184) we see that the adverb comes after the verb rather than
before it. The result is that the sentence-scope reading is no longer available:

(184)   Jovan **je**   odgovorio   pravilno Mileni
            Jovan 3SG.AUX answered.LPART correctly Milena

            a. 'Jovan gave Milena a correct answer'

            b. *'Jovan did the right thing in answering Milena'

The same patterning is found when the subject is omitted and the main verb
appears in initial position:

(185)   Odgovorio   **je**   pravilno Mileni
            answered.LPART 3SG.AUX correctly Milena

            a. 'He gave Milena a correct answer'

            b. *'He did the right thing in answering Milena'

Bošković also argues that a purely phonological account can't work because
there are constructions that ought to be identical phonologically but that behave
differently with respect to clitic placement.

On the face of it, there might seem little difference between positing a 'weak
syntactic' and a 'weak phonological' model. However, what Bošković means by
'weak syntactic' model is crucially a model that permits phonological operations
to reorder syntactic elements. This is considered to be an unacceptable 'mixing
of levels' (to echo the American Structuralists). The understandable desire is

to maintain a maximally simple and mechanical view of syntax and to account for idiosyncratic variability elsewhere in the system. Principles of phonology are supposed to establish what is pronounceable. We should therefore no more expect phonological rules to reorder syntactic elements than we would expect syntactic rules to specify the pronunciation of a word or phrase. Permitting phonological rules to reorder words and phrases is thus a kind of category error.

The other difference, in Bošković's typology, between the weak syntactic and the weak phonological approach is that the weak syntactic approaches generally need to provide a unitary definition of the intermediate and ultimate positions of clitics. For instance, it is often assumed that clitics cluster in the same kind of position in which verbs appear in a verb-second language such as German. This is often taken to be the 'C' or 'Complementizer' position, preceded by a speci-fier phrase (which then functions as the host for the clitics). However, Bošković offers a number of arguments from Serbian/Croatian to show that there simply is no unitary position for clitics.

We can see how this model is supposed to work by considering some sim-ple examples from the pronominal clitic systems of Bulgarian and Macedonian. Recall that in Bulgarian the clitics are found most commonly sandwiched between the first phrase of the domain (the clause in the case of pronominals) and the verb group (that is, the main verb preceded, if appropriate, by non-clitic auxiliary verbs). In Macedonian, on the other hand, the clitics always precede the (finite) verb even if that verb is in sentence-initial position. Bošković assumes that clitics originate in a lower phrase position next to their verb and that various movements take place to the left (i.e. upwards). The term 'movement', how-ever, is misleading in the Minimalist Program, because the effects of movement are achieved in two independent stages: first an element lower down the tree is copied in a higher position, as often as necessary. Then (sometimes) the origi-nal element and some or all of these copies get deleted. However, exactly which copies get deleted (if any) depends on various language-specific factors.

Consider the Bulgarian and Macedonian expressions in (186):

(186) a.   Dade **mi**   **go**
              gave to.me it
              'S/he gave it to me' [Bulgarian]
    b.   **Mi**   **go** dade
              to.me it gave
              'S/he gave it to me' [Macedonian]

Bošković assumes that such expressions are built up by taking a verb and build-ing a VP, then merging this with a functional head housing the direct object pronominal, *go*, AGRdoP: [$_{\text{AGRdoP}}$ *go* [$_{\text{VP}}$ *dade*]]. Then, the verb is copied under the AGRdoP node: [$_{\text{AGRdoP}}$ *go+dade* [$_{\text{VP}}$ *dade*]]. This phrase is then merged with the indirect object pronominal under the phrase AGRioP: [$_{\text{AGRioP}}$ *mi* [$_{\text{AGRdoP}}$ *go+dade* [$_{\text{VP}}$ *dade*]]], after which the AGRdoP is copied under the AGRioP node.

This gives the structure (187) for both languages:

(187)   [$_{AGRioP}$ *mi+go+dade* [$_{AGRdoP}$ *go+dade* [$_{VP}$ *dade*]]]

For Macedonian this is sufficient because we can now delete the unwanted copies
and obtain:

(188)   [$_{AGRioP}$ *mi+go+dade*[$_{AGRdoP}$ ~~*go+dade*~~[$_{VP}$ ~~*dade*~~]]]
                = mi go dade

For Bulgarian we need to assume that the whole phrase is copied again to give

(189)   [$_{AGRioP}$ *mi+go+dade* [$_{AGRioP}$ *mi+go+dade* [$_{AGRdoP}$ *go+dade* [$_{VP}$ dade]]]]

By deleting those copies that violate the phonological principles of Bulgarian
we obtain the characteristic Tobler–Mussafia element order:

(190)   ~~*Mi + go*~~+*dade* [$_{AGRioP}$ *mi+go+dade*[$_{AGRdoP}$ ~~*go+dade*~~[$_{VP}$ ~~*dade*~~]]]
                = dade mi go

Bošković writes (2001, 185), "Since the pronunciation of the highest copies of
the pronominal clitic would lead to a PF violation, the clitics are pronounced in
a lower position". This means that there is no need for Prosodic Inversion or for
rightward syntactic movement.

To account for the Serbian/Croatian type of Wackernagel patterning Bošković
assumes a general principle which states that clitics have to occur in the second position within their Intonational Phrase (p. 65). Recall that the Intonational
Phrase is the highest of the phonological domains of Prosodic Phonology (Nespor and Vogel 1986). This is the phonological unit over which intonation patterns
are defined. For example, when a phrase or sentence is interrupted by a parenthetical expression, that expression defines a new Intonational Phrase. The portions
of the utterance that it interrupts are therefore Intonational Phrases themselves.
For instance, a simple sentence such as *Mary likes olives* will normally be
pronounced as a single Intonational Phrase. However, when we interrupt the
utterance with a parenthetical phrase such as *as far as I know*, both *Mary* and
likes olives have their own intonational contours and each defines a separate
Intonational Phrase:

(191)   ($_I$ Mary) ($_I$ as far as I know) ($_I$ likes olives)

Bošković uses examples such as these in Serbian/Croatian to justify his claim
that the Intonational Phrase is a crucial part of the explanation of second-position
placement.

Szczegielniak (2005) applies Bošković's notion of a phonological filter
('phonological buffer') to the placement of auxiliary clitics in Polish (the
so-called floating inflections). Recall, too, that the role of prosodic phrases has
also been stressed for an entirely different language, the Austronesian language
Chamorro, by Chung (2003).

8.10   Clitic doubling

In this section we investigate the way that clitic doubling has been handled in PPT accounts, an early topic of debate in PPT treatments of clitics.[46]

In the earlier generative literature on clitics, as represented particularly by Kayne (1975), it was largely taken for granted that clitics are pronouns that originate in the same position with respect to the verb as any other argument and that they are moved to their special positions by syntactic rules. In part, no doubt, this assumption arose because Kayne was principally interested in French, which disallows clitic doubling. However, it was later noticed that certain dialects of Spanish permitted the kind of clitic doubling in which the clitic takes on very much the appearance of an agreement element (for instance, Jaeggli 1982). It was also observed that, in general, Spanish requires the doubling full noun phrase to be marked by a preposition *a* 'to'. This led to the so-called 'Kayne–Jaeggli Generalization', that such doubling is only possible when the doubling noun phrase receives 'case' from a preposition. The facts of Greek (Anagnostopoulou 1999), Macedonian (Lyons 1999), Pirahã (Everett 1987), the Porteño dialect of Spanish (Suñer 1988) and Yagua (Everett 1989) demonstrated that the Kayne–Jaeggli Generalization is false, given normal PPT assumptions about such pronominal systems. In some cases doubling depends on obscure semantic properties of referentiality/specificity/topicalization or whatever, but Balkan languages such as Macedonian and Romanian are particularly damaging to the 'generalization', since in those languages indirect objects with specific interpretation are obligatorily doubled by clitics.

Subsequent research explored the possibility that in such cases the doubling noun phrases are not really arguments of the verb, but are rather adjuncts, somewhat in the manner of dislocated phrases such as *that man* in *I've seen him before, that man*. However, Anagnostopoulou (1999) presents evidence that this could not be the whole story for Greek, for instance. She argues that doubled noun phrases are genuine arguments when definite but that they are indeed dislocated phrases when they are indefinite.

Clitic doubling thus remains a thorn in the side of syntactically based analysis of clitic constructions: on the one hand clitics seem to be in complementary distribution with overt argument phrases and on the other hand they sometimes appear as agreement-like elements, tightly linked to a doubling argument phrase. An influential account of clitics that aims at 'squaring the circle' is that of Sportiche (1996). He claims that it is possible to develop a model in which clitics are both base-generated and undergo movement. The reason why movement is necessary in Sportiche's model is that the dependency between a clitic and a phrase that it is associated with often has restrictions reminiscent of those dependencies generally analysed as movement. For instance, in French it is not possible to strand a preposition in a *wh*-question construction:

(192) a.   Jean a   voté pour Maastricht
            Jean has voted for   Maastricht
            'Jean voted for Maastricht'
      b.   * Quel traité Jean a-t-il voté pour
            which treaty Jean has-he voted for
            (Intended:'Which treaty has Jean voted for?')

Similarly, it is not possible for a clitic pronoun to 'strand' a preposition:

(193) a.   Jean a   voté pour lui
            Jean has voted for   him
            'Jean voted for him'
      b.   * Jean **lui**   a   voté pour
            Jean him.CL has voted for
            (Intended:'Jean voted for him')

Interestingly, it is possible to have a sentence-final preposition when the object of the preposition is interpreted generically: *Jean a voté pour* 'Jean voted "for"'.

Sportiche argues that we should assume that clitics head their own projections (which he refers to as Clitic Voices, with a different voice for each 'case', nominative, accusative, dative and so on). The basic structure is conveniently represented by Anagnostopoulou (1999, 779) as (194) for an 'accusative case' clitic:

(194)

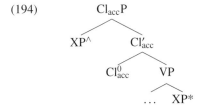

The XP* is the argument phrase that the clitic Cl^0_{acc} has a dependency with (and in some cases may double). That XP* has to move to the Specifier position of $Cl_{acc}P$, $XP^\wedge$, because the dependency has to be expressed as a Specifier-Head relationship in this type of model. The fact that movement is required for all clitics captures the fact that the dependencies shown by the clitic obey similar restrictions to those of, say, *wh*-phrases and their dependents. In languages that show genuine clitic doubling, the XP* can be overt. In those that do not permit doubling, the XP* has to be covert (it is not immediately apparent to us how this restriction is guaranteed). In the surface structure of clitic-doubled expressions the XP* is generally in the position expected of such arguments. This means that it has to move to the $XP^\wedge$ position covertly, at 'Logical Form' (LF).[47]

Much of the debate concerning clitic doubling centres around the question of whether we are dealing with a type of agreement or not. As we saw in Chapter 6, agreement systems that look uncontroversially affixal can sometimes show restrictions that are reminiscent of those operating on clitic doubling systems. Formal frameworks therefore sometimes propose representations that

allow us to treat pronominal clitics as having some of the properties of full pronouns and some of the properties of agreement markers. Cardinaletti and Starke
(1999, 169), for instance, claim that it is only their class of clitics that permit doubling, not the weak or the Strong pronouns. We saw above how Sadler proposes
to treat the doubling of the Welsh clitics by an overt pronominal by permitting
the clitic to have a PRED value (making it akin to a weak or Strong pronoun)
but optionally. Where it lacks the PRED value it lacks the potential to show
the kinds of semantic properties associated with Strong(er) pronominals and full
noun phrases.

A rather different proposal is presented by Uriagereka (2000). Clitic doubling in Spanish is somewhat similar in its semantic import to the much more
widespread clitic doubling found in Balkan languages such as Macedonian and
Albanian discussed in Chapter 6. In Spanish, too, the clitic that doubles a noun
phrase induces a fully referential reading, ruling out the doubling of indefinites, quantified phrases or question words, and also ruling out interpretations
that involve 'attributive' reference in the sense of Donnellan (1966) (Uriagereka
2000, 414):[48]

(195) a.   **Lo/le**   ve a tu   hermano?
            3SG.M.ACC/DAT see to your brother
            'Can he see your brother?'

     b.   * **Lo/le**   ve a un hermano de Juan?
            3SG.M.ACC/DAT see to a   brother of Juan's
            (Intended: 'Can he see a brother of Juan's?')

(196) a.   No **lo/le**   ve a Juan?
            Not 3SG.M.ACC/DAT see to Juan
            'Can't he see Juan?'

     b.   * No **lo/le**   ve a nadie?
            Not 3SG.M.ACC/DAT see to nobody
            (Intended: 'Can't he see anybody?')

(197) a.   A Juan **lo/le**   ve
            To Juan 3SG.M.ACC/DAT see
            'Juan, he sees'

     b.   * A quién **lo/le**   ve?
            To whom 3SG.M.ACC/DAT see
            (Intended: 'Who does he see?')

     c.   No **lo/le**   conozco   al   asesino de Smith
            Not 3SG.M.ACC/DAT know/meet to-the murderer of Smith
            (With doubling) 'I am not acquainted with Smith's murderer'

     d.   No conozco   al   asesino de Smith
            Not know/meet to-the murderer of Smith
            (Without doubling) 'I do not know whoever Smith's murderer is'

Uriagereka argues that there is an intrinsic relation between clitic doubling (in
Spanish, at least) and inalienable possession. He proposes (p. 412) the principle
in (198) (which he introduces, disarmingly, as "a leap of faith"):

(198)   The Inalienable Double Hypothesis (IDH): All doubles stand in an inalienable possession relation with regards to the referent of the clitic they double.

Thus, the sentence (199), in which the clitic *la* doubles the full pronoun *ella* (with the preposition *a* 'to'), is interpreted as something along the lines of 'Juan saw her persona':

(199)   Juan **la** vio a ella/a mi madre
          Juan her saw to her/to my mother
          'Juan saw her/my mother'

Uriagereka argues that his IDH entails the facts about referentiality seen above. If the doubling clitic is elliptical for 'someone's (inalienably possessed) persona', then that expression must strictly refer. He presents some interesting examples of the failure of such strict reference. In (200) we see an example in which the expression *a mi madre* 'my mother' does not actually refer to the speaker's mother as such. Outside of contexts of hallucination, a sentence such as this cannot be taken to mean that the speaker actually sees some representation of his/her mother, but rather that the addressee resembles the speaker's mother in some respect:

(200)   Al   ver**te**   a ti, vi   a mi madre en tu   sonrisa
          at.the seeing.you to you I.saw to my mother in your smile
          'Upon seeing you, I saw my mother in your smile'

A resemblance reading of this sort is impossible with clitic doubling in those dialects of Spanish that permit doubling of a whole noun phrase:[49]

(201)   Juan **la** vio a mi madre (#en tu   sonrisa)
          Juan her saw to my mother in   your smile
          'Juan saw my mother (in your smile)'

With the adjunct 'in your smile' the sentence becomes bizarre, because it can only be interpreted as referring directly in some sense to the speaker's mother.

Intriguing though Uriagereka's observations are, it is difficult to see what generality they might have beyond Spanish. He himself starts from the observation that clitics are pronominal elements and that pronominals have certain properties in common with determiners such as definite articles (p. 406). Indeed, in Romance languages both elements are generally derived from the same set of (emphatic) demonstrative pronouns/adjectives in Vulgar Latin. But it is not necessary for a language to have parallel definite articles and doubling clitics: in Macedonian and Bulgarian, for instance, the definite article system has developed from an entirely different set of demonstratives from the pronouns. The clitics involved in doubling in Welsh seem to have nothing to do with the definite article in that language. It is not even necessary for a language to have a determiner system to show clitic doubling: Pirahã, for instance, has no articles. Moreover, as we saw in Chapter 6, the precise details of clitic doubling differ considerably even for closely related languages or dialects (such as Macedonian/Bulgarian), and those facts are only imperfectly mirrored in any of the varieties of Spanish that Uriagereka discusses.

8.11   Clitic climbing

8.11.1   Complex predicates and clitic climbing

We pointed out in Chapter 6 that the phenomenon of clitic climbing has been taken to provide proof that a syntactic analysis of clitics is required. Since the clitic is in complementary distribution with an overt noun phrase such as *il libro*, the argument runs, it must have moved from the position of direct object of the lower verb to its higher position. That argument was undermined, of course, by the fact that the 'climbing' phenomenon isn't exclusive to clitics. As we saw in Section 6.3, languages may exhibit 'long-distance agreement', in which the same construction is found as in (66b) but with unequivocally affixal morphology. Moreover, there are now numerous analyses of clitic climbing (also applicable, of course, to agreement climbing) that do not involve movement of an argument clitic pronoun to a higher clause. In such analyses the clitic placement rules are able to make more or less direct reference to the complex predicate. For instance, in LFG we can say that a complex predicate is formed at f-structure or at an argument structure level of representation, independently of its instantiation in phrasal syntax (c-structure) (see, for instance, Alsina 1997 and Matsumoto 1998 for discussion). Below we will briefly sketch a typical HPSG analysis.[50] The value of selecting such an analysis is that it is relatively explicit about the structures involved. In many respects, however, the same leading ideas are deployed by all frameworks that broach the issue of clitic climbing.

Monachesi (2005, 139) notes that a number of syntactic structures have been proposed for auxiliary constructions in European languages. The standard assumption, still current in Minimalist analyses, has been that the auxiliary is a higher functional head which takes the lexical verb phrase (or the phrase headed by the next auxiliary down) as its complement. This is shown schematically in (202):

(202)

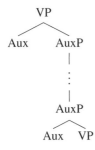

For Romanian, however, Monachesi notes that the auxiliaries behave rather differently from those in other Romance languages. For French and Italian, for instance, it makes sense to adopt a flat (phrase structure) structure for the auxiliary + lexical verb complex (Abeillé and Godard 2002):

(203)   VP

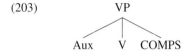

          Aux   V   COMPS

In Romanian the auxiliary forms a much tighter unit with the lexical verb. For example, it can only be separated by one of five monosyllabic adverbs, *mai* 'again', *cam* 'little', *prea* 'very/too much', *şi* 'also/already', *tot* 'still' (Monachesi 2005, 175), while in other Romance languages the auxiliary can be freely separated from the lexical verb. In fact, the auxiliaries appear to be clitics, hosted by the lexical verb. Monachesi (2005, 159) cites the examples in (204) as instantiating two types of clitic cluster:

(204) a.   Să nu **o**   mai fi văzut
           that not ACC.CL again be seen
           'That I should not have seen her again'
     b.   Nu **l**   ar   mai fi întrebat
           not ACC.CL would again be asked
           'He wouldn't have asked him again'

The cluster can be summarized as having the form

(205)   COMPLEMENTIZER < NEGATION < PRONOUN < AUX1 < ADV <
         AUX2

However, Monachesi (2005, 147) argues that in fact we should assume a syntactic structure in which the auxiliary and the lexical verb form a constituent:

(206)   VP

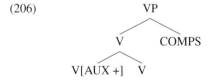

          V   COMPS

    V[AUX +]   V

She then argues that the non-auxiliary clitics are prefixed to the auxiliary.[51]

   Monachesi begins her discussion of Restructuring verbs with a summary of Rizzi's (1982b) influential paper on the subject. Rizzi shows that in structures where a clitic has climbed to a higher predicate, it is no longer possible for certain syntactic processes to target the infinitival complement on its own. For instance, Rizzi (1982b, 7) notes the contrasts in (207):

(207) a.   Questi argomenti, dei quali ti   verrò   a parlare
            these topics,   about which to.you.CL I.will.come to speak
                al più presto ...
                as soon as possible

'These topics, about which I will come to talk with you as soon as possible ...'

b.   Questi argomenti, a parlar=ti   dei   quali verrò
       these   topics,   to speak=to.you.CL about which I.will.come

       al più presto ...
       as soon as possible

       [Lit.] 'These topics, to talk with you about which I will come as soon as
       possible ...'

c.   * Questi argomenti, a parlar dei   quali ti=verrò
       these   topics,   to speak about which to.you.CL=I.will.come

       al più presto ...
       as soon as possible

In (207a) we have an ordinary relative clause beginning with the wh-phrase *dei quali*. In (207b) we see that it is possible to front the infinitival complement along with the wh-phrase (so-called 'Pied-piping'). However, (207c) shows that Pied-piping the infinitive is impossible if *ti*, the clitic pronoun complement of *parlare*, has climbed up to the matrix verb of the subordinate clause, *verrò*. Rizzi points out that these contrasts can be understood if we assume that the complex, restructured predicate *ti verrò a parlare*, with the clitic attached to the matrix verb, forms a single constituent. This will mean that we have the following underlying (initial) structures for (207a, b):

(208) a.   Questi argomenti, [s verrò [a parlarti dei quali] ...]

      b.   Questi argomenti, [s [ti verrò a parlarti] dei quali ...]

Clearly, in (208b) the string *a parlarti dei quali* fails to form a constituent, so it can't be Pied-piped. Rizzi identifies a number of other syntactic processes which likewise demonstrate that *a parlarti dei quali* is not a constituent.

Monachesi (2005, 223) proposes a flat phrase structure for the clitic climbing structures, and a hierarchical one for the structures in which the clitic remains in situ:

(209)   Phrase structure for Restructuring and non-Restructuring constructions

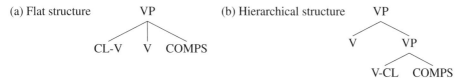

(a) Flat structure   VP   (b) Hierarchical structure   VP

          CL-V   V   COMPS   V   VP

                                                   V-CL   COMPS

Restructuring verbs have a different lexical representation from non-restructuring verbs, in that they show argument composition. This is a device frequently used in HPSG analyses to permit an auxiliary or a higher matrix verb to express some or all of the arguments of one of its dependent predicates. In

(210) we see a highly oversimplified representation of the sort of feature structure that is used to represent argument composition:

$$(210) \quad \text{volere:} \begin{bmatrix} \text{SUBJ} \\ \text{COMP} & \left\langle \begin{bmatrix} \text{SUBJ} \\ \text{COMP} \boxed{1} \end{bmatrix} \right\rangle \oplus \boxed{1} \end{bmatrix}$$

This representation states that the verb VOLERE has a subject and a (clausal) complement. When the clausal complement itself has a complement that complement is appended to the list of complements of the VOLERE itself. This is indicated by the $\oplus$ operator which appends the COMP argument labelled $\boxed{1}$ to the list of COMPs of VOLERE. For the use of VOLERE in which no clitic climbing has taken place, and hence no Restructuring, we would simply have a standard entry without the argument sharing, as in (211):

$$(211) \quad \text{volere:} \begin{bmatrix} \text{SUBJ} \\ \text{COMP} & \begin{bmatrix} \text{SUBJ} \\ \text{COMP} \end{bmatrix} \end{bmatrix}$$

The restructured representation can now be subjected to the Complement Cliticization Lexical Rule (122) described earlier in connection with Romanian. The result will be that the clitic complements of the infinitival verb will appear as complements of the Restructuring verb.

8.12   Clitic cluster ordering

As we have seen, a characteristic feature of many clitic systems is that the clitics are placed in a set order with respect to each other, even in languages with otherwise very free word order. In this respect, clitics most resemble morphological elements (affixes). To many linguists the relative ordering of clitics demonstrates that we are dealing with a largely morphologized system, in which there may be at best typologically mandated tendencies governing the ordering but which otherwise represents idiosyncratic systems that just have to be memorized and can't be derived from deeper principles of organization. For other linguists, however, the idiosyncratic nature of clitic ordering is an intellectual challenge spurring various ingenious proposals for deriving the ordering from more general principles. In a morphologically oriented approach, clitic order is no more or less problematic than affix order. In a syntactically oriented approach, clitic order can pose serious descriptive problems whether or not the analyst is able to propose general principles to account for the ordering. This is because the linearization principles that govern the ordering of clitic pronominals, clitic auxiliary verbs and other clitic elements are usually completely different from those governing otherwise very similar non-clitic pronominals, full-form auxiliary verbs and so on.

A full discussion of how ordering is achieved in different theoretical frameworks would require a separate monograph in itself, and a full survey of the proposals found in the literature would require us to present a historical survey of recent theories of syntax (this is particularly so of PPT models, which have changed radically over the past three decades and in which there is rather little consensus about a number of relevant technical issues). We will therefore just briefly sketch the kinds of approach that are possible in these models without discussing any details.

One of the earliest works within the generative framework to address the question of clitic ordering seriously is the study on Spanish clitic clusters by Perlmutter (1971) (see also Perlmutter 1970). In the model of syntax that was dominant at the time of his study it was generally assumed that a sentence was built up from a Deep Structure representation, which abstracted away from much of the detail realized by inflections and function words, and which was transformed into a Surface Structure by means of syntactic transformations. Perlmutter argued that this machinery was insufficient to account for the clitic system of Spanish. That system is very similar in many respects to the clitic system of Italian, in that the clitics form a cluster, with clitics occurring in particular positions in the cluster depending on the properties that they realize.

Perlmutter therefore argued that the syntactic component of the grammar should be enriched with a filter in the form of a template, and a set of statements regulating the order in which clitics are allowed to occur. For standard Spanish that template is (with typical examples):

(212)   Perlmutter's (1971) clitic template for Spanish

REFL	I	II	III.DAT	III.ACC
se	me	te	le	lo

Perlmutter then noted that a variety of cluster-specific alterations are required to generate precisely the right set of clitics. In particular, some of the expected combinations fail to appear, as we noted in our discussion of Monachesi's analysis of Italian in Chapter 5. For instance, in a number of languages a 1st/2nd person direct object (accusative) clitic cannot precede a 3rd person indirect object (dative) clitic, a prohibition Perlmutter calls the *me lui constraint, after one of the prohibited sequences in French. Similarly, certain combinations of clitics give rise to allomorphic variants. The expected sequence for 3SG.M.ACC+3SG.M.DAT would be le lo, but this is not possible in Spanish. In that sequence the first clitic is replaced by an allomorph that is homophonous with the reflexive to give se lo. Perlmutter refers to this as the 'Spurious-se rule'. We have already seen very similar allomorphic alternations (presumably motivated by the need to avoid phonological assonance in various degrees) in Italian (*ci ci ⇒ vi ci) and Serbian/Croatian (*je je ⇒ ju je).

The idea of a template describing the behaviour of clitic clusters has been widely adopted by linguists working in a variety of traditions. It is advocated in an influential paper by Simpson and Withgott (1986). They explicitly compare the clitic cluster templates required for Romance languages and for certain Australian languages such as Warlpiri with the position class templates that are sometimes proposed for describing affix sequences in languages such as Navajo. The filter idea also lies behind the analysis of clitic sequences in Catalan by Bonet (1991), working within a PPT framework, and templates or position classes are essentially what are being described by Optimality Theoretic approaches such as those of Anderson (2005) or Legendre (1996, 2000a, 2000b, 2001).

However, the idea of a surface template, with positive or negative restrictions, is not generally accepted by practitioners of PPT syntax, where the overriding concern appears to be to find a purely derivational syntactic explanation for all morphosyntactic patterning. As a consequence, the order of grammatical elements in PPT models is determined by constituent structure. Syntactic constituents are either non-branching or binary branching. The order of functional elements (including clitics) is determined first by the order in which functional elements are 'merged' with another c-structure tree in the course of syntactic derivation. The higher an element is in a tree the further to the left it will appear in surface structure, all else being equal. However, syntactic structures are subject to various 'displacements', which are generally handled by permitting certain elements lower in the tree to move to the left and adjoin to elements higher in the tree. This will then mean that the position of the moved element will be further to the left in linearized structure. The movement of such an element is triggered by the presence of an 'uninterpretable feature' on that element. Such a feature has to be 'checked' against a similar feature on the host to which the element adjoins. A further complication is that the morphological component (usually taken to be some form of Distributed Morphology, Halle and Marantz 1993) is also able to effect shifts in linear order, as we saw in our sketch of Noyer's (2001) discussion of Nunggubuyu.

By the judicious deployment of uninterpretable features it is possible to describe a considerable variety of clitic cluster types. One important feature of such analyses is that they make absolutely no appeal to the notion of a clitic cluster itself. The cluster effects, together with the overall placement of the cluster (e.g. as a verb-oriented cluster in Romance languages, or as a Wackernagel cluster in Slavic) is determined by the complex interaction of basic syntactic structure and the individual movement of individual functional heads. Mixed clitic/affix systems such as that of European Portuguese therefore pose a particularly interesting challenge to such models (see Costa 2000 for a number of papers discussing Portuguese clitics).

A particularly troubling case is that of South Slavic auxiliary clitics: as we saw in Chapter 3 in Serbo-Croat and Bulgarian the auxiliary clitic (forms of the present tense of the verb BE) occupy leftmost position in the clitic cluster, with the exception of the 3rd singular form, which occupies the rightmost position. (In Macedonian, both 3rd singular and 3rd plural forms occupy the rightmost position. As Franks and King (2000, 211) point out, it is a striking peculiarity of Slavic auxiliary clitics that either they are null forms or the 3sg form occupies the rightmost position in the cluster.) This problem is addressed in detail by Bošković (2001). He handles the problem of the aberrant placement of the 3sg auxiliary clitic in Serbian/Croatian by arguing that, in fact, its 'real' position is with the other auxiliary clitics, at the left of the cluster. In his terms this means that it is placed 'high' in the tree structure that represents the clause. The evidence he adduces for this conclusion is based on ellipsis phenomena, as discussed in Stjepanović (1998). As in many languages (such as English), it is possible to elide repeated material in the verb phrase of the second conjunct of a coordinated clause:

(213)   Ona **mu**   **ga je**   predstavila, a   i   on **je**
             She to.him him AUX.3SG introduced and also he AUX.3SG
             ~~**mu ga** predstavila~~
             (to.him him introduced)
             'She introduced him to him, and he did too'

As we can see, the elided material includes the two pronominal clitics and the lexical verb from the first conjunct. What is not possible is to elide the lexical verb together with the auxiliary clitic, leaving behind the two pronominals:

(214)   *Ona **mu**   **ga je**   predstavila, a   i   on **mu**   **ga**
             She   to.him him AUX.3SG introduced and also he to.him him
             ~~**je** predstavio~~
             (AUX.3SG introduced)
             (Intended: 'She introduced him to him, and he did too')

Bošković remarks (p. 127), "The data in <(214)> clearly show that *je* must be higher than pronominal clitics in the syntax". He proposes shortly afterwards the following (p. 130): "Suppose now that there is a low level constraint on the final PF representation requiring that in a clitic cluster, *je* must follow all other clitics". This illustrates one of the principal problems with syntactically based analyses of these sorts (albeit in the case of Bošković one that is supplemented by appeal to prosodic structuring). It is extremely difficult to state such 'PF' conditions on clitics without appealing to the notion of 'clitic', and yet such a notion is, *ex hypothesi*, more or less impossible to reconstruct if clitics are mere epiphenomena, as is assumed by Bošković and many others. Analyses of this kind run a serious risk, therefore, of falling into circularity.[52]

Franks (2008, 112–17) addresses the problem of the 3rd person auxiliary clitic placement in Bulgarian, offering a number of criticisms of Bošković's proposals (some of them admittedly aesthetic and/or theory internal[53]). He proposes instead a purely syntactic account of the placement of the 3rd person auxiliary. While other auxiliaries appear in the 'subject agreement' position AgrS, as in (215a), the 3rd person form (which in Bulgarian is *e*), appears under the Tense head, T, as shown in (215b).

(215)   a.   AgrS'   b.   AgrS'

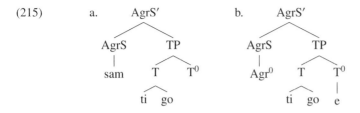

Modest empirical support for this analysis is provided by those rare occasions in Bulgarian in which a small adverb such as *už* 'maybe' or *več* 'already' can be interpolated in the clitic cluster. Such elements may not break up a string of pronominal clitics (216b), though they can split the auxiliary clitic from the pronominals as in (216a) and they can split the whole cluster from the lexical verb (Franks 2008, 116):[54]

(216) a.   Az **săm**   už   **ti**   **go** dala
           I   AUX.1SG maybe to.you it   given
      b.   * Az **săm ti** už **go** dala
      c.   Az **săm ti go** už dala
           'I have maybe given it to you (reportedly)'

However, such elements are unable to split the pronominal clitics from the cluster-final 3rd person auxiliary:

(217) a.   * Tja **ti**   už   **go e**   dala
            she to.you maybe it   AUX.3SG given
      b.   * Tja **ti**   **go** už   **e**   dala
            she to.you it   maybe AUX.3SG given
      c.   * Tja **ti**   **go e**   už   dala
            she to.you it   AUX.3SG maybe given
            'She has maybe given it to you (reportedly)'

In Franks' analysis the pronoun + auxiliary cluster *ti+go+e* occurs as a string under the Tense node, and for this reason cannot be split by an adverb.[55]

One line of research in HPSG factors out linear order entirely from constituent structure and defines linearization in terms of a separate grammatical property under the heading of order domains. Originally this device was developed for the description of clause-internal word order variation in German (Kathol 2001), but it has been co-opted by Crysmann (2000, 2002) in his study of the Portuguese mixed clitic system.

In a sense, OT accounts were developed precisely in order to address the problem of clitic ordering within the cluster. Constraint ranking can be a descriptively very rich device when combined with a more-or-less limitless collection of specific constraints. It is therefore relatively easy in principle to state the clustering property of the Serbian/Croatian 3sg auxiliary: all that is needed is a constraint specific to that verb form which aligns it to the right of a set of clitics rather than to the left. By ranking that constraint higher than the default constraint for auxiliaries we can then permit the more specific constraint to pre-empt the more general auxiliary alignment constraint.

8.13   Conclusions

One striking feature of a number of analyses of clitic constructions, particularly, though not exclusively, those framed in the PPT model of syntax, is the extent to which authors seek to present what are sometimes highly idiosyncratic clitic phenomena as explicable in terms of synchronic grammatical relationships. The morphologically-based analyses are generally far less likely to present themselves as 'explanations'. For many morphologists, (including us) the true explanation of a given morphological pattern will often be as much the caprice of history as any property of the language faculty (innate or otherwise). However, on the fairly rare occasions when a syntactician makes an explicit comparison between the syntactic approach and some kind of morphological approach it is customary for the morphological approach to be criticized as merely descriptive.

The question is addressed directly by Heggie and Ordóñez (2005, 3–5) in their introduction to a volume devoted (for the most part) to articles that propose syntactic accounts of clitic ordering and placement. They outline the Zwickly–Pullum criteria for clitics vs affixes and then present a variety of 'problems' for that typology from Romance verbal clitics. In the case of all but one of the generalizations they discuss there are phenomena in Romance that make the clitics look more like affixes. The authors' conclusion seems to be that the criteria don't work very well (they speak of 'counterexamples' to those criteria). But an equally reasonable response is to say, as many have, including us (Klavans 1985, Miller and Sag 1997, Monachesi 1999, 2005, Luís and Spencer 2005 and many other references), that the Romance verbal clitics really are best viewed as (sometimes degenerate) affixes and certainly not as words or syntactic heads.

Later in their survey, where they are introducing research by syntacticians as a response to morphologically based analyses, Heggie and Ordóñez consider the way that pronominal clitic order is often affected by the person/number features expressed. They claim that there is a strong cross-linguistic tendency for 1st/2nd person dative clitics to be ordered before 3rd person accusative clitics. They then ask (Heggie and Ordóñez 2005, 23): "If ordering is arbitrary,[56] why would we not find a change in the reverse direction?" Such remarks are likely to be very surprising for those who are aware of the veritable typological industry that exists for explaining precisely such patterning in terms of a universal hierarchy such as Silverstein's (1976) Animacy Hierarchy. More generally, if, as many morphologists and typologists believe, linguistic patterning is often the result of forces that drive language change, then there is no mystery here: considered as a dynamic system, we would expect clitic systems to evolve in one way but not necessarily in another way. But this sort of information doesn't have to be available to the language learner. All she needs is the descriptive wherewithal to be able to describe those patterns that are actually found in her language and generalize from them appropriately (and to only a limited extent in the case of clitic systems). Thus, the language itself as a system can behave in what seems to be a lawful fashion, while the synchronic description can be as arbitrary as it needs to be to get the facts right. To us this seems the only reasonable way to approach the logical problem of language acquisition: compared with genuine syntax, clitic systems are finite systems (much like morphological systems) and therefore don't require the language learner to have access to universal patterns of diachronic change. Indeed, it would be a grave mistake to try to plug such knowledge into the child's language faculty, and it is very difficult to see how doing so could possibly lead to a viable model of language acquisition.

9 Envoi

9.1   Do clitics exist?

To conclude, we summarize what we see as the crucial issues surrounding the notion of clitic. We will conclude that the notion is often a useful one in description but that it's difficult to justify setting up any universal category of clitic or clitichood.

First, we have to conclude that traditional typology is not of much help in identifying a universal category of clitic. The most promising way of establishing a typology of clitics in the classical sense would be to set up an implicational scale of some sort. When we set up such a scale, we find some property that implies the existence of some other property. For instance, in morphology if a language distinguishes a trial number then it will also have a dual and a plural distinction and so we can set up a scale along the lines trial → dual → plural. Cases such as Polish show that there is little chance of finding a set of implicational scales for clitics and affixes. The Polish floating inflections show typically clitic properties of wide scope and (completely) promiscuous attachment. On the other hand, unlike special clitics in most languages, they don't really show any special syntactic behaviour. They can appear in almost any position in the clause, much like the (non-clitic) unstressed pronominals in that language or the Russian conditional mood marker *by*, which makes them look more like function words than clitics. However, they trigger idiosyncratic allomorphy on their hosts in the manner of a typical, highly morphologized affix. Indeed, they are more affix-like in this regard than are the regular English verb suffixes *-s*, *-ed*, *-ing*. It's therefore difficult to imagine any sense in which we could define a set of implications along the lines 'if an element displays clitic property P_c then it will not display affix property P_a', or conversely 'if an element displays affix property P_a then it will not display clitic property P_c'.

Within the framework of Canonical Typology discussed in the previous chapter we can ask what are the canonical properties of affixes and of weak function words and then define a canonical clitic as an element with the distributional properties of a canonical function word but the phonological properties of a canonical affix. This means that it shows the (function) word-like properties of not being phonologically integrated into its host and being distributed with respect to syntactic phrase structure. It shows the affixal properties of being smaller than a function word, and lacking prosodic structure of its own, and hence being immune to focussing and being obligatorily attached to a host (Spencer and Luís 2012).

However, for practical analysis it's probably better to think in terms of prototypical properties of function words, clitics and affixes. This is much more difficult than defining canonical properties. Canonical criteria for membership of a class are intended to be obvious and uncontroversial. The way they combine and interact is what is of crucial interest. But it's much more difficult to reach agreement on what is 'typical' behaviour for a category or a construction. If we wish to be relatively certain that we're dealing with an affix rather than a clitic we might appeal to the fact that affixes quite often attach to bound stems or bound allomorphs of stems, and quite often induce idiosyncratic allomorphy on those stems. These are not, however, canonical properties of affixes, and therefore a canonical typology of clitics would have nothing to say about this criterion. In practice, therefore, we need to ask what are the typical properties of function words and affixes and to what extent a putative clitic shares those properties. Let's therefore consider the kinds of questions we might want to ask when investigating an element that we think might be a good candidate for clitichood. To begin with let's assume we are looking at exponents of inflection-like functions. The properties we are interested in are phonological, morphological and syntactic.

The phonological questions we need to ask concern the phonological form of the clitic, the phonological form of its host, the phonology of the context in which the clitic is found and the phonology of the clitic-host combination. A clitic will typically be short and (therefore?) non-prominent; indeed, it will often be shorter than the minimal word for that language. This is a property that clitics generally share with affixes and function words. If we encounter a candidate clitic that is longer than typical function words or more prominent prosodically we therefore have to decide whether it's really a clitic. We've seen this problem with the Italian pronominal *loro*. When we speak of the phonological environment and the phonology of the clitic-host combination we mean what unit on the Prosodic Hierarchy governs clitic formation and placement and what kind of prosodic unit does the clitic-host consist of. For instance, is our candidate clitic attracted to a particular prosodic unit such as a Prosodic Word (as in the case of Bulgarian *li*)? Is the domain of cliticization defined in terms of a prosodic unit such as the Intonational Phrase (as in the case of Chamorro or Serbian/Croatian)? Does the clitic-host combination behave like a Prosodic Word, a Phonological Phrase or some different prosodic unit that could be called a Clitic Group? Here, when we rely on considerations of typical phonological behaviour, we encounter some intriguing definitional problems. To distinguish clitics prosodically from function words the clitic has to have more affix-like phonological properties than a typical function word has. To distinguish a clitic prosodically from a typical affix the clitic has to have more function-word-like phonological properties. Ideally, this means that there should be some easily defined third, intermediate phonological category, say, the Clitic Group, which served to individuate clitics

from affixes/function words. But as we've seen, the Clitic Group is a controversial construct that has been rejected by a number of researchers, and even
its proponents would have to admit that we need subtle and careful analysis to
detect the presence of such a unit. We can put matters in an oversimplified, but
reasonably true-to-life form in the following way. In one language description
we might find that an element is defined as a clitic because it is outside the stress
domain of ordinary words and therefore can produce surface violations of normal
stress patterns, thereby distinguishing it from an affix (as in the case of Spanish
pronominal clitics). In another language description we might find that a similar element is defined as a clitic because it is incorporated into the prosody of
the word and respects the word-level stress rules of that language, thereby distinguishing it from a function word (as in the case of the Lucanian dialect of
Italian, or Latin clitic conjunctions). Depending on the details of the language,
both descriptions may well be perfectly sound accounts of the structure of the
language (or conversely, both may be equally misguided, of course). The point is
that there is no simple set of universal criteria that we can apply to any language
to individuate its clitics prosodically.

A similar problem of demarcation emerges when we consider the morphology of clitics. Clitics often form clusters, and within those clusters they often
interact in ways in which normal function words don't interact. For instance,
they can trigger and undergo idiosyncratic allomorphy, often unique to that particular clitic. This helps differentiate the clitics from function words, but it also
makes it more difficult for us to distinguish clitics from affixes. On the other
hand, we've seen that elements that have most of the properties of affixes can
sometimes exhibit behaviour more typical of clitics or even non-clitic function
words. Affixes can sometimes be conjoined with each other, and can sometimes
take wide scope over conjoined phrases (the suspended affixation property).

At the syntactic level matters ought to be more simple. If we can define
the standard syntax for function words of a given category (including prepo-
sitions/postpositions very often), then we can take the candidate clitics and
examine the extent to which their syntax differs from that of the typical function word. Here we encounter the problem of different theoretical models. On
the PPT models there is no concept of a function word syntax that would be
distinct in kind from clitic syntax (and in some PPT models there is no syntactic difference between function words and affixes). At a more superficial level,
where we are concerned merely with the basic surface distribution of elements,
things look a little more promising. The phonological or simple clitics are just
function words with particular prosodic/phonological requirements, so by definition they can't be distinguished syntactically from function words. However,
the special clitics show special distributional properties. In principle we might
find that similar functions are subserved by clitics and by non-clitic functions in
one and the same language. This is the case in Bulgarian, for instance, in which
the present tense forms of the auxiliary verb sǎm 'be' are part of the clitic cluster,
while other tense forms of the same auxiliary are not clitics and have a syntax

that is much closer to that of normal lexical verbs. However, even here we find that certain elements pose intriguing difficulties of classification. The Bulgarian future tense particle *šte*, and the negation word *ne*, for example, seem to be part of the clitic cluster, but, unlike all the other clitics, they can also serve as the host for the rest of the cluster. Thus, these are the only clitics in Bulgarian that can appear clause-initially. It's therefore moot whether we should really call them clitics. But then it becomes unclear how else we should label them.

These problems of definition become more acute when we look at the various types of 'mixed system' discussed in Chapter 8 and elsewhere. The English auxiliary clitics combined with pronominal subjects, the European Portuguese pronominal clitics and the Udi subject markers all illustrate the way that one and the same element can behave like a typical clitic in some constructions and like a typical affix in other constructions.[1] We can draw a number of different conclusions from cases such as these. For Udi, Harris (2000, 2002), as we saw, started from the observation that the subject markers behave like prototypical clitics when attached to non-verbal hosts, and from this concluded that they are categorially clitics under all circumstances. This means, among other things, that we can have endoclitics, breaking up monomorphemic roots. If we further adopt the assumption that a clitic's distribution is a matter of syntax then this means that we must accept the existence of rules of syntax that break up words, in violation of the Lexical Integrity Hypothesis. That reasoning relies on the idea that there is an underlying classification of formatives into non-clitic function words, clitics and affixes and that once an element is classified it retains that classificatory feature under all circumstances. However, we argued that a different perspective is possible. If we think of clitics as morphological objects, then it's not surprising if they sometimes behave just like affixes. The Udi subject markers are then unusual because they are affixes that can sometimes escape the confines of the verb and attach as phrasal affixes to another constituent, as in the analysis proposed by Crysmann (2002) and alluded to in Luís and Spencer (2005).

One technical way of cleaning up the problem of mixed clitics is the least interesting: in principle, we can identify two distinct types of the same category, say [SubjectMarkerType:clitic] and [SubjectMarkerType:affix] and then state the privileges of occurrence of each subtype. However, even this brute force descriptive solution is of no avail in the case of the floating inflections of Polish. These elements simultaneously show affix-like and clitic-like behaviour in all their occurrences. There is therefore no way in which we could subtype these elements.

9.2   Clitics: syntax or morphology?

The typological puzzles we have just mentioned are of direct relevance for grammatical descriptions of clitic systems. As we've pointed out several times, one of the recurrent themes in the research literature on clitics is the question of whether a clitic is best thought of as a word, distributed by syntactic principles, or whether it should be thought of as a morphological object or process of some kind, such as an affix. The variety of behaviour shown by clitics demonstrates that it will not be easy to pursue either the syntactic or the morphological approach in its pure form. To conclude we will briefly summarize what we see as the main problems for each approach.

9.2.1 Problems for a syntactic approach to clitics

Syntactic approaches generally have to assume something like a morpheme-based approach to clitics because otherwise it's not clear what the syntactic rules and principles would be defined over. This brings with it all the theoretical and descriptive difficulties that are associated with morpheme-based morphology, many of which spill over into clitic systems, as we've seen throughout Chapter 5. Perhaps the main problem for syntactically based approaches is the linear placement of clitics. Syntax generally aims to state general principles based on the behaviour of classes of words and phrases, but the ordering of clitics tends to be highly idiosyncratic. This is not a unique problem, of course. The existence of frozen, phrase-like idioms poses similar problems to syntactic theory. But the problem of clitics is more acute because it's harder to relegate clitic systems to some memorized portion of the lexicon (or rather, it's easy to adopt that ploy, but then that would be equivalent to admitting that clitics are essentially a morphological phenomenon).

The close relationship between clitics and phonology, especially Prosodic Phonology, also means that it's becoming increasingly difficult to motivate a purely syntactic approach to cliticization. Thus, whether a purely syntactic analysis of any kind of clitic system can be justified remains to be seen. At the same time, permitting syntactic analyses to be meshed with phonological representations, as, say, in the approach of Bošković (2001), doesn't really address the problems raised by the morphology-like behaviour of clitics or their idiosyncratic ordering. Even when enriched with appeal to phonological structure, such syntactic accounts still have to explain how clitics are recognized by the highly idiosyncratic processes of copying/deletion that are supposed to give rise to their special linear orders. This is a difficult challenge and it's hard to see how it can be met without introducing circularity into the argumentation.

9.2.2 Problems for a morphological approach to clitics

Anderson (1992, 2005) has advanced perhaps the most thoroughgoing and consistent version of the morphological approach to clitics. However, there are important challenges for this approach too. Some of these challenges relate specifically to Anderson's a-morphous approach under which all special clitics are phrasal affixes. For instance, he is forced to treat the enclitic clusters of European Portuguese as phrasal affixes when in fact they behave more like real affixes. Other challenges relate to the inferential-realization class of models, while some of the problems are shared by all morphologically based approaches.

There is one challenge that is presented by a phenomenon that is equally challenging for syntactic accounts, namely, the idiosyncratic positioning of the 3rd person auxiliary clitic in certain South Slavic languages, notably Serbian/Croatian. Recall that the clitic auxiliaries come at the left edge of the cluster followed by the pronominal clitics, but the 3sg auxiliary, *je*, occurs at the right edge, after all the pronominals. This patterning has all the hallmarks of a highly morphologized affixal system (despite being a typical 2P clitic cluster). However, we noted that Stjepanović (1998) has observed that the 3sg auxiliary form behaves just like the other auxiliary clitics under conditions of VP ellipsis, suggesting that, in some abstract sense, the 3sg form occupies the same syntactic position as the other auxiliaries. This sort of evidence is potentially more damaging to a morphological approach than the existence of clitic climbing or the complementary distribution of pronominal clitics and overt arguments, because we've seen that those phenomena are mirrored in affixal agreement systems.

Now, it must be admitted that the syntactic arguments are very theory-dependent, and there is far from a consensus on how best to analyse such VP-ellipsis constructions. It's therefore unclear whether such phenomena would really pose a serious challenge to a morphological approach when studied in detail (or, indeed, whether they would really turn out to support a syntactic approach, after all). We will therefore remain agnostic about such cases.

On the other hand, Kambera (Section 8.5) may well pose rather more problems for morphologists. The Acc → Dat referral for object clitics following a genitive clitic is a serious challenge to any inferential-realizational morphological model, because such models don't countenance morphemes, that is, pieces of inflection that have lexically specified properties pre-associated with them in their lexical representations. For models such as Paradigm Function Morphology or Anderson's A-Morphous Morphology the phenomenon is particularly challenging because those models don't even countenance morphs. On the other hand, Distributed Morphology might well be able to state fairly easily the conditions under which the syncretism operates, because on that model there are morphemes ('Vocabulary Items') which are furnished with feature content, so that it would, in principle, be possible for the grammar to recognize a genitive clitic. To express the syncretism DM would have to delete the 'Acc' marking on the alternating clitic and replace it with the marking 'Dat'. Unfortunately, though, syncretisms are handled by means of the device of Impoverishment in Distributed Morphology. This means that the 'Dat' marking would have to be presented as the default form for direct objects, an unappealing conclusion given the nature of Kambera grammar. It's difficult, therefore, to see how these models could easily handle these facts. Presumably, an account in LFG that treated the clitics as lexically represented pronominals would be able at least to state the conditions under which the referral takes place.

Another set of challenges to the a-morphous variant of the morphological analysis of clitics comes from clitics with their own semantic or pragmatic properties, that is, clitics that seem to express a lexical meaning (such as place adverbs) or which determine a discourse function for the utterance, rather than realizing inflection-like morphosyntactic properties of lexemes. Anderson, as we have seen, has recognized this problem and we have already made some critical observations about his solution (Section 8.3).

One solution is to abandon the a-morphous assumptions that underly the morphological model. In other words, suppose we reject the assumption that the morphological rules realizing inflectional properties perform solely the operation of changing the phonology of the stem (say, by adding a piece of phonology to it in the form of an affix). Instead, suppose we allow morphological rules and principles to be defined over morphs, that is, objects with their own morphological properties. This would not require us to resurrect the morpheme concept because there's no suggestion that the morphs necessarily have to be lexical entries with a semantic/featural content of their own. However, it might be necessary to make some sort of concession to traditional morpheme-based approaches. In Spencer (2005b, 2008, 2010) it is argued that, even for ordinary inflection, we must take seriously Geert Booij's (1996b) notion of 'inherent inflection' and accept that some inflectional pieces are associated not just with a morphosyntactic property or feature, but with a meaning, in the sense of a semantic predicate that is added to the semantic representation of the inflected lexeme.

If such a concession is made it opens up the road to providing a compromise analysis between the purely a-morphous morphological model and the traditional morpheme-based approaches or their modern descendants (such as Distributed Morphology or Minimalist Morphology). Some of the clitics would realize morphosyntactic properties (interpreted semantically in the way that any other inflectional properties get interpreted in a realizational model), while other clitics would bring their own semantic or pragmatic force to the representation (in much the same way that Spencer 2008 argues that some of the Hungarian case suffixes are more like 'fused postpositions' which add a locational predicate to the meaning of the base noun).

However, the idea that some inflections might be meaningful is a very controversial proposal among advocates of realizational morphology, and the idea would have to be developed in much more detail before it could be accepted.

9.3   How to think of clitics

Echoing Zwicky (1994, xiii), we have reached the conclusion that, while the CATEGORY of clitic may not exist, some sort of CONCEPT of clitic remains ubiquitous, both in theoretical discussion and in descriptive studies, as an umbrella term. The reason for this is probably that the term usefully points to elements that cannot easily be classified as normal affixes or normal function words. Moreover, in many languages it's helpful to identify that group of elements which pattern together, say, in forming a 2P cluster. But, as with the results of any process of grammaticalization or morphologization there are generally intermediate cases that fail to behave in the same way as the rest of the group and which therefore defy adequate categorization. The problem of defining clitics in, say, English, is therefore not much different from the problem of defining auxiliary verbs and distinguishing them from lexical verbs: there are clear cases (modal auxiliaries, for instance), there are elements which belong to both categories (*do*, *have*), there is an element that has the form and morphosyntax of an auxiliary verb even when it's the (sole) main verb of the clause (*be*), and there are notorious 'semi-auxiliaries', which have some of the auxiliary properties but not all (*daren't, needn't, ought* ...).

The clitic, then, is a potentially useful descriptive construct, best characterized in canonical terms (Spencer and Luís 2012), as an element that has the distribution of a function word and the phonological properties of an affix. In addition, it might show special distribution within its domain, especially 2P distribution. But having said that, in any given language an element might lack any of the prototypical clitic properties and still have sufficiently many other clitic properties to warrant being included in the list of clitic elements of that language. For any given candidate clitic it might still be necessary to provide a detailed specification of its phonological, morphological, syntactic and perhaps even semantic/pragmatic properties. It is this flexibility that makes clitic systems such a challenge for descriptive grammarians and theoreticians alike.

Notes

1. Preliminaries

1. Quite often we will make the direction of attachment clear by placing an 'equals' sign = before an enclitic and after a proclitic: host=**enclitic**, **proclitic**=host.
2. See Culicover and Jackendoff (2005) for discussion of this point, from a specific syntactic point of view.
3. For those who are familiar with the different types of computer operating systems, a light-hearted analogy comes to mind to illustrate some of the difficulties we face. HPSG is rather like the Linux system – you can express more or less what you like but it's not easy if you're not a computer programmer. LFG is rather like the Mac OS used by Apple-Macintosh computers. LFG is closely related to HPSG (they are based on the same underlying engineering principles) but it has a much more intuitive user interface. Although the experts can readily access and tweak the system it can be employed even by those with little computational background. PPT, of course, is rather like the Windows operating system: its format, its default settings and even its name change fairly frequently and programs written for one version may well not be compatible with earlier versions.

2. The functions of clitics

1. However, as Franks and King (2000, 104) note, this particle has a certain amount of freedom within the second position clitic cluster itself.
2. A good many languages can use both strategies, e.g. Turkish.
3. When typologists don't wish to distinguish between prepositions and postpositions they often refer to them as adpositions. However, there is no harm in calling both prepositions, given the semantic opacity which is typical of linguistic terminology.
4. The notation '*(go)' means that the sentence is grammatical with the clitic *go*, but ungrammatical without. The notation '(*go)' means by contrast that the sentence is grammatical without the clitic, but ungrammatical with it.
5. Unfortunately, it is necessary to have a reading knowledge of Greek to appreciate fully Denniston's exhaustive analyses, but even with just an ability to decipher the Greek alphabet the effort is rewarding.
6. We use the standard transliteration for Weir Smyth's examples, but omitting grave accents.
7. We reproduce Garrett's transliteration.
8. Hittite was written in cuneiform, an essentially syllabic writing system developed for writing the unrelated language Sumerian. The Hittite words presented in capital letters represent Sumerograms, that is, hieroglyph representations of entire words taken from the Sumerian language. They would have been read as Hittite words but are conventionally represented in transcripts as though they were Sumerian words.
9. Lauffenburger's grammar is a conveniently available précis of Friedrich (1960).

3. Types of clitic system

1. In fairness to colleagues and students who have cited Wackernagel's opus without actually reading it, a large proportion of the text consists of Ancient Greek examples without glosses, so that it is more or less unintelligible to those who don't know Greek.
2. The transcription is normalized.
3. A further entertaining instance of prescience on Wackernagel's part is his suggestion concerning the historical origins of second-position placement for the discourse particles in Ancient Greek. He proposes (pp. 377–8) that these were originally clause-initial and moved to second position under the influence of the clitic pronouns, citing the case of Homeric *dē* 'already' as a word which is attested in first position in earlier texts and then moves to second. In other words, Wackernagel is anticipating, as a type of historical change, what was later proposed by Halpern (1995) as a synchronic process, under the name of Prosodic Inversion.
4. This assumes that the Romance pronominal clitics are best thought of as clitics and not affixes. As we will see later in Chapter 5 and Chapter 8, this assumption has been questioned.
5. Among the critical discussions of Klavans' typology we should mention Marantz (1988), Sadock (1991) and Billings (2002).
6. Indeed, he argues that affixal morphology generally can be handled by a similarly parametric approach to placement, which emphasizes still further the morphological nature of cliticization. See also Luís and Spencer (2005) for a concrete instantiation of this idea with respect to European Portuguese pronominal proclitics.
7. We tend to get more freedom of ordering with discourse marker clitics or with clitics whose meanings can combine, such as certain types of aspectual clitic.
8. We have put scare-quotes around the term 'periphrastic' because that term usually applies to a construction that is realized by two or more words (a 'multiword combination'). However, it isn't clear that a clitic can really be called a word (this is one of the reasons why clitics are an interesting phenomenon). As we will see throughout the book, and especially in Chapter 5, clitics are in many respects like inflectional affixes and not like proper words. For this reason it isn't necessarily appropriate to think of the past tense formed with a clitic auxiliary as periphrastic (i.e. 'multiword').
9. In Czech orthography, the symbol ě is equivalent to the sequence *je* and the acute accent ´ indicates a long vowel. Note that clitic forms as well as full forms can have a long vowel.
10. Hock (1996, 229) argues for a clitic cluster template with the intriguing property that it imposes a pattern of alternating accented and unaccented clitics within the cluster. However, as observed by Schäufele (1996, 458) this accentual pattern is at best a tendency and not a rigid constraint.
11. Schachter and Otanes (1972, 184) note that the *ang*-forms are not clitics when they are used as Inverted Topics, which shows that we can't straightforwardly label each set of forms as 'clitic' or 'non-clitic'.
12. We don't gloss the grammatical markers *ay, ang, ng* in the Tagalog examples.
13. The symbol ă is the conventional way of transliterating a letter which represents a schwa in Bulgarian cyrillic. This is also sometimes written as â.
14. We slightly amend the English free translation in Avgustinova's examples by rendering *sigurno* as 'probably', rather than 'certainly' as in the original text.
15. In the version of Minimalism she endorses syntax is allowed to effect head movement, though in more recent versions of Minimalism head movement is regarded as a type of phonological adjustment and not as part of syntax sensu stricto.
16. The third person forms of BE are null when the verb is used as an auxiliary in Macedonian and they only appear when it is used as a copula.
17. Transcription slightly normalized.
18. One might be tempted to call such an element a 'Wackernagel afffix', but that term has been appropriated for the very interesting case of Lithuanian, in which reflexive verbs are

marked by an affix which is always second *in the prefix string attached to that verb form.* See our discussion of Nevis and Joseph 1993 in Chapter 7.

19. Karlsson's own emphasis.

20. We'll see in Section 8.4 that the Austronesian language Chamorro defines second position as 'after the first phonological phrase'.

4. Clitics and phonology

1. It's misleading to speak of syllables in Japanese because the phonology works in terms of timing units or moras. A more precise characterization of the facts would therefore substitute the word 'mora' for 'syllable' throughout.

2. 'H' means 'high level pitch', 'L' means 'low level pitch' and 'M' means 'mid level pitch'.

3. Pashto is ergative in perfective tenses. This means that the pronominals in those tenses are absolutive markers, cross-referencing either the direct object or the intransitive subject.

4. We preserve Polish orthography, adding IPA transcriptions in square brackets [] where necessary. Note that the acute accent in Polish on *ó* is purely conventional and has nothing to do with stress. To avoid confusion we represent stressed syllables with underlining in the Polish examples. Elsewhere we use an acute accent.

5. The particle is cognate with the Russian conditional marker that we discuss in Chapter 7. The Russian and Polish particles have somewhat different behaviour with respect to the clitic systems, however.

6. Needlesss to say, there is debate in the philological and theoretical literature over the exact nature of the prosodic patterning, particularly since the clitics left no trace in the later Romance languages, so that scholars have to rely on the writings of ancient grammarians such as Varro (first century BC). For a very interesting discussion of these matters, see Plank (2005).

7. It won't do, for instance, merely to say that the clitics add "enough material to build a new foot <...> and thus to create a new stress" (Anderson 2005, 26). That observation certainly accounts for the fact that the clitics can be considered as 'clitics' and yet still receive stress. And there's nothing unusual about constructing disyllabic stress feet over an extended word. But the grammar of Greek still has to include a stipulation somewhere stating that it is possible for clitics to be incorporated into the stress domain, otherwise it will be impossible to distinguish Greek from, say, Standard Spanish or Standard Italian.

8. The syllabic obstruents [ḍ, ɣ] are often pronounced with a schwa, of course: [əd, əv], as are the syllabic sonorants.

9. One issue we won't address is the question of whether phonological principles ever need to make direct reference to syntactic structures, or whether such apparent references are always mediated through a level of phonological (prosodic) structure. Some have argued for 'direct reference' to syntactic structure in certain cases (Odden 1987, 1990, Chen 1990). We will ignore this problem here, though it principle it might ultimately prove important for understanding the phonology of clitics.

10. Vogel renames the Clitic Group 'Composite Group' in Vogel (2010).

11. Misprint in (59) corrected.

12. As Wolfgang Dressler points out to us, example (60) with truncation is homophonous with *vuole scriver=gli indirizzi* 'wants to write him addresses', where the truncation is obligatory.

5. Clitics and morphology

1. In standard varieties. In Irish English this form is, in fact, attested.

2. The Nahuatl conjugation system is described in a number of sources. These examples have been taken from Sullivan (1988) and Andrews (1975).

3. The digraphs 'ch', 'tz' represent single affricate phonemes, corresponding to English 'ch', 'ts', IPA tʃ ts; 'x' corresponds to English 'sh', IPA ʃ; 'tl' is a single segment, a lateral

affricate, IPA ƛ or t͡l, 'kw' is a labialized 'k', hence a single segment, 'kʷ', 'h' is a glottal stop and the colon : indicates a long vowel.

4. There is a plural indirect object form *loro*, sometimes described as a 'semi-clitic', which behaves slightly differently from the rest of the system. We discuss that form briefly below.
5. The accents over the vowels represent tones, found only in full lexical items, not on clitics.
6. This is a special colloquial form available only for the copular use of the verb.
7. Anderson makes a number of suggestions for dealing with the special phonological effects of the possessor construction but concedes that there are still uncertainties surrounding the data themselves. This seems to be a corollary of the informal law in linguistics which states that the confidence we have in the empirical data for a given language is inversely proportional to the number of published descriptive grammars available for that language.
8. Strictly speaking tone is distributed with respect to moras rather than syllables.
9. The 'C' represents a voiced pharyngeal fricative [ʕ] in Somali orthography.
10. Anderson (2005, 96), Churchward (1953, 150); the column labels are Anderson's.
11. Further, very interesting, discussion of this point can be found in Anderson (2005, 94–101). See also Anderson 1992, 212–15.

6. Clitics and syntax

1. It seems that on occasions a variant word order will be used just for the sake of variety. When a speaker repeats him/herself because the original utterance wasn't audible or was misunderstood, it's very common for the word order to be changed without any change in emphasis.
2. It is very clear that languages such as English, French or German are typologically rather less common than null-subject languages, so it would have been more reasonable to single out those languages and call them 'obligatory subject languages'.
3. The original justification for the PRO-drop parameter was that it was supposed to be associated with a host of other properties, such as the possibility of extracting question words out of finite clauses, but it appears that all of these properties are independent of the PRO-drop property.
4. One prediction is that languages respecting the PP will not be able to have true infinitives. Two of the languages (or language groups, better) that Baker explicitly discusses, Chukchee (Chukotkan) and Rembarrnga (non-Pama-Nyungan Australian), clearly do have infinitives, however (see Spencer 1999 and Nordlinger and Saulwick 2002 respectively).
5. SM = Subject Marker, FV = 'final vowel'; numerals before nouns denote noun class; FOC = focus marker, APPL = applicative marker.
6. We have corrected a misprint in the Russian gloss, which has *snesnjat'sja* for *stesnjat'sja* 'to be embarrassed'.
7. There is no gender in Chukchee, so the pronouns could in principle refer to men or women. Inenliqej and Nedjalkov translate them throughout as 'he', but we have substituted 's/he' throughout except in the examples (27), where translating as 'she', especially in (27b), would be culturally very odd.
8. Poletto glosses this merely 'SCL', her abbreviation for 'subject clitic'. However, it is clearly 2pl in form (as is the verb). It is therefore presumably an instance of a Type 4 'number clitic', though one of the rare types that realizes 2pl.
9. Marušič and Žaucer (2010a) open their paper citing what they call 'Bošković's Generalization': all languages that have clitic doubling have definite articles. This 'generalization' is flatly contradicted by a number of languages, including the totally unrelated Luiseño, Pirahã, Udi, Warlpiri and Yagua.
10. For an introduction to Relational Grammar, see Blake (1990).
11. A useful and concise overview of these phenomena is provided by Kroeger (2004, chapter 8).

12. Rizzi (1982b, 27–9) explicitly argues that the rule responsible for Restructuring predicates based on modals, aspectuals and motion verbs is distinct from that which gives rise to *fare*-causatives in Italian. Our point here is that typologically causatives often create complex predicates of the type that might license clitic climbing, long-distance agreement and so on, even if there are clear specific differences between these constructions within a single language, or cross-linguistically.
13. This is true of long-distance agreement, too. It is obligatory in Hungarian, for instance, but optional in Hindi-Urdu.
14. Recall that encliticization of the object clitic to the infinitive gives rise to stem allomorphy, *troncamento*, discussed in Section 4.6.
15. Franks and King's exposition is very detailed and includes a good deal of discussion of examples that are regarded as dubious or unclear by native informants or on which there is native speaker disagreement. This variability is very interesting in itself, of course (as well as being all too characteristic of clitic systems), but in the interests of clarity we will limit ourselves to relatively clear-cut cases, leaving the reader to explore the full empirical richness from the cited sources.
16. One might also want to describe the complementizer *da* as part of the clitic cluster, but we are just concentrating on the pronominal clitics here.
17. English glossing corrected.
18. See Franks and King (2000, 131, 157, 179–80) for further examples respectively from Slovak, Polish and Sorbian.
19. Schachter and Otanes (1972, 461–63) also describe four sentence-final discourse particles, *a* 'contrary to expectation', *e* 'you see; on the contrary; unfortunately', *ha* expressing importunity, and *o* expressing emphasis.
20. The glosses are extremely approximate. Typically, these particles show considerably polysemy, if not homonymy.
21. A calabaw is a type of buffalo.
22. Schachter and Otanes' gloss for (97b) lacks the adverb *too*, so we have supplied it.

7. Clitics, affixes and words

1. The analysis of *ðe(n)/θa* and the pronominals as affixes is still controversial. For instance, the standard English-language reference grammar of Greek, Holton et al. (1997), refers to the pronominals as 'weak pronouns' and as 'clitics' (pp. 97, 303–7; see also the glossary entry for 'clitic pronoun', p. 506) and refers to the negative and future markers as 'particles', and they explicitly speak of the future construction as 'periphrastic' (p. 226), implying that the *θa* marker is an independent word.
2. This article is republished as Aronoff and Sridhar (1987).
3. See Paster (2009, 35) for a different view on the Afar facts.
4. An Applicative form turns a prepositional complement into a direct object. In English we could think of *give* in *Harriet gave Fido a bone* as the Applicative form of the *give* in *Harriet gave a bone to Fido*.
5. Rice (2000) presents a remarkably detailed study of the relationship between affix order and semantic scope in the Athapaskan group of languages. While her claims are controversial (see Spencer 2003b for discussion), they are meticulously worked out, demonstrating a virtuoso command of notoriously complex data. Stump (1997) aims to handle all cases of order-driven scope effects in terms of the order of application of realization rules.
6. Glossing conventions: 1 = 1st person, 2 = 2nd person, 3 = 3rd person, A = Actor argument, ADD = additive focus marker ('too'), AMB = 'ambulative' ('walk around'), DU = dual, EX = exclusive, NEG = negation, NPAST = nonpast, NS = nonsingular, P = primary object, S = sole argument of intransitive (i.e. subject).
7. Misaligned diacritics corrected.
8. See below for natural coordination.
9. The capital letter 'E' in *lEr* stands for the vowel harmony variants {e, a}.

10. Or sometimes in groups of one or two depending on rather complex factors – see Orgun (1996a, b) for discussion.

11. In contrast to Turkish, the Hungarian suffix *-talan/telen* observes vowel harmony even when suspended. Thus, we have *erkély- és kémény-telen* 'balcony- and chimney-less', with front vowels, but not **ajtó- és kémény-telen* or **erkély- és ablak-talan* with mixed back/front harmony roots.

12. Page references are to Harris (2002).

13. There is also a partial set which is labelled 'Question' set (Harris 2002, 28).

14. We have reconstructed example (70b) from Harris' discussion.

15. Verb-final placement also takes place with a very small set of suppletive roots consisting entirely of a single consonant (e.g., *b-esa-n* [LV-PRES-3SG] 'she makes', *p-e-ne* [LV-AORII-3SG] 'she said') and with irregular forms of other verbs (e.g. *aba-t'u* 'she knows' the shortened form of *aba-t'u-bak-e* [know-INV.3SG-be-AORII]).

16. We italicize the PMs in these examples since they take the appearance of affixes rather than clitics, but bear in mind that for Harris these are still genuine clitics.

17. We follow Harris in glossing the parts of the discontinuous root twice with different subscript numbers. The examples are adapted from Harris (2002, 125), examples (43)–(46).

18. For recent discussion of periphrasis, see Ackerman and Stump (2004).

8. Approaches to clitics

1. A very detailed survey of theoretical approaches to clitics in Slavic, which is very relevant to the study of clitic systems generally, is presented in Franks and King (2000, chapters 10–12). Slavic clitics provide a particularly good window on clitic systems generally. Even without considering historical forms of the languages, the modern standardized forms of Slavic languages offer examples of classical Wackernagel clitics (Czech, Slovak, Slovene, Serbian/Croatian), a Tobler–Mussafia system, that is, a 2P system in which the finite verb has to follow immediately after the clitic cluster (Bulgarian), verb-oriented clitics that are essentially loosely cohering affixes (Macedonian), and a typologically unusual system of floating affixes realizing auxiliary verb functions and pronominal arguments (Polish), as well as an entire subgroup that lacks the pronoun/auxiliary clitics of the other languages but which has a variety of clitic prepositions and particles (the East Slavic group, Russian, Belarusian, Ukrainian).

2. This use of *loro* is somewhat different from that illustrated above in (1), where the *loro* is used as a subject pronoun, not an indirect object pronoun as in (4). For detailed discussion, see Maiden and Robustelli (2000, 116–119). They also discuss the complex factors of register, written/formal vs spoken/informal, that influence judgements on these constructions.

3. Yagua doesn't actually have determiners, it has pronominal clitics which double certain complement noun phrases and which encliticize to the word immediately preceding that complement. See Section 6.4 for discussion.

4. See Lidz (1995) for interesting observations on Romance reflexive verbs and event structure/argument structure representations.

5. The publications list on Professor Insler's webpage records a reference Insler (1997) which we have not seen.

6. The orthography is to be read as follows: *nh* = [[ɲ] *ng* = [ŋ], *y* = [j]].

7. Anderson (2005, 114–116) discusses Chung's analysis.

8. Pronunciation: ä = [æ], ' = [ʔ], ch = [ts], y = [dz], ñ = [ɲ].

9. Chung (2003, 562–8) argues on the basis of such facts that it isn't possible to account for the Chamorro data by appeal to the devices discussed elsewhere in this chapter, namely, phonological repair in the form of Prosodic Inversion or a PF filter of the kind advocated for Serbian/Croatian by Bošković (2001).

10. The Aṣṭādhyāyī or 'Eight Books'. The Wikipedia article on Pāṇini is very detailed and informative.
11. The inferential~lexical, realizational~incremental typology is due to Stump (2001, 1–2).
12. For more detailed discussion of Russian declensional syncretism, see Baerman et al. (2005, 38–39).
13. In addition, we immediately notice that, for a given lexeme, several of these forms have the same endings: the nominative/accusative forms for ZAKON in both singular and plural and the nominative/accusative forms of KOMNATA in the singular are identical. More detailed study of Russian declension would reveal that this is a (well-known) systematic fact about nominals in Russian and hence constitutes a genuine syncretism. There are various ways of capturing the syncretism which we won't explore here.
14. It probably isn't necessary for Minimalist Syntax to adopt the Distributed Morphology model, and in fact the Minimalist approach originally envisaged a lexicalist model of inflection (Chomsky 1995b), which effectively would make it compatible with an inferential-realizational model.
15. In order to see precisely how OT can be deployed to implement an inferential-realizational account of a large and complex dataset, the reader is therefore advised to consult the analyses of Géraldine Legendre devoted to the clitic systems of Bulgarian, Macedonian and Romanian referred to above.
16. Page references are to Klamer (1997) unless otherwise stated. We modify Klamer's glossing conventions for the sake of uniformity.
17. We have added missing brackets to some of the examples. Kambera has no gender as so we gloss 3sg pronouns as 's/he'.
18. We correct a typo in Klamer's original morpheme gloss for (57a), which is misprinted as '3sG'.
19. This may be a misprint for 'S/he'll surely give …'
20. This fused double clitic functioning as the exponent of continuative aspect is notated '3s.CONT' in Klamer (1997). The abbreviation 'CONT' is explained in Klamer (1998a).
21. We have renumbered the columns in this table so as to correspond to Bonami and Boyé's labelling of PFM rule blocks.
22. Bonami and Boyé write their rules using the notational innovations in Paradigm Function Morphology introduced by Ackerman and Stump (2004). We have slightly rewritten these rules in a simplified form of Stump's (2001) original notation for ease of comparison with earlier PFM analyses.
23. Noting that the negative particle *ne* is a clitic, Jones (1996, 225, fn. 4) observes, "Since *ne* always precedes the verb, we may postulate that its presence in Standard French has the effect of attracting all the other clitics to the preverbal position, whereas its absence in colloquial French allows clitic pronouns to follow the verb in line with the pattern positive imperatives."
24. The formalism Stump uses in his 1993 exposition is slightly different from that which he uses in Stump (2001) and it would take us too far afield to provide a version of the 1993 metarule normalized to the 2001 formalism.
25. We presume Vigário is referring to *Partido Comunista Português*, not to be confused with *Partido Comunista de Portugal (Marxista-Leninista)*.
26. It's actually not clear from Noyer's discussion why he regards these as clitics rather than verbal prefixes. This is how they are described, for instance, by Whitman (1991, 623–5) in his Government-Binding analysis.
27. Noyer's data are taken for the most part from Heath (1984).
28. This brings with it a strong prediction (though one that is difficult to establish in practice): all syncretisms will involve a 'retreat to the unmarked'. It is impossible to have a syncretism in which, say, a feature bundle including the value [Number:plural] is neutralized to a [Number:dual] form. Another way of stating this prediction is to say that there are no stipulated directional syncretisms, that is, syncretisms in which the direction of neutralization is arbitrary and not derivable from some general markedness principle: any such

stipulated syncretism would be a frank counterexample to the Impoverishment thesis. Unfortunately, Baerman et al. (2005) provide a good many reasonably secure examples of precisely such counterexamples. Indeed, the astute reader will have noticed that our example of the Latin Class III future/subjunctive 1sg syncretism (which Baerman et al. don't discuss) would entail that the subjunctive mood was less marked than the indicative on an Impoverishment account.

29. Noyer here appeals to Marantz's (1988) notion of Morphological Merger.

30. Milićević (2009) presents an analysis of Serbian clitics with interesting observations about the interaction of clitic placement and focus, within the Meaning⇔Text model of Igor Mel'čuk (2009).

31. The abbreviation *cl-ss* stands for 'clitic synsem'. This denotes the HPSG SYN and SEM values of the representation of the clitic, that is, the 'lexical entry' for the clitic ignoring its phonological form.

32. A useful descriptive comparison can be found in Mišeska Tomić (2006).

33. Those who endorse the movement approach to cliticization have adopted one of two positions with respect to the nature of the clitic pronouns that get moved. Either the clitics are phrases or they are just heads. A Head Movement analysis of pronominal and auxiliary clitics in Slavic and both medieval and modern varieties of a number of Romance languages is proposed by M.-L. Rivero and her colleagues, for instance Lema and Rivero (1989), Rivero (1994, 1991). That approach was always controversial because it relies on a notion of Long Head Movement under which a head moves across another head, in violation of the Head Movement Constraint, a key architectural feature of PPT in the 1980s. The question of whether clitics are heads or phrases is rendered redundant on the perspective of Cardinaletti and Starke discussed below, because for them all pronominals are phrases of some sort.

34. Note the following patterns in Welsh orthography: c = [k], ff = [f], f = [v], dd = [ð], ph = [f], th = [θ], ch = [x], mh = [m̥], nh = [n̥], ngh = [ŋ̊], ll = [ɬ], rh = [r̥]; y = [ə], u = [i], w = [u]. For details of Welsh clitics and morphosyntax generally, see Borsley et al. (2007).

35. However, the types of mutation found in Scots/Irish Celtic (Goidelic) are somewhat different from the types found in Welsh and Breton (Brythonic).

36. The symbol ∅ means 'initial consonant deleted', '—' means 'no change'. The table in (129) is adapted from the Wikipedia entry, http://en.wikipedia.org/wiki/Colloquial _Welsh_morphology#Initial_consonant_mutation, accessed 7 November 2010.

37. The form *fe* is the allomorph of *e* found after a vowel-final word.

38. We normalize and adapt Sadler's representations slightly for uniformity of exposition.

39. This assumption is common to LFG, HPSG and Government-Binding syntax, but is not made in the Minimalist Program espousing the Bare Phrase Structure model of Chomsky (1995a).

40. For LFG treatments of that phenomenon, see Barron (1998), Sadler (1998) and Wescoat (2002).

41. We must stress that Anderson, at least, would reject such an edge inflection interpretation of the English group genitive.

42. In speech, if not writing, the 3SG.NEUT pronoun *it* has the s-form /ɪts/. The generic pronoun has the *'s* form, *one's*.

43. A number of factors contribute to grammaticality judgements on group genitives. The University of Manchester project on the *s*-possessive in Germanic languages investigates a number of these (www.llc.manchester.ac.uk/research/projects/germanic-possessive-s/ last accessed 4 December 2010). See also Rosenbach (2005) for discussion.

44. Although Anderson has now explicitly recognized the existence of edge inflection, he analyses the English possessive as instances of phrasal affixation. The original conceptual motivation for this in Anderson (2005) is one of parsimony, to relieve linguistic theory of the need to recognize an additional construction type. But this argument is now invalid, given the recognition of edge inflection.

45. Anderson (2005, 116–23) provides a helpful short summary of Bošković's analysis, together with discussion of its consequences for Anderson's own approach to clitics. Bošković's proposals are also discussed throughout Part III of Franks and King (2000). A very detailed and insightful review is that of Billings (2004).
46. Kallulli and Tasmowski (2008) is an interesting collection of articles dealing with doubling phenomena in the Balkan languages, where we find particularly rich instances. Mišeska Tomić (2006) is a survey of the morphosyntax of the Balkan languages with extensive discussion of clitic doubling and its conditioning factors. Everett (1996, chapter 3) provides detailed discussion of clitic doubling across a wide variety of languages while his chapter 4 discusses the way subject clitics are doubled by overt noun phrases in some varieties of Romance, a topic we return to below.
47. Puzzlingly, one of the options available in such a system is for a covert XP* to move covertly to XP^. We find it difficult to see what empirical consequences there could be to such a choice.
48. We have rewritten the examples for perspicuity and normalized Uriagereka's interlinear glosses. The variation between *lo/le* is stylistic/dialectal.
49. Uriagereka (2000, 413) identifies these dialects as Argentinian and Northern Castilian. The symbol # means 'semantically anomalous'.
50. For recent, and contrasting, Minimalist analyses of clitic climbing in Serbian/Croatian and Czech, see Stjepanović (2004), Lenertová (2004).
51. A similar structure is said to account for the Portuguese mesoclisis phenomenon (Monachesi, 2005, 152–8). We would reject that analysis, however, for the same reason we have rejected the analysis of Vigário (2003).
52. This risk is highlighted when Bošković remarks a little later in his discussion (2001, 131) on the gradual process of grammaticalization that has given rise to these idiosyncratic placement facts: "We thus have an explanation for the PF requirement on *je* proposed above. The requirement has developed as a consequence of *je* losing its clitichood." This apparently harmless remark demonstrates how easy it is to imagine that one has explained something when in fact one has merely provided a cumbersome redescription of the facts.
53. One of these is that the idiosyncratic placement of the 3rd person auxiliary is treated as accidental. However, it can only be regarded as systematic if some kind of system can be identified. Whether Franks has succeeded in this we leave to Minimalist syntacticians to decide, but it seems to us that his own account simply writes the idiosyncrasy into unmotivated starting assumptions.
54. Glosses slightly amended.
55. However, since Franks does not actually provide a detailed analysis of the structure of the elements under T^0 it is not entirely obvious that this really does constitute an explanation.
56. By 'arbitrary' Heggie and Ordóñez apparently mean 'described in terms of a morphological template or OT constraints'.

9. Envoi

1. The Tagalog *ang*-form clitics, which aren't clitics in Inverted Topic sentences, may be another example of such mixing.

References

Abeillé, Anne, and Godard, Danièle. 2002. The syntactic structure of French auxiliaries. *Language*, **78**(3), 404–52.

Abraham, Werner (ed.). 1991. *Discourse Particles: Descriptive and Theoretical Investigations on the Logical, Syntactic and Pragmatic Properties of Discourse Particles in German*. Amsterdam: John Benjamins.

Ackerman, Farrell, and Stump, Gregory T. 2004. Paradigms and periphrastic expression: a study in realization-based lexicalism. In Sadler, Louisa, and Spencer, Andrew (eds.), *Projecting Morphology*. Stanford, CA: Center for the Study of Language and Information, pp. 111–58.

Aikhenvald, Alexandra Y. 2003. *The Tariana Language of Northwest Amazonia*. Cambridge: Cambridge University Press.

Aissen, Judith. 1974. *The Syntax of Causative Constructions*. PhD thesis, Harvard University. Reprinted New York: Garland Press, 1979.

Akinlabi, Akinbiyi. 1996. Featural affixation. *Journal of Linguistics*, **32**, 239–89.

Akmajian, Adrian, Steele, Susan M., and Wasow, Thomas. 1979. The category AUX in Universal Grammar. *Linguistic Inquiry*, **10**(1), 1–64.

Alpher, Barry. 1991. *Yir-Yoront Lexicon: Sketch and Dictionary of an Australian Language*. Berlin: Mouton de Gruyter.

Alsina, Alex. 1997. A theory of complex predicates: evidence from causatives in Bantu and Romance. In Alsina, Alex, Bresnan, Joan, and Sells, Peter (eds.), *Complex Predicates*. Stanford, CA: CSLI Publications, pp. 203–46.

Anagnostopoulou, Elena. 1999. Conditions on clitic doubling in Greek. In van Riemsdijk, Hendrik C. (ed.), *Clitics and the Languages of Europe*. Berlin: Mouton de Gruyter, pp. 761–98.

Anderson, Stephen R. 1982. Where's morphology? *Lingustic Inquiry*, **13**(4), 571–612.

Anderson, Stephen R. 1984. Kwak'wala syntax and the Government-Binding theory. In Cook, E.-D., and Gerdts, Donna B. (eds.), *The Syntax of Native American Languages*. Syntax and Semantics 16. New York: Academic Press, pp. 21–75.

Anderson, Stephen R. 1992. *A-Morphous Morphology*. Cambridge: Cambridge University Press.

Anderson, Stephen R. 1993. Wackernagel's revenge: clitics, morphology, and the syntax of second position. *Language*, **69**, 68–98.

Anderson, Stephen R. 2005. *Aspects of the Theory of Clitics*. Oxford Studies in Theoretical Linguistics. Oxford: Oxford University Press.

Anderson, Stephen R., Brown, Lea, Gaby, Alice, and Lecarme, Jacqueline. 2006. Life on the edge: there's morphology there after all! *Lingue e Linguaggio*, **5**(1), 1–16.

Andrews, Avery. 1990. Unification and morphological blocking. *Natural Language and Linguistic Theory*, **8**(4), 507–57.

Andrews, J. Richard. 1975. *Introduction to Classical Nahuatl*. Austin: University of Texas Press.

Aronoff, Mark. 1976. *Word Formation in Generative Grammar*. Cambridge, MA: The MIT Press.

Aronoff, Mark. 1994. *Morphology by Itself: Stems and Inflectional Classes*. Cambridge, MA: The MIT Press.

Aronoff, Mark, and Sridhar, S. 1983. Morphological levels in English and Kannada; or atarizing Reagan. In *Papers from the Parasession on the Interplay of Phonology, Morphology, and Syntax*, vol. 19. Chicago Linguistic Society, pp.3–16.

Aronoff, Mark, and Sridhar, S. 1987. Morphological levels in English and Kannada; or atarizing Reagan. In Gussmann, Edmund (ed.), *Rules and the Lexicon: Lublin*. Redakcja Wydawnictw Katolickiego Uniwersytetu Lubelskiego, pp. 9–22.

Avgustinova, Tania. 1994. On Bulgarian verbal clitics. *Journal of Slavic Linguistics*, **2**, 29–47.

Avgustinova, Tania. 1997. *Word Order and Clitics in Bulgarian*. Saarbrücken Dissertations in Computational Linguistics and Language Technology 5. Saarbrücken: Deutsches Forschungszentrum für Künstliche Intelligenz and Universität des Saarlandes.

Avgustinova, Tania, and Oliva, Karel. 1995. The position of sentential clitics in the Czech clause. Technical Report 68. Universität des Saarlandes.

Awbery, Gwen. 1976. *The Syntax of Welsh: A Transformational Study of the Passive*. Cambridge: Cambridge University Press.

Baerman, Matthew, Brown, Dunstan, and Corbett, Greville G. 2005. *The Syntax-Morphology Interface: A Study of Syncretism*. Cambridge: Cambridge University Press.

Baker, Mark. 1996. *The Polysynthesis Parameter*. Oxford: Oxford University Press.

Baker, Mark, Johnson, Kyle, and Roberts, Ian. 1989. Passive arguments raised. *Linguistic Inquiry*, **20**(2), 219–51.

Barešić, Jasna. 1988. *Dobro došli: Gramatika hrvatskog ili srpskog jezika*. Zagreb: Škola za Strane Jezike.

Barron, Julia. 1998. 'Have' contraction: explaining 'trace effects' in a theory without movement. *Linguistics*, **36**(2), 223–51.

Benacchio, Rosanna, and Renzi, Lorenzo. 1987. *Clitici slavi e romanzi*. Padua: Dipartimento di Linguistica dell'Università di Padova e del Centro per gli Studi di Fonetica del C. N. R.

Bennett, David. 1986. Towards an explanation of word-order differences between Slovene and Serbo-Croatian. *The Slavonic and East European Review*, **64**, 1–24.

Berendsen, Egon. 1986. *The Phonology of Cliticization*. Dordrecht: Foris.

Bermúdez-Otero, Ricardo, and Luís, Ana R. 2009a. Cyclic domains and prosodic spans in European Portuguese encliticization. Paper given at the Old World Conference in Phonology 6, University of Edinburgh.

Bermúdez-Otero, Ricardo, and Luís, Ana R. 2009b. Cyclic domains and prosodic spans in the phonology of European Portuguese functional morphs. Talk given at the Workshop on the Division of Labour between Morphology and Phonology, Meertens Instituut, Amsterdam, 16–17 January 2009.

Beukema, Frits, and den Dikken, Marcel (eds.). 2000. *Clitic Phenomena in European Languages*. Linguistik Aktuell 30. Amsterdam: John Benjamins.

Bickel, Balthasar, Banjade, Goma, Gaenszle, Martin, Lieven, Elena, Paudyal, Netra Prasad, Rai, Ichchha Purna, Rai, Manoj, Rai, Novel Kishore, and Stoll, Sabine. 2007. Free prefix ordering in Chintang. *Language*, **83**, 43–73.

Billings, Loren A. 2002. Phrasal clitics. *Journal of Slavic Linguistics*, **10**, 53–104.

Billings, Loren A. 2004. Review of Bošković 2001. *Journal of Slavic Linguistics*, **12**, 285–321.

Blake, Barry J. 1990. *Relational Grammar*. London: Routledge.

Blakemore, Diane. 2002. *Relevance and Linguistic Meaning: The Semantics and Pragmatics of Discourse Markers*. Cambridge: Cambridge University Press.

Bögel, Tina. 2010. Pashto (endo)clitics in a parallel architecture. In Butt, Miriam, and King, Tracy Holloway (eds.), *The Proceedings of the LFG10 Conference*. University of Stanford, CA: CSLI, pp. 85–105.

Bonami, Olivier, and Boyé, Gilles. 2007. French pronominal clitics and the design of Paradigm Function Morphology. In Booij, Geert, Ducceschi, Luca, Fradin, Bernard, Guevara, Emiliano, Ralli, Angela, and Scalise, Sergio (eds.), *On-line Proceedings of the Fifth Mediterranean Morphology Meeting (MMM5) Fréjus 15–18 September 2005*. Bologna: Università degli Studi di Bologna, pp. 291–322.

Bonet, Eulàlia. 1991. *Morphology after Syntax: Pronominal Clitics in Romance*. PhD thesis, MIT, Cambridge, MA.

Bonet, Eulàlia. 1995. Feature structure of Romance clitics. *Natural Language and Linguistic Theory*, **13**, 603–47.

Booij, Geert. 1985. Coordination reduction in complex words: a case for prosodic phonology. In van der Hulst, Harry, and Smith, Norval (eds.), *Advances in Non-linear Phonology*. Dordrecht: Foris, pp. 143–60.

Booij, Geert. 1988. Review article on Nespor and Vogel 1986. *Journal of Linguistics*, **24**, 515–25.

Booij, Geert. 1996a. Cliticization as prosodic integration: the case of Dutch. *The Linguistic Review*, **13**, 219–42.

Booij, Geert. 1996b. Inherent versus contextual inflection and the split morphology hypothesis. In Booij, Geert, and van Marle, Jaap (eds.), *Yearbook of Morphology 1995*. Dordrecht: Kluwer Academic Publishers, pp. 1–16.

Booij, Geert. 2007. *The Grammar of Words: An Introduction to Morphology*. 2nd edn. Oxford: Oxford University Press.

Booij, Geert, and Lieber, Rochelle. 1993. On the simultaneity of morphological and prosodic structure. In Hargus, Sharon, and Kaisse, Ellen M. (eds.), *Studies in Lexical Phonology*. San Diego, CA: Academic Press, pp. 23–44.

Booij, Geert, and Rubach, Jerzy. 1987. Postcyclic versus postlexical rules in lexical phonology. *Linguistic Inquiry*, **18**(1), 1–44.

Borer, Hagit. 1984. *Parametric Syntax: Case Studies in Semitic and Romance Languages*. Dordrecht: Foris Publications.

Borer, Hagit (ed.). 1986. *The Syntax of Pronominal Clitics*. Syntax and Semantics 19. Orlando: Academic Press.

Borer, Hagit, and Grodzinsky, Yosef. 1986. Syntactic cliticization and lexical cliticization: the case of Hebrew dative clitics. In Borer, Hagit (ed.), *The Syntax of Pronominal Clitics*. Syntax and Semantics 19. Orlando: Academic Press, pp. 175–217.

Börjars, Kersti. 1998. Clitics, affixes, and parallel correspondence. In Butt, Miriam, and King, Tracy Holloway (eds.), *Proceedings of the LFG '98 Conference*. www.CSLi-publications. stanford. edu/LFG/2/lfg 98-toc.html

Borsley, Robert D. 1993. On so-called verb-nouns in Welsh. *Journal of Celtic Linguistics*, **2**, 35–64.

Borsley, Robert D., Tallerman, Maggie, and Willis, David. 2007. *The Syntax of Welsh*. Cambridge: Cambridge University Press.

Bošković, Željko. 2001. *On the Nature of the Syntax-Phonology Interface: Cliticization and Related Phenomena*. Amsterdam: Elsevier.

Bresnan, Joan. 1998. Morphology competes with syntax: explaining typological variation in weak crossover effects. In Barbosa, Pilar, Fox, Danny, Hagstrom, Paul, McGinnis, Martha, and Pesetsky, David (eds.), *Is the Best Good Enough? Optimality and Competition in Syntax*. Cambridge, MA: The MIT Press and MIT Working Papers in Linguistics, pp. 59–92.

Bresnan, Joan. 2001a. The emergence of the unmarked pronoun II. In Legendre, Geraldine, Grimshaw, Jane, and Vikner, Sten (eds.), *Optimality-Theoretic Syntax*. Cambridge, MA: The MIT Press, pp. 113–42.

Bresnan, Joan. 2001b. *Lexical-Functional Syntax*. Oxford: Blackwell Publishers.

Bresnan, Joan, and Mchombo, Sam. 1986. Grammatical and anaphoric agreement. In Farley, A.M., Farley, P.T., and McCullough, K.-E. (eds.), *Papers from the Parasession on Pragmatics and Grammatical Theory at the Twenty-Second Annual Regional Meeting of the Chicago Linguistic Society*. Chicago: Chicago Linguistic Society, pp. 287-97.

Bresnan, Joan, and Mchombo, Sam A. 1987. Topic, pronoun, and agreement in Chicheŵa. *Language*, **63**(4), 741–82. Reprinted in Iida, Masayo, Wechsler, Steven, and Zec, Draga (eds.), *Working Papers in Grammatical Theory and Discourse Structure: Interactions of Morphology, Syntax, and Discourse*. Stanford, CA: CSLI Publications, pp. 1–59.

Bresnan, Joan, and Moshi, Lioba. 1990. Object asymmetries in comparative Bantu syntax. *Linguistic Inquiry*, **21**(2), 147–85. Reprinted in Mchombo, Sam A. (ed.), *Theoretical Aspects of Bantu Grammar 1*. Stanford, CA: CSLI Publications, pp. 47–91.

Browne, Wayles. 1974. On the problem of enclitic placement in Serbo-Croatian. In Brecht, Richard D., and Chvany, Catherine V. (eds.), *Slavic Transformational Syntax*. Ann Arbor, MI: Michigan Slavic Materials, pp. 36–52.

Browne, Wayles. 1993. Serbo-Croat. In Comrie, Bernard, and Corbett, Greville G. (eds.), *The Slavonic Languages*. London: Routledge, pp. 306–87.

Buchholz, Oda, and Fiedler, Wilfried. 1987. *Albanische Grammatik*. Leipzig: VEB Verlag Enzyklopädie.

Butt, Miriam. 1995. *The Structure of Complex Predicates in Urdu*. Stanford, CA: CSLI.

Cardinaletti, Anna, and Roberts, Ian. 2002. Clause structure and X-second. In Cinque, Guglielmo (ed.), *Functional Structure in DP and IP: The Cartography of Syntactic Structures*, vol. 1. Oxford: Oxford University Press, pp. 123–65.

Cardinaletti, Anna, and Starke, Michal. 1999. The typology of structural deficiency: a case study of the three classes of pronouns. In van Riemsdijk, Hendrik C. (ed.), *Clitics and the Languages of Europe*. Berlin: Mouton de Gruyter, pp. 145–233.

Carstairs, Andrew. 1987. *Allomorphy in Inflexion*. London: Croom Helm.

Chen, Matthew Y. 1990. What must phonology know about syntax? In Inkelas, Sharon, and Zec, Draga (eds.), *The Phonology-Syntax Connection*. Stanford, CA: CSLI Publications, pp. 19–46.

Chomsky, Noam. 1973. Conditions on transformations. In Anderson, Stephen, and Kiparsky, Paul (eds.), *A Festschrift for Morris Halle*. New York: Holt, Reinhart, and Winston, pp. 232–86.

Chomsky, Noam. 1981. *Lectures on Government and Binding*. Dordrecht: Foris.

Chomsky, Noam. 1995a. Bare phrase structure. In Webelhuth, Gert (ed.), *Government and Binding Theory and the Minimalist Program*. Oxford: Blackwell Publishers, pp. 383–439.

Chomsky, Noam. 1995b. *The Minimalist Program*. Cambridge, MA: The MIT Press.

Chomsky, Noam. 2001. Derivation by phase. In Kenstowicz, Michael (ed.), *Ken Hale: A Life in Language*. Cambridge, MA: The MIT Press, pp. 1–52.

Chomsky, Noam. 2008. On phases. In Freidin, Robert, Otero, Carlos, and Zubizarreta, Maria-Luísa (eds.), *Foundational Issues in Linguistic Theory: Essays in Honor of Jean-Roger Vergnaud*. Cambridge, MA: The MIT Press, pp. 133–66.

Chung, Sandra L. 2003. The syntax and prosody of weak pronouns in Chamorro. *Linguistic Inquiry*, **34**, 547–99.

Churchward, Clerk M. 1953. *A Tongan Grammar*. Oxford: Oxford University Press.

Cole, Peter. 1982. *Imbabura Quechua*. Lingua Descriptive Studies 5. London: Routledge.

Condoravdi, Cleo, and Kiparsky, Paul. 2001. Clitics and clause structure. *Journal of Greek Linguistics*, **2**, 1–40.

Condoravdi, Cleo, and Kiparsky, Paul. 2004. Clitics and clause structure. The Late Medieval Greek system. *Journal of Greek Linguistics*, **5**, 159–83.

Corbett, Greville G. 1991. *Gender*. Cambridge: Cambridge University Press.

Corbett, Greville G. 2003. Agreement: the range of the phenomeon and the principles of the Surrey Database of Agreement. *Transactions of the Philological Society*, **101**(2), 154–202.

Corbett, Greville G. 2006. *Agreement*. Cambridge: Cambridge University Press.

Corbett, Greville G. 2007. Canonical typology, suppletion, and possible words. *Language*, **83**(1), 8–42.

Corbett, Greville G., and Fraser, Norman M. 1993. Network morphology. *Journal of Linguistics*, **29**, 113–42.

Costa, João (ed.). 2000. *Portuguese Syntax: New Comparative Studies*. Oxford: Oxford University Press.

Crysmann, Berthold. 2000. Clitics and coordination in linear structure. In Gerlach, Birgit, and Grijzenhout, Janet (eds.), *Clitics in Phonology, Morphology, and Syntax*. Amsterdam: John Benjamins, pp. 121–59.

Crysmann, Berthold. 2002. *Constraint-Based Coanalysis: Portuguese Cliticisation and Morphology-Syntax Interaction in HPSG*. Saarbrücken Dissertations in Computational Linguistics and Language Technology 15. Saarbrücken: Deutsches Forschungszentrum für Künstliche Intelligenz and Universität des Saarlandes.

Culicover, Peter, and Jackendoff, Ray. 2005. *Simpler Syntax*. Oxford: Blackwells.

Cysouw, Michael. 2005. Morphology in the wrong place: a survey of preposed enclitics. In Dressler, Wolfgang U., Kastovsky, Dieter, Pfeiffer, Oskar E., and Rainer, Franz (eds.), *Morphology and its Demarcations*. Amsterdam: John Benjamins, pp. 17–37.

Dalrymple, Mary. 2001. *Lexical Functional Grammar*. San Diego, CA: Academic Press.

Dalrymple, Mary, and Nikolaeva, Irina A. 2006. Syntax of natural and accidental coordination. *Language*, **82**(4), 824–49.

Daniel, Michael, and Spencer, Andrew. 2009. The vocative – an outlier case. In Malchukov, Andrej, and Spencer, Andrew (eds.), *The Oxford Handbook of Case*. Oxford: Oxford University Press, pp. 626–34.

de Bruyne, Jacques. 1995. *A Comprehensive Spanish Grammar*. Oxford: Blackwell Publishers.

Denniston, J. D. 2002. *The Greek Particles*. Revised edition edited by K. J. Dover. London: Bristol Classical Press.

Der Grosse Duden. 2006. *Die Grammatik. Band 4*. Mannheim/Leipzig/Vienna/Zürich: Bibliographisches Institut & F. A. Brockhaus AG.

Dixon, R. M. W., and Aikhenvald, Alexandra. 2002. *Word: A Cross-Linguistic Typology*. Cambridge: Cambridge University Press.

Donnellan, Keith S. 1966. Reference and definite descriptions. *The Philosophical Review*, **75**, 281–304.

Donohue, Mark. 1999. *A Grammar of Tukang Besi*. Berlin: Mouton de Gruyter.

Doron, Edit. 1988. On the complementarity of subject and subject-verb agreement. In Barlow, Michael, and Ferguson, Charles A. (eds.), *Agreement in Natural Language: Approaches, Theories, Descriptions*. Stanford, CA: CSLI Publications, pp. 201–18.

Dryer, Matthew S. 2005a. Position of case affixes. In Haspelmath, Martin, Dryer, Matthew S., Gil, David, and Comrie, Bernard (eds.), *World Atlas of Linguistic Structures*. Oxford: Oxford University Press, pp. 210–13; available at http://wals.info/.

Dryer, Matthew S. 2005b. Position of pronominal possessive affixes. In Haspelmath, Martin, Dryer, Matthew S., Gil, David, and Comrie, Bernard (eds.), *World Atlas of Linguistic Structures*. Oxford: Oxford University Press, pp. 234–8; available at http://wals.info/.

Dzokanga, A. 1979. *Dictionnaire lingala-français, suivi d'une grammaire lingala*. Leipzig: Verlag Enzyklopädie.

Embick, David, and Noyer, Robert Rolf. 2001. Movement operations after syntax. *Linguistic Inquiry*, **32**, 555–95.

Embick, David, and Noyer, Robert Rolf. 2007. Distributed morphology and the syntax-morphology interface. In Ramchand, Gillian, and Reiss, Charles (eds.), *The Oxford Handbook of Linguistic Interfaces*. Oxford: Oxford University Press, pp. 239–88.

Erschler, David. 2009. Modularity and 2P clitics: arguments from Digor Ossetic. In Falk, Yehuda N. (ed.), *Proceedings of the Israel Association for Theoretical Linguistics 25*. Israel Association for Theoretical Linguistics, www.linguistics.huji.ac.il/IATl/25/TOC.html

Evans, Nicholas. 2003. Typologies of agreement: some problems from Kayardild. *Transactions of the Philological Society*, **101**(2), 203–34.

Evans, Nicholas, Brown, Dunstan, and Corbett, Greville. 2001. Dalabon pronominal prefixes and the typology of syncretism: a Network Morphology analysis. In Booij, Geert, and van Marle, Jaap (eds.), *Yearbook of Morphology 2000*. Amsterdam: Kluwer Academic Publishers, pp. 187–231.

Everett, Daniel L. 1987. Pirahã clitic doubling. *Natural Language and Linguistic Theory*, **5**, 245–76.

Everett, Daniel L. 1989. Clitic doubling, reflexives, and word alternations in Yagua. *Language*, **65**, 339–72.

Everett, Daniel L. 1996. *Why There are No Clitics: An Alternative Perspective on Pronominal Allomorphy*. Arlington, TX: Summer Institute of Linguistics and University of Texas at Arlington Publications in Linguistics.

Fischer, Susann. 2003. Rethinking the Tobler-Mussafia Law. Data from Old Catalan. *Diachronica*, **20**, 259–88.

Fontana, Josep M. 1996. Phonology and syntax in the interpretation of the Tobler-Mussafia Law. In Halpern, Aaron, and Zwicky, Arnold (eds.), *Approaching Second: Second Position Clitics and Related Phenomena*. Stanford, CA: CSLI Publications, pp. 41–83.

Franks, Steven. 2000. Clitics at the interface: an introduction to *Clitic Phenomena in European Languages*. In Beukema, Frits, and den Dikken, Marcel (eds.), *Clitic Phenomena in European Languages*. Linguistik Aktuell 30. Amsterdam: John Benjamins, pp. 1–46.

Franks, Steven. 2008. Clitic placement, prosody, and the Bulgarian verbal complex. *Journal of Slavic Linguistics*, **16**, 91–127.

Franks, Steven, and King, Tracy Holloway. 2000. *A Handbook of Slavic Clitics*. Oxford: Oxford University Press.

Fried, Mirjam. 1994. Second-position clitics in Czech: syntactic or phonological? *Lingua*, **94**, 155–75.

Friedman, Victor A. 1994. Variation and grammaticalization in the development of Balkanisms. In *Papers from the 30th Regional Meeting of the Chicago Linguistic Society*, vol. 2: *The Parasession on Variation in Linguistic Theory*. Chicago: University of Chicago Press. (Reprinted in *Studia Albanica*, **32** (1995–99), 95-110.)

Friedrich, Johannes. 1960. *Hethitisches Elementarbuch. Erster Teil: Kurzgefasste Grammatik*. 2nd revised edn. Heidelberg: Carl Winter Verlag.

Fulmer, Sandra Lee. 1991. Dual-position affixes in Afar: an argument for phonologically-driven morphology. In Halpern, Aaron (ed.), *Proceedings of the 9th West Coast Conference on Formal Linguistics*. Stanford, CA: CSLI Publications, pp. 198–203.

Fulmer, Sandra Lee. 1997. *Parallelism and Planes in Optimality Theory: Evidence from Afar*. PhD thesis, University of Arizona.

Gaby, Alice. 2005. Some participants are more equal than others: case and the composition of arguments in Kuuk Thaayorre. In Amberber, Mengistu, and de Hoop, Helen (eds.), *Competition and Variation in Natural Languages: The Case for Case*. Oxford: Elsevier, pp. 9–40.

Garrett, Andrew. 1996. Wackernagel's Law and unaccusativity in Hittite. In Halpern, Aaron, and Zwicky, Arnold (eds.), *Approaching Second: Second Position Clitics and Related Phenomena*. Stanford, CA: CSLI Publications, pp. 85–133.

Gerlach, Birgit. 2002. *Clitics between Syntax and Lexicon.* Amsterdam: John Benjamins.

Gerlach, Birgit, and Grijzenhout, Janet (eds.). 2000. *Clitics from Different Perspectives.* Amsterdam: John Benjamins.

Ghomeshi, Jila. 1997. Non-projecting nouns and the ezafe construction in Persian. *Natural Language and Linguistic Theory*, **15**, 729–88.

Göksel, Aslı, and Kerslake, Celia. 2005. *Turkish: A Comprehensive Grammar.* London: Routledge.

Good, Jeff C., and Yu, Alan C. 2005. Morphosyntax of two Turkish subject pronominal paradigms. In Heggie, Lorie, and Ordóñez, Francisco (eds.), *Clitic and Affix Combinations.* Amsterdam: John Benjamins.

Greenough, J. B., Kittredge, G. L., Howard, A. A., and D'Ooge, B. L. 1983. *Allen and Greenough's New Latin Grammar for Schools and Colleges, 1903.* New Rochelle, NY: Aristide D. Caratzas.

Grimshaw, Jane. 1997. The best clitic: constraint conflict in morphosyntax. In Haegeman, Liliane (ed.), *Elements of Grammar.* Dordrecht: Kluwer Academic Publishers, pp. 169–96.

Grimshaw, Jane. 2001. Optimal clitic positions and the lexicon in Romance clitic systems. In Legendre, Géraldine, Grimshaw, Jane, and Vikner, Sten (eds.), *Optimality-Theoretic Syntax.* Cambridge: Cambridge University Press, pp. 205–40.

Gussmann, Edmund. 2007. *The Phonology of Polish.* The Phonology of the World's Languages. Oxford: Oxford University Press.

Hale, Mark. 1996. Deriving Wackernagel's Law: prosodic and syntactic factors determining clitic placement in the language of the Rigveda. In Halpern, Aaron, and Zwicky, Arnold (eds.), *Approaching Second: Second Position Clitics and Related Phenomena.* Stanford, CA: CSLI Publications, pp. 165–97.

Hall, T. Alan, and Kleinheinz, Ursula (eds.). 1999. *Studies on the Phonological Word.* Amsterdam: John Benjamins.

Hall, T. Alan, Hildebrandt, Kristine A., and Bickel, Balthasar (eds.). 2008. *Theory and Typology of Words.* Special issue of *Linguistics*, **46**(2).

Halle, Morris, and Marantz, Alex. 1993. Distributed morphology and the pieces of inflection. In Hale, Kenneth, and Keyser, Samuel J. (eds.), *The View from Building 20: Essays in Honor of Sylvain Bromberger.* Cambridge, MA: The MIT Press, pp. 111–76.

Halpern, Aaron. 1995. *On the Placement and Morphology of Clitics.* Dissertations in Linguistics. Stanford, CA: CSLI Publications.

Halpern, Aaron. 1998. Clitics. In Spencer, Andrew, and Zwicky, Arnold (eds.), *The Handbook of Morphology.* Oxford: Blackwell Publishers.

Halpern, Aaron, and Zwicky, Arnold (eds.). 1996. *Approaching Second: Second Position Clitics and Related Phenomena.* Stanford, CA: CSLI Publications.

Harris, Alice. 2000. Where in the word is the Udi clitic? *Language*, **76**, 593–616.

Harris, Alice. 2002. *Endoclitics and the Origins of Udi Morphosyntax.* Oxford: Oxford University Press.

Haspelmath, Martin. 2000. Periphrasis. In Booij, Geert, Lehmann, Christian (in collaboration with Wolfgang Kesselheim, Joachim Mugdan and Stavros Skopeteas) (eds.), *Morphologie/Morphology: Ein internationales Handbuch zur*

Flexion und Wortbildung/An International Handbook on Inflection and Word-formation. Berlin: Walter de Gruyter.

Hauge, Kjetil Rå. 1976. *The Word Order of Predicate Clitics in Bulgarian*. Oslo: Universitet i Oslo, Slavisk-Baltisk Institutt.

Hauge, Kjetil Rå. 1999. *A Short Grammar of Contemporary Bulgarian*. Bloomington, IN: Slavica Publishers Inc.

Heath, Jeffrey. 1984. *Functional Grammar of Nunggubuyu*. Canberra: Australian Institute for Aboriginal Studies.

Heggie, Lorie, and Ordóñez, Francisco (eds.). 2005. *Clitic and Affix Combinations*. Linguistics Today 74. Amsterdam: John Benjamins.

Heggie, Lorie, and Ordóñez, Francisco. 2005. Clitic ordering phenomena: the path to generalizations. In Heggie, Lorie, and Ordóñez, Francisco (eds.), *Clitic and Affix Combinations*. Amsterdam: John Benjamins.

Hock, Hans. 1996. Who's on first? Toward a prosodic account of P2 clitics. In Halpern, Aaron, and Zwicky, Arnold (eds.), *Approaching Second: Second Position Clitics and Related Phenomena*. Stanford, CA: CSLI Publications, pp.199–270.

Hockett, Charles F. 1965. What Algonquian is really like. *International Journal of American Linguistics*, **32**, 59–73.

Holton, David, Mackridge, Peter, and Philippaki-Warburton, Irene. 1997. *Greek: A Comprehensive Grammar of the Modern Language*. London: Routledge.

Hosokawa, Komei. 1991. *The Yawuru Language of West Kimberly: A Meaning-Based Description*. PhD thesis, Australian National University, Canberra.

Huddleston, Rodney, and Pullum, Geoffrey K. 2002. *The Cambridge Grammar of the English Language*. Cambridge: Cambridge University Press.

Hyman, Larry M. 2003. Suffix ordering in Bantu. In Booij, Geert, and van Marle, Jaap (eds.), *Yearbook of Morphology 2002*. Dordrecht: Kluwer Academic Publishers, pp. 245–81.

Inenliqej, Pjotr I., and Nedjalkov, Vladimir P. 1967. Iz nabljudenij nad ėrgativnoj konstrukcij v čukotskom jazyke. In Žirmunskij, V. M. (ed.), *Ėrgativnaja konstrukcija predloženija v jazykax različnyx tipov. Issledovanija i materialy*. Leningrad: Nauka, pp. 246–60.

Inkelas, Sharon. 1989. *Prosodic Constituency in the Lexicon*. PhD thesis, Stanford University.

Insler, Stanley. 1997. The phonological organization of the Rigvedic clitic chain. In Kaiser, Lizanne (ed.), *Yale A-Morphous Linguistics Essays: Studies in the Morphosyntax of Clitics*. New Haven, CT: Department of Linguistics, Yale University, pp. 75–88.

Jaeggli, Osvaldo A. 1982. *Topics in Romance Syntax*. Dordrecht: Foris Publications.

Jaeggli, Osvaldo A. 1986. Three issues in the theory of clitics: case, doubled NPs, and extraction. In Borer, Hagit (ed.), *Syntax and Semantics 19: The Syntax of Pronominal Clitics*. New York: Academic Press, pp. 15–42.

Jakobson, Roman. 1971. Les enclitiques slaves. In *Selected Writings II: Word and Language*. The Hague: Mouton, pp. 16–22.

Jelinek, Eloise. 1984. Empty categories, case, and configurationality. *Natural Language and Linguistic Theory*, **2**, 39–78.

Johannessen, Janne Bondi. 1998. *Coordination*. Oxford: Oxford University Press.

Jones, Michael A. 1993. *Sardinian Syntax*. London: Routledge.

Jones, Michael A. 1996. *Foundations of French Syntax*. Cambridge: Cambridge University Press.

Joseph, Brian D. 1988. Pronominal affixes in Modern Greek: the case against clisis. In Macleod, Lynn, Larson, Gary, and Brentari, Diane (eds.), *Papers from the 24th Annual Regional Meeting of the Chicago Linguistic Society. Part One: The General Session*. Chicago: Chicago Linguistic Society, pp. 203–14.

Joseph, Brian D., and Philippaki-Warburton, Irene. 1987. *Modern Greek*. Beckenham: Croom Helm.

Kabak, Barış. 2007. Turkish suspended affixation. *Linguistics*, **45**, 311–27.

Kager, René. 1999. *Optimality Theory*. Cambridge: Cambridge University Press.

Kaisse, Ellen M. 1981. Separating phonology from syntax: a reanalysis of Pashto cliticization. *Journal of Linguistics*, **17**, 197–208.

Kaisse, Ellen M. 1985. *Connected Speech*. New York: Academic Press.

Kallulli, Dalina, and Tasmowski, Liliane (eds.). 2008. *Clitic Doubling in the Balkan Languages*. Amsterdam: John Benjamins.

Kanerva, Jonni. 1987. Morphological integrity and syntax: The evidence from Finnish possessive suffixes. *Language*, **63**(3), 498–521. Reprinted in Iida, Masayo, Wechsler, Stephen, and Zec, Draga (eds.), *Working Papers in Grammatical Theory and Discourse Structure*. Stanford: CSLI Publications, 1987, pp. 61–91.

Kari, Ethelbert Emmanuel. 2003. *Clitics in Degema: A Meeting Point of Phonology, Morphology, and Syntax*. Tokyo: Research Institute for Languages and Cultures of Asia and Africa (ILCAA), Tokyo University of Foreign Studies.

Karlsson, Fred. 1987. *Finnish Grammar*. 2nd edn. Helsinki: Werner Söderström Osakeyhtiö.

Kathol, Andreas. 2001. *Linear Syntax*. Oxford: Oxford University Press.

Kayne, Richard S. 1975. *French Syntax: The Transformational Cycle*. Cambridge, MA: The MIT Press.

Kenesei, István. 2007. Semiwords and affixoids: the territory between word and affix. *Acta Linguistica Hungarica*, **54**, 263–93.

Kiefer, Ferenc. 1998. Morphology and pragmatics. In Spencer, Andrew, and Zwicky, Arnold (eds.), *The Handbook of Morphology*. Oxford: Oxford University Press, pp. 272–79.

Kiparsky, Paul. 1982. Word-formation and the lexicon. In Ingemann, F. (ed.), *Proceedings of the 1982 Mid-America Linguistics Conference*. Lawrence: University of Kansas, pp. 3–29.

Klamer, Marian. 1997. Spelling out clitics in Kambera. *Linguistics*, **35**, 895–927.

Klamer, Marian. 1998a. *A Grammar of Kambera*. Berlin: Mouton de Gruyter.

Klamer, Marian. 1998b. Kambera intransitive argument linking. *Studia Linguistica*, **52**, 77–111.

Klavans, Judith. 1979. On clitics as words. In Clyne, Paul R., Hanks, William F., and Hofbauer, Carol L., *Papers from the 15th Regional Meeting of the Chicago Linguistic Society*. Vol. 2: *'The Elements': A Parasession on Linguistic Units and Levels*. Chicago: University of Chicago, pp. 68–80.

Klavans, Judith L. 1982. *Some Problems in a Theory of Clitics*. Bloomington, IN: Indiana University Linguistics Club.

Klavans, Judith L. 1985. The independence of syntax and phonology in cliticization. *Language*, **61**, 95–120.

Koutsoudas, Andreas, Sanders, Gerald, and Noll, Craig. 1974. The application of phonological rules. *Language*, **50**, 1–29.

Kroeger, Paul. 1993. *Phrase Structure and Grammatical Relations in Tagalog*. Dissertations in Linguistics. Stanford, CA: CSLI Publications. Revised and corrected version of 1991 Stanford University dissertation.

Kroeger, Paul. 2004. *Analyzing Syntax: A Lexical-Functional Approach*. Cambridge: Cambridge University Press.

Kuhn, Jonas. 2001. *Formal and Computational Aspects of Optimality-theoretic Syntax*. PhD thesis, Universität Stuttgart.

Kupść, Anna. 2000. An HPSG Grammar of Polish Clitics. Unpublished PhD dissertation, Université de Paris 7 and Polish Academy of Sciences.

Kupść, Anna, and Tseng, Jesse. 2005. A new HPSG approach to Polish auxiliary constructions. In Müller, Stefan (ed.), *The Proceedings of the 12th International Conference on Head-Driven Phrase Structure Grammar, Department of Informatics, University of Lisbon*. Stanford, CA: CSLI Publications, pp. 253–73.

Lapointe, Steven. 1980. *A Theory of Grammatical Agreement*. PhD thesis, University of Massachusetts at Amherst.

Lapointe, Steven G. 1990. EDGE Features in GPSG. In *Papers from the Twenty-Sixth Regional Meeting of the Chicago Linguistic Society*. Chicago: Chicago Linguistic Society, pp. 221–35.

Lapointe, Steven. 1992. Life on the EDGE: arguments in favor of an autolexical account of edge inflections. In *Papers from the Twenty-Eighth Regional Meeting of the Chicago Linguistic Society*. Chicago: Chicago Linguistic Society, pp. 318–32.

Lauffenburger, Olivier. 2008. *Hittite Grammar*.

Laughren, Mary. 2002. Syntactic constraints in a 'free word order' language. In Amberber, Mengistu, and Collins, Peter (eds.), *Language Universals and Variation*. Westport, CT: Praeger Publishers, pp. 83–130.

Launey, Michel. 1999. *Introduction à la langue et à la littérature aztèques. Tome 1: grammaire*. Paris: L'Harmattan.

Legate, Julie Anne. 2008. Warlpiri and the theory of second position clitics. *Natural Language and Linguistic Theory*, **26**, 3–60.

Legendre, Géraldine. 1996. *Clitics, Verb (Non)-Movement, and Optimality in Bulgarian*. Technical Report JHU-CogSci-95-5. Johns Hopkins University, Baltimore.

Legendre, Géraldine. 2000a. Optimal Romanian clitics: a cross-linguistic perspective. In Motapanye, Virginia (ed.), *Comparative Studies in Romanian Syntax*. Oxford: Elsevier Publishers, pp. 227–64.

Legendre, Géraldine. 2000b. Positioning Romanian verbal clitics at PF: an Optimality-Theoretic analysis. In Gerlach, Birgit, and Grijzenhout, Janet (eds.), *Clitics in Phonology, Morphology and Syntax*. Amsterdam: John Benjamins, pp. 219–54.

Legendre, Géraldine. 2001. Morphological and prosodic alignment of Bulgarian clitics. In Dekkers, Joost, van der Leeuw, Frank, and van de Weijer, Jeroen (eds.), *Optimality Theory: Syntax, Phonology, and Acquisition*. Oxford: Oxford University Press, pp.219–54.

Lema, José, and Rivero, María Luísa. 1989. Long head movement: ECP vs. HMC. *Cahiers Linguistiques d'Ottawa*, **18**, 61–78.

Lenertová, Denisa. 2004. Czech pronominal clitics. *Journal of Slavic Linguistics*, **12**, 135–71.

Lewis, G. L. 1967. *Turkish Grammar*. Oxford: The Clarendon Press.

Lidz, Jeffrey. 1995. On the non-existence of reflexive clitics. In Dainora, Audra, Hemphill, Rachel, Luka, Barbara, Need, Barbara, and Pargman, Sheri (eds.), *Papers from the 31st Regional Meeting of the Chicago Linguistic Society*. Vol. 2: *The Parasession on Clitics*. Chicago: Chicago Linguistic Society.

Luís, Ana. 2004. *Clitics as Morphology*. PhD thesis, University of Essex, Department of Language and Linguistics.

Luís, Ana, and Otoguro, Ryo. 2004. Proclitic contexts in European Portuguese and their effect on clitic placement. In Butt, Miriam, and King, Tracy Holloway (eds.), *The Proceedings of the LFG '04 Conference*. www.csli-publications.stanford.edu/LFG/2/lfg04-toc.html

Luís, Ana, and Sadler, Louisa. 2003. Object clitics and marked morphology. In Beyssade, Claire, et al. (eds.), *Empirical Issues in Formal Syntax and Semantics 4*. Paris: Presses de l'Université de Paris, Sorbonne, pp. 133–54.

Luís, Ana, and Spencer, Andrew. 2005. A paradigm function account of 'mesoclisis' in European Portuguese. In Booij, Geert, and van Marle, Jaap (eds.), *A Yearbook of Morphology 2004*. Dordrecht: Springer, pp. 177–228.

Luís, Ana R. 2009. Para uma (re)definição da sufixação no Português Europeu: a adjunção prosódica de enclíticos pronominais. *Biblos: Revista da Faculdade de Letras, Universidade de Coimbra*, 451–70.

Luís, Ana R., and Otoguro, Ryo. 2011. Inflectional morphology and syntax in correspondence: evidence from European Portuguese. In Galani, Alexandra, Tsoulas, George, and Hicks, Glyn (eds.), *Morphology and its Interfaces*. Amsterdam: John Benjamins, pp. 97–134.

Luutonen, Jorma. 1997. *The Variation of Morpheme Order in Mari Declension*. Helsinki: Suomalais-Ugrilainen Seura.

Lyons, Christopher. 1999. *Definiteness*. Cambridge: Cambridge University Press.

Maiden, Martin, and Robustelli, Cecilia. 2000. *A Reference Grammar of Modern Italian*. London: Edward Arnold.

Marantz, Alec P. 1988. Clitics, morphological merger, and the mapping to phonological structure. In Hammond, Michael, and Noonan, Michael (eds.), *Theoretical Morphology*. San Diego, CA: Academic Press.

Marten, Lutz, Kula, Nancy C., and Thwala, Nhlanhla. 2007. Parameters of morphosyntactic variation in Bantu. *Transactions of the Philological Society*, **105**, 253–338.

Marušič, Franc, and Žaucer, Rok. 2010a. Clitic doubling in a determinerless language with second position clitics. In Zybatow, Gerhild, Dudchuk, Philip, Minor, Serge, and Pshehotskaya, Ekaterina (eds.), *Formal Studies in Slavic Linguistics, Proceedings of FDSL 7.5*. Frankfurt am Main: Peter Lang Verlag, pp.101–15.

Marušič, Franc, and Žaucer, Rok. 2010b. On clitic doubling in Gorica Slovenian. In Franks, Steven, Chidambaram, Vrinda, and Joseph, Brian (eds.), *A Linguist's Linguist: Studies in South Slavic Linguistics in Honor of E. Wayles Browne*. Bloomingdale, IN: Slavica Publishers, pp. 281–95.

Matsumoto, Yo. 1998. A reexamination of the cross-linguistic parameterization of causative predicates: Japanese perspectives. In Butt, Miriam, and King, Tracy Holloway (eds.), *The Proceedings of the LFG '98 Conference*. www.csli-publications.stanford.edu/LFG/2/lfg98-toc.html

McCarthy, John. 2002. *A Thematic Guide to Optimality Theory*. Cambridge: Cambridge University Press.

McCloskey, James, and Hale, Ken. 1984. On the syntax of person-number inflection in modern Irish. *Natural Language and Lingustic Theory*, **1**, 487–534.

Mel'čuk, Igor A. 2009. Dependency in natural language. In Polguère, Alain, and Mel'čuk, Igor A.(eds.), *Dependency in Linguistic Description*. Amsterdam: John Benjamins, pp.1–110.

Milićević, Jasmina. 2005. Clitics or affixes? On the morphological status of the future-tense markers in Serbian. In Dressler, Wolfgang U., Kastovsky, Dieter, Pfeiffer, Oskar E., and Rainer, Franz (eds.), *Morphology and its Demarcations*. Amsterdam: John Benjamins, pp. 39–52.

Milićević, Jasmina. 2009. Linear placement of Serbian clitics in a syntactic dependency framework. In Polguère, Alain, and Mel'čuk, Igor A. (eds.), *Dependency in Linguistic Description*. Amsterdam: John Benjamins, pp. 235–76.

Miller, Philip. 1992. *Clitics and Constituents in Phrase Structure Grammar*. New York: Garland Publications.

Miller, Philip H., and Sag, Ivan A. 1997. French clitic movement without clitics or movement. *Natural Language and Linguistic Theory*, **15**(3), 573–639.

Mithun, Marianne. 2003. Pronouns and agreement: the information status of pronominal affixes. *Transactions of the Philological Society*, **101**(2), 235–78.

Mišeska Tomić, Olga. 2006. *The Balkan Sprachbund: Morpho-syntactic Features*. Dordrecht: Springer Verlag.

Monachesi, Paola. 2000. Clitic placement in the Romanian verbal complex. In Gerlach, Birgit, and Grijzenhout, Janet (eds.), *Clitics in Phonology, Morphology and Syntax*. Amsterdam: John Benjamins, pp. 255-93.

Monachesi, Paola. 2005. *The Verbal Complex in Romance*. Oxford: Oxford University Press.

Monachesi, Paula. 1999. *A Lexical Approach to Italian Cliticization*. Stanford, CA: CSLI Publications.

Muysken, Peter. 1981. Quechua word structure. In Heny, Frank (ed.), *Binding and Filtering*. Cambridge, MA: The MIT Press, pp. 8, 279–327.

Neeleman, Ad, and Szendrői, Krisztina. 2007. Radical pro drop and the morphology of pronouns. *Linguistic Inquiry*, **38**, 671–714.

Nelson, Diane. 1998. *Grammatical Case Assignment in Finnish*. New York: Garland Publications.

Nespor, Marina. 1999. The phonology of clitic groups. In van Riemsdijk, Hendrik C. (ed.), *Clitics and the Languages of Europe*. Berlin: Mouton de Gruyter.

Nespor, Marina, and Vogel, Irene. 1986. *Prosodic Phonology*. Dordrecht: Foris Publications.

Nevis, Joel A. 1986. *Finnish Particle Clitics and General Clitic Theory*. PhD thesis, The Ohio State University.

Nevis, Joel A. 2000. Clitics. In Booij, Geert, Lehmann, Christian, and Mugdan, Joachim (eds.), *Morphology: An International Handbook on Inflection and Word-Formation*, vol. 1. Berlin: Walter de Gruyter, pp. 388–404.

Nevis, Joel A., and Joseph, Brian D. 1993. Wackernagel affixes: evidence from Balto-Slavic. In Booij, Geert, and van Marle, Jaap (eds.), *Yearbook of Morphology 1992*. Dordrecht: Kluwer Academic Publishers, pp. 93–111.

Nevis, Joel A., Joseph, Brian D., Wanner, Dieter, and Zwicky, Arnold M. 1994. *Clitics: A Comprehensive Bibliography 1892–1991*. Amsterdam: John Benjamins.

Nikolaeva, Irina A. 2012. Towards a typology of finiteness: a canonical approach. In Brown, Dunstan P., Chumakina, Marina, and Corbett, Greville C. (eds.), *Canonical Morphology and Syntax*. Oxford: Oxford University Press.

Nordlinger, Rachel, and Sadler, Louisa. 2006. Case stacking in realizational morphology. *Linguistics*, **44**, 459–88.

Nordlinger, Rachel, and Saulwick, Adam. 2002. Infinitives in polysynthesis: the case of Rembarrnga. In Evans, Nicholas, and Sasse, Hans-Jürgen (eds.), *Problems of Polysynthesis*. Berlin: Akademie Verlag, pp. 185–201.

Noyer, Robert Rolf. 2001. Clitic sequences in Nunggubuyu and PF convergence. *Natural Language and Linguistic Theory*, **19**, 751–826.

Odden, David. 1987. Kimatuumbi phrasal phonology. *Phonology Yearbook*, **4**, 13–36.

Odden, David. 1990. Syntax, lexical rules, and postlexical rules in Kimatuumbi. In Inkelas, Sharon, and Zec, Draga (eds.), *The Phonology-Syntax Connection*. Stanford, CA: CSLI Publications, pp. 259–78.

Orgun, Cemil Orhan. 1996a. *Sign-based Morphology and Phonology with Special Attention to Optimality Theory*. PhD thesis, University of California, Berkeley.

Orgun, Cemil Orhan. 1996b. Suspended affixation: a new look at the phonology-morphology interface. In Kleinheinz, Ursula (ed.), *Interfaces in Phonology*. Berlin: Akademie Verlag, pp. 251–61.

Paster, Mary. 2009. Explaining phonological conditions on affixation: evidence from suppletive allomorphy and affix ordering. *Word Structure*, **2**(1), 18–47.

Payne, Doris L., and Payne, Thomas E. 1990. Yagua. In Derbyshire, Desmond C., and Pullum, Geoffrey K. (eds.), *Handbook of Amazonian Languages*, vol. 2. Berlin: Mouton de Gruyter, pp. 249–74.

Payne, John. 2009. The English genitive and double case. *Transactions of the Philological Society*, **107**(3), 322–57.

Payne, John, and Huddleston, Rodney. 2002. Nouns and noun phrases. In Huddleston, Rodney, and Pullum, Geoffrey (eds.), *The Cambridge Grammar of the English Language*. Cambridge: Cambridge University Press, pp. 323–523.

Peperkamp, Sharon. 1997. *Prosodic Words*. HIL dissertations 34. The Hague: Holland Academic Graphics.

Perlmutter, David. 1970. Surface structure constraints in syntax. *Linguistic Inquiry*, **1**, 185–255.

Perlmutter, David. 1971. *Deep and Surface Structure Constraints in Syntax*. New York: Holt, Reinhart, and Winston.

Pesetsky, David. 1985. Morphology and logical form. *Linguistic Inquiry*, **16**, 193–246.

Pierrehumbert, Janet B. 1980. The Finnish possessive suffixes. *Language*, **56**, 603–21.

Plank, Frans. 2005. The prosodic contribution of clitics: focus on Latin. *Lingue e Linguaggio*, **4**, 281–92.

Poletto, Cecilia. 1997. Pronominal syntax. In Maiden, Martin, and Parry, Mair (eds.), *The Dialects of Italy*. London: Routledge, pp.137–44.

Poletto, Cecilia. 2000. *The Higher Functional Field: Evidence from Northern Italian Dialects*. Oxford: Oxford University Press.

Polinsky, Maria. 2003. Non-canonical agreement is canonical. *Transactions of the Philological Society*, **101**(2), 279–312.

Polinsky, Maria, and Potsdam, Eric. 2001. Long-distance agreement and topic in Tsez. *Natural Language and Linguistic Theory*, **19**, 583–646.

Poser, William J. 1985. Cliticization to NP and Lexical Phonology. In Goldberg, J., MacKaye, S., and Wescoat, Michael (eds.), *Proceedings of the West Coast Conference on Formal Linguistics 4*. Stanford, CA: CSLI Publications, pp. 262–72.

Prinz, Michael. 1991. *Klitisierung im Deutschen und Neugriechischen: Eine lexikalisch-phonologische Studie*. Tübingen: Niemeyer.

Progovac, Ljiljana. 1996. Clitics in Serbian/Croatian: Comp as the second position. In Halpern, Aaron, and Zwicky, Arnold (eds.), *Approaching Second: Second Position Clitics and Related Phenomena*. Stanford, CA: CSLI Publications, pp. 411–28.

Radanović-Kocić, Vesna. 1996. The placement of Serbo-Croatian clitics: a prosodic approach. In Halpern, Aaron, and Zwicky, Arnold (eds.), *Approaching Second: Second Position Clitics and Related Phenomena*. Stanford, CA: CSLI Publications, pp. 429–45.

Reed, Irene, Miyaoka, Osahito, Jacobson, Steven, Afcan, Paschal, and Krauss, Michael. 1977. *Yup'ik Eskimo Grammar*. Fairbanks: Alaska Native Language Center/ Yup'ik Language Workshop, University of Alaska.

Rhys Jones, T. J. 1977. *Living Welsh*. London: Hodder and Stoughton.

Rice, Keren D. 2000. *Morpheme Order and Semantic Scope: Word Formation in the Athabaskan Verb*. Cambridge: Cambridge University Press.

Rivas, Alberto Mario. 1977. *A Theory of Clitics*. PhD thesis, Massachusetts Institute of Technology, Cambridge, MA.

Rivero, María Luisa. 1991. Long head movement and negation: Serbo-Croatian vs. Slovak and Czech. *The Linguistic Review*, **8**, 319–51.

Rivero, María Luisa. 1994. Clause structure and V-movement in the Clause structure and V-movement in the languages of the Balkans. *Natural Language and Linguistic Theory*, **12**, 63–120.

Rizzi, Luigi. 1982a. *Issues in Italian Syntax*. Dordrecht: Foris Publications.

Rizzi, Luigi. 1982b. A restructuring rule. In *Issues in Italian Syntax*. Dordrecht: Foris Publications, pp. 1–48.

Rizzi, Luigi. 1986. On the status of subject clitics in Romance. In Jaeggli, Osvaldo A., and Silva-Corvalán, Carmen (eds.), *Studies in Romance Linguistics*. Dordrecht: Foris Publications, pp. 391–419.

Roberts, Ian. 2010. The pronominal domain: DP-NP structure, clitics and null subjects. In D'Allessandro, Roberta, Ledgeway, Adam, and Roberts, Ian (eds.), *Syntactic Variation: The Dialects of Italy*. Cambridge: Cambridge University Press, pp. 3–27.

Rosenbach, Anette. 2005. Animacy versus weight as determinants of grammatical variation in English. *Language*, **81**, 613–44.

Rudin, Catherine. 1997. Agr-O and Bulgarian pronominal clitics. In Lindstedt, M., and Franks, S. (eds.), *Formal Approaches to Slavic Linguistics: The Indiana Meeting 1996*. Ann Arbor, MI: Michigan Slavic Publications, pp. 224–52.

Ryding, Karin C. 2005. *A Reference Grammar of Modern Standard Arabic*. Cambridge: Cambridge University Press.

Sadler, Louisa. 1988. *Welsh Syntax*. Beckenham: Croom Helm.

Sadler, Louisa. 1997. Clitics and the structure-function mapping. In Butt, Miriam, and King, Tracy Holloway (eds.), *Proceedings of LFG97*. Stanford, CA, CSLI Publications: www.csli-publications.stanford.edu/LFG/2/lfg97-toc.html.

Sadler, Louisa. 1998. English auxiliaries as tense inflections. *Essex Research Reports in Linguistics*, **24**, 1–16.

Sadock, Jerrold M. 1991. *Autolexical Syntax: A Theory of Parallel Grammatical Representations*. Chicago: The University of Chicago Press.

Saeed, John. 1999. *Somali*. Amsterdam: John Benjamins.

Sag, Ivan, Wasow, Thomas, and Bender, Emily. 2003. *Syntactic Theory: A Formal Introduction*. Stanford, CA: Center for the Study of Language and Information.

Samvelian, Pollet. 2007. A (phrasal) affix analysis of the Persian Ezafe. *Journal of Linguistics*, **43**(3), 605–45.

Schachter, Paul. 1973. Constraints on clitic order in Tagalog. In Gonzalez, A. B. (ed.), *Parangal kay Cecilio Lopez*. Manila: Linguistic Society of the Philippines, pp. 214–31.

Schachter, Paul, and Otanes, Fe T. 1972. *Tagalog Reference Grammar*. Berkeley: University of California Press.

Schäufele, Steven. 1996. Now that we're all here where do we sit? Phonological ordering in the Vedic clause-initial string. In Halpern, Aaron, and Zwicky, Arnold (eds.), *Approaching Second: Second Position Clitics and Related Phenomena*. Stanford, CA: CSLI Publications, pp. 447–75.

Schegloff, Emanuel A. 2007. *Sequence Organization in Interaction: A Primer in Conversation Analysis*. Cambridge: Cambridge University Press.

Selkirk, Elisabeth O. 1984. *Phonology and Syntax: The Relation between Sound and Structure*. Cambridge, MA: The MIT Press.

Selkirk, Elisabeth O. 1995. The prosodic structure of function words. In Beckman, Jill N., Dickey, Laura W., and Urbanczyk, Suzanne (eds.), *Papers in Optimality Theory*, vol. 18. University of Massachusetts Occasional Papers in Linguistics. Amherst: Graduate Linguistic Student Association (GLSA), University of Massachusetts.

Sells, Peter. 1995. Korean and Japanese morphology from a lexical perspective. *Linguistic Inquiry*, **26**, 277–325.

Short, David. 1993. Czech. In Comrie, Bernard, and Corbett, Greville G. (eds.), *The Slavonic Languages*. London: Routledge, pp. 455–532.

Siegel, Dorothy. 1974. *Topics in English Morphology*. PhD thesis, Massachusetts Institute of Technology, Cambridge, MA.

Siewierska, Anna. 2012. Refining the canonical characterization of the passive. In Brown, Dunstan P., Chumakina, Marina, and Corbett, Greville C. (eds.), *Canonical Morphology and Syntax*. Oxford: Oxford University Press.

Silverstein, Michael. 1976. Hierarchy of features and ergativity. In Dixon, R.M.W. (ed.), *Grammatical Categories in Australian Languages*. Canberra: Australian Institute for Aboriginal Studies, pp.112–71.

Simpson, Jane. 1991. *Warlpiri Morpho-Syntax*. Dordrecht: Kluwer Academic Publishers.

Simpson, Jane, and Withgott, Margaret. 1986. Pronominal clitic clusters and templates. In Borer, Hagit (ed.), *The Syntax of Pronominal Clitics*. Syntax and Semantics 19. Orlando: Academic Press, pp. 149–74.

Spencer, Andrew. 1989. Morpholexikalische phonologie. In Prinzhorn, Martin (ed.),
    Phonologie. Special Issue of *Linguistische Berichte*. Wiesbaden: Westdeutscher
    Verlag, pp. 164–97.
Spencer, Andrew. 1991. *Morphological Theory: An Introduction to Word Structure in
    Generative Grammar*. Oxford: Blackwell Publishers.
Spencer, Andrew. 1993. Review of Sadock 1991. *Journal of Linguistics*, **29**, 143–55.
Spencer, Andrew. 1999. Chukchee and polysynthesis. In Raxilina, Ekaterina V., and
    Testelec, Jakov G. (eds.), *Tipologija i teorija jazyka – ot opisanija k ob"jasneniju.
    K 60-letiju Aleksandra Evgen'eviča Kibrika*. Moscow: Jazyki russkoj kul'tury,
    pp. 106–13.
Spencer, Andrew. 2000. Inflection and the lexeme. *Acta Linguistica Hungarica*, **47**,
    335–44.
Spencer, Andrew. 2001. Verbal clitics in Bulgarian. A Paradigm Function Morphology
    approach. In Gerlach, Birgit, and Grijzenhout, Janet (eds.), *Clitics in Phonology,
    Morphology, and Syntax*. Amsterdam: John Benjamins, pp. 355–86.
Spencer, Andrew. 2003a. Periphrastic paradigms in Bulgarian. In Junghanns, Uwe, and
    Szucsich, Luka (eds.), *Syntactic Structures and Morphological Information*.
    Berlin: Mouton de Gruyter, pp. 249-82.
Spencer, Andrew. 2003b. Putting some order into morphology: reflections on Rice
    (2000) and Stump (2001). *Journal of Linguistics*, **39**, 621–46.
Spencer, Andrew. 2005a. Inflecting clitics in Generalized Paradigm Function
    Morphology. *Lingue e Linguaggio*, **4**, 179–93.
Spencer, Andrew. 2005b. Towards a typology of 'mixed categories'. In Orgun,
    C. Orhan, and Sells, Peter (eds.), *Morphology and the Web of Grammar: Essays in
    Memory of Steven G. Lapointe*. Stanford, CA: CSLI Publications, pp. 95–138.
Spencer, Andrew. 2008. Does Hungarian have a case system? In Corbett, Greville G.,
    and Noonan, Michael (eds.), *Case and Grammatical Relations*. Amsterdam: John
    Benjamins, pp. 35–56.
Spencer, Andrew. 2009. Case as a morphological phenomenon. In Malchukov, Andrej,
    and Spencer, Andrew (eds.), *The Oxford Handbook of Case*. Oxford: Oxford
    University Press, pp. 185–99.
Spencer, Andrew. 2010. Lexical relatedness and the lexical entry – a formal unification.
    In Müller, Stefan (ed.), *Proceedings of the HPSG10 conference*. Stanford, CA:
    CSLI Publications, pp. 322–40.
Spencer, Andrew, and Luís, Ana. 2012. The canonical clitic. In Brown, Dunstan P.,
    Chumakina, Marina, and Corbett, Greville C. (eds.), *Canonical Morphology and
    Syntax*. Oxford: Oxford University Press.
Sportiche, Dominique. 1996. Clitic constructions. In Zaring, Laurie Ann, and Rooryck,
    Johan (eds.), *Phrase Structure and the Lexicon*. Dordrecht: Kluwer Academic
    Publishers, pp. 213–76.
Sproat, Richard. 1998. Morphology as component or module: mapping principle
    approaches. In Spencer, Andrew, and Zwicky, Arnold (ed.), *The Handbook of
    Morphology*. Oxford: Oxford University Press, pp. 335–48.
Steele, Susan. 1976. On the count of one. In Juilland, A. (ed.), *Studies Presented to
    Joseph Greenberg on his 60th Birthday*. Saratoga, CA: Alma Libri, pp. 591–614.
Steele, Susan. 1978. The category AUX as a language universal. In Greenberg,
    Joseph H., Ferguson, Charles, and Moravcsik, Edith A. (eds.), *Universals of*

Human Language, vol. 3: *Word Structure*. Stanford, CA: Stanford University Press, pp. 7–45.

Steele, Susan, Akmajian, Adrian, Demers, Richard, Jelinek, Eloise, Kitagawa, Chisato, Oehrle, Richard, and Wasow, Thomas. 1981. *An Encyclopedia of AUX*. Cambridge, MA: The MIT Press.

Stjepanović, Sandra. 1998. On the placement of Serbocroatian clitics: evidence from VP-ellipsis. *Linguistic Inquiry*, **29**, 527–37.

Stjepanović, Sandra. 2004. Clitic climbing and restructuring with 'finite clause' and infinitive complements. *Journal of Slavic Linguistics*, **12**, 173–212.

Stump, Gregory T. 1984. Agreement vs. incorporation in Breton. *Natural Language and Linguistic Theory*, **2**, 289–426.

Stump, Gregory T. 1993. Position classes and morphological theory. In Booij, Geert, and van Marle, Jaap (eds.), *Yearbook of Morphology 1992*. Dordrecht: Kluwer Academic Publishers, pp. 129–79.

Stump, Gregory T. 1997. Template morphology and inflectional morphology. In Booij, Geert, and van Marle, Jaap (eds.), *Yearbook of Morphology 1996*. Dordrecht: Kluwer Academic Publishers, pp. 217–41.

Stump, Gregory T. 1998. Inflection. In Spencer, Andrew, and Zwicky, Arnold (ed.), *The Handbook of Morphology*. Oxford: Oxford University Press, pp. 13–43.

Stump, Gregory T. 2001. *Inflectional Morphology: A Theory of Paradigm Structure*. Cambridge: Cambridge University Press.

Sullivan, Thelma D. 1988. *Thelma D. Sullivan's Compendium of Nahuatl Grammar*. Translated by Thelma D. Sullivan and Neville Stiles, edited by Wick R. Miller and Karen Dakin. Salt Lake City: The University of Utah Press.

Suñer, Maria. 1988. The role of agreement in clitic-doubled constructions. *Natural Language and Linguistic Theory*, **6**, 391–434.

Sussex, Roland. 1980. On agreement, affixation and enclisis in Polish. In Chvany, Catherine V., and Brecht, Richard D. (eds.), *Morphosyntax in Slavic*. Columbus, OH: Slavica Publishers, pp. 187–203.

Szczegielniak, Adam. 2005. Clitic positions within the left periphery: evidence for a phonological buffer. In Heggie, Lorie, and Ordóñez, Francisco (eds.), *Clitic and Affix Combinations*. Amsterdam: John Benjamins, pp. 283–99.

Taylor, Ann. 1996. A prosodic account of clitic position in Ancient Greek. In Halpern, Aaron, and Zwicky, Arnold (eds.), *Approaching Second: Second Position Clitics and Related Phenomena*. Stanford, CA: CSLI Publications, pp. 477–503.

Tegey, Habibullah. 1977. *The Grammar of Clitics: Evidence from Pashto and Other Languages*. PhD thesis, University of Illinois.

Testelets, Yakov G. 2003. Are there strong and weak pronouns in Russian? In Browne, Wayles, Kim, Ji-Yung, Partee, Barbara H., and Rothstein, Robert A. (eds.), *Formal Approaches to Slavic Linguistics: The Amherst Meeting 2002*. Ann Arbor, MI: Michigan Slavic Publications, pp. 515–38.

Toivonen, Ida. 2000. The morphosyntax of Finnish possessives. *Natural Language and Linguistic Theory*, **18**(3), 579–609.

Toivonen, Ida. 2003. *Non-Projecting Words: A Case Study of Swedish Particles*. Dordrecht: Kluwer.

Toman, Jindřich. 1986. Cliticization from NPs in Czech and comparable phenomena in French and Italian. In Borer, Hagit (ed.), *Syntax and Semantics 19: The Syntax of Pronominal Clitics*. New York: Academic Press, pp. 123–45.

Truckenbrodt, Hubert. 1999. On the relation between syntactic phrases and phonological phrases. *Linguistic Inquiry*, **30**, 219–56.

Uriagereka, Juan. 2000. Doubling and possession. In Gerlach, Birgit, and Grijzenhout, Janet (eds.), *Clitics in Phonology, Morphology and Syntax*. Amsterdam: John Benjamins, pp. 405–31.

van Riemsdijk, Hendrik C. 1999. Clitics: a state of the art report. In van Riemsdijk, Hendrik C. (ed.), *Clitics and the Languages of Europe*. Berlin: Mouton de Gruyter, pp. 405–31.

van Riemsdijk, Hendrik C. (ed.). 1999. *Clitics and the Languages of Europe*. Berlin: Mouton de Gruyter.

Vanelli, Laura, and Renzi, Lorenzo. 1997. Personal pronouns and demonstratives. In Maiden, Martin, and Parry, Mair (eds.), *The Dialects of Italy*. London: Routledge, pp. 106–15.

Vasil'eva, Anna Nikolaevna. 1974. *Particles in Colloquial Russian (Manual for English-speaking Students of Russian)*. Moscow: Progress Publishers.

Veselovská, Ludmila. 1995. *Phrasal Movement and X^0-morphology*. PhD thesis, Palacky University, Olomouc.

Vigário, Marina. 2003. *The Prosodic Word in European Portuguese*. Berlin: Mouton de Gruyter.

Vogel, Irene. 2009. The status of the Clitic Group. In Grijzenhout, Janet, and Kabak, Barış (eds.), *Phonological Domains: Universals and Deviations*. Berlin: Mouton de Gruyter, pp. 15–46.

Vogel, Irene. 2010. The phonology of compounds. In Scalise, Sergio, and Vogel, Irene (eds.), *Cross-disciplinary Issues in Compounding*. Amsterdam: John Benjamins, pp. 145–63.

Wackernagel, Jacob. 1892. Über ein Gesetz der indogermanischen Wortstellung. *Indogermanische Forschungen*, **1**, 333–436.

Wälchli, Bernhard. 2005. *Co-compounds and Natural Coordination*. Oxford: Oxford University Press.

Weir Smyth, Herbert. 1920. *A Greek Grammar for Colleges*. New York: American Book Company.

Werle, Adam. 2009. *Word, Phrase, and Clitic Prosody in Bosnian, Serbian, and Croatian*. PhD thesis, University of Massachusetts at Amherst, GLSA, Department of Linguistics.

Wescoat, Michael T. 2002. *On Lexical Sharing*. PhD thesis, Stanford University.

Wescoat, Michael T. 2009. Udi person markers and lexical integrity. In Butt, Miriam, and King, Tracy Holloway (eds.), *Proceedings of the LFG09 Conference*. Stanford, CA: CSLI Publications, pp. 604–22.

Weydt, Harald. 1969. *Abtönungspartikel: Die deutschen Modalwörter und ihre französischen Entsprechungen*. Berlin: Gehlen.

Whitman, John. 1991. Argument positions and configurationality. In Georgopoulos, Carol (ed.), *Interdisciplinary Approaches to Language: Essays in Honor of S.-Y. Kuroda*. Dordrecht: Kluwer Academic Publishers, pp. 615–28.

Wunderlich, Dieter. 2001. A correspondence-theoretic analysis of Dalabon transitive paradigms. In Booij, Geert, and van Marle, Jaap (eds.), *Yearbook of Morphology 2000*. Kluwer Academic Publishers, pp. 233–52.

Wunderlich, Dieter, and Fabri, Ray. 1995. Minimalist Morphology: an approach to inflection. *Zeitschrift für Sprachwissenschaft*, **14**, 236–94.

Zec, Draga, and Inkelas, Sharon. 1991. The place of clitics in the Prosodic Hierarchy. In Bates, Dawn (ed.), *Proceedings of the 10th West Coast Conference on Formal Linguistics (WCCFL)*. Stanford, CA: CSLI Publications, pp. 505–19.

Zwicky, Arnold. 1987. Suppressing the Z's. *Journal of Linguistics*, **23**(1), 133–48.

Zwicky, Arnold M. 1977. *On Clitics*. Bloomington, IN: Indiana University Linguistics Club.

Zwicky, Arnold M. 1985a. Clitics and particles. *Language*, **61**(2), 283–305.

Zwicky, Arnold M. 1985b. How to describe inflection. In Niepokuj, Mary, Van Clay, Mary, Nikiforidou, Vassiliki, and Feder, Deborah (eds.), *Proceedings of the Eleventh Annual Meeting of the Berkeley Linguistic Society*. Berkeley: University of California at Berkeley.

Zwicky, Arnold M. 1986. The general case: basic form versus default form. In Nikiforidou, Vassiliki, VanClay, Mary, Niepokuj, Mary, and Feder, Deborah (eds.), *Proceedings of the Twelfth Annual Meeting of the Berkeley Linguistics Society*. Berkeley, CA: Berkeley Linguistics Society, University of California, pp. 305–14.

Zwicky, Arnold M. 1994. What is a clitic? Nevis, Joel A., Joseph, Brian D., Wanner, Dieter, and Zwicky, Arnold M. (eds.), *Clitics: A Comprehensive Bibliography 1892–1991*. Amsterdam: John Benjamins, pp. xii–xx.

Zwicky, Arnold M., and Pullum, Geoffrey K. 1983. Cliticization vs. inflection: English *n't*. *Language*, **59**, 502–13.

Index of names

Abeillé, Anne, 312
Abraham, Werner, 34
Ackerman, Farrell, 334, 335
Aikhenvald, Alexandra, 13, 20
Aissen, Judith, 162, 332
Akinlabi, Akinbiyi, 134
Akmajian, Adrian, 50
Alpher, Barry, 235
Alsina, Alex, 311
Anagnostopoulou, Elena, 188, 307, 308
Anderson, Stephen, 7, 12, 13, 40, 43–4, 44–7, 58, 59, 66, 71, 78, 95, 98, 103, 126, 127, 130, 131, 134, 145, 150, 151, 153, 218, 220, 221, 228–31, 235, 238, 244, 246–9, 250, 254, 260, 268, 288, 291–4, 304, 316, 325–7, 331, 334, 336, 337
Andrews, Avery, 283
Andrews, J. Richard, 115–6, 331
Aronoff, Mark, 188–9, 238, 333
Avgustinova, Tania, 12, 61–3, 168, 277, 331
Awbery, Gwen, 281

Baerman, Matthew, 243, 273, 335
Baker, Mark, 4, 143, 332
Barešić, Jasna, 122
Barron, Julia, 336
Benacchio, Rosanna, 12, 41
Bennett, David, 54
Berendsen, Egon, 13
Bermúdez-Otero, Ricardo, 267
Beukema, Frits, 12
Bickel, Balthasar, 193–6
Billings, Loren, 330, 337
Blake, Barry, 333
Blakemore, Diane, 34
Bögel, Tina, 287
Bonami, Olivier, 244, 250, 256–63, 275, 335
Bonet, Eulàlia, 12, 270, 316
Booij, Geert, 85, 102–3, 201, 229, 327
Borer, Hagit, 12, 169–70, 275, 278
Börjars, Kersti, 220
Borsley, Robert, 145–6, 279, 281, 336

Bošković, Željko, 12, 47, 100, 246, 300, 303–6, 317, 325, 332, 334, 337
Boyé, Gilles, 244, 250, 256–63, 275, 335
Bresnan, Joan, 146–7, 161, 219, 274
Browne, Wayles, 2, 41, 49
Buchholz, Oda, 187
Butt, Miriam, 162

Cardinaletti, Anna, 28, 221–5, 228, 278, 309, 336
Carstairs, Andrew, 242
Chen, Matthew, 331
Chomsky, Noam, 7, 274, 335, 336
Chung, Sandra, 47, 236–7, 306, 334
Churchward, C. M., 132–3, 332
Cole, Peter, 20
Condoravdi, Cleo, 208
Corbett, Greville, 139, 141, 143–4, 208, 232, 238, 243
Costa, João, 316
Crysmann, Berthold, 12, 208, 277, 318, 324
Culicover, Peter, 329
Cysouw, Michael, 46, 65, 66, 69

Dalrymple, Mary, 198, 274–5
Daniel, Michael, 23
de Bruyne, Jacques, 153
den Dikken, Marcel, 12
Denniston, J. D., 12, 34, 176, 329
Dixon, R. M. W, 13
Donnellan, Keith, 309
Donohue, Mark, 21
Doron, Edit, 144, 146
Dryer, Matthew, 21, 23
Dzokanga, A., 191

Embick, David, 65, 220, 243, 277
Erschler, David, 212
Evans, Nicholas, 141, 273
Everett, Daniel, 12, 150, 159, 161, 307, 337

Fabri, Ray, 246
Fiedler, Wilfried, 155
Fischer, Susann, 64

Index of languages

Afar, 190
Albanian, 74, 154–157, 185, 186, 276, 309
Ancient Greek, *see* Greek
Arabic, 22, 24
Argentinian (Spanish), 337
Athabaskan, 144
Avestic, 57

Balto-Slavic, 142
Belarusian, 334
Bemba, 147
Breton, 144, 145, 218, 336
Bulgarian, 12, 21–23, 32, 47, 59–62, 64, 68, 69,
  73, 74, 82, 83, 88, 104, 105, 118, 124, 125,
  128–130, 137, 142, 144, 154–157, 191, 203,
  214, 228, 236, 246, 247, 249, 264, 274, 276,
  277, 288, 303, 305, 306, 310, 311, 316–318,
  322–324, 330, 334, 335

Catalan, 12, 34, 64, 85, 270, 316
Celtic, 144–146, 279
Chamorro, 47, 84, 146, 218, 236, 237, 306, 322,
  331, 334
Chicheŵa, 146
ChiMwi:ni, 162
Chinese, *see* Mandarin Chinese
Chintang, 178, 190, 194–196
Chukchee, 30, 31, 142, 148, 332
Chukchi, *see* Chukchee
Chukotkan, *see* Chukchee
Classical Nahuatl, *see* Nahuatl
Czech, 18–20, 41, 53, 54, 60, 70, 118, 123, 124,
  142, 166–168, 170, 179, 213–215, 231, 330,
  334, 337

Daghestanian, 29, 147
Dalabon, 273
Dutch, 201

English, 1–5, 9, 15–24, 33, 34, 42–44, 66, 68, 73,
  91–102, 107–109, 111–114, 126–128, 139,
  140, 142, 143, 146, 147, 155, 163, 165, 166,
  169, 178–180, 188, 189, 193, 195, 201, 204,
  205, 215, 220, 225, 227–229, 239, 240, 263,
  268, 284, 286–288, 291–294, 301, 304, 317,
  321, 324, 328, 332, 333, 336
  Irish~, 331
Equadorian Quechua, *see* Quechua
Eskimoan, 144
Estonian, 228

Farsi, *see* Persian
Finnish, 19, 52, 53, 70–72, 101, 109, 178, 181,
  182, 184, 185, 193, 228, 274
French, 3, 4, 9, 13, 21, 22, 28, 33, 34, 63, 112,
  125, 140, 142, 143, 145, 150, 152, 153, 163,
  200, 215, 222, 228, 254, 256–261, 263, 275,
  278, 286, 292, 307, 312, 315, 332, 335

German, 22, 27, 29, 30, 34, 40, 92, 93, 95, 96,
  137, 141, 142, 178–180, 188, 215, 286, 305,
  318, 332
  Swiss ~, 193
Greek, 9, 69, 72, 74, 91, 104, 105, 118, 178,
  186–188, 207, 307, 331, 333
  Ancient ~, 12, 23, 34–36, 39, 40, 53, 73, 84, 87,
  176, 235, 329, 330
Gunwinyguan, 270, 273

Hebrew, 146, 169, 218
Hindi-Urdu, 22, 76, 333
Hittite, 36, 329
Hungarian, 20, 21, 147, 148, 184, 201, 239, 327,
  333, 334

Imbabura Quechua, *see* Quechua
Indo-Aryan, 22
Indo-European, 17, 39, 40, 57, 58, 73, 142, 176,
  186
Indo-Iranian, 57, 78, 79, 212
Irish, 145, 283, 336
Italian, 34, 85, 163, 164, 166, 189, 191, 200, 221,
  223, 230, 254, 258, 259, 275, 278, 312, 315,
  322, 323, 333

Japanese, 19, 22, 70, 74–76, 142, 331

Kambera, 72, 244, 250–252, 254, 326, 335

Index of subjects